Diversity in Counseling

Robert Brammer
West Texas A&M University

THOMSON
BROOKS/COLE

Australia • Canada • Mexico • Singapore • Spain
United Kingdom • United States

THOMSON
★
BROOKS/COLE

Executive Editor: Lisa Gebo

Acquisitions Editor: Julie Martinez

Assistant Editor: Shelley Gesicki

Editorial Assistant: Amy Lam

Marketing Manager: Caroline Concilla

Advertising Project Manager: Tami Strang

Project Manager, Editorial Production: Cathy Linberg

Print/Media Buyer: Doreen Suruki

Permissions Editor: Robert Kauser

Production Service: Kim Vander Steen

Text and Cover Designer: Lucy Lesiak

Copy Editor: Janet Tilden

Cover Image: Ian Woodstock/Illustration Works/Getty Images

Compositor: Lucy Lesiak

Printer: Transcontinental Printing/Louiseville

Photo Credits: page 1: ©Nik Wheeler/CORBIS; page 29: Jon Bradley/Stone/Getty Images; page 163: © CORBIS SYGMA, "BOYS DON'T CRY" ©1999 Twentieth Century Fox. All rights reserved.; page 321: Holos/The Image Bank/Getty Images

Printed in Canada

3   4   5   6   7   06

For more information about our products, contact us at:
Thomson Learning Academic Resource Center
1-800-423-0563
For permission to use material from this text, contact us by:
Phone: 1-800-730-2214
Fax: 1-800-730-2215
Web: http://www.thomsonrights.com

Library of Congress Control Number: 2002113037

ISBN 10: 0-87581-449-2

ISBN 13: 978-0-87581-449-0

Brooks/Cole—Thomson Learning
10 Davis Drive
Belmont, CA 94002
USA

Asia
Thomson Learning
5 Shenton Way #01-01
UIC Building
Singapore 068808

Australia/New Zealand
Thomson Learning
102 Dodds Street
Southbank, Victoria 3006
Australia

Canada
Nelson
1120 Birchmount Road
Toronto, Ontario M1K 5G4
Canada

Europe/Middle East/Africa
Thomson Learning
High Holborn House
50/51 Bedford Row
London WC1R 4LR
United Kingdom

Latin America
Thomson Learning
Seneca, 53
Colonia Polanco
11560 Mexico D.F.
Mexico

Spain/Portugal
Paraninfo
Calle/Magallanes, 25
28015 Madrid, Spain

Contents

Preface

The United States has often opened its doors to diverse cultural groups, but the dominant power structure and social foundations have been established and maintained by European immigrants. As the population continues to diversify and more minority groups find stronger voices, the cultural landscape is changing. In counseling, this process has evoked an intense debate about the drawbacks of applying traditional mental health techniques to people from different cultures. For the past 30 years, psychologists, social workers, psychiatrists, and counselors have acknowledged the limitations of therapeutic theories, but there is still no consensus as to what techniques best fit various ethnic and cultural groups. For that matter, many students in the helping professions are European Americans who have limited experience with minority groups.

Diversity in Counseling was written to provide clear illustrations and details about cultural dynamics. The need for more specific knowledge of different cultures has become increasingly apparent in the new millennium, as the world becomes smaller and more interactive. Providing information is not enough; students must be encouraged to scrutinize their personal biases and perspectives as they are introduced to various worldviews. They must also realize that multicultural competency will require ongoing self-evaluation. For some students who had already worked through many of their biases, new prejudices surfaced after terrorists destroyed the World Trade Towers. They may feel uneasy about working with Muslims or Middle Easterners, but they are also likely to dismiss these negative thoughts and bury their feelings. I understand these reactions well. Shortly after September 11, 2001, I was interviewed about the role of Islam in fostering violence. I talked about Islam's exaltation of peace above all other virtues, but I added that peace, according to the Qur'an, comes through submission to Allah rather than through cooperative individualism, as in Western cultures. I remember feeling angry as the interview progressed, an emotion that greatly surprised me. Over the next few days, I had time to reflect on my feelings. I had studied Islam for a decade, had dozens of Muslim friends, and felt well qualified to discuss Muslim culture. But listening to months of reports about "Muslim terrorists" had subtly affected my psyche. I found myself questioning their religion, fearing their passion, and feeling frustrated by their views on apostasy. In just a few months, the media had fundamentally affected my views, and the change had occurred without my self-examination or conscious awareness.

In this text, first-hand stories are provided to introduce students to the experiences of people from different cultures. Insight exercises are offered to stimulate self-examination of assumptions and biases. Often students are encouraged to compare their cultural identity with others. We explore similarities and differences in Islamic and Christian perspectives, and we compare European American views with those of Native American and African American cultures. The text comprehensively addresses cultural groups and provides a window into various ways of life.

Ethnic and Gender Issues

In addition to ethnicity, gender and sexual orientation have an enormous impact on our cultural identities. Men and women are treated differently from birth, yet they are more similar than different. Transgendered individuals try to bridge the gender gap and sometimes find themselves stuck in the middle. Gays and lesbians maintain their gender identities but often experience intense social pressure because they find themselves attracted to members of their own sex. Are bisexuals accepted within gay culture? Are cross-dressing males accepted by societies of surgically transgendered individuals? Do men grasp the association of excessive dieting with social and personal powerlessness? Do women understand why men are more likely to display narcissism than depression? This book explores these topics and many others.

Organization of the Text

The book is divided into 11 chapters grouped into four parts. Part I provides an introduction to the theory behind multicultural counseling. Students are encouraged to look at the field as a whole. They are also introduced to worldviews, biases, and the history of the field. Part II explores various ethnic groups (African Americans, Latin Americans, Asian Americans, Native Americans, and European Americans). Within these chapters, multicultural theory is explored as it relates to each group. In Part III, gender and sexual orientation issues (i.e., gays and lesbians, transgendered persons, women, and men) are examined. Part IV explores mixed cultural identities (i.e., bicultural issues, people with disabilities, and ageism).

In order to explore ethnic and gender issues comprehensively, each chapter includes the following sections:

- History of oppression
- Family (structure and dynamics)
- Economics
- Education
- Health
- Cultural uniqueness
- Psychological issues
- Within-group differences
- Counseling issues

Although the scope of this book is wide-ranging, it is an introductory text. It is designed to provide graduate faculty with a comprehensive, multicultural curriculum for mental-health-related disciplines (e.g., counseling, psychology, social work, and psychiatry). Although detailed information is provided regarding various cultural worldviews, the text consistently returns to self-examination. Imagine how risky studying diversity could be if students only accumulated knowledge without doing any kind of self-exploration. They could easily focus on a group's common problems without considering the underlying causes. The end result could be therapists, social workers, or other professionals who had the potential to cause more harm than good. To confront this issue, this text constantly encourages students to reexamine their prejudices with the hope of training them to appreciate their cultural history while respecting the diversity of those around them.

Special Features

- *Insight Exercises:* Each chapter begins with a thought-provoking story designed to stimulate self and group exploration. Usually, these stories depict problems an individual has with the dominant culture and end by asking the reader to reflect on the issues involved.
- *Religion as diversity:* Surveys often indicate that religion is one of the most important determinants of gender and ethnic culture. In each chapter, there is a discussion of the ways religious involvement shapes cultural perspectives and behaviors.
- *Personal stories:* Each chapter includes a story depicting life from a specific cultural perspective. Stories range from a mother's attempt to fight the social stigma directed at her HIV-infected bisexual son to a Latino's struggle to understand the different values of his European American wife.

- *Questions to Consider:* Chapters close with key questions. Some cover debates that have been thoroughly discussed in the text, while others expect students to go beyond the information provided.

Acknowledgments

Throughout the construction of this text, Richard Welna, Vice President and Publisher of F. E. Peacock Publishers, provided steadfast support and direction. He also teamed me up with Janet B. Tilden, who edited this text and provided numerous suggestions and insights.

The reviews by Deryl F. Bailey (University of Georgia), Donna S. Davenport (Texas A&M University), and Pamela Highlen (Ohio State University) significantly shaped the structure and content of this text, and their expertise and guidance is greatly appreciated.

The three contributing authors (Alfonso Galan, Gwen Williams, and Gabi Clayton) offered key insights, and their openness enhanced the quality and depth of the text.

Editor's Note: Wadsworth is pleased to welcome Robert Brammer to our publishing family through our recent acquisition of the former F. E. Peacock Publishers, Inc. We also thank Ted Peacock, Richard Welna, and their entire staff for their contribution to this work and to the field of social work.

PART I

Aspects of Diversity

*W*hat images come to mind when you hear the word *diversity?* Do you think of exotic foods, eclectic radio stations, or modern art? The first image that comes to my mind is Venice, California. This beach community is home to wealthy movie stars, successful business owners, homeless drug addicts, prostitutes, and hundreds of others. The area attracts thousands of tourists—not for the waterfront, but for the people. The suburban high school students want to see the "freaks," the homeless people want to see the clueless high school students, and everyone somehow survives and enjoys this unique landscape and menagerie.

Diversity in counseling involves a similar range of people and behaviors. One of the terms most often associated with diversity is "race," an anthropological concept used to classify people according to physical characteristics, such as skin and eye color, or the shape of certain body parts such as head, eyes, ears, lips, or nose (Hernandez, 1989). The term "race" also has a social meaning that is often accompanied by stereotyping; it suggests one's status within the social system and introduces power differences as people of different "races" interact with one another (APA Task Force, 1998). Today, some people argue that the concept of race no longer applies to humanity because we have become an integrated racial society. They believe that forcing people with diverse ancestry into a specific category serves little purpose other than to construct a genetic social hierarchy. The term has also fallen out of favor because the grouping of individuals into "races" is arbitrary. It is not uncommon for political groups

1

to create definitions of race that serve their interests (e.g., separating those of Irish ancestry from those of Scandinavian origin). You will notice, throughout this text, that when the term *race* is used, it is often applied when one group is attempting to demonstrate the inferiority of another physically different group.

Without a concept of race, the notion of diversity becomes very complex. Diversity becomes something subtle and transitory, rather than endemic. Groups, to some degree, are self-defined, coming together for a variety of reasons. Someone born into a mixed racial background, for example, may seek out and explore the cultural history of all her ancestors, or she might simply identity herself with a single legacy, even if it is not associated with visible physical features, such as skin tone or hair texture. Other people strongly believe that certain cultural groups look and act different from others. Stereotyping and prejudice has caused people to lose jobs, houses, relationships, and sometimes even their lives. No one can evaluate diversity without taking into consideration the active internal facets of identity and the socially stigmatizing elements. We must also evaluate our reactions when encountering members of different groups. With some groups, we are more willing to accept their internal definitions of selfhood than we are with others. Keep this idea in mind as you read this book, and try to identify the factors that cause you to change your views.

1

Introduction to Diversity

*I*n the past, psychologists and counselors have inadequately integrated diversity into practice and theory. In many ways, our early attempts to understand minority cultures caused more harm than good.

Generally, the fields of counseling and psychology have actively explored diversity issues since the 1950s. Erikson (1950) referred to the need to broaden our perspective beyond mainstream America, but the approach, at this early stage, maintained a Eurocentric nature. Most multicultural authors, however, focused on racial differences and sought to find ways to indoctrinate cultural minorities into the "mainstream." At first, the investigation into multiculturalism addressed specific groups. The original goal of the movement was the assimilation of blacks into mainstream America, especially into the work force, but this assimilation process proved harmful (Jackson, 2001). In the 1960s, counseling and psychotherapy began to examine multicultural issues more formally (Atkinson, Morton, & Sue, 1998). By the 1970s, the number of empirical studies on ethnicity increased (Baruth & Manning, 1999) and professional organizations began to develop specialties in multicultural counseling, including sexual orientation and ethnic divisions.

As exploration into diversity continued, the quest to understand how various groups interacted led to a movement away from the "melting pot" philosophy. This expression assumes that immigrating individuals assimilate into the dominant culture and identify solely with that culture. Although there may be some advantages to such an environment, it has not existed for many years. Prior to the 1880s, the melting pot idea was viewed as the goal. Each group entering the mostly Anglo Americas would be fused into the dominant culture. Between 1880 and 1950, the theme of assimilation turned to "Americanization" or acculturation. This idea began after the mass immigration of eastern European people. By this time, the Anglo-American culture was dominant and viewed as the "true America." Other groups were expected to fit into this culture.

Acculturation theory had serious flaws. The most significant was the fact that acculturation systematically alienated minorities from the dominant and minority cultures. This alienation occurs, in part, because the dominant culture never fully accepts minority members. Even when they adopt the dominant culture's values, members of minority groups continue to experience prejudice and discrimination (Fuller, 1995). Eventually, they realize that assimilation is impossible. However, in the process of attempting to conform to the dominant culture, they appear "different" from their peers and find themselves regarded as traitors. This alienation sometimes leaves the individual feeling as if she is without a culture, trapped between two worlds that cannot accept or understand her struggles.

The Case of Alma

When I moved to a small town in Texas, I realized that things were going to be different. My husband, who is White, had taken a job in a mostly White community and I really didn't think it was going to be that difficult for me. For a while I didn't understand why I was so discouraged. I had a nice house, wonderful family, but something was missing. The missing part became evident when I was at the grocery store and heard someone speaking in Spanish. I felt my heart jump as if that person held the key to lifting the depression that controlled me. I walked over to her and started a conversation. We talked about what brought us to the little town, the foods we missed, what it was like for our families, and other similar issues. As the conversation continued, she told me that she lived in one of the poorer areas of town. Such conditions made little difference to me, but I soon realized that our living conditions would create a wall between us. When I told her that I lived in the nicest area of town, I could visually see her pull away. When she learned that I worked at the university, she quickly ended the conversation and walked away. She viewed me as a gringo, even though we each had something that the other needed. Apparently, I had been corrupted by the White world and, in her mind, would never be able to understand or accept her.

Alma's story is relatively common and makes the process of assimilation relatively difficult. Contemporary theories of acculturation de-emphasize any assimilation process. Rather than lose their ethnic or cultural identity, members of minority groups incorporate only those pieces of the dominant culture that are necessary for survival. From this point of view, individuals who attempt to blend cultures may never identify with the dominant culture and instead may become bitter and hostile.

Rather than move toward Americanization or acculturation, the current model advocates cultural pluralism. This change has occurred partly because there is a growing awareness that people remain distinct and maintain primary friendships within various cultural groups. Rather than form a single shared culture, multifarious societies seem to exist as a collection of distinct components, intermixed and adding flavor to the overall dish. The current global community has been described as a multicultural "salad bowl" (Pope, 1995) or "mosaic" (Sciarra, 1999). Authors such as Glazer and Moynihan (1970) have effectively argued that the salad bowl provides the best explanation for why ethnic groups, such as Jews, Italians, and the Irish, can be segregated within a city and maintain their old-world heritages. Each component is viewed as different from the others but none is viewed as deficient (Baruth & Manning, 1991). The blending of the cultures, like a mosaic or salad bowl, becomes more beautiful or tasty as additional elements are added. The task is not to create a single global culture but to allow all cultures to benefit and enrich themselves by sharing in the wealth provided by others.

The shift toward pluralism has occurred, in part, because the dominant culture never successfully created an integrated melting pot. A European American homeowner may accept his African American neighbor and they may even become friends, but in most cases, the two cultures will remain distinct. Hartup and Stevens (1997) found that friendships across cultures are usually based on "homophilies," or physical similarities. They found that most people choose friends based on similarities in age, gender, ethnicity, and abilities. Beyond the obvious physical differences between racial groups, they also noted that by the time children reach adolescence they seek out friendships with those who share some of their own interests and experiences. Given the effects of prejudice and discrimination, such preferences would further increase the number of intra-ethnic relationships. Such findings are similar to those revealed by Hallinan and Williams (1989), who, in their massive examination of more than 1,000 public and private high schools across the United States, found that fewer than 3.5 percent of the 18,000 friendships identified by students occurred between African American and European American teenagers.

If you are like most students exploring this area for the first time, you may be thinking, "Why can't we just accept each other and call ourselves Americans (or Canadians, British, etc.)?" You may also be thinking that an exploration into diversity only panders to irresponsibility and makes excuses for people who have yet to succeed in this country. As you continue to read this book, however, you may begin to realize the importance of culture in relation to identity. For many multicultural researchers, such as Derald Sue (2001), monoculturalism, or the tendency to apply the dominant cultural worldview to all cultural groups, may be one of the most insidious types of racism. Perhaps the best way to begin expanding your worldview is to examine how you have been shaped by your own culture.

Let's assume that you recognize the cultural differences of the people you encounter and you realize that addressing such differences could assist in the therapeutic process. What you may not realize is that none of us can effectively reach the point of accepting or fully understanding another person's culture. Our cultural worldview, as created by our values, belief systems, lifestyles, modes of problem solving, and decision-making processes, affects how we see each other and the world (Baruth & Manning, 1991). For example, many European American males have learned to control their emotions and emphasize words. They have been rewarded for containing their feelings of anger, sadness, and frustration and learning to speak politely and calmly, even if the words are incongruent with their feelings. When African American females have interacted with European American men, they have learned to interpret the tones of the expression and the intention of the speaker. They have listened to such men speak politely and calmly while actually seething with anger, and they have come to believe that the tones behind the words more accurately represent the speaker's feelings. Both communication styles are reasonable, considering their ethnic histories. European American males often have the privilege of being judged by their words, so they will concentrate on the verbal message conveyed. African American females often face prejudice and discrimination from European Americans who speak politely and calmly to them. If African American women trusted everyone they met, they would find themselves in precarious situations.

Such experiential differences as those encountered by dominant and minority group members have created different loci of control and responsibility. Sue and Sue (1999) argued that minority group members were more likely than European Americans to have an external locus of control and an external locus of responsibility. In other words, they viewed the world as a powerful force that would continue in its current path regardless of their individual actions (i.e., external locus of control). They were also more likely to believe that because of their limited resources and power, it was the responsibility of the system itself to create change (i.e., external locus of responsibility).

European Americans have the privilege of being judged by their actions, and because of this, they are more likely to have an internal locus of control and responsibility. They believe that they can change their environment and, possibly more importantly, they believe they have the responsibility to change a dysfunctional system. It should be clear, however, that these positions flow from the manner in which people are treated. When members of a group notice that their actions actually change the way society functions, they will seek to create other such changes. The converse is also true, which makes intercultural relationships more difficult.

Let's look at the notion of responsibility and control a little differently. In Table 1.1, the dimensions of responsibility and power are viewed as either dictated by the world or by the self. Imagine the difference these assumptions would make in a person's life. The person who believes she is able to carry out her dreams is much more likely to feel motivated in counseling than the person who sees himself as a victim of fate, buffeted about by forces he cannot control.

With such prominent differences in cultural worldviews and behaviors, it should come as no surprise that interracial counseling is generally more difficult than counseling with racially matched clients and counselors (Sodowsky & Parr, 1991; Sue, 1998). Our basis of understanding mental health and psychological growth is shaped by our culture. When someone presents with a different cultural history and worldview, it takes great insight on the part of the therapist to

TABLE 1.1 *Attribution of Power and Responsibility*

		RESPONSIBILITY	
		Self	*World*
POWER	*Self*	I alone am responsible for my fate and I have the ability to carry out my dreams.	My family, culture, and community will help me find my life path, but I have the power to follow through with my plans.
	World	I alone am responsible for my fate, but when I make plans the world often interferes with the process. Fate will decide how successful I am.	People in my life will help me find a path, and they will also dictate how successful I am in life. In many ways I am a passive observer.

separate cultural biases from clinical insights. For example, Russell et al. (1996) examined the relationship between therapist-client ethnic match and the therapists' evaluations of overall client functioning based on the Global Assessment Scale. Their enormous sample consisted of more than 9,000 adults in the Los Angeles County mental health system. Their findings indicated that ethnically matched therapists were more likely to judge their clients as having higher mental health functioning than did mismatched therapists.

How can therapists learn to prevent their biases from affecting their counseling? Increasing one's diversity skills is more difficult than it appears. According to Ottavi, Pope-Davis, and Dings (1994), clinical hours in multicultural settings, workshops, and multicultural supervision are all considerably less effective than coursework in building self-reported multicultural skills and knowledge. Maybe the classroom setting provides an opportunity to examine the issues from an objective or academic point of view. Whatever the reason, it appears that time is an important factor because acquiring such skills happens slowly.

The association between multicultural knowledge and skill is not accidental. Pedersen (2000) argued for a three-stage model of multicultural training: Awareness, Knowledge, and Skill. Similarly, Holcomb-McCoy (2000) examined the underlying factors of multicultural competencies. She surveyed 151 professional counselors who were members of the American Counseling Association. An exploratory factor analysis revealed five multicultural competency factors: awareness, knowledge, definitions of terms, racial identity development, and skills. It appears that knowledge and awareness must precede the development of skills, which might explain why Ottavi, Pope-Davis, and Dings (1994) found coursework more productive. The longer exposure to the topics offers more time to address awareness and identity issues.

Exposure to various cultural dynamics is only the beginning. We must actively fight against the perception that the views of one culture should be placed above those of another. This topic will be explored in great detail in the chapter on European American culture, but for now, it is important to realize that certain guidelines should be followed in order to become an effective multicultural counselor. The Society for the Psychological Study of Ethical Minority Issues (1982), or Division 45 of the American Psychological Association, came up with the following principles:

I. All individuals exist in social, political, historical, and economic contexts and the influence of racial and ethnic socialization upon individual identity may be paramount to understanding oneself as a psychologist and others (students, colleagues, clients, research subjects, and institutional administrators) in this pluralistic society. Culturally proficient psychologists value and affirm the inherent diversity and uniqueness of self and others as "persons-in-contexts."

II. Professional ethics demand that psychologists be knowledgeable about a range of differences in beliefs and practices introduced by racial and ethnic socialization and how these will necessarily affect the practice, education, and research of psychology (American Psychological Association, 1992).

III. Culturally proficient psychologists strive to recognize the interface between individuals' racial and ethnic socialization and psychological theory and research, practice, and education.

IV. Culturally proficient psychologists strive to recognize the intersection of racial and ethnic socialization with other dimensions of identity (e.g., gender, age, sexual/affectional orientation, physical disability, and socioeconomic status) and of psychological theory and research, practice, and education.

V. Culturally proficient psychologists strive to be aware of the impact of social dimensions of influence based on Eurocentric, historically-derived models and theories, and cultural deficit approaches (e.g., not valuing certain human differences) that have influenced research, practice, and education while simultaneously minimizing and or rendering invisible the role of ethnicity and race.

VI. Culturally proficient psychologists strive to be aware of their impact on others, the influence of their role in society and the concomitant responsibility to serve as agents of prosocial change.

Basically, what must occur for an individual to understand how to effectively interact with different cultural groups is an ability to see oneself differently. This notion of self-development is part of the constructivist philosophy that is gaining momentum in multiculturalism. The hermeneutical (or interpretative) shift spawned by Dilthy and others has led to the understanding that individuals create or interpret their sense of reality (Sciarra, 1999). Culture provides part of the context for such interpretations and rewards or punishes people for their creative powers, and each culture (or collection of individual inter-pretations) will view reality differently.

What would you think of a Latina who believed the ghost of her mother spoke to her regarding the inappropriateness of her pending marriage? Would such an "encounter" be regarded as a hallucination? If so, the number of Latina schizophrenics would be much higher than reported, because such experiences are relatively common. Counseling must be a collaborative effort in which the counselor and client attempt to co-construct alternate meanings and stories in order to create harmony between the client's experiences and cultural world-view (Sciarra, 1999). When counselors impose their cultural worldview upon a client, the richness of the collaboration is lost, and the session will eventually force the client to choose between the worldviews presented.

Use of Social Influence in Counseling Diverse Clients

Mark's Story

Taking this class (Diversity in Counseling) reminds me why I grew up hat-ing therapists. I was 15 when my mother sent me to a psychologist because she thought I was out of control. It's almost funny to think about it now. She [my mother] was drinking and the victim of physical abuse (my step-father hit her regularly), but *I* was the one who was out of control.

When I met the shrink, he looked me over like he was trying to make out the kind of person I was. I had to hold back my laughter because this honky could never understand my life, but he still sat there, with an arrogant look on his face, thinking he could save me from myself. I didn't realize it at the time, but I didn't need saving. I just needed a little guidance and support. What he offered was less than helpful.

At the time, I was convinced that when I grew up I was going to be a lawyer. My father was arrested when I was three, and I was determined to make him the last innocent Black man who would serve time. Maybe I was a little idealistic, but I was sincere. When Dr. Smith learned about my goals, he asked, "Do you think your grades are good enough to get into law school?" I knew what he was *really* asking. He was thinking, "What college is going to let an ignorant Black man like you into law school?" That was the end of the therapy for me. No matter what he said, it would never get through.

Mark's story, like most of the narratives in this book, is based upon my own encounters with students. The stories have been edited to preserve anonymity, but the events and tones closely match those expressed. In this case, "Mark" judged his therapist on the basis of a single question regarding his college aspi-rations. Do you think he was justified in doing so? Maybe Mark believed Dr.

Smith had a mocking tone in his voice that is not apparent in the transcript. Maybe Mark had heard similar statements from his White teachers that had sensitized him to the opinions others expressed. Whatever the reasons, the therapeutic process ended because Mark lost trust in his therapist.

In forming multicultural relationships, effective therapists will use social influence to their advantage. Social Influence theory (Strong, 1969) involves three relational dimensions: attraction, trustworthiness, and expertness/competence. Each element affects how a given relationship will function.

- *Attraction:* Although this may include physical attractiveness, it is usually the ability to see within the other something appealing. It implies understanding, acceptance, warmth, and the ability to create a relational bond. Attraction is the opposite of repulsion. It represents two objects being drawn toward each other.
- *Trustworthiness:* In addition to believing that the individual will maintain confidentiality, trustworthiness implies a lack of threat to cause harm.
- *Expertness/competence:* The therapist is able to project the training, experience, and professionalism to assist the individual in need.

All three of the above components are important when working with minority clients, but trustworthiness seems to play the most critical role, especially in mixed-ethnic sessions. A lack of trust may be caused by any of the following factors:

- Limited experience of the counselor with members of the client's cultural group;
- Sustained employment or housing discrimination;
- Sustained economic or political discrimination;
- Limited knowledge of minority issues on the part of the counselor.

After trust has been lost, reestablishing it may prove to be quite difficult. In such cases, therapists without much multicultural experience are likely to attempt to reconstruct the therapeutic alliance by distancing themselves from their feelings and striving to appear knowledgeable. This approach may further distance the therapist from the client and have a negative effect on the intervention. To engage in therapy successfully, clients must believe that the therapist is able to understand their plight. Such a belief is possible only when attraction and trustworthiness are blended into the presentation provided to the client.

With regard to the case mentioned above, after Mark felt insulted, an "expert" intervention would have had little chance of restoring the relationship. Suppose the therapist responded to Mark's emotional withdrawal by saying, "It looks like something I said offended you—would you like to talk about it?" Mark would probably regard this as further proof that the counselor could not understand him. Instead, an approach emphasizing attraction and trustworthiness would be more productive. A better therapeutic intervention would be to say, "Hey, man, I screwed up there and I can see it bothered you. It must be hard to talk to White people when they come across like they have all the answers. It won't happen again." This approach not only focuses on building a relationship, but it incorporates a promise to avoid harming the client in the future. Such admissions are likely to restore client confidence.

Sometimes the mechanism for regaining trust may come from an unexpected source. While I was working at a California veterans' hospital, a client asked me where I attended school. When he discovered that I attended the University of Southern California, located in the heart of Los Angeles, he seemed relieved. At the time, I, being an ignorant White male, interpreted the change in his affect as respect for the institution, but I was wrong. Nearly a year later, when we had successfully reached the therapeutic goals, he stated that he had felt comfortable working with me because my school was close to his home. To him, this meant that I "understood the plight of living in Watts" (the ghetto south of the university).

Anyone familiar with USC knows that the wealthy university is quite different from the impoverished community surrounding it. The students generally come from exclusive homes and have little first-hand knowledge of the ghetto culture. In this case, however, the location of the school communicated to the client that I had some notion of what it meant to be an economically deprived African American, and it was this belief that had kept him in therapy.

Recognizing Cultural Bias

If expertness is emphasized above all else, the counselor is acting upon the client by performing a set of techniques, rather than engaging the client in a therapeutic relationship. Taking an "expert" approach is unlikely to help multicultural clients because the techniques often taught in graduate schools are culturally biased. Sue and Sue (1999) rightly assert that counseling is a political endeavor, which implies that therapists who attempt to help people live their lives more effectively must first have some idea how life should be lived. Although various theoretical orientations purport varying levels of objectivity, each also introduces new biases into the counseling process. Psychoanalysts emphasize the effects of childhood and parental interaction, REBT theorists champion logical thought, Gestalt therapists advocate thinking "outside the box," multimodal therapists require a scientific foundation, and cognitive-behavioral therapists view thoughts as the foundation of emotions. All theoretical perspectives provide a framework upon which all human action can be interpreted, and they have developed standardized techniques that theoretically can be applied to all people. With most therapists being of European descent, this has meant counselors inevitably and inadvertently have applied European values to people of other groups.

Most existing counseling techniques were developed to assist European American clients, but these techniques may not be effective or acceptable for the fastest growing segments of Americans. The emphasis on talk therapy alone, without action or family involvement, is likely to appear stale and threatening to many clients (Sue & Sue, 1999). Sadly, exploration of alternatives is wrought with additional problems. Even the research into cross-cultural counseling is biased and requires a new framework (Sue & Sundberg, 1996). The problem with our current understanding of psychology is that it depends upon cultural stereotypes of mental health. We view various ethnic groups from a Eurocentric perspective, which decreases the likelihood of finding effective interventions for minority groups. This bias may explain, in part, why members of various minority groups tend to terminate counseling earlier than European American clients do (Ridley, 1989).

The same biases may appear when writing or reading texts on the subject of multiculturalism. Emphasizing "scientific" or "historical" methods may simply pass along inaccurate findings to a new generation. In many cases, problems arise when attempting to interpret information that was accurately uncovered. For example, what happens if researchers find that people from one group are less athletic, empathetic, merciful, or intelligent than members of another group? Should those findings be accepted, or should they be considered biased falsehoods?

Deficit Hypothesis

Of all the differences emphasized between cultural groups, intelligence has been the most widely discussed. What happens when someone truly believes that a client is innately less intelligent, insightful, or wise than someone from another culture? Such a position is often referred to as the deficit hypothesis, which Thomas and Sillen (1972) defined as predetermined deficiencies that relegate a group member to an inferior status. The alleged deficit may be attributed to a genetic inferiority, such as inferior brain power or limited mental development, or a cultural deficit in which the individual's ethnic lifestyle is thought to be debilitating. Both theories have taken many forms over the past century, but staunch opponents have challenged them scientifically, philosophically, and theoretically. Although a thorough analysis of the deficit hypothesis is beyond the scope of this text, the argument requires a brief summary.

The most recent reincarnation of the deficit hypothesis has been the debate surrounding Richard Herrnstein and Charles Murray's (1996) text, *The Bell Curve: Intelligence and Class Structure in American Life*. In this text, the authors begin by arguing that the construct of intelligence plays an important role in an individual's life. Intelligence, as a single construct, represents the ability to reason, plan, solve problems, think abstractly, comprehend complex ideas, learn quickly, and learn from experience. An individual with a high IQ has an advantage in life because virtually all activities require some reasoning and decision making. Conversely, a low IQ is often a disadvantage, especially in disorganized environments. From a practical point of view, a high IQ becomes more important as an individual confronts more complex situations. Fluid jobs often involve management or utilizing professional skills. However, the advantages are less noticeable for someone involved in a setting requiring routine decision making or simple problem solving.

When IQ scores for all the people from a given population are represented graphically, they form what is known as a bell curve. Most people cluster around the middle, with the average IQ score of 100 representing the 50th percentile. On either extreme of the scale, representing either mental giftedness or borderline mental dullness, the curve becomes flat. Less than 3 percent of Americans receive "superior" intelligence scores of 130 or above, and about the same percentage score 70 or below, the threshold for mental retardation.

Given this understanding of intelligence testing, if people from various ethnic groups are innately equal in abilities, then a test measuring such capabilities should not reveal any differences between groups. This would be especially true of tests such as the Weschler Adult Intelligence Scales (WAIS) that are believed to measure genetically endowed intelligence. Kaufman (1990) reports various comparisons between test scores from identical and fraternal twins and lists the broad heritability estimates. Estimates ranged from 74 percent for full-scale IQ scores for eight-year-old children to 82 percent for full-scale IQ scores for Norwegian adults. These figures are especially noteworthy because they roughly compare with the heritability estimates for height (80 percent) and are significantly higher than the estimates for weight (48 percent).

Sadly, the findings reported in *The Bell Curve* do not support the hypothesis that WAIS-R scores are equivalent for different cultural groups. Instead, they indicate that while members of all racial-ethnic groups can be found at every IQ level, the *average* score for some groups (Jews and East Asians) are centered somewhat higher than for European Americans in general. Other groups (African Americans and Latinos) are centered significantly lower than non-Hispanic Whites.

The average IQ score for European Americans is roughly 100, but the average score for African Americans is approximately 85. Few people will contest this point, but the controversy focuses on what causes the difference (Boodoo et al., 1995) and what the difference means. Is intelligence an inherited trait that remains very stable throughout the course of life? Based on the available research, it is difficult to tell. A task force from the American Psychological Association (Boodoo et al., 1995), which was formed to debate this point, concluded that differences in genetic endowment contribute substantially to individual differences in psychometric intelligence, but they also noted that the pathway by which genes produce their effects is still unknown. However, we also know that environmental factors contribute substantially to the development of intelligence (Nagoshi, 1997), but it is not clearly understood what those factors are or how they work. Attendance at school is certainly important, for example, but it is not known what aspects of schooling are critical. Additionally, family size was inversely related to verbal IQ scores for African and European American children, and these differences in intelligence did not vary by ethnicity (Steelman & Doby, 1983).

Regardless of the cause, socioeconomic status and obvious biases in test construction and administration can explain only part of the substantial difference between the mean intelligence test scores of African Americans and European Americans (Boodoo et al., 1995). This picture is not positive, but it does not encompass the whole story. Myerson, Rank, Raines, and Schnitzler (1998) used the same data Herrnstein and Murray used, but rather than finding a genetic explanation for the deficit, they found a social one. One of their most significant findings involved the differences between African Americans and European Americans who attend college. When comparing students in their final year of high school, they found, as Herrnstein and Murray did, that European Americans tended to outscore African Americans by as many as 15 IQ points. But among college graduates, the IQ scores of African American students increased four times more than did the scores of their European American classmates. European American students still scored about 7 points higher, but the diminishing gap between average IQ scores implies that IQ has a strong social component.

Neisser (1998) argues that this diminishing gap between various groups also occurs in areas other than college. For the past 20 years, IQ scores for all groups have increased, but they have increased most rapidly among African Americans. The trend appears to correspond to the growth in social programs instituted for young minority students. These trends could also be attributable to changes in nutrition or advances in technology. Whatever the reason, something is reducing the gap between cultural and racial groups. These changes pose serious challenges to the deficit hypothesis, and imply that the differences between groups may be eliminated in the next 50 years.

From a counseling perspective, it is important to realize that just because an individual client belongs to a group whose average IQ score is currently lower than that of another group, it does *not* imply that he or she is less intelligent. African Americans, as well as every other ethnic group, are represented among the highest intellectual groups, just as European Americans and Asian Americans are represented among the lowest intellectual groups. Stereotyping individuals to fit group norms is harmful to everyone involved.

Ogbu (Gibson & Ogbu, 1991; Ogbu, 1990) proposed one of the most widely accepted theories for differences in intelligence scores. He argued that performance differences in academics and other achievement areas stem from a group's history of opposition. This explains why African Americans (an involuntary minority), who were brought to America as slaves, traditionally performed below Asian Americans (an immigrant minority) who came voluntarily. The descendants of oppressed racial groups tend to lack the vision of potential success that members of nonoppressed groups possess. These doubts concerning their abilities extend to their performance in school, in society, and in the workplace. Many students from oppressed groups do not envision success in their future and, therefore, are not inspired to exceed the cultural limitations placed on them. Because of its historical and cross-cultural appeal, this explanation has been well received by academics, although key implications of the theory have not been carefully tested. In fact, there is recent evidence to suggest that this widely accepted theory may be wrong.

Ainsworth-Darnell and Downey (1998) investigated Ogbu's theories on oppositional culture. For the first time, their study investigated a large longitudinal sample of African American, Asian American, and non-Hispanic White high school sophomores. As expected, they found that individuals from historically oppressed groups (involuntary minorities) had lower achievement scores than those from groups who freely came to the host country (immigrant minorities). What they did not find was support for the foundational elements of the theory. It was hypothesized that involuntary minorities signify their antagonism toward the dominant group by resisting school goals, and individuals from the dominant group and immigrant minorities maintain optimistic views of their chances for educational and occupational success. Ainsworth-Darnell and Downey found that these constructs did not accurately predict successful performance in academic or occupational settings.

While looking for other possible explanations, Richman et al. (1997) examined the effects of current prejudices on various groups. They instructed European American fourth-year teachers-in-training to estimate the grade point average and intelligence of either four African American or four European American school children. They found, as expected, that the African American students were rated less favorably, but the racial attitudes of the student teachers predicted the differences in their scores. Basically, the more prejudiced they were, the lower they rated their African American students. Their racist beliefs, or lack thereof, also predicted how much pleasure they derived from reading a short story or a poem supposedly written by an African American author. If such biases are present among researchers and counselors, the findings reported above could create significant problems for minority clients and students.

It is also important to realize that tests such as the WAIS-R, WAIS-III, and WISC-III may be culturally biased. They may provide higher scores for mental processes that mimic highly functional European Americans. Saccuzzo, Johnson, and Russell (1992) found that even gifted (highly intelligent) African American children tended to emphasize different language skills from European Americans, and consequently their verbal IQ scores were lower than expected in some cases. Vincent (1991) also argues that educational and economic opportunities that have opened up in the United States over the past two decades have lessened the gap between the intelligence scores of African and European American children. The fact that social changes have decreased the gap, he suggests, means that the IQ differences are not caused by genetic factors and instead may reflect bias in the instruments themselves.

Probably the most interesting, and the most disconcerting, studies involving the deficit hypothesis relate to the way test takers perceive the tests themselves. Claude Steele and Joshua Aronson (2000) performed an interesting test on the psychology of self-perception. They gave an exam to two mixed-race groups of students. The first group was told that the exam was a simple problem-solving exercise; the other group was told that their scores would show how smart they were. The European American students from the two groups obtained similar scores, but the African American subjects who believed they were taking an intelligence test performed considerably worse than those who thought they were taking a nondiagnostic test. In a sense, the African American subjects not only accepted the stereotype that they were less intelligent, they acted upon this prejudice with a self-fulfilling prophecy.

To overcome the biases found in research, counselors, researchers, and teachers must begin by engaging in intense self-evaluation. Before counselors can realize what it means to be a member of a different ethnic/cultural group, they must learn how their ethnic/cultural/gender worldview influences their perception of the other group. Some counselors may choose to assume that they have transcended their heritage to attain greater objectivity, but our views will always be influenced by our histories.

Appreciating Divergent Worldviews

The deficit model of diversity counseling basically assumes that one culture lacks something that is present in another culture. While it is true that one culture may possess strengths lacking in another, these differences do not mean that one culture is better than the other. Each cultural system must be viewed in its entirety before it can be dissected into parts. One method of accomplishing such an overview, as recommended by Ibrahim (1985), is to explore *value orientations*. Each culture will create different orientations with respect to time, activity, relationships, and ecology. Table 1.2 describes a variety of value orientations.

Each orientation has its own unique strengths. A society adopting any of these can succeed and flourish, but cultures with conflicting orientations may have difficulties interacting with one another. Consider the example of a Native American therapist who is counseling a European American client. Many Native American cultures value the past and present more than the future. They will maintain their present path, if it seems productive, rather than switch to a new task, because they believe each task should be brought to fruition. Many European American cultures value the present and future more than the past. Rigidly maintaining schedules and appointments is viewed as respectful

TABLE 1.2 *A Model of Values*

Dimensions	Value Orientations		
Time	*Past*: We must be guided by history, and especially our personal and cultural experiences.	*Present*: We should emphasize the here and now. Other time frames are distractions pulling us away from the moment.	*Future*: We must focus on our goals (teleology). Without goals and direction, our present actions are ineffectual.
Action	*Being*: Our actions should be secondary to the condition of our soul, mind, or psyche.	*Active becoming*: Our behaviors should be focused on the development of an inner self.	*Doing*: Actions are essential. Working hard and behaving morally is more important than finding inner peace.
Family	*Dependence*: We should always remain attached to our family, respecting our parents and trusting their wisdom.	*Interdependence*: Family should be used as consultants, but not depended upon. We should be there for each other when necessary.	*Independence*: Families help to equip fully functional members of society who are ready to face the world on their own.
Spirituality	*Pantheism*: God is part of nature and acts in and through all living things.	*Humanism*: Spirituality may be of value, but the evidence of the divine is in the hearts and actions of humanity.	*External deity*: God exists beyond nature. The divine is something we should seek and follow but we can never be identified with it.
Ecology	*Life force*: Nature is holy and should be preserved, respected, and honored.	*Co-existence*: Nature is valuable, but so is humanity's progress.	*Androcentric*: Humanity's progress is more important than the preservation of nature. Nature will adapt to our demands of it.
Sexuality	*Polyamorous*: Multiple sexual partners help to increase our sexual satisfaction and awareness of ourselves.	*Serial monogamy*: Stay with people until the relationship loses passion, and then move on to the next relationship.	*Monogamy*: Avoid premarital sex and stay with one mate for life.
Gender roles	*Feminist*: Women and men should feel comfortable interchanging any and all social roles.	*Developmental*: Gender roles are likely to shift over time, with each person playing several roles over a lifetime.	*Patriarchal*: Men should be the leaders of the family. Women should focus on raising children and maintaining household stability.

of others. If the Native American therapist is working with another client who is making considerable progress during a session and requires more time than the allotted hour, she may be willing to work longer with this client. The European American client in the waiting room may become frustrated by the delay because he feels disrespected and believes the therapist to be unprofessional. Such value differences could cause friction if not discussed.

A European American therapist who values independence may have difficulty understanding and appreciating a Latina client who feels ashamed because she is distant from her mother. A Taoist client, who views his strength as coming from a divine encounter with nature, might clash with the humanistic therapist who denies any supernatural powers. A liberal European American therapist may feel that her fundamentalist, African American client is limiting herself by letting her husband act as the household leader. No matter what value is being addressed, contrasting values can be difficult to understand, let alone appreciate. Conscious effort must be made to step into the client's perceptions and see the world through his or her eyes.

In addition to ethnicity, other factors affect how people conceive their world. Class, usually determined by socioeconomic level, also plays a role in how the world is perceived. Lower-class individuals are often less time oriented and are motivated by immediate, concrete reinforcement (Peterson & Nisenholz, 1987). Middle- or upper-class therapists may have difficulty understanding the cultural differences between their views and those of clients from different socioeconomic backgrounds. Sometimes class values will intermix with ethnic values, but both are important components of how individuals see the world.

Recognizing Your Prejudices

What does it mean to be "White" or "Black" in America? The answer to this question addresses the notion of ethnic identity, which is the sum total of group members' feelings about those values, symbols, and common histories that identify them as a distinct group (Rice, 2001). Ethnic identity is an essential human need. It is related to self-esteem, coping mechanisms, and one's sense of belonging in the world (Smith, 1991). For many European Americans, the path to identity is one of assimilation, in which immigrants learn to identify with the dominant society and relinquish ties to their ethnic culture. Such a path, as mentioned earlier, is untenable for many minority group members because they are unlikely to be fully accepted by the dominant culture. Instead, they must choose between the following three options: integration, separation, or marginality (Rice, 2001). As shown in Table 1.3, integration involves identification with both the dominant society and one's traditional ethnic culture. Separation, as the name implies, involves exclusive focus on the cultural values and practices of the ethnic group and a complete rejection of the dominant society. Marginality is simply the absence or loss of one's culture of origin combined with lack of acceptance by the dominant society.

Marginality is most likely to occur when the individual attempts to connect with the dominant society but is pushed away unexpectedly. A few years ago, a colleague of mine worked with a college football team. While preparing for an away game, the team piled into the coach's hotel room to watch a pay-per-view boxing match together. The event featured one "White" and one "Black"

TABLE 1.3 *Paths to Ethnic Identity*

		DOMINANT CULTURE	
		Rejection	*Acceptance*
TRADITIONAL ETHNIC CULTURE	*Acceptance*	Separation	Integration
	Rejection	Marginality	Assimilation

fighter, who appeared evenly matched during most of the fight. As the fight drew to a close, one contender took a commanding lead.

As the crowd awaited the officials' decision, the students made predictions regarding the victor. All of the students believed the "Black" fighter had won. After a few minutes, the referee announced that the "White" boxer had won by decision. The students of European descent (comprising about half of the team) erupted. They could not understand how something like this could happen. All of the African American students, however, walked out of the room with their heads lowered. When questioned, one of the Black students commented, "That's life." Throughout their lives, they had faced similar oppression and injustice. The boxing incident simply served to remind them that they could not change the prejudices of society. The playing field was not level. Some people have never had the chance to earn their position in life because someone would knock them down before they ever made a move.

If African Americans identify completely with the dominant society, marginality is more likely to occur. Events such as the boxing story described above will interfere with their sense of identity. However, separation and integration are more likely and stem from an awareness of their cultural identity. By the time they enter college, most minority students will have some idea what it means to be a member of a cultural group. They have faced discrimination and often learned to take pride in their history and heritage. European Americans, however, may have given the matter little thought and simply accepted what they view as the American culture, which really means the dominant culture. When asked about their cultural identity, they typically respond with statements such as, "I've never really thought of it before," or "it's no different from being like anyone else." Both of these replies indicate assimilation. Other clues come by asking students to describe themselves. Most European Americans will offer descriptions such as American, person, adult, man/woman, their job title, religion, or other generalized criteria. Non-White students, however, tend to offer more ethnically related answers (Fuller, 1995).

In addition to accepting the dominant culture, European Americans often believe they have never really benefited by the color of their skin. For the most part, they are either unaware or in denial of their political and social privileges. When asked, they cannot recall any instance in which someone gave them something without their having earned it, and therefore, they believe they have not lived a privileged life. Some will even strongly protest the accusation that they received any of their success because of the color of their skin. They argue that they worked hard for what they desired, and others can freely do the same. However, this line of thinking has a serious flaw. Social privilege does not equal unmerited favors. In the case of racism and discrimination, social privilege means that an individual can earn social rewards.

Let's back up a little and provide some definitions. The *Random House Dictionary of the English Language* (Second Edition, 1987) offers the following definitions:

(a) *Prejudice*: (1) An unfavorable opinion or feeling formed beforehand or without knowledge, thought, or reason. (2) Any preconceived opinion or feeling, either favorable or unfavorable. (3) Unreasonable feelings, opinions, or attitudes, especially of a hostile nature, regarding a racial, religious, or national group. (4) Such attitudes considered collectively; e.g., the war against prejudice is never-ending.

(b) *Stereotype*: (4) A simplified and standardized conception or image invested with special meaning and held in common by members of a group: e.g., the cowboy and Indian are American stereotypes.

(c) *Racism*: (1) A belief or doctrine that inherent differences among the various human races determine cultural or individual achievement, usually involving the idea that one's own ethnicity is superior and has the right to rule others. (2) A policy, system of government, etc., based upon or fostering such a doctrine; discrimination. (3) Hatred or intolerance of another ethnic group. (Though not defined by Random House, *institutional racism* is also an important concept; it is a covert form of racism that is embedded in the development of political policies and decision-making practices.)

(d) *Discrimination*: (2) Treatment or consideration of, or making a distinction in favor of or against, a person or thing based on the group, class, or category to which that person or thing belongs rather than on individual merit: e.g., racial and religious intolerance and discrimination.

(e) *Sexism*: (2) Discrimination or devaluation based on a person's sex, as in restricted job opportunities; esp., such discrimination against women.

(f) *Heterosexism*: A prejudiced attitude or discriminatory practices against homosexuals by heterosexuals.

Of these terms, the idea of prejudice is the most important to therapists because it is fundamental to understanding the concepts of discrimination and racism. Without prejudice there is no racism. The term *prejudice* literally means to have a preconceived judgment or opinion without sufficient knowledge to render such a claim (Axelson, 1999). As such, prejudices can be positive as well as negative, although most theorists use the term to describe negative judgments (Ridley, 1989). Imagine you are walking down the street, and you see a gray-haired, 50-year-old male, carrying a stack of books, and wearing a sports coat with leather patches at the elbows. Your first impression may be that this person is a professor. Such a judgment may be positive, but it is still made without sufficient reasoning to support your claim. The judgment may in fact be accurate, but it forces the individual into a contrived category.

Although prejudices of any form can be harmful, they are also necessary. We learn what types of people to fear, respect, appreciate, and dominate. If we could not characterize people based on stereotypes and prejudices, it would be impossible to function within a society. As social creatures, we judge people based on their presentation. This does not mean, however, that as enlightened creatures, we cannot attempt to examine our prejudices and remove all those that we can identify. The trick rests in identifying the prejudices that we have long accepted or ignored.

More than a decade ago, on the way home from a lecture, I found myself gazing at the driver next to me as we waited for the light to change. He drove a new BMW, wore an expensive suit, and looked in peak physical condition. Instantly, I thought to myself, "He's just like me." As he drove away, I realized that his new car moved a little faster than my old, very abused Honda. I looked down and noticed that I was wearing shorts with a T-shirt and looked a little disheveled. The other difference between us was the color of our skin. I began to wonder what impression I might have had if he had been of another ethnicity. After very little thought, I realized that I considered us socially equal only because his skin was dark. Had his skin been lighter, I probably would have considered him my social superior, although even this would have been problematic. This event took place 15 years ago, but I remember it vividly. It forced me to realize that even when we feel close to members of different ethnic groups or gain knowledge regarding cultural differences, the prejudices running rampant in society take hold of our subconscious minds.

Let me offer another illustration. Imagine you are visiting the Museum of Tolerance in Los Angeles, California. As you enter the building, there are two doors at the end of a long hallway. To the left, there is a massive, beautifully decorated door bearing the inscription "nonprejudiced people enter here." The other door is plain, about four feet tall, two feet wide, and rather unattractive. Above this modest door, the plaque reads, "Prejudiced people enter here." Those who have the self-confidence and nerve to open the large door find it quite impenetrable. All patrons wishing to enter the building must crouch down and humbly enter through the smaller door.

The large door represents the myth of the unprejudiced person—he or she doesn't really exist. When we enter counseling sessions under the false assumption that we lack biases, we deceive ourselves and potentially harm our clients. We are also likely to project our prejudices onto others. When we refuse to acknowledge our potential for bias, we open ourselves up to acting upon our prejudices. Discrimination is the act of making a distinction in favor of or against a person based on the group, class, or category to which that person belongs rather than upon individual merit. It is this active form of prejudice that explains why minority clients are frequently diagnosed with more severe disorders and are given less favorable prognoses (Zane, Enomoto, & Chun, 1994). To reverse these patterns, knowledge must be paired with personal growth. We must learn to identify our biases, even the suspicion of bias, if we are to become successful multicultural counselors. Doing so demonstrates wisdom, sound judgment, and a healthy respect for one's client. Failure to recognize our prejudices, on the other hand, leads to inevitable biases and ultimately harmful discrimination.

Consider the following comment from a student in a multicultural graduate class:

> The only problem I would possibly have with multicultural education would be in cases where micro-cultural identification leads to separatism and favoritism. The fear of offending any one particular group (and I think there are almost as many groups as there are individuals) has brought the practice of "political correctness" to laughable extremes in some cases. Other than that, I think the objective of teaching each student according to his need and learning styles, as dictated partially by his cultural background, is an objective that is worth pursuing. And, as for the "political correctness" of using "his" in the previous sentence: "he" is the appropriate generic pronoun that may be used in a sentence of that nature.

At this point in his education, this student is certain he knows what is right and merely wants to better understand the plight of some "less fortunate" individuals. However, his limited ability to examine himself has created some dangerous obstacles. Are there so many different "groups" that he need not fear offending any of them? He alludes to this by stating that the pronoun "his" adequately applies to all students and that no apology is necessary for its use. Why is this the case? What makes the term "his" more acceptable than the feminine term "she"? Would it offend male students to be included in the global pronoun "she"? If so, what is so frightening about identifying with womanhood, and is this fear something that girls will inevitably internalize? Could his use of the term "his" be an attempt to establish a masculine hierarchy and view women as lesser creatures? Whatever the case, he refuses to acknowledge or investigate his prejudices and instead is likely to pass them along to the next generation.

Regardless of an individual's ethnic background or identity, prejudices and stereotypes are buried deep within every person's mind. These unacknowledged prejudices often interfere with counseling by creating "micro-aggressions" hidden beneath the counselor's conscious awareness (Falicov, 1998). Subconscious prejudices or cultural biases can hinder the flow of a counseling session by tacitly denigrating an individual's self-worth. If you are not aware of your own prejudices, how will you know when to refer clients to a different therapist? Unfortunately, this is a very difficult question to answer, but increasing your awareness of your prejudices will assist you in the decision-making process.

Ethnicity Models

Do we simply accept prejudice as a way of life and move on to other topics? To do so would undermine any effective intervention. All people are prejudiced and have discriminated against others. Realizing our potential for unfair and prejudicial actions allows us to actively explore new ways of thinking and acting. In order to fully understand our biases, we must first examine the lessons we have learned from our cultural background.

Most people tend to take their culture for granted. Aries et al. (1998) sought to examine college students' awareness of the cultural differences and similarities around them. The researchers specifically examined the conditions under which college students were most likely to notice the gender, racial, or ethnic constitution of their peers. For an entire week, participants carried beepers and notified the researchers whenever they had an impression regarding the racial makeup of their present group. In general, when the individuals mixed with people from their own ethnic group and gender, they were unaware of the cultural makeup of the group. Certain situations seemed to highlight the awareness of cultural differences, too. The participants in this study were most aware of cultural differences when in a public setting or during athletic involvement. It is also interesting to note that European Americans were more aware of ethnicity when they were in the racial minority. The situation was just the opposite for members of minority groups. The non-White participants were more aware of ethnicity when they were in the racial majority. We learn to identify differences when we encounter situations that differ from our expectations.

There are factors that can help people overcome the effects of their own prejudices. Phinney, Ferguson, and Tate (1997) examined the ways eighth- and eleventh-graders viewed themselves and those outside their cultural group. Rather than examine the avenue for negative prejudice, they used a path analysis to help identify the mechanisms by which people develop positive views of ethnic identity. They found two distinct pathways leading to positive out-group attitudes. In the first, simply growing older led the 133 African Americans, 219 Latinos, and 195 Asian Americans involved in the study to have a stronger sense of ethnic identity. The eleventh-graders had more positive in-group attitudes, and, in turn, this positive conception of their own group contributed to more positive out-group attitudes. The second pathway revealed that children who spent more time with peers from other cultures *outside of school* were involved in more cross-cultural interaction during school. The fact that only relationships outside of school correlated with positive out-group attitudes implies that children must feel free to interact with those they view as different.

Do we really need in-groups and out-groups within a pluralistic society? It appears that we do. We may hope to someday reach a level where color, language, gender, or sexual orientation no longer play a role in forming friendships and identity, but this seems unlikely to occur. If anything, there is a growing acceptance that our conception of in-groups intensifies throughout our lives. Should diversity counselors attempt to help individuals from minority groups conform to the majority group's expectations, or should counselors help individuals learn to develop their self-concept and continue to identify with their minority group? There is no clear answer. Each group and individual will require one mode or the other. What is clear is that individuals will create an ethnic identity of some type, and counselors should be sensitive to the decisions their clients make.

To better understand the development of an individual's ethnic identity, it may be helpful to compare it to the growth of a tree. Even from a young age, a tree is identifiable as a specific type, but no two trees are exactly alike. Some face greater hardships and must adapt to limited water supplies, poor soil, or inadequate sunlight. Others are damaged by animals, pruned by gardeners, or played upon by children. All of these factors will change the structure of the tree. In some cases, the tree may change so much that it no longer resembles others of its kind. In the same way, our view of our ethnicity and our view of the world around us is shaped as we develop. Many Latino groups, for example, learn to accept the hardships of life as a matter of fate, which helps them to cope with overwhelming obstacles. Many European American groups believe the individual is required to change social structures that create hardship, a belief that stems from growing up in a well-nurtured and reasonably protected environment (Draguns, 1989).

In order to investigate how acculturation works for different groups, we must examine each group individually. There should also be an attempt to separate demographic variables from issues related to mental health. For example, African Americans have historically been more likely to drop out of high school. Is this related to the prejudice they experience from the dominant society, the added pressure of financial hardship, unique physical health issues that are relatively unknown to European Americans, or something else? Without exploring how each of these individual factors contributes to the larger picture of their mental health, we may be creating additional biases by simply purporting psychological dysfunction. Similar arguments could be made for gender issues. The structure of the family has a significant effect on the way men and women perceive themselves. Such factors also influence how men and women perceive their occupational or academic roles and how they spend the majority of their time. In order to explore these issues more thoroughly, the remainder of this text is divided into two parts (racial/ethnic components and gender/sexuality issues). Each chapter explores the following areas:

- History of oppression
- Family structure and dynamics
- Economics
- Education

- Health
- Cultural uniqueness
- Psychological issues
- Within-group differences
- Counseling issues

Admittedly, some of these headings are value laden. Psychological labels, for example, have been used to stereotype African Americans in socially deprecating ways. During the time of slavery, Samuel Cartwright created a diagnostic category for runaway slaves (*draptemania*, or flight from madness) because he believed only insane African Americans would run from their protective homes. This mentality migrated into the modern age. Even psychological giants such as C. G. Jung published racist theories concerning African Americans and Jews. As president of the Nazi New German Society of Psychotherapy, he argued that members of the Jewish race (as it was often called) were "genetically inferior" to those of European descent (Alexander & Selesnick, 1966, p. 408).

Problems with underdiagnosing must also be explored. If clients have experienced difficulty acculturating to the dominant society, they are likely to wrestle with feelings of displacement, poor self-esteem, or disillusionment. Such conditions could mask a comorbid clinical depression that is unrelated to the adjustment issues. Therapists, attempting to be sensitive to the oppression their clients have faced, may overlook or minimize valid psychological or psychiatric factors. Allowing the depression to continue could also interfere with the client's acculturation, which would marginalize the entire intervention.

Given these historical and practical warnings, any discussion of psychological, relationship, and counseling issues requires extreme sensitivity, but this does not alter the fact that people of different racial groups are likely to present with different psychological complaints. For example, the alcoholism rate for Native Americans living on reservations significantly exceeds that of other population groups. The wise multicultural counselor will use these statistics to explore areas of possible psychological risk without stereotyping individual clients. All of these topics will be explored with sensitivity, and ideally this text will challenge you to reevaluate your views of many diverse population groups.

You may have realized, by this point, that the preceding introduction to "diversity" lacks sufficient depth into gender issues. There is a two-fold reason for this: (1) most people are aware of their gender identity and believe they have a grasp of maleness and femaleness, and (2) a conceptual understanding of ethnicity undergirds our gender identity. As we begin to discuss gender issues more thoroughly, however, I hope you will start to realize that gender and sexual identity are more complex than they appear. Ideally, you will acquire a deeper understanding of the ways in which gender, which is really a social construction of our sexuality, is based upon the roles instituted by our ethnic culture.

When we begin to discuss gender issues, readers should be aware that their perceptions may be challenged. Exploring issues such as homosexuality, transvestism, bisexuality, spousal abuse, and other such topics can threaten our religious positions, make us question our sexual relationships, or force us to reopen old wounds. Although these topics may be difficult to examine, imagine what they are like for the client who is wrestling with them. For now, you may want to see if you can answer all of the following questions:

- How can you counsel men who are abusing their spouses?
- Would you treat a woman with depression differently from a man with the same diagnosis?
- Are children with cross-sexed behaviors likely to become gay, lesbian, or transsexual in adulthood?
- When counseling parents of a child who was born with a penis but with female chromosomes, should you recommend raising the child as a boy or a girl?

It would be impossible to fully investigate all the gender issues a counselor is likely to encounter professionally; instead, this book takes a sampling across three broad categories of gender/sexual identity: (1) gay, lesbian, and transgendered clients, (2) women's issues, and (3) men's issues. Each chapter in this part of the book examines the group's common history of oppression, etiology of problems, family dynamics, economics, education, health, cultural uniqueness, within-group differences, psychology, and counseling issues. As with all topics in psychology, any discussion of common group behaviors should not be applied to every individual in the group. For example, when investigating economic issues, we find that gay men are likely to have incomes above the national average while lesbian women have a mean income that is closer to the poverty level. This trend exists because men still tend to earn more than women, and therefore two men are likely to earn a higher combined income than two women. However, the gay or lesbian client who begins therapy with you may not meet this profile. Trends are discussed only to provide a framework for understanding issues certain groups are likely to face.

In the chapters on sexuality and gender identity, special care must be taken with the sections on psychological issues and a new topic, etiology. Both of these headings appear value laden, but they are used to address trends within a given population as indicated in contemporary research. For example, women are twice as likely as men to receive a mood disorder diagnosis, and men are more likely to seriously injure or kill their spouses. In these sections, statistics and trends are emphasized over the rationale for the behavior. We will address the possibility of diagnostic bias, but our main focus will be on the skills needed to counsel clients with these presenting problems.

Achieving Multicultural Competence

When exploring the various cultural groups, we should pay special attention to the diversity of the culture at hand. The various groups are profiled to provide a unique window into each group's stereotypical customs, beliefs, and functioning. To effectively incorporate this information into your worldview, it is necessary to heed the following guidelines:

- Culturally diverse individuals and groups should be the primary source of information about their situation, condition, or direction (Locke, 1998). This text should be treated as an introduction and should be a catalyst, not a replacement, for interaction with members of other cultures.

- Multicultural skills must be personalized. There are recommendations in this book regarding interventions with diverse clients. Using them exactly as they are expressed is unlikely to produce the desired response. Multicultural clients will respond best to your interventions if they are both *knowledgeable* and *personalized*. Your intervention must be tailored to fit your personality and that of your client.

- Learn from your mistakes (Hanna, Bemak, & Chung, 1999). If the information provided in this text does not apply to your client, you would be wise to say something like, "My culture tends to look at that differently. I'm interested to know more about your culture's perceptions."

- Learn to reframe problems. Often, minority cultures will internalize negative views about their culture. Learning to help the client embrace the positive elements can help to create a better therapeutic direction. For example, many Native American cultures emphasize the present over scheduled plans. Rather than making them "lazy," this time orientation often shows a greater commitment to completing the task at hand.

- Recognize your prejudices and cultural perceptions. Even though we have already discussed this topic, one more example may help illustrate this point. One European American student, while taking a multicultural graduate class, described her painful childhood and the mistreatment she bore at the hands of several African Americans. She ended by saying, "It took me a long time to get over this, but I can honestly say that I'm no longer prejudiced." Following her disclosure, we asked her why she had made eye contact with virtually everyone in the room except the African American student sitting next to her. At first, she denied it. When we asked the African American student if he was aware of it, he lit up and said, "Ohhhhhhh, yeah." Be open to learning from your fellow students, professors, and friends.

- Start to view psychological problems as social constructions: Western psychology tends to assign responsibility for an individual's mental health entirely to the individual. Many non-Western cultures scoff at this approach and place partial responsibility on society, family, God, demons, and other factors. It is important to realize that the Western view of mental health is simply one perspective among many.

- Examine cultures as facets and wholes. Each culture comprises countless facets. In many ways, these facets are each cultures in themselves but are uniquely combined for an individual. An African American woman, a wealthy Native American, a gay European American man, and an unemployed bi-cultural woman will each have a unique point of view. It may take some time before therapists can view their clients' histories from both micro and macro perspectives.

Therapists who are able to incorporate the above-mentioned components into their counseling interventions are more likely to succeed at multicultural therapy. In addition to this list, you could also add personal characteristics such as tolerance, humor, and wisdom. Above all, however, effective multicultural counselors will continually expand their cultural knowledge and surround themselves with diversity.

Questions to Consider

1. Social influence theory (i.e., the dimensions of attraction, trustworthiness, and expertness/competence) takes on additional importance when dealing with minority clients. Which of these factors is likely to be the most important?

2. How does the deficit hypothesis explain why people from different cultures appear to have different levels of intelligence?

3. If assimilation into the dominant culture is no longer considered helpful for minority clients, what should be the new focus?

4. How would you work with a client who believes society is responsible for his plight in life and feels impotent to change the conditions around him? What difficulties might arise in therapy?

5. Can you imagine ways multicultural clients might be overdiagnosed? How might views of ghosts, herbal healing, drug use, gambling, spanking children, diet, and education be associated with specific cultures?

6. What responsibility should therapists take for helping clients build productive in-group and out-group beliefs?

7. How important is a client's worldview to the way he or she interacts with the therapist?

PART II

Counseling Ethnic Populations

"*E*thnicity" connotes a common culture and shared meaning. It includes feelings, thoughts, perceptions, expectations, and actions of a group resulting from shared historical experiences. Pedersen (2000) defined ethnicity as a cultural heritage that is preserved from one generation to another as a means of classification or identification. Ethnicity can include religious groups (e.g., Jews), country of origin (e.g., Africa), or any other facet passed down to children. Diversity even extends to our culture, which includes components such as our geographic community, religion, gender, sexual orientation, and socioeconomic status. Herskovits (1948) referred to culture as that part of our environment created by people. As such, it is not explicitly taught but rather absorbed through socialization and reinforced by lifelong incidental learning.

These varying definitions of diversity (summarized in the table below) make counseling an inherently multicultural process. A woman counseling a man, marital therapy with an interracial couple, a single man counseling a full-time mother, or virtually any other combination falls under the auspices of multiculturalism. Attempting to understand all such possible groups, however, would be impossible. Instead, we strive to develop an appreciation of cultural groups as a whole. This is especially important in America, where the ethnic and racial structure is shifting. In 1996, the estimated U.S. population was 271 million. This total comprised 195.8 million Whites, 32.8 million Blacks, 2.0 million American Indians, 9.9 million Asians, and 29.6 million Hispanics (Tomes, 1998). If all non-White groups were added together, such "people of color" would comprise about 28 percent of the total population. In the 2000 census, the number of non-Whites increased to 30.8 percent, and the number jumped to 39.1 percent for children under 18 years of age (Annie E. Casey Foundation, 2001). By the year 2035, the population is projected to be 358 million, with people of color making up about 41 percent of that total. By mid-century, the total is projected to be 394 million, with people of color representing nearly half (48 percent) of that total. The resulting changes will affect the general population faster than they will influence the field of psychology. What does this mean to therapists? It means that therapists, especially European American therapists, must learn as much as they can about minority worldviews because there will not be enough minority psychologists to fill the potential need (Tomes, 1998). Knowing about ethnic groups requires more than understanding stereotypical behaviors. It requires therapists to put themselves into the lives of people from different cultures and ethnicities. We must learn to understand the culture from the inside out. How are people treated in school? What is the basis of their relationships? How does the dominant society treat them? As you read through the following chapters, try to imagine you are experiencing the information firsthand. Let yourself become angry, sad, or excited.

Examples of Terms Used to Indicate Identity

Term	Examples
Race	American Indian Black (African American) Pacific Islander (Asian) White Biracial
Ethnicity	Ancestry from a specific country or continent Membership in some social (ethnic) religious group (e.g., Jewish)
Culture	Geographic community Religion Gender Sexual orientation Class (socioeconomic status)

2

African Americans

INSIGHT EXERCISE Imagine today started differently from most days. Soon after leaving home, you begin to feel that everyone is looking at you critically. You check your outfit, smell your clothes, and convince yourself that you are okay and that there must be something wrong with *them*. You drive your car into the service station and notice that the attendant instantly starts watching you. He looks down when you make eye contact but then continues staring again when you look away. Strange!

At lunch, you notice that the hostess seats you away from the main crowd and frequently casts suspicious glances toward you. She never asks if you want something—instead, she hovers, as if you are about to steal a menu. After work, on your way to your counseling session, you are pulled over by the police. The officer informs you that you have a low tire and might need to refill it soon. He never once looks at you as he provides this courteous advice. Instead, his eyes roam about the car. Could he be looking for drugs?

As you enter your counselor's office you feel relieved that you can finally tell someone about the events of your day. Before you are able to tell the tale, you notice, only for a second, the same critical expression in the eyes of your counselor. Is it safe to talk with this person?

History of Oppression

The 1976 publication of Alex Haley's *Roots* gave the world a frightening glimpse into the life of the African American slave. The story of Kunta Kinte was filled with graphic depictions of men and women being stolen from their homes, shipped to America in chains as human cargo languishing in urine-, vomit-, and feces-filled chambers below the decks of slave vessels, and forced into slavery. African men and women were chained, branded, separated from their families, separated from their tribes, raped, and forbidden to speak. Teaching slaves to read and write was punishable by imprisonment, and relationships between members of the perceived racial groups almost always led to dangerous levels of harassment and death for both partners. There can be no doubt that such trauma left an indelible impact on African American slaves and their descendants for generations to come.

Much of the violence perpetrated against the African American slaves of long ago still festers in our society today. The story of James Byrd, Jr., testifies to the ongoing influence of racism. Mr. Byrd, a 49-year-old African American from Jasper, Texas, was walking down a dusty highway during the summer of 1998. As he walked, three young White men drove their pickup past him. He apparently asked for or was offered a ride. They drove to a remote spot in the pine forest outside Jasper. Soon thereafter, an altercation occurred. Only three people will ever know exactly what took place, and even if the events of that day could be known, few would want to know them. We do know that Mr. Byrd's body was found the following Sunday. His head and other body parts were strewn across a country road ten miles from his home. Each part took some time to discover. His head was eventually found a mile away from the rest of his body. It is believed that Mr. Byrd was tied to the back of the truck and forced to run as the vehicle accelerated. When he could no longer keep pace, the drivers allowed his body to be dragged along the road. All three men received the death penalty for their crime of hate, which was motivated by racism.

Stories like Mr. Byrd's are so horrific that they may cause us to overlook the more subtle and pervasive forms of racism, hate, and discrimination. These hidden forms of racism perpetuated by the dominant society affect nearly every African American to varying degrees. Schools in many African American communities lack funds for supplies; school locker rooms and restrooms are in deplorable condition; extreme poverty is often a way of life. The very perpetuation of the common African American stereotypes can damage the African American psyche.

In a powerful short story, African American author Brent Staples (1992), described a typical nightly walk taken by a Black man. The narrator saw a young White woman who showed fear because his walking pattern happened to match hers. He witnessed a dark-skinned man being dragged from his car at gunpoint because the police suspected him of murder. Day after day, year after year, these incessant negative images forced him to realize that the world viewed him as a threat. To reassure people that he was not a mugger or aggressor, he learned to hum Vivaldi's "Four Seasons." But no amount of education, money, or status would ever eliminate the dissenting impression many European Americans formed of him. Over time, he learned to "smother the rage" that stemmed from being treated like a criminal. Messages such as these frequently run through the minds of many African Americans. Are they perceived as threatening or inherently inferior to their lighter-skinned peers?

A sense of inferiority has become common for many African Americans. In the 1940s, when America faced the possibility of integrating African American and European American school children, those in favor of desegregation needed evidence demonstrating that "Black schools" harmed African Americans. After a long search, they found K. B. Clark and M. K. Clark (1947), who were conducting research on children's racial attitudes. The researchers presented European American and African American school-aged children with two dolls, one dark-skinned and the other light-skinned. The children were asked questions such as, "Which is the smart doll?" "Which is the pretty doll?" Which is the bad doll?" Both African Americans and European Americans identified the dark-skinned doll as bad and ugly and the light-skinned doll as smart and pretty. Many of the questions in this study elicited intense emotional responses from the young participants. For example, one young girl, when asked to identify the "bad" doll, attempted to refuse. After some time, she lowered her head, wept, and silently pointed to the dark-skinned doll.

The 1940s have passed and schools are now integrated, thanks to the Supreme Court's decision in *Brown v. Board of Education* (1954) and many other efforts. We no longer have separate drinking fountains or separate bus seats for light- and dark-skinned individuals, but the negative impressions remain. In 1985, the Clark and Clark doll study was repeated to see if political and social changes had altered European Americans' and African Americans' perceptions of dark-skinned individuals. Powell-Hopson and Derek (1988) tested 105 African American and 50 European American preschoolers and found that a majority of the participants still chose a White doll when asked preference questions. They noted that these preferences could be changed, at least temporarily, by employing basic learning principles and psychoeducation. They found it disturbing that American society had been unable to promote positive images of African Americans despite many years of desegregation.

The targets of racism and discrimination are not dolls but living human beings. As African American children grow up, many tend to project negative impressions of their ethnic group upon each other. Some African American children use derogatory statements such as "You're darker than charcoal" to insult one another, and they learn to view light skin as evidence of intelligence, morality, and success. This negativity is pervasive and shared by many other ethnic groups. For example, when examining how people view the homeless, Whaley and Link (1998) found that European Americans were more likely to attribute the potential for violence to African Americans who are homeless than to non-Blacks who are homeless. When asked which ethnic group is most likely to commit rape, various ethnic groups identified African Americans as those most likely, and many African Americans themselves placed the highest culpability on their own group (Varelas & Foley, 1998), while no mention was made of the fact that African Americans are most likely to be rape victims themselves (Rennison, 2000).

African Americans, while internalizing some of the negative messages conveyed to them, also feel the need to fight against the images forced upon them by the dominant society. Nowhere has this been more evident than in public attitudes toward the O. J. Simpson trial. When the acclaimed African American football player and actor was acquitted of murdering his blonde-haired, blue-eyed ex-wife, Nicole Simpson, the Associated Press (1997) reported that 30 percent of European Americans and more than 85 percent of African

Americans viewed the verdict as "right." Fifteen months after the acquittal, Simpson testified for the first time at his civil trial. The Associated Press conducted a second poll to reinvestigate the effects of ethnicity. This time, only 18 percent of Whites and 58 percent of Blacks still considered the verdict right. Even though both groups were less likely to view Mr. Simpson as innocent in the second polling, in both instances, most African Americans polled viewed him as innocent, and most European Americans polled viewed him as guilty. Clearly, ethnicity often colors our perspectives of truth and reality.

Regarding the O. J. trial, Mary Stanley, a 48-year-old African American resident of Downey, California, said, "I think this man is innocent. This is a Black man being framed, abused by the White people, by the world. It's all about money— bloodthirsty money" (Associated Press, 1997). Another African American interviewee (Brammer, 1994) said, "It doesn't matter if he's guilty; enough innocent Black men have gone to jail to pay for White men's crimes." This latter statement captures a sentiment of anger and frustration that permeates African American society, and there is evidence to support it. Of African Americans in their twenties, roughly one-third will spend time in jail, on probation, or on parole (Sue & Sue, 1999). Are these statistics the result of justice or prejudice?

Cathy Harris (Brammer, 1997), an African American woman from Amarillo, Texas, said, "My mother always told me, believe none of what you hear and half of what you see." African Americans have learned to focus on the tones they hear and the nonverbal communication they observe. Experience has taught them that words are filled with lies. People say, "Color doesn't matter to me," or "I've always respected your people," but their mildly sarcastic tones, poor eye contact, and physical distance communicate the real message. Simply to survive, African Americans have learned that words are not to be trusted, which makes interracial counseling all the more difficult.

> During the early 1970s the television show *Candid Camera* had White and Black young men walk down a sidewalk opposite White women. In the show, the women moved their purse strap to the shoulder away from the Black male, but they did not alter their behavior when the White male passed by. The behavior was so entrenched that some of the women actually moved their shoulder strap when the Black male passed on the opposite side of the street! If this experiment were conducted again today, do you think similar behaviors would be observed?

Family

The distrust that African Americans feel for European Americans has contemporary roots as well. Seppa (1996) noted that during the early 1970s, when psychologists were attempting to help African Americans rebuild after the Watts riots, parent training was offered to help reduce the high divorce rate and decrease the use of corporal punishment. At the time, he noted that African Americans overused corporal punishment and even used it as a teaching (non-punishment) tool for children. He noted that the behavior dates back to slave days when Black children were taught not to "sass" Whites. The psychologists' attempts to reduce the use of physical punishment and lower divorce rates were completely unsuccessful. Today, African American males show more support for corporal punishment than females and European Americans (Flynn, 1998). More than half of African American children grow up in single-parent households (Seppa, 1996). From an external perspective, the use of corporal punishment and high numbers of single parents could be seen as entirely negative. The solutions might also seem relatively simple, yet reality is more complex than it seems.

Thirty years of research have indicated that when European American children are physically punished, they tend to become more aggressive. With the increased violence within the African American community, it seems natural to trace the origins of this trend back to the punishment styles of parents. However, emerging research is indicating that African American children do not become more aggressive when they are punished physically by their parents (Deater-Deckard, Dodge, Bates, Pettit, 1998). There is even emerging research indicating the physical discipline may be negatively correlated with behavioral problems in African Americans (Whaley, 2000). Apparently, European American children view physical punishment as hostile or lacking in warmth, whereas African American children may not identify physical punishment with these negative qualities. Deater-Deckard et al. also found that while African American children were more likely to come from single-mother and lower-income households, these children did not behave more aggressively in school. Similarly, it appears that African American children are less likely to use drugs when they come from single-parent families than from families headed by both of the biological parents (Amey & Albrecht, 1998).

Why do African American families function well even though they appear to have all the signs of disaster? Before answering this question, we must first decide to what extent the problems are related to ethnicity. Pinderhughes et al. (2000) argued that culture, per se, had less of an effect on the type of discipline used than the intervening effects of parenting beliefs, stress, perception of the child, and cognitive/emotional processes. Their path analysis comparing African American and European American households showed that socioeconomic status was more important in creating these intermediary variables than culture or ethnicity. African American families use physical discipline because they are more likely to be poor or less educated, but their culture may also help to protect them from the negative effects of such discipline.

Nancy Boyd-Franklin (Martin, 1995) argues that mental-health experts fail to recognize the power of the African American extended family, the intensity of Black spirituality, and the advantages of a united African American community. In many European American families, the mother-father dyad dictates the family's direction. In traditional African American families, grandmothers and grandfathers, aunts and uncles, and fathers and boyfriends often share power. This power structure is evidenced by Lee, Peek, and Coward's (1998) study, which examined the beliefs of older parents (i.e., those over 65 years of age) regarding expectations of support from their children. African Americans demonstrated significantly higher expectations of their children than did European Americans. They expected their children to take care of them in their old age and to provide for them, and, in general, accepted a higher level of "fill-in" responsibility than European American grandparents (Lee, Peek, & Coward, 1998).

Although many of the negative perceptions of African American families can be debunked, some must be acknowledged. For example, 60 percent of all African American births are to teenagers. These young families face over-whelming pressures and are often run solely by the young mother. African American girls do not appear to be more sexually active than other girls, but they appear to be less likely to use condoms or other forms of protection at the time of their first intercourse (Ford, Rubinstein, & Norris, 1994). By the time they felt they knew their partners well, less than half of the 1,425 participants in Ford, Rubinstein, and Norris' study reported using a condom. African American boys do not help in this process. Young African American men reported the earliest initiation of sexual activity of all groups studied, and they had the greatest number of sexual partners (Ford & Norris, 1993).

With so many women heading African American families, these young mothers often face additional stereotypes. Gloria Naylor (1993) writes about the myth of the matriarch. African American women are expected to be strong, independent from men, and domineering. Naylor traces this contemporary image to the slave days when African American women performed "women's" duties but also worked alongside the men in the fields. They were regarded as mentally weaker than Whites, but they were treated as though they were hardier than European American women, who were seen as too delicate to work outside the home. The perpetuation of this image prevents many African American mothers from giving themselves permission to simply collapse. Once the kids are put to bed, all parents deserve the right to do something as simple as to cry.

Economics

Homeless African American men tend to be better educated, less psychi-atrically impaired, and have better job skills than their European American peers (Davis & Winkleby, 1993). Can you think of a possible explanation for this phenomenon?

The struggles faced by African American families are paralleled, and partially created by, economic concerns. African Americans are three times more likely to live in poverty than European or Asian Americans (Paschall & Hubbard, 1998). According to the U.S. Bureau of the Census (1995), racism and discrimination directly create many financial hardships. Huffcutt and Roth (1998) examined 31 studies involving employment interviews with European American, African American, and Latino job applicants. Their meta-analysis revealed that both African Americans and Latinos received interview ratings slightly below those of European American applicants. In order to examine whether these results were reasonable, the researchers also tested the mental abilities of the participants. Although some differences were present, the differences in interview ratings were considerably greater than discrepancies on mental ability tests. This forcefully implies that racism is a chief contributor to high unemployment rates among African Americans (11 percent, versus 5 percent for European Americans, according to the U.S. Bureau of the Census, 1995). Racism is also responsible for problems obtaining housing, which may be the most important economic concern facing African American families.

A 1997 Census Bureau survey (Fisher, 1999) conducted in North Carolina found home ownership rates of 62 percent among Whites and 37 percent among Blacks. Even more disturbing is the fact that the White home ownership rate has risen almost two percentage points since the 1970 Census, while the Black rate has fallen 7 points during the same time period. Part of this trend is caused by the financial state of many African American families. White households are twice as likely as Black ones to include a married couple. Among married people only, the Black-White gap in home ownership is cut in half, to about 14 percentage points. Additionally, when comparing only affluent households (i.e., those making between $50,000 and $70,000 a year), the racial gap in home ownership is less than 8 points. Even with these controls, there is still a substantial gap. Why is this the case? Racism seems to be the most likely explanation.

Fisher (1999) tells the story of Stowe and his wife, who are both Black, and their experience of moving to Raleigh, N.C. In 1994, they purchased a house in an integrated neighborhood and expected a relatively smooth transition. Soon after their move, Stowe was gardening in his front yard when a White neighbor approached him. Assuming that she intended to welcome him to the neighborhood, he walked over to her "with my best Southern-hospitality face on."

Without introducing herself, the woman stated, "You are doing wonderful work!" As she began leading up to a job offer, he explained that he was not a gardener but the owner of the house. The woman then launched into a story about her father's good treatment of a Black household servant. She concluded by stating that Stowe would have no problems in Berwick if he "promised to be good." Obviously, Stowe found the encounter deflating.

Although racism and job discrimination present serious obstacles to economic success, many African Americans thrive. The number of middle- and upper-class African Americans is growing, and this group is likely to hold values that are similar to those of the dominant culture (Hildebrand, Phenice, Gray, & Hines, 1996). However, even when African Americans are able to find adequate employment and earn high incomes, they may be reluctant to move into affluent neighborhoods. South and Crowder (1998) examined a sample of 2,613 African Americans and 3,123 European Americans to identify the characteristics that predicted where they would live. They found that a number of factors keep people in the neighborhoods where they grew up, such as age, home ownership, being married, and having children. However, the most surprising finding of their study involves the small effect created by socioeconomic status. Only a small proportion of the racial differences in the probability of moving from a racially mixed to a predominantly European American tract can be attributed to differences in socioeconomic status, life-cycle characteristics, or geographic location. Even when African Americans earn more money, they realize they may not be accepted in traditionally "White" areas.

Mr. and Mrs. Williams, a young African American couple who had moved to a mid-sized southwestern city, were shopping for homes with their realtor. As they toured various neighborhoods, the realtor began to express some concern. "Now, this area might not work for you," she remarked nonchalantly. "There really aren't very many Blacks on this street." As they reached the house, the realtor nervously unlocked the door and showed the family around. When they made their way to the backyard, they noticed an African American man mowing a yard across the alley. When they approached, he ceased mowing and quickly went inside. The realtor immediately called the police, because "there aren't any Blacks living on this block." The police arrived and attempted to arrest the mower. As they escorted him through the house, he frantically grabbed family pictures from the wall to demonstrate that he was the owner of the house.[1]

With continued obstacles preventing African Americans from leaving impoverished communities, a price must be paid. What happens when African Americans are forced to remain in largely impoverished communities? One of the results seems to be an increase in neighborhood violence. This is a delicate and important subject that requires careful examination. Is the violence due to poverty, an inherent restlessness among African Americans, or something else? The violence in African American urban areas appears to reflect the violence endemic in many impoverished communities, but recent studies suggest that economics do not have a direct effect on violent behavior.

Paschall and Hubbard (1998) examined the effects of neighborhood poverty on family conflict and a propensity for violent behavior. After examining 188 African American adolescents and their mothers, their path analysis revealed that neighborhood poverty did *not* directly affect adolescents' propensity for violent behavior. Instead, economic levels appear to play an indirect role in elic-

---

[1] This anecdote was relayed to the author during a conversation with Gwen Williams.

iting violent behavior. Paschall and Hubbard found that family stress and conflict tended to decrease an adolescent's sense of self-worth. When these effects were combined with impoverished living conditions, adolescents appeared to react against the forces at large, finding identity and a sense of significance through membership in violent gangs and dealing in illegal drugs. Similarly, Bergesen and Herman (1998) found that when economic conditions and the racial/ethnic composition of a neighborhood were statistically controlled, ethnic succession seemed to be associated with the emergence of riots. Specifically, the more African Americans left an area and were replaced with Latinos and Asians, the greater the likelihood of community violence. Apparently, the ethnic rivalry between neighborhood factions polarized the various minority groups and inspired them to defend *their* turf against rivals. This implies that changes in economics alone will not eliminate violence in impoverished neighborhoods. Hope for real change rests in better education, improved economic opportunities, and interracial tolerance.

Education

> When you were in elementary school, middle school, and high school, were any of your friends African American? Did you view them as intelligent? Did the teacher treat them the same way he or she treated European American students? If you don't know the answer to these questions, is it because the treatment of African American students was undifferentiated from that of other students? Might it also be because you were less concerned about the treatment of these students because you were treated fairly?

One of the most important elements associated with violence among young people is an inability to complete high school. In the 1970s, 11 percent of African American teenagers dropped out of high school. In 1994, that number had been reduced to just 5 percent (U.S. Bureau of the Census, 1995), which is not significantly different from the rate for European Americans. Although this trend is encouraging, and should help to decrease violence within African American communities, other academic problems remain. Largely because of prejudice and racism, many African American students perform below their abilities. Ford and Harris (1995) found that the academic success of African American students is influenced more by personal and environmental factors than by actual ability. These influences include ethnic ideology, relationships with teachers and counselors, ambivalent feelings about school, experiences of discrimination, and negative peer relationships. These factors have led approximately 80 percent of gifted African American children to perform below their abilities academically.

The tendency for African Americans to perform below their intellectual ability has caused many to question whether standardized intelligence tests should be used to place Black children in various academic levels (i.e., special education or gifted programs). In 1970, Hispanic students in California complained that their rights were being violated because IQ tests designed for English-speaking subjects were being used to place them in special education classes. After the ruling on *Diana v. State Board of Education* (February 3, 1970), such tests could no longer be used for students whose primary language was not English. This was not the end of the debate, however, because Latinos were only one of the minority groups overrepresented in special education programs. In *Larry P. v. Riles* (1979), the California Supreme Court heard arguments that IQ tests should not be used for academic placement of African American students. The court decided that racial bias resulted from the practice, and the California Board of Education declared a moratorium on the use of intelligence tests because the tests are biased against Black children and tend to place them in stigmatizing programs for the mentally retarded. As a result of this proceeding, and others, the Education of the Handicapped Act (1975) was passed, which required the identification of deficits in adaptive behaviors as well as a below-average intelligence score for the diagnosis of mental retardation.

In addition to performing below their abilities, African Americans' academic performance is below that of children from other ethnic groups. The reasons for this discrepancy are multifaceted, but part of the explanation involves societal expectations. For example, the aspirations of African American and Latino students regarding college are likely to wane as they progress through junior high and high school. Such attitudes can be traced in part to the fact that their families are more likely to be of a lower socioeconomic status than those of their peers (Stevenson, 1998). In addition, the educational aspirations of African American students are typically less concrete than those of their European American and Asian American peers. Focus group discussions with African American adolescents support quantitative findings that, compared to European Americans and Asians Americans, they are relatively uninformed about college admission procedures, which reduces their odds of reaching their educational goals (Kao & Tienda, 1998).

Without clear academic goals, African Americans tend to downplay the importance of higher education. When African Americans believe that education is not important, they are more likely to drop out of school. This is especially troubling because African American boys are more likely than Latino and European American students to lose interest in academics during middle and high school (American Psychological Association, 1998).

Girls also have special problems with motivation in high school. Low individual educational performance measures, such as lower test scores and lower grades, predict a higher risk of early motherhood. Similarly, girls who are held back or repeatedly change schools are at greater risk of having children early in life (Moore, Manlove, Glei, & Morrison, 1998). If girls become pregnant, they are less likely to complete high school. Stevenson, Maton, and Teti (1998) examined the factors associated with keeping African American pregnant teens in high school. She found that internal factors, such as depression, self-esteem, mastery, and parental and friend support, did not predict dropout rates. Instead, students who received at least passing grades and perceived a high school degree as "very important" elected to complete their studies. This perception of school was so significant that African Americans who viewed school as very important received higher average grades than European American students did.

Unfortunately, it is difficult to communicate the importance of a high school diploma to some African American students. Jason Osborne (1998) followed nearly 25,000 students from eighth grade through high school and found that the interaction between self-esteem and grades predicted levels of academic identification. Improved self-esteem and grades helped to instill academic identification. If students' self-esteem remained constant or rose while their grades fell, then their level of academic disidentification would also increase. The relationship between grades and academic interest remained relatively stable in Osborne's study, with one exception. As African American boys approached high school graduation, grades became increasingly less important to their self-esteem. Could it be that they had experienced too many failures or regarded school as a White world? Whatever the rationale, they shifted their interest to social activities and attempts to impress their peers.

Other studies have found just the opposite to be true for African American girls. In Ekrut's study (Murray, 1996), academic achievement was the strongest predictor of high self-worth among African American girls. These high-achieving girls also considered themselves to be the most socially accepted and romantically appealing of all the ethnic/racial groups investigated.

A number of components appear helpful in promoting academic achievement among African American adolescents. For both boys and girls, parental involvement in the academic process and high academic expectations help children stay focused on academics. African American parents can also have a significant impact on their children by providing strict discipline, combined with nurturing and community connectedness. These mechanisms appear to counteract the potentially negative influences of neighborhood peers, inadequate schools, and racist messages from society (Maton, Hrabowski, & Greif, 1998).

When African Americans make their way to college, other difficulties may surface. Although college is likely to improve the cognitive skills of African Americans as much as the gains reported by European Americans (Myerson, Rank, Raines, & Schnitzler, 1998), other problems arise. As undergraduate students, they appear less willing to disclose much of themselves to non–African American faculty (Noel & Smith, 1996). The reasons for this reluctance are relatively clear. The hardship and racism African Americans face throughout life has taught them to distrust people of different ethnicities. There is reason for this distrust, but many European Americans have difficulty understanding the emotion. "I haven't done anything to them," one future teacher commented during a course. As a result of their life experiences, European American students tend to expect honesty, fairness, and opportunity, while African American students are likely to expect prejudice, discrimination, and inequality.

Even after African Americans begin to believe that they can expect fairness from their teachers, prejudices or miscommunication often reemerge. Consider the following statement from an anonymous graduate student:

> As an English teacher, as well as a history teacher, I have tried to incorporate the literature and history of non-White ethnic groups into my classes. Usually this has been generally accepted and has enhanced understanding between the various cultures, but not always. In one particular class, I had problems first with the Black students. Once I had included their culture in the class they began to see this as a victory on their part, believing that everything would be Black power from then on, excluding any White viewpoints at all. They even wanted the Whites in the class to suffer the blame for their ancestors' enslavement. Needless to say, a backlash started to occur, not only from the White students, but also from me. We used it as a means to gain patience and understanding of the worst qualities an ethnicity may have to offer as well as trying to appreciate the good qualities.

In this example, the African American students initially came to believe that the teacher was willing to explore history and English topics from both African and European perspectives. Soon thereafter, intense friction developed and a cultural rift appeared. The teacher viewed the students' excitement as a statement of arrogance, and she could not understand why the African American students would want their peers to take responsibility for their ancestors' (and perhaps their own) suffering. Eventually, the situation degraded to the point where the "White" members of the class (including the teacher) felt they needed to rise above the issue by taking a condescending attitude toward the impatience of their African American classmates. The end result of these actions is not difficult to imagine. The African American students likely felt betrayed and wounded. They had pulled closer together to create a common front and had defended their position as best they could. Throughout the conflict, though, they probably felt inadequate, unappreciated, and inferior to the students who won the favor of their teacher.

Health

Pressures from discrimination also have a direct impact on physical health. David Williams and James Jackson (1997) found that physical health problems appear to result from persistent and repeated stressors. They referred to these problems as "everyday discrimination," as opposed to episodic "major discrimination." In their study, African Americans suffered from nearly twice as many health problems and were considerably more likely than European

Americans to describe their health as "fair" or "poor" (23.3 percent versus 12.8 percent). They were also less likely than European Americans to describe their health as "very good" or "excellent" (48.4 percent versus 59.8 percent).

Complicating the increased health problems is a lack of confidence in the health profession. As many as 40 percent of African Americans lack health insurance of any kind (Giachello & Belgrave, 1997), and those who have insurance are less likely to undergo corrective surgeries or major therapeutic procedures (Sue & Sue, 1999). It is possible that African Americans view the health care system as "White" and untrustworthy. This distrust may also extend to White psychotherapists, a topic that will be covered in the last section of the chapter.

In addition to general, physical concerns and underutilization of health care, African Americans also face mortality risks greater than those of any other group. African Americans are highly overrepresented among AIDS clients (Talvi, 1997) and face other lethal challenges from their own communities. The high rate of violence among urban African American youth has led to increased mortality rates among this group (Sanders-Phillips, 1996), but other, subtler effects have emerged as well. Exposure to violence can result in feelings of powerlessness, hopelessness, and alienation. Each of these factors can significantly limit an individual's motivation, involvement, and persistence in overcoming barriers to health-promoting behaviors (Sanders-Phillips, 1996).

With health hazards coming from multiple areas, it might be expected that the coping skills of African Americans have been systematically worn away. Rather than strip African Americans of their coping mechanisms, however, the pressures from prejudice and violence have often led to new strengths. African American adolescents report the lowest incidence of illicit drug use initiation, and unlike teenagers from other ethnic groups, disruptions in their home life are seldom enough to make them turn to drugs (Gil, Vega, & Biafora, 1998) or cigarettes (Griesler, Kandel, & Davies, 2002).

Why are African Americans able to fend off the impulses toward substance abuse that plague other ethnic groups? Maybe because they have learned how to cope with the daily pressures placed upon them. Facing racism and discrimination from such an early age may help African Americans adapt to pressures and weather many of life's storms. However, these adaptive skills have their limitations. Even though African Americans may cope with daily struggles well, the pressures placed on them by society can become quite overwhelming. According to a study conducted by the National Institutes of Health (Strong STARTS program combats unhappiness among Black youth, 1998), the suicide rate among young African American males has jumped by nearly 300 percent since 1980. The reasons for the increase are unclear, but poverty, single-parent households, and societal stress are probably the chief influences. Adolescence can be difficult for anyone, but imagine the pressures stemming from sideways glances, inflammatory names, and discriminatory employment and school experiences. The cumulative effect of these pressures, when heaped upon the already tumultuous lives of many African Americans, may cause them to lose hope. These issues are not unique to African Americans, however, and we will discuss suicide rates for other cultural groups in later chapters. For now, though, it is important to consider how you, as a therapist, can help to reduce the turmoil caused by discrimination and prejudice. At the very least, we need to refrain from adding to our clients' negative experiences.

Cultural Uniqueness

No discussion of African American culture would be complete without exploring the topic of language. All too often, stories arise of young African Americans being told by teachers that they should not consider attending college because they have "poor language skills." The frequency of these stories has led psychologists such as Robert Williams to fight for an acceptance of "Black English" dialects in order to limit academic discrimination against African Americans. "Ebonics," the term most frequently used to describe the African American Vernacular English, is sometimes viewed as a distinct language, though there is considerable debate regarding this position. Williams (Burnette, 1997) observed that African Americans score significantly better on tests when the questions are written in Ebonics. Williams also argues that providing such tests on a regular basis could significantly enhance students' self-esteem and, in turn, boost their academic performance. This position reached its apex in 1996 when the Oakland Unified School Board in California flirted with recognizing Ebonics as the primary language of African American students. The Black-majority school board's announcement that African American students should speak their own second language was motivated, in part, by a desire to garner a share of federal funds for bilingual education. Acceptance of this initiative would have required teachers to use Ebonics when assisting African American students in learning English and other subjects. It was hoped that if teachers recognized the language of African American children, instead of telling them that their language usage was incorrect, the students would develop more positive self-images and become more interested in school.

Whether tolerating or encouraging Ebonics would actually help African American students remains uncertain, but it does bring up some important historical references. For example, in the once autonomous country of Scotland, the Scots created a dialect of the Gaelic language, which was introduced by the Irish invaders. When Anglo-Saxon invaders drifted in, they brought with them their own Germanic language. The Scottish people ended up speaking an interesting hybrid language, which is now called "Scots English," or simply "Scots." For a while it looked like Scotland could have a language and a national literature all its own, but the English eventually conquered Scotland and made it part of their "United Kingdom." Standard British English supplanted the Scottish dialect, although many Scots can still understand the old Scots English and there is a small but growing number of people in Scotland who speak the older Gaelic language. Is the old Scottish English inferior to the official British English? It would be difficult to make such an argument. Similarly, judgments against Ebonics are difficult to justify. The Ebonic dialect may serve a purpose in uniting a splintered ethnic group; however, Ebonics is unlikely to become an officially recognized language. Standardized tests that are used primarily to screen students out of institutions of higher learning do not recognize or include Ebonics. In light of this fact, teaching or promoting the use of Ebonics may serve only to reduce opportunities for African Americans to enter or succeed in colleges and universities.

One of the reasons the Ebonics movement gained momentum was its contribution to a sense of ethnic pride and identity. For some Black groups, especially the Nation of Islam, the establishment of a language system is only one step toward freedom from White rule. For the Nation of Islam, only the creation of an independent country for African Americans will provide Blacks with social and intellectual freedom.

The Nation of Islam is one of three dominant religious groups among African Americans. Although there are unique elements to Black Protestantism and Catholicism, the Nation of Islam requires special attention because of its advocacy of separation from White America and its culture (Lovinger, 1996).

Wallace D. Fard, also known as Wallace Fard Muhammad, founded the Nation of Islam. In 1930, he opened a mosque in Detroit and taught his followers that they should reject Christianity because it was the "slave-master's religion." In 1934, Fard disappeared and was succeeded by Elijah Muhammad (Elijah Poole).

According to the Nation of Islam, the White race stems from the tribe of Adam and is associated with the Devil (Yakub) whom they chose to follow. After Adam and Eve were evicted from the Garden of Eden, or the Holy Lands (which consists of Egypt, Jordan, and Syria), they were driven into the hills and caves of West Asia, or as it is now called, Europe. The Adamic race was allowed to reign for 6,000 years, but they were not allowed to return to the tree of life (i.e., the Nation of Islam), and the sword of Islam (the Muslim Army) prevented the Adamic race from crossing the border between Europe and Asia.

The Nation of Islam is a group of American Blacks who view themselves as descendents of the tribe of Shabazz (Evanzz, 1999). The Tribe of Shabazz, according to the religion, descends from nature herself, and she is the wife of the most high, Allah (God) himself. Unlike the White race, which stems from Adam and Eve, the Shabazz tribe has no mother or father, and predates all societies. It has a proud history and would have remained proud had the White man not deceived the tribe in the mid-sixteenth century.

According to Elijah Muhammad (1997), the movement's founder (1897–1974), Black men were taken into captivity in 1555. This is 65 years prior to the first recorded captivity of Africans. Who were these early captives? They were people from a great nation in what is now known as Syria. They had their own name, country, flag, language (Hebrew), religion (Islam), and, most of all,

God, who is Allah. Elijah Muhammad writes that the White man had to remove the Black man's history in order to effectively enslave the Black man. To this end, many Blacks, from Africa, were brought during 1600 to mix with the God Tribe. The new Africans spoke an African dialect, which made it impossible to understand members of other tribes. The plantations were then used as indoctrination camps to complete the robbery of the Black man's identity. Children were taken from their mothers and raised by White women or very trusted Black nannies. Given this history, referring to Black Americans as "African Americans" would be offensive. They do not believe they are from Africa and they have little identity with America.

The prophet, Elijah Muhammad (1997), writes that the White men alone are not to blame for the captivity of the Black race. Though they were vicious and beat, kicked, busted skulls, and hung Black people, those actions were designed to show a love for their own kind. The prophet continues by adding that if the Black man had demonstrated pride for himself and love for his own kind, he would have bashed in the head of the White man and hung him on a tree and earned his respect today.

Today, the White race is viewed as the worst enemy of the Nation of Islam, and it will never be the chosen people of Allah. In this view, Black people are often deceived into trusting this devil race (i.e., Whites). Gullible Blacks believe that White education will assist them, intermarriage will help them gain status, and interracial friendships will create helpful alliances, but these efforts are part of an elaborate attempt to control the Black race and prevent them from creating their own nation.

Jews are viewed in an especially bad light. In 1991, the Nation of Islam published *The Secret Relationship Between Blacks and Jews*. Here the authors observe that no single ethnic group has faced blanket expulsion in so many places around the world as have the Jews. Rather than attribute this fact to the enduring legacy of anti-Semitism, however, the authors provide a list of "reasons" for these expulsions: the Jews were monopolizers, usurers, they engaged in "sharp practices" and sold "cheap" goods, they filed for frequent bankruptcies. Each of these charges, of course, stems from the timeless stereotype that Jews are inherently untrustworthy and obsessed with money, a stereotype the Nation of Islam apparently accepts as reasonable.

Female European American therapists may have the most difficult time working with male members of the Nation of Islam. In general, Elijah Muhammad believed that a woman's job was to stay in the house and rear her children. This would apply to White women as well. Beyond this basic precept, there is an assumption that the White woman is the Universal Delilah. She is the seductress who attracts and tempts Black men, drawing them away from their heritage and their birthright.

No matter which religious tradition they choose, African Americans are more likely to turn to a clergy member than to a psychologist in times of trouble (Religious institutions play a central role in African American life, 1996). In fact, some of the problems a mental health worker would label as mental illness may not be recognized as such within the Black community. Depression, for instance, is sometimes viewed as a spiritual problem caused by sinful behavior or the failure to pray (Religious institutions play a central role in African-American life, 1996). If mental health professionals attempt to explain potentially spiritual issues in psychological terms, they are likely to be viewed as anti-spiritual and therefore threatening. Regardless of the religious affiliations of African Americans, spirituality tends to play an important role in the lives of many families, and it is foundational in helping youth define their identity (Chadiha, Veroff, & Leber, 1998).

The intensity of any cultural differences, however, will depend in part on the client's level of acculturation. Cross (1971, 1991, 1995) developed a four-stage model of Black identity development in which individuals progress through stages described as pre-encounter, encounter, immersion-emersion, and internalization (see Table 2.1). Each stage refers to an individual's understanding and level of acceptance with his or her individual and corporate cultural identity.

In the pre-encounter stage of identity development, individuals have yet to consider the value of cultural identity. They tacitly accept the pervasive prejudices of the dominant culture, which leads to a devaluation of their culture and an uncritical acceptance of European American culture.

At the beginning of the encounter stage, a crisis occurs. The form that it takes may vary among individuals. For some, a fellow African American might confront them and encourage them to reject the European American culture. For others, a "White" subculture may reject them and make them feel different.

Picture Jermaine, a young high school student who takes considerable pride in his clothing. He wears only designer labels, drives expensive cars, and plans to inherit his father's business. One day when he walks out to his car, he finds the word "nigger" scrawled in lipstick upon the windshield. Even though he had followed the cultural mores of his peers, someone still could not accept

TABLE 2.1 *Cross's Black Identity Model*

	View of minority culture	*View of dominant culture*
Pre-encounter	Not really considered.	The dominant culture is viewed as the only true culture.
Encounter	The minority culture is viewed as an alternative path to identity but one that is not fully embraced.	Something from the dominant culture pushes them away. They are no longer able to identify with it.
Immersion-emersion	The minority culture is embraced.	Components of the dominant culture are rejected and sometimes abhorred.
Internalization	The minority culture is still embraced.	Some elements of the dominant culture are reintroduced and embraced, but only those that are not prejudicial.

him simply because his skin was dark. This event triggered his encounter. He begins to reinterpret his friendships, social interactions, and views of himself, constantly shifting between guilt and anger. He starts to feel guilty for living the way others expected him to live and angry at the culture that futilely attempted to conform him to its standards.

The end of the encounter stage is often very confusing. Jermaine realizes he does not fit within the dominant culture, but he knows very little about African American culture. As he begins to explore this topic, Jermaine enters the third stage, immersion-emersion. Here, Jermaine attempts to eliminate European influences and submerge himself in the perceived African culture. He may choose to attend an African American school or join an African American social group. If such options are not available, he may surf the Internet to learn about African tribes or civil rights leaders. During this stage of identity development, African American clients may also come to view a European American counselor as part of the "White" establishment. Multiculturally sensitive counselors may also contribute to the problem if they attempt to portray themselves as part of the "Black" culture. Counselors must wait for the client to piece together a sense of cultural identity, which happens during the final stage, internalization.

During the internalization stage, Jermaine attempts to resolve the conflict between old and new identities. Is it acceptable to join a mostly "White" country club when so many of the members demonstrate prejudices against African Americans? Should he live in an African American neighborhood? Each individual will find his own answers to such questions and gradually learn to accept pieces of the dominant culture while taking pride in his African American roots. He may collect African art, poems, or other artifacts. He may volunteer to work with African American teens, financially support Africans in crisis, or even begin teaching multicultural classes.

Cross (2001) recently noted that this course of acculturation and identity varies among individuals. For some African Americans, a racial-cultural identity may never be important, despite the importance for most people of color. He also noted that, for most African Americans, self-hatred is a minor, rather than a central, theme in everyday life. Given this diversity, it is important to avoid viewing his model of identity development, or any other cultural model, "as if" it applied to all Black people. In reality, the diversity of cultural identity is quite profound, and African Americans hold a wide variety of views concerning what it means to be Black.

Psychological Issues

Cultural differences also make psychological and educational assessments difficult. When Jensen (1968) released his controversial findings that African Americans were less intelligent than European Americans, the nation was appalled. Jensen argued that biological differences between the races could hinder efforts to discover optimal instructional procedures for students of varying abilities. In other words, culture and biology make it impossible to use a single teaching style to teach all children.

Jensen's data were carefully scrutinized, and many contested his methodology. Light and Smith (1969) critiqued Jensen's hypothesis that inherited factors may be "implicated" in observed racial differences in measured intelligence. Instead, they proposed that other factors, such as the presence of racism and oppression, could better explain the differences in intelligence scores. Arguments such as these quieted the commotion Jensen created, but most researchers still realized that there were legitimate differences between the intelligence scores of various groups. These known differences led to the removal of many standardized intelligence tests from public school settings. The tests were apparently biased and inappropriate for determining a child's academic potential.

The acceptance of intelligence tests as inherently biased remained unchallenged until a new argument arose. In 1996, Herrnstein and Murray published *The Bell Curve: Intelligence and Class Structure in American Life*, which reaffirmed the possibility of biological causes for differences in intelligence scores. They reviewed findings from multiple cultures and controlled for level of income and still found differences between various racial and ethnic groups. Something creates differences, albeit subtle, in the way members of different ethnic groups think or respond to questions. Whether these are differences in actual intelligence or simply in broader thinking styles remains to be seen, but we should realize that different cultural groups may score differently on standardized tests, and interpretations of these tests should be made in light of these facts.

Controlling for education and socioeconomic status reduces many of the discrepancies between African and European American intelligence scores. Ethnic group differences on measures of figure memory, verbal abstraction, category fluency, and visual-spatial skill may remain (Manly et al., 1998). Such tests are important measures of dementia, and significantly lower scores by African Americans may lead to overdiagnosis of that group. Even standardized screening tests, such as the mini mental status examination (MMSE), appear to have ethnic biases. Leveille et al. (1998) noted that the MMSE was effective in identifying dysfunction among European American women but not among African American women. Similarly, the MacAndrews Alcoholism Scale (MAC) of the MMPI-2, an indication of alcohol and drug use, is also artificially higher for African Americans. Whether these differences are attributable to test biases or actual differences, practitioners should realize that African Americans are more likely to receive false positives on dementia and some personality screenings. Because of these biases, tests such as the Black Intelligence Test of Cultural Homogeneity, which assesses a child's knowledge of African folklore, history, and dialect, and the Themes Concerning Black (TCB), which measures certain personality components, have emerged. For younger children, these are often preferred means of assessing personality and intelligence.

The overly negative scores of African Americans on certain tests should not be viewed as an indication of increased pathology. In general, African Americans cope with stress better than European Americans. As already mentioned, their exposure to chronic, repetitive stressors may lead to health problems. When facing significant, episodic pressures, however, African Americans demonstrate an impressive emotional flexibility. They also tend to have better support mechanisms than European Americans and are connected to others in the community through religious involvement (Williams & Jackson, 1997). Nevertheless, the strain of discrimination wears on them and tends to create problems with depression and anxiety. Reed, McLeod, Randall, and Walker (1996) found that nearly 58 percent of the African American women they surveyed demonstrated symptoms of depression. They attributed these findings to discrimination, higher-stress environments (e.g., urban, low income, and high crime rates) and lack of institutionalized community support (e.g., hospitals, shopping centers, and recreational facilities).

Differences in coping skills between European Americans and African Americans led Sue and Sue (1990) to acknowledge the presence of a *cultural paranoia*. In making such a claim, they asserted that African Americans, as a result of their historical and present mistreatment, have learned to distrust people, are often depressed, and may appear resistant to certain therapists. Rather than diagnose this as a pathological condition, it appears that it may be more appropriate to recognize it as an adaptive skill that people have developed to cope with a world that will undoubtedly hurt them.

Within-Group Differences

African Americans may trace their lineage through any number of African countries. In addition to these differences, some received added cultural influences when they migrated through Latin America or Europe or when they endured enslavement. "African descent" describes people beyond those who have dark skin, broad noses, and full lips. There are hundreds, if not thousands, of ethnicities that make up Black Africa, as well as a wide spectrum of languages and religions. Some Black North Africans have blond hair and blue eyes. These differences are only the beginning of the diversity among Black people. Jamaicans are different from Trinidadians, who are different from South American Blacks, who are different from West African Blacks, who are different from Egyptians, who are different from Tanzanians, and so on.

In the Caribbean, there is a unique group of African descendants. Many had constructed their own dialect, a form of Creole English. In recent years, the Creole spoken by past generations has been transformed into newer variants of English. British Black English, also known as patois, is a modified version of Creole. Its use is often associated with Rastafarianism (a variant of the Ethiopian Orthodox Christian faith using the Holy Piby as its sacred text) and reggae. Although speakers sometimes call it Jamaican, it is different from Jamaican Creole.

In addition to the differences between cultural groups, gender and age issues must be considered. Over the years, African American women have encountered great difficulty creating their identity. When the African American civil rights movement emerged in the 1960s, African American women found themselves fighting for freedoms that appeared to affect only their male counterparts. Black women still received unequal pay in employment, were expected to stay at home and raise their children, and often experienced inequality within the family structure. When the feminist movement achieved mainstream status, most feminist groups seemed to focus predominantly on the concerns of European American women. In both the civil rights and feminist movements, African American women represented a fringe group—accepted by each but failing to achieve equal status. This discrepancy led authors such as bell hooks (1991) to decry any attempt to separate gender from the minority status of African American women. For hooks, the use of phrases such as "women and minorities" belittles the experiences of African American women who are both women *and* members of an ethnic minority group. Both their ethnic and gender status affect how the world sees them. A professor at West Texas A&M University was once asked, "Do you find your status challenged more often because you are Black or because you are a woman?" She responded simply, "I can't answer that question—I am an African American woman."

Early civil rights groups tended to overlook the unique struggles of African American women, and early feminist groups were regarded as primarily White organizations. In one subsample of 36 African American women, intercorrelations revealed that these women felt an ongoing conflict between their racial identification and their identity as feminists (Myaskovsky & Wittig, 1997). However, there is also a theory that minority group membership can be a catalyst for the development of feminist attitudes. Hunter and Sellers (1998) found that a feminist ideology, although not necessarily a feminist identity, was common among both African American women and men, although women were more likely than men to hold feminist ideals.

In addition to gender issues, developmental issues also play a critical role in defining an African American's identity. Prejudice and segregation lead African American children to define themselves in terms of being *different*. African American adolescents, for example, are likely to feel distant from their non-Black peers because of differences in dialect, family structure, academic achievement, and other such issues (Baruth & Manning, 1999). They may be experiencing discrimination for the first time when applying for employment, which may significantly affect their self-esteem and self-concept. Such social pressures often afflict adolescent girls less than boys, who often feel displaced from society (Murray, 1996).

At the other end of the developmental cycle, new complications arise. By the time African Americans reach retirement age, their skills in dealing with racism and discrimination have helped them to cope with many other hardships. They are overrepresented among the poor, have high rates of divorce and marital separation, and face significant health problems that often require more frequent and prolonged hospitalizations. They have also learned to distrust non–African Americans, and are likely to prefer counselors who resemble them in personality, ethnicity, and temperament.

Counseling Issues

Taking account of the history of injustice experienced by African Americans, mental health practitioners must carefully consider how a lifetime of dealing with prejudice has affected their clients' development. Therapists must find ways to demonstrate their awareness of the hardships their clients have experienced. One way to do this is by asking for the client's life story and noting the patterns of abuse. If the narrative contains no mention of prejudice, therapists may well wonder if their presentation or demeanor is perceived as threatening by the client.

Identifying the effects of prejudice, however, can also create problems in therapy. In some cases, therapists may find themselves acting paternally (Sue & Sue, 1990). They start to interpret all of the client's problems as stemming from racism or their minority status, and seek to protect or comfort the client in this battle. Such a position may lead to a distortion of the client's mental-health issues. Clients with major depression, anxiety disorders, and possibly even psychotic disorders may be misdiagnosed and provided with inadequate treatment plans because all their negative behaviors are wrongly attributed to environmental causes. When such distortions arise, therapy often takes a dangerous turn. Therapists may attempt to protect their clients from exploring the painful aspects of their lives, which may render sessions stagnant and unproductive.

In establishing guidelines for effective therapy, Gibson and Mitchell (1999) recommend that therapists carefully identify the expectations of African Americans. How do these clients feel about being in therapy? Do they believe in catharsis, dreams, schemata, or systemic forces? If the dominant theme of the therapist's theoretical orientation is incompatible with the client's worldview, the therapist should explain any differences. Clarifying these issues early in the therapeutic process can save both the therapist and client from significant hardship.

If the therapist is not an African American, he or she should also ask the client how he or she feels about working with someone from a different ethnic group. Treat these investigations seriously, and pay careful attention to nonverbal cues. Many African Americans may feel threatened by a European American therapist and will comply with therapy without actually feeling safe. They may state that they are comfortable with their therapist but maintain poor eye contact, position themselves several feet away, and speak in a quiet voice. These behaviors do not necessarily imply tension in the relationship, but they should be explored with sensitivity.

The value of exploring the client's multicultural comfort level should also be viewed in light of the client's developing identity. Early in therapy, it is important for therapists to ascertain which stage their client is in. Clients in stages antithetical to "White" society are considerably less likely to benefit from mixed-racial interventions. Regardless of the stage, however, a number of other cultural differences may prove frustrating for therapist and client. For example, it is important to realize that many African American clients are likely to attribute their problems to external causes (Gibson & Mitchell, 1999; Sue & Sue, 1999). The reason for this external locus of responsibility, and possibly an external locus of control, is that they have been unable to change many of the negative issues in their lives. They cannot control racism, discrimination, or even prejudices. Many people in White society will perceive them negatively because of the color of their skin. By the time they reach adulthood, most have come to accept unfairness as a fact of life. Acceptance, however, does not indicate approval. Often hostility, verging on rage, lies just beneath the surface calm of many African Americans. They have been mistreated for generations, and these hardships have made their lives more difficult than they should be.

An equally dangerous error is to overemphasize the client's feelings in an attempt to achieve catharsis. Many African American clients are well aware of the painful experiences in their lives, and, as noted, they have accepted them. A nondirective, affect-oriented approach is often rejected as unproductive and ineffectual because it merely teaches them what they already know. Consider the following interaction:

Client: I just find myself crying all the time. I can't seem to stop. (light sob)

Counselor: I can tell that you are feeling overwhelmed. It must be very difficult to feel trapped under such a heavy burden.

Client: Yes, I don't know what to do—what can I do?

Counselor: (softly) That's a question you will have to answer for yourself. I'm just here to help you find your own answers.

Client: (heavy sigh)

During this discussion, the client wanted specific, practical advice for dealing with her problems. She did not wish to discuss her depression or cry during the session. In this session, the therapist continued to help the client explore her feelings. This approach resulted in a premature termination from the client. She could cry at home. From her therapist, she wanted something more.

For many African Americans, the purpose for coming to therapy is to receive some practical steps to ease their pain. This may take the form of education and job training, drug treatment, or parenting skills. Therapeutic interventions will work best when connected with related services. For example, vocational training may be useless if not connected to jobs that are financially and mentally rewarding. Likewise, drug rehabilitation must be connected to practical changes in other lifestyle arenas. For example, considering the influence of religion in the lives of many African Americans, it is not surprising to find treatment programs such as Alcoholics Anonymous commonly advocated in African American communities. Such programs define mental health within a spiritual context, and reaching a deeper level of spiritual awareness is viewed as a crucial aspect of recovery. Consequently, many clergy and members of the faith community have recognized the role of spirituality in prevention, intervention, and treatment of alcoholism and substance dependence and have responded with innovative programs.

In addition to practical solutions and spiritual awakening, African Americans seek lasting mental health interventions. Therapists need to address the individual within the context of her family, neighborhood, and city. At the very least, therapists should make an effort to involve a client's immediate family in the therapeutic process. Family members can provide reassurance, support, guidance, and stability. When attempting to involve members of an individual's community, the mechanisms for therapy may need to be altered. Therapists must learn to meet their clients where they are—both literally and figuratively. Meeting children on the basketball court, playground, schoolyard, street corner, or video arcade may help to demonstrate solidarity. African American children, especially, may view non–African American therapists as distant, naïve, and ignorant. Meeting the child in a familiar setting conveys a willingness to view the world from the client's reality. Some therapists may dismiss such modifications to traditional therapy as being unnecessary. Shouldn't a good counselor be able to look past the color of a person's skin and treat all clients the same way? The answer is both yes and no.

Many non–African Americans assert, "We should be blind to color." In the context of an individual's value, such a statement would be accurate, but in the context of an individual's identity, factors such as ethnicity, culture, and appearance play important roles. Take something as simple as a productive relationship between the client and the therapist. African American clients are likely to be more guarded with a non–African American therapist. Years of prejudice and discrimination have forced these clients to reveal themselves cautiously. A failure to recognize the origins of this response and deal with it appropriately will attenuate the productivity of the intervention. In fact, sensitivity to the client's preference for gradual disclosure will demonstrate what Sue and Sue (1999) refer to as cultural competence, which has been shown to be even more important to African Americans than the ethnicity of their therapist. Having cultural competence doesn't mean that you should colorfully adapt your language by making statements such as, "Why you ain't tell me?" It means that you may need to honestly express your feelings, revealing your thoughts faster and more openly than you would with a client from your own ethnic group.

Imagine you are working with a client who is concerned about the treatment she is receiving from coworkers. "None of them seem to understand me, and I think Kathy has it in for me." As the client makes these statements, you begin to wonder whether these are real or imagined social problems. Before you can react, the client remarks, "You think I'm paranoid—I can see it in your eyes." This situation happened to me, sadly. The truth was that I was indeed wondering whether the client was paranoid, but I didn't want her to see my concern, so I remained silent. When she commented on the expression in my eyes, my initial reaction was one of defensiveness and denial. What a horrid thing to view a client so negatively. After thinking about the situation for a second or two, I realized that I needed to take a different route. I smiled, and said, "You seem to have some special gifts. Yes, I was thinking that you were seeing problems that didn't really exist, but now that you have read me so perfectly, I'm starting to think that Kathy might really have it in for you!" The client smiled at this statement, and our relationship improved. Rather than feel threatened by my negative view, she felt comfortable with my trustworthiness.

Part of understanding a culture is considering the perspective of those inside the culture. When you read about Gwen's experiences, consider how she must have felt when she decided to turn down her friend's request. It is also important to ponder what it must be like to feel trapped between cultures.

Gwen's Story

I am often surprised when I talk with White people about Blacks. They don't seem to truly understand. One of my White friends asked me to come join a rally against the Ku Klux Klan. She stated that it was my duty to help fight against the prejudice and discrimination caused by this hideous group. When I turned her down, she became angry. "How can you expect it to end if you won't stand up for what is right?" she asked. All I could think about is what might happen if I, as a Black woman, marched against the KKK; I would have to fear for my life and my family's. After all, they have masks on when they ride—I wouldn't. I know the reality of being hunted down and having crosses burned on your front lawn. I know that the KKK kills little Brown and Black girls and that they hide bombs under church benches. My friend simply doesn't understand the price I would pay—the price I *have* paid.

My friend does not know that my family has already experienced the midnight raids of the KKK. She does not know what it is like to throw babies from the upstairs floor of an apartment to escape the flames of the KKK. She does not know what it is like to walk on the wrong side of the street. Nor does she know the pain I've felt in my heart and in my soul after having awakened only to find my cousin hanged by the neck from his very own pecan tree. I was afraid; I am still very afraid.

I realize that people are filled with prejudice. I'm still prejudiced against White teenagers, although I realize that most are kind, wise children with no intent to harm. My experiences have led me to believe that some White people are dangerous and I know it would be silly for me to believe otherwise. People say and do harmful things. It's just a way of life. I don't think most White people can ever grasp how frightening it is for a Black person to walk down the street or simply go shopping. We try to blend in, but it never works.

Some of the people I know have learned to hum Mozart and to purchase only designer clothes. Many have learned to straighten the kinky curls from their hair with chemical relaxers and hot combs. Their intent was simply to look as "White" as possible, which poses an entirely new set of problems. No matter what their profession, clothing, or mannerisms, they never really had a chance to be accepted by White people. For all of us, there are sideways glances hiding subtle terror buried in their eyes. They see a person of color, any person of color, and suspect some danger.

In addition to losing the battle to fit into White culture, many of us have felt banished from African cultures as well. One African American woman told me that I was an Oreo cookie—Black on the outside but White on the inside—because I attended a wealthy, historically White college. At the time, she was teaching at that same college and apparently saw no conflict between her profession and her identity. But for me, as a student, being "one" with all these wealthy White kids—I was betraying my culture. Apparently, she thought I should have attended a "Black school." Somehow, we need to find out how to form an acceptance of ourselves, and other Black Americans. We must do this on our own because White society may never understand our needs.

Questions to Consider

1. Do you believe that the hardships African Americans endured 100 years ago continue to affect their culture today?

2. Does it seem likely that African Americans follow a process of identity development? Do you think Cross's model accurately describes the experiences of many African Americans?

3. Why does physical discipline seem to be less harmful to African American children than it is for European Americans?

4. African Americans are graduating from high school at record levels. What factors do you believe to be responsible for this change?

5. Despite their increased rate of high school graduation, African Americans have seen little improvement in the status of their wages. What factors could be continuing to hold them back in the work force?

6. Traditionally, African American women have had difficulty fitting into some feminist organizations. Why do you think this is the case?

7. Why is insight-oriented therapy often less helpful than solution-focused approaches when working with African American clients?

8. How do prejudice and discrimination affect the educational and occupational experiences of African Americans?

9. Is it possible (or desirable) to be a "color-blind" therapist?

10. On August 28, 1963, while standing on the steps of the Lincoln Memorial in Washington, D.C., Martin Luther King, Jr., made his most memorable speech. He declared, "I have a dream that one day this nation will rise up and live out the true meaning of its creed—'We hold these truths to be self-evident, that all men are created equal.'" Later in the same speech, he stated, "I have a dream that my four little children will one day live in a nation where they will not be judged by the color of their skin but by the content of their character." Do you believe that today is the day that he dreamed of? If not, will this day ever take place?

3

Latin Americans

Juanita's grandmother appeared to her last night. It wasn't a dream. She simply appeared, glowing and holding a cempazuchitl (a yellow marigold, the symbol of death). After her eyes adjusted, Juanita sat up and concentrated on the woman. Before Juanita could react or leave her bed, the woman began to speak!

"Juanita, you are making a mistake," the figure stated in a concerned voice. "You should not marry José; he is not your soulmate—beware of your lust and wait for the right man!" With that, the apparition vanished, and Juanita fainted. When she awoke, Juanita ran to her mother and recounted the story to her. Her mother explained that ghosts rarely appear outside of Día de los Muertos (the Day of the Dead) unless the message provided was urgent and necessary. Given this commentary, Juanita cancelled her wedding and broke off her relationship with José. Do you believe this was a healthy or wise decision?

The term "African American" underwent several derivations before reaching its final form. It represents a location of origin (Africa) rather than physical characteristics. With Latin Americans, the term is more difficult for many outsiders to understand. Why Latino? Why not Hispanic, Mexican, or Cuban? The explanation is a little complicated.

In most Latin American countries, there are usually at least three distinct groups present: the indigenous group that continues to speak the native language; the *mestizo*, or blended group that shares indigenous and Spanish blood and culture; and those who are direct descendants of Spanish colonizers (Falicov, 1998). The term "Hispanic" best depicts the direct descendants of the Spanish conquerors, but applies only partially or not at all to other Latin groups. When the term is applied to the *mestizo* groups, it may imply that their Spanish heritage is more important or valuable than their native roots. For members of native cultures, the term may simply insult their uniqueness and individuality. In order to avoid all of these pitfalls, the terms "Latino" (masculine) and "Latina" (feminine) were employed to provide an unbiased and more universal means of identifying an enormously diverse group of individuals. Why refer to such groups as Latinos? The regions in the Western Hemisphere south of the United States—Mexico, Central America, the West Indies, and South America—comprise a territory referred to as *Latin America*. In each of these regions, the official languages (Spanish, Portuguese, and French) are derived from the Latin language. Latin is a significant cultural umbrella that is shared by these multifarious groups, even though none of the regions actually speak Latin.

Although the term "Latinos" adequately identifies people with Latin American roots, in some cases, it is not the preferable method of identification. For example, many Mexicans prefer to be called Mexican or Mexican American rather than Latino/a. The various Latin American countries have distinct cultures and traditions that make them unique. Many immigrants fight to hold onto their nationalistic identities, which are more specific than ethnicity. As generations become further removed from the country of origin, however, they may distance themselves from their ancestors' homeland. Consider the following narrative from a college student in southern California:

> My parents are from Mexico and are very proud of their Mexican heritage. When we came to America, they understood very little English, but they wanted us to learn because, they said, "You must speak English to survive here." As I studied with the Anglo students, I never felt as though I was different. I was accepted. At least, I was until junior high school. One day, a boy ran up behind me, pulled my hair, and called me a spick. I didn't know what the word meant, but there was an intense anger in his voice. I wanted to be like everyone else, but something about me was different—painfully different. By the time I started college, I had started to learn about the richness of the Latino culture. I wanted to understand my people and how they viewed themselves. The more I learned, the prouder I became. Eventually, I decided to call myself "Latina" rather than Mexican-American, because I wanted to identify with all Latino cultures. This hurt my parents deeply, and continues to hurt them to this day, because they thought I was abandoning my Mexican heritage. On the contrary, I believe I was fulfilling it.

The position taken by this student was one of the reasons why some Latinos started calling themselves "Chicanos." The term arose in the late 1960s, when the English-speaking children of Mexican immigrants realized they were not fully Mexican or American. They wanted a term that reflected the special history of Mexican Americans and paid tribute to both cultural influences (Falicov, 1998). The term fell out of favor during the 1990s because it was associated with poverty and gangs. Still, it is important to realize that the term a Latino/a client selects to define himself or herself is very powerful. These labels are not chosen arbitrarily. They reflect elements of the client's past, culture, and identity.

History of Oppression

The region of Latin America is made up of South America, Mexico, Central America, and the West Indies. Within this region are nearly three dozen independent nations as well as colonies and other political units that have special ties with the United States, Great Britain, France, or the Netherlands. At the time of the Europeans' arrival in the New World in 1492, from 60 to 75 million people lived in Latin America. Most of them inhabited the highlands of the central Andes and the region between northern Central America and central Mexico. These areas were under the control of the Inca, Maya, and Aztec peoples. Within 50 years after the arrival of the Europeans, more than half the Indians had perished. Within a century, no more than a fourth remained. The disappearance of the native population has often been attributed to cruel treatment by the Spaniards. However, the introduction of European diseases such as smallpox and measles, against which the Indians had no natural immunity, had an equally devastating effect.

To provide a supply of labor in places uninhabited by Indians, the Portuguese—and, to a lesser degree, the Spaniards—imported African slaves. After 1650, settlers from the colonizing nations of northern Europe transported slaves into the territories they had seized from the Spaniards in the West Indies. During the three centuries prior to 1850, as many as 14 million slaves may have been introduced into Latin America, compared with about 500,000 brought into the United States. In Latin America, most of the slaves were taken to northeastern Brazil and the islands of the Caribbean, where they worked on sugar plantations.

Spanish and Portuguese colonies in Central and South America became independent during the first half of the nineteenth century. Haiti, the first Latin American country to win independence, gained its freedom from France in 1804. In 1821, Mexico won its independence from Spain and governed California until the end of the Mexican-American War in 1848. At that time the Treaty of Guadalupe Hildalgo was signed, promising the rights of citizenship and land ownership to the Mexicans living in the territories that became part of the United States. In reality, many rights were denied and land was confiscated (Novas, 1994). It is important to realize that many Latino residents of the southwestern United States may be offended at being considered immigrants. Their families may predate the arrival of European Americans to this region.

Non-Latinos, however, either forgot or overlooked the long history of Latinos with their land. During the depression of the 1930s, an estimated half a million Mexican Americans, including those whose families had been living in the U.S. for centuries, were deported to Mexico. Most were never fully integrated into Mexican society, and many returned when labor shortages developed during World War II. At that time, the United States instituted the Bracero program to encourage Mexicans to work in the fields on a seasonal basis (Kanellos, 1994).

Skin color, as with African Americans, may play a role in the history of discrimination against Latinos. González de Alba (1994) theorized that the arrogant Spanish colonizers might have created this prejudice. White (or *güero*) individuals are viewed as descendants of the Spaniards, and as such, are born into power, privilege, and a higher social class. Darker skin (or *indio*) signifies suppression, inferiority, and lack of social power (Falicov, 1998).

The possibility of Latinos classifying themselves as "Black" may surprise many European Americans. Until 1954, Latinos were considered "White" according to American census data (Falicov, 1998). In 1954, they, as well as African Americans and Asians, were labeled a "colored minority." The distinction was used for less than noble purposes. European American school systems fighting to keep African Americans out of their schools could argue that they were already integrated because they accepted "Hispanics." Still, the designation as a minority group provided a political advantage to Latinos, who could now secure federal funding and political representation.

Recognition from the American government, however, does not imply acceptance by the broader society. Mary Margaret Navar (Davis, 1990) tells the story of her "assimilation" during the 1950s. As part of a young immigrant family struggling to gain acceptance, she was allowed to speak only English. She was given an American name and expected to learn American culture. Still, she found herself labeled as different. Store owners refused to assist her, and others politely redirected her to Spanish-speaking attendants. Still others simply provided racist comments and feedback.

She describes a shopping trip to a hosiery store for stockings. She began browsing for brownish colors that would accentuate her olive skin and dark hair. As she continued her search, a saleswoman intervened: "Honey, no offense, but your complexion is dark, not too dark—but you know what I mean, you have to be careful, watch what you wear, you don't want it to look (pause) you know what I mean. Why don't you get a light hose; you'll look so much better." The implication was clear: if you wear dark-colored hose you will look different. This single event convinced her that she would never be fully accepted in America.

Virtually any physical or noticeable characteristic may evoke intolerance from European American society. It could be a person's manner of dress, Spanish accent, Latin surname, immigrant status, or skin color. Of these, however, skin color seems to play the most significant role. When examining housing segregation, Massey and Denton (1993) found that darker-skinned Latinos tended to become more segregated than their lighter-skinned peers were. Lighter-skinned Latinos earned a segregation index of 52, mixed-race Latinos received a score of 72, and darker-skinned Latinos received an index of 80, which was similar to that found for African Americans.

The same prejudice that leads to housing segregation creates other problems. Darker-skinned Latinos tend to be diagnosed with mental illnesses more frequently than are their lighter-skinned peers (Rabkin & Struening, 1976), and, as we will see, experience more prejudice from within and outside their community. (This does not mean that lighter-skinned Latinos can easily assimilate into the Anglo community.)

Cowan, Martinez, and Mendiola (1997) investigated the views of California college students regarding a then-recent case of police brutality. The case received considerable exposure in the local press, and was frequently compared with the Rodney King beatings. Two illegal immigrants were struck several times by police before being arrested and later deported. The researchers wanted to know what factors might lead college students, averaging 26.76 years of age, to support the police action. Some common themes quickly emerged. Students were more likely to condone the brutality if they held racist beliefs, harbored negative stereotypes toward Latinos, or lacked humanitarian values. Students who found the brutality acceptable were also likely to hold similar views regarding other issues involving illegal immigrants.

Family

> Imelda came in for counseling because she was concerned about her 13-year-old son, Juan, and his social problems at school. It seems his fellow students, who are mostly non-Hispanic, have been teasing him for his "quietness." As the interview continues, you find that Juan sleeps in the same bed with Imelda and her husband, as he has done since he was a baby. Would you seek to change the family's sleeping arrangement?

In the example of "Juanita," which was presented at the beginning of the chapter, the young woman is warned by a ghost not to marry her boyfriend. A possible intervention for this case may involve asking Juanita how her family handled her marriage announcement. Did her boyfriend ask her father for her hand in marriage? If not, the ghost (or guardian angel) may have been helping her to realize that her fiancé lacks the cultural insight or manners to blend into her Latino family.

More than any other American cultural group studied, Latino Americans appear to have the closest family ties. For social and economic reasons, immigrants from Mexico are the cultural group most likely to live with extended kin or unrelated persons (e.g., family friends) upon recent arrival to the United States (Blank, 1998). After immigrating, Latinos are more likely than European Americans to describe their personal networks and social support in terms of kinship (Schweizer, Schnegg, & Berzborn, 1998). They define their selfhood by their familial ties, and consider these relationships more important than autonomy.

Falicov (1998) refers to family ties between Latinos as *familismo*, which implies a combination of collectivism and interdependence. Rather than function as united individuals, members of a Latino family view themselves as a unit. All family members share functions such as rearing children, earning money, and providing companionship. Even household objects tend to be viewed as collectively owned. Family members hold culturally determined roles, but they will share these roles when necessary. The husband/father may be the primary financial provider, but many other family members are likely to contribute to the process. To outsiders, such shared burdens might appear unhealthy, especially when one person's desires are placed beneath the will of the family. Some Latinas, for example, may silently "sacrifice" themselves— possibly even abandoning their desires and wishes to attend to help the family financially and emotionally. European American therapists may view this self-sacrificial lifestyle as destructive or co-dependent, but for many Latino families the gender-assigned roles and corporate identity are accepted facts of life.

Familismo extends beyond the nuclear family to encompass grandparents, extended family members, and, in some cases, even maids (Falicov, 1998). This view of family is evidenced, in part, by the celebration of *la comida semanal* (the weekly meal). For this day of feasting, family members may have dinners at both grandparents' homes. All offspring, their spouses, children, and special friends are expected to attend the event. In America, *la comida semanal* is less frequently practiced because many families lack the financial resources or household space to host the event. However, many middle- to upper-class immigrants from Mexico, Puerto Rico, and Cuba still continue some form of the gathering. Even in these cases, however, more acculturated Latinos typically adopt the nuclear-family model and spend most of their time and money on immediate family members (Blank, 1998).

When Latino families demonstrate the intimate ties described above, European Americans or other non-Latino therapists are often quick to label them as enmeshed. It is important to note that what constitutes "excessively" close in one culture may be completely acceptable in another. One of my clients, a 24-year-old Mexican American woman, lived with her mother and her eight brothers and sisters. Although three of her brothers were older than she was, they were expected to live at home until they were married. Rather than view this as a lack of preparation for the "real world," they believed that living with each other provided them with the social skills to be successful in marriage.

Close family ties offer clear advantages, yet there are potential disadvantages. The most significant cost associated with close family ties involves increased risk for sexual exploitation. Latino sexual molestation rates by extended family members are generally higher than rates found in other ethnic groups (Moisan, Sanders-Phillips, & Moisan, 1997). A therapist may wonder if molestation might be present in the case introduced at the beginning of this section. Perhaps Imelda's son Juan is quiet because he is the victim of sexual abuse and is having difficulty coping with the shame and pressure of the relationship. The potential for abuse should be explored, yet it is highly unlikely that Juan's problems stem from the family's sleeping arrangement. Latino children are simply more likely to share a bed with their parents even up to puberty. In most cases, co-sleeping creates few problems for the family and is the result of two conditions: (1) the strong desire for intimacy in Latino homes, and (2) the limited financial status of some Latino families. In Juan's case, he was insecure and quiet because he feared his English was "not good enough." After interacting for a few weeks with his therapist, he gained confidence and began to talk more readily with his peers.

Despite the desire for close ties between family members, traditional, or "old school" Latino families hold views on sexual intimacy that differ from those of European Americans. Fidelity is mandatory for a wife, but infidelity by a husband can be overlooked or forgiven (Falicov, 1998). This double standard is underscored by the fact that Latinas' risks of contracting sexual diseases increases within a committed relationship, while European American women's risks are increased by sex outside of their current relationship and by their sexual practices (Wyatt, Forge, & Guthrie, 1998). One Latino client described the sexual double standard to me in the following way:

> When I'm with my wife, I can't help but think of her as the mother of my children. I love her, but I feel like I need something more. I need passion and excitement, not just comfort and support.

Often, the male partner is reluctant to discuss these issues with his wife. When conducting marital therapy, it is important for the therapist to recognize when one partner feels unusually uncomfortable. In such cases, issues should be explored privately and brought into marital therapy later. It should be noted that the double standard described above is significantly less common within the younger generation of Latinos. Younger Latinos, while aware of their parents' and grandparents' extramarital views, tend to view such beliefs as archaic.

Economics

When infidelity occurs, many couples stay together. They may even undergo marital counseling to preserve the family. In addition to cultural mandates, economic necessity also compels families to remain intact. Many Latinos struggle with issues related to poverty, and if their families were to disband, their financial struggles would be made more acute.

The causes of their economic struggles are multi-faceted. It is easy to hypothesize that language barriers, acculturation, or immigration create poverty among many Latinos, but these factors explain only part of the problem. For example, many Latinos come to America with the hope of stabilizing their economic situation. If adjustment difficulties create or sustain their poverty, future generations should enjoy greater economic success. For many families, this is not the case. Although many poor Latinos come to America, their prospects for economic success do not improve as they continue to work. Latino immigrants tend to fall into greater poverty with each successive generation. Third-plus-generation Latinos have the greatest chances of being in poverty (Padilla, 1997). Additionally, a number of other conditions seem to have little effect on Latino poverty. For example, the number and presence of young children (under six years of age), marital status, citizenship, and English usage all have marginal effects on income levels (Kirschner-Cook & Welsh-Jordan, 1997). What, then, creates and sustains poverty? The two most important considerations are the types of jobs sought and levels of educational attainment.

Employment, unsurprisingly, plays an important role in fending off poverty. Both the number of hours a person works and having a managerial or professional job decrease the risk of poverty (Kirschner-Cook & Welsh-Jordan, 1997). Additionally, the jobs held by young people may significantly affect the type of work they will find themselves doing later. If Latinos seek professional employment from an early age (as opposed to more menial employment), they may develop high-level skills that will create more opportunities in the future. Opportunities are also more plentiful for employees who are willing to leave their communities. Latinos who chose to migrate in search of job opportunities are the least likely to find themselves among the very poor (Padilla, 1997).

When Latinos succeed in overcoming financial barriers, their success is often associated with a change in identity. Eckman, Kotsiopulos, and Bickle (1997) investigated how changes in income levels influence changes in cultural values. Their results showed that higher-income Latinos (those earning at least $30,001 per year) resembled their European American counterparts in many other consumer aspects. They were more likely to shower their children with Christmas gifts, join health clubs, purchase expensive health-related products, and travel to exotic places. However, such attempts at assimilation are less common among darker-skinned Latinos, who are significantly less likely to escape poverty (Novas, 1994).

It should also be noted that economics play a significant function in defining gender roles. Falicov (1998) reported that a couple came into her office complaining about each other's failures. The husband stated that his wife had failed in her "wifely duties" (a euphemism for sex). The wife responded, "If you fulfilled your husbandly duties of supporting the family, things would be different." In this situation, both the husband and wife worked, and the wife derived considerable satisfaction from her employment. Still, she viewed her husband as less of a man because she *had* to work. Latina feminists, though striving for equal access to work and salaries, still cherish traditional Latino values, including caring for their family and community. For many Latino males, being respected and considered masculine are tied to financially supporting their families. When they are unable to earn adequate wages, they may attempt to exert more control over their family (physically or verbally) or begin to drink heavily (Falicov, 1998).

Education

> *Segura, age 16:* I don't understand what all the fuss is. I'm not saying I want to work for $8.50 an hour for the rest of my life, but I don't need an education to do better. I'm going to start a rock band, and school would just slow me down.

The most effective way for Latinos to overcome financial hardships is to attain the best possible education. Simply put, the more education Latinos and many other groups obtain, the greater their chances for economic success (Kirschner-Cook & Welsh-Jordan, 1997). However, Latino education itself is fraught with tremendous obstacles, and education comes at a considerable cost for Latinos.

One of the more devastating costs involves linguistic issues. Are Latinos robbed of their language if they are forced to study in English? Do they fall too far behind academically if they receive their training in Spanish? Since the mid-1970s, when the Supreme Court case *Lau v. Nichols* mandated private schools to provide adequate training to non-English-speaking students, bilingual education programs flourished across the country. More recently, however, short-term alternatives have been implemented to replace long-term programs. California, for example, had a 30-year history of offering bilingual education, but in 1998 the citizens voted to ban long-term programs in favor of providing a one-year transitional English immersion program. After completing this course, students from all linguistic heritages will complete the rest of their training in English.

It is hoped that changes such as these will help to reduce the staggering Latino dropout rate. Currently, nearly one third of Latino students fail to complete high school. This rate is three times that of European Americans and twice as high as the dropout rate for African Americans. For children of migrant workers, the situation is even worse, with only about 10 percent finishing high school (Sue & Sue, 1999). One quarter of Latinos have repeated at least one year of school by the time they reach eighth grade, and they are overrepresented in special education programs.

Language difficulties contribute to the poor academic performance of Latinos. Some Latino children are bilingual but have only a limited command of the English language. In such cases, their friends and family are likely to speak Spanish, which further complicates matters. The language barrier, while having a direct effect on the student's ability to understand classroom material, also has an indirect effect on the student's academic performance. It provides non-Latino students with further evidence that the student is "different."

Beyond language differences, there is a broader cultural difference affecting Latino educational achievement. In a brief article in *U.S. News and World Report*, Headden (1997) quoted a young Santa Fe teenage girl as saying that doing well in school was considered "Anglo" or "nerdy." With beliefs such as these readily accepted, Latinos face tremendous peer pressure to do poorly in school or to drop out. In order to combat negative attitudes toward school among Latino students, teachers and other educators can alter their instructional strategies to better fit the child's cultural values. For example, instead of saying, "You did well—you should be very proud of yourself," a teacher could say, "Your family should be very pleased with your work" (Sue & Sue, 1999). Involving the family in the educational process creates a bridge between the "Anglo" academic world and the child's Latino culture. Culturally sensitive interventions may help to support the student's development of an academic identity.

In addition to confirming the positive effects of parental support, there is some evidence that information from counselors, teachers, college materials, preparatory classes, friends, and extracurricular activities play a role in the college planning process for Latino students (Hurtado & Gauvain, 1997). Acculturation through these avenues is predictive of actual college attendance among Mexican American adolescents. In many ways, information received outside the family plays a more significant role in college attendance than comments offered by parents. Even though many Latino parents want their children to attend college (Retish & Kavanaugh, 1992), if parents have not completed college themselves, their children are less likely to do so. This cycle is difficult to reverse because parents' educational attainment tends to have a strong influence on their children's college aspirations and planning behaviors (Hurtado & Gauvain, 1997).

Even when Latinos decide to attend college, they face additional obstacles. Latino undergraduate students appear less willing to disclose much of themselves to non-Latino faculty. All racial groups express a preference for intraracial faculty, but African Americans and Latinos express a significantly higher discomfort level with interracial teaching staff than do European Americans (Noel & Smith, 1996). Lack of trust may keep them from interacting with faculty. With less faculty contact, Latinos face an increased struggle to finish their schooling. Increasing the number of Latino faculty would likely ease this problem, but at present, only 1.5 percent of all college faculty are Latino (Kavanaugh & Retish, 1991).

If schools are successful in gaining the trust of their Latino students, the students may place more value on academic achievement. For example, Osborne (1998) found that Latina girls were the only group he studied that became more identified with academics as they progressed through their academic careers. Members of every other ethnic group tended to distance themselves from academic success and identify themselves with social groups, occupations, or some other type of affiliation. One method of creating trust and encouraging a sense of belonging is by adopting and supporting programs sponsored by the National Council of La Razas (NCLR) Center for Community Educational Excellence. The NCLR works to bridge the gap between communities and schools in order to strengthen the quality of education for Hispanic students, and to involve Hispanic families in the education of their children. The NCLR has been relatively successful in helping Latinos stay in school.

Health

Latinos are less likely to finish the same academic curriculum that European Americans pursue, and they are also less likely to adopt the European American understanding of medicine. Rather than adopt medical interpretations for illnesses, they are more likely to believe in "folk illnesses." For example, *mal de ojo* (the evil eye) is a belief that a jealous, malicious, or powerful person can steal someone's ability to control their own actions. This condition may even arise from more innocuous means. In Mexican culture, if a person comments on the attractiveness of an infant, that person is then required to physically touch the baby. Failing to contact the baby may curse the young child with *mal de ojo*. The victim may experience severe headaches, uncontrollable weeping, fretfulness, insomnia, and fevers (Falicov, 1998). Other folk concepts such as witchcraft *(mal puesto)*, fright, indigestion *(empacho)*, and natural illnesses *(males naturales)* are considered the best explanation for many health-related problems.

Other folk illnesses are thought to cause a number of mental-health-related problems. *Nervios* (nerves) is thought to exist because one's "brain aches." Headaches, sleep difficulties, trembling, tingling sensations, and dizziness may be associated with the disorder. Although these are symptoms for a number of DSM-IV diagnoses (e.g., post-concussional disorder, inhalant intoxication, panic disorder, etc.), some Latinos may be unfamiliar with such diagnoses and favor their cultural explanation.

Physical problems may also be associated with folk illnesses. For example, many Latinos, especially Puerto Ricans, still believe in the "hot and cold" theory of illness. According to this view, physical and mental health are promoted by an equilibrium of hot and cold in one's body and environment. Too much heat, such as that caused by ironing clothes with wet hands, is thought to cause arthritis. Strong psychological reactions, such as fright, are said to create heat and are relieved by consuming cool herbal teas. These unique views concerning the etiologies of many health problems make traditional health care less attractive to Latinos. This attitude, in itself, may pose a serious health threat to many Latin Americans.

In the case of *empacho* (indigestion), an elder may bring an individual into a dark room, rub the victim's back with ashes, and pinch the skin around the spinal cord. If the cause is more serious than a stomachache—say, appendicitis—this treatment could pose a serious health risk.

Folk beliefs regarding other illnesses have created an epidemic among certain groups. Ailinger and Dear (1997) investigated the effects of tuberculosis infection on Latinos. One third of the world's population is infected with tuberculosis (TB), costing Americans more than $700 million per year. Latinos are a high-risk group, in part because they appear to have a limited understanding of the disease, but also because they are typically less likely than members of other minority groups to be able to afford medical evaluations and treatment. This financial limitation means that Latino immigrants are unlikely to seek preventative intervention, and many infected Latino immigrants did not know the cause of their infection. A similar lack of awareness has been noted regarding the use of illicit drugs, alcohol, and tobacco. Gil-Rivas, Anglin, and Annon (1997) examined ethnic drug use differences among 2,738 incarcerated individuals (aged 18 to 82 years). Although fewer Latinos were arrested under the influence of drugs, nearly 50 percent of Latinos reported drug use in the year prior to their arrest. They were also the most likely group to report a history of abuse (e.g., cocaine, heroin, PCP). These problems are also found among non-incarcerated Latino men. While rates remained relatively stable for men from other ethnic groups, rates among Latino men rose from 9 percent in 1984 to 16 percent in 1995 (Caetano & Clark, 1998). Despite these high rates of abuse, most Latino drug users believed drug treatment was unnecessary (Gil-Rivas, Anglin, & Annon, 1997) and they were less likely than other groups to attend Alcoholics Anonymous meetings (Arroyo, Westerberg, & Tonigan, 1998). It appears that their most positive treatment intervention came from formal alcohol treatment centers, but even in these cases, the treatment was effective only in decreasing the intensity and quantity of alcohol use, rather than increasing the number of abstinent days.

Alcohol use for Latinos is related, in part, to the use of alcohol in ceremonies and holidays. In nearly all Latino celebrations, alcohol is involved. People who refuse to drink on such occasions are often stigmatized as inhospitable, antisocial, or dull. The alcohol industry has recently begun to use this trend to push for increased use during Cinco de Mayo celebrations.

High rates of alcohol use among Latinos are somewhat understandable, but it is less clear why there are increasing rates of usage of illegal substances within this community. One explanation for drug use may involve efforts to seek relief from acculturation difficulties and economic problems. When entire families find themselves impoverished and disassociating themselves from their cultural roots, the chances increase that a given family member will start trying illicit drugs (Gil, Vega, & Biafora, 1998). Polednak (1997) found that the more acculturated Latinos became, the more likely they were to drink on a weekly basis. Women were the most likely to increase their drinking in America as they took advantage of newfound freedoms and opportunities, but men also increased their drinking. It would be easy to assume that the drinking stems from a high American tolerance for the behavior, but there may be other reasons as well. As Latinos lose part of their culture and are simultaneously rejected by the dominant culture, they are likely to feel isolated and abandoned. These factors may increase a sense of hopelessness, which in turn may increase self-medicating efforts such as drinking. If this is the reason for excessive drinking, it may explain why Latinos who abuse alcohol tend to downplay the significance of the problem. Their "drinking" may not be the problem. Instead, the underlying problem is the self-prejudice they have internalized from a racist society. Drug treatment interventions are often ineffective because they fail to address the underlying roots of the behavior.

In support of an acculturation model for alcohol and drug use, we know that depression contributes to illicit drug use among Latino males. Galaif, Chou, Sussman, and Dent (1998) compared Latino and European American males and females to discover factors that led to what they called "gateway" substances (legal drugs such as cigarettes and alcohol) as well as "hard substances" such as marijuana, cocaine, stimulants, and inhalants. For Latinas, their depression was likely to be correlated with suicidality but not drug use. For male Latinos, however, depression predicted both gateway and hard substance use. Both the suicidality of Latinas and the drug use of Latinos are forms of escapism. Depression, fed by acculturation problems, may cause people to engage in self-destructive behaviors such as suicide attempts and substance abuse.

When providing an intervention for drug use among Latinos, providers would be wise to simultaneously treat depression. For example, Spanish-speaking Latinos find it easier to end smoking when they also receive help managing their depression. Munoz, VanOss-Marin, Posner, and Perez-Stable (1997) mailed a self-administered mood-management-smoking-cessation intervention program to 136 Spanish-speaking Latino smokers. The participants were randomly assigned to groups that received either a smoking cessation guide (the *Guia*) or the *Guia* plus a written and audiotaped mood management intervention *(Tomando Control de su Vida)*. After three months, 23 percent of those assigned to the *Guia* plus mood-management group reported abstaining from smoking for at least a week. Only 11 percent of the control group could say the same. Clients with prior major depressive episodes reported an even higher abstinence rate in the *Guia* plus mood-management condition.

Depression and acculturation issues may even manifest themselves in physical symptoms. Abraido-Lanza (1997) examined the effects of social role identity on the ways low-income Latinas coped with arthritis. She found that depression and other negative feelings were more common when the women's sex roles were challenged. When they could base their identities on being homemakers, mothers, and grandmothers, their self-esteem and self-efficacy rose, which in turn contributed to psychological well-being and mediated the effects of arthritic pain.

There are other positive trends in the health patterns of Latinos as well. Suinn (1999) observed that Latinas born in 1995 will have the highest life expectancy of any racial or gender group because of the cultural value of prioritization of family, extended families providing emotional support, good nutritional habits, and fewer negative health habits. Such information helps us identify the factors associated with long life, and it also confirms the benefits provided by a strong cultural foundation.

Cultural Uniqueness

Assessing levels of acculturation among Latinos is considerably different from doing so for African Americans. Most African Americans readily identify themselves as "Black." Latinos often find themselves trapped between various racial groups. According to the U.S. Bureau of the Census (1991), when Latinos were given the choice between identifying themselves as "White," "Black," or "other," 52 percent identified themselves as White, 3.4 percent considered themselves Black, and the rest checked the "other" box. Many of the Latinos who come from the Caribbean islands share a significant history with darker-skinned individuals. For example, Puerto Ricans, who were originally dark-skinned, mixed with lighter-skinned immigrants to create a range of racial characteristics and colors. These differences have led some to refer to Puerto Ricans as "rainbow people" (Falicov, 1998).

The differences between skin colors have also triggered racism between Latino groups. Many Latino groups hold firmly established views of ethnic hierarchies. Shorris (1992) referred to this form of intra-group discrimination as *racismo*, and he noted that many of these beliefs stem from myths about the prestige of a Latino's national origin. From his observations, Cubans living in Miami are often regarded as conceited and arrogant. They are viewed as cultural traitors and more closely akin to European Americans than their fellow Latinos. Given their increased potential for economic success, they may flaunt their economic progress or use it to denigrate other Latino groups.

Mexicans, according to Shorris, are most likely to be prejudiced against dark-skinned Puerto Ricans and other dark-skinned Latinos. This trend towards a visually oriented bias also applies to the Puerto Ricans. Although Puerto Ricans tend to be critical of the United States in general, there is also a social bias against African Americans. This may seem contradictory, considering the number of dark-skinned Puerto Ricans who self-identify as Black. Why would someone do this? The answer is complex, but it involves way we view ourselves. If we are dark-skinned, we have two choices. We can either ignore our physical presence or embrace it. Learning to embrace it in the face of social disapproval takes significant coping skills and self-determination. Imagine you were a dark-skinned Latino hearing the following advice:

> You should know, my son, that you are very, very dark. Now that you are going to move (from Guadalajara) and come to live here in Mexico City and you soon will have a girlfriend, you must find one who is very, very White so that in case you get married you will have White children (González de Alba, 1994, p. 28).

The inner conflict upon hearing such statements is profound. On the one hand is the desire to maintain a sense of heritage, cultural identity, and ethnic pride. On the other hand is the wish to attenuate heartache and discrimination. There are no easy answers in the resolution of these conflicts.

In addition to racial hierarchies, there are also gender hierarchies among Latinos. Regardless of their national origin, families treat young Latinas differently from Latino boys. Every family member must protect the emerging woman from the sexual threats around her. Various family members emphasize the need for young women to follow special rules, preserve their virginity, and prepare for their role in creating a new family. Villarruel (1998) notes that these customs and rules, while consistently observed in Latino households, are not directly associated with religious doctrine or practice. Regardless of a family's religious affiliation, they seek to protect their daughters and sisters from pregnancy and assault.

Family members are likely to maintain a protective role towards young Latinas, yet these girls also undergo a form of liberation. Immigrant mothers tend to accept the "Americanization" of their girls and welcome the freedom they experience (Falicov, 1998). However, many older Latinas take great pride in housework and traditionally feminine activities, which may send mixed messages to girls. They are told to exceed the limitations of their mothers but also expected to maintain the prescribed feminine roles of their culture. Forging a new definition of womanhood that bridges these two worlds is often quite difficult and requires all family members to make compromises.

Changes in Latina roles have led to greater flexibility in the culturally assigned gender roles of Latino males. This flexibility is evident, in part, in the games played by young boys. In 1982, young boys living in Mexico City refused to play the game *lavando la muñeca* (washing the doll), saying it was only for "sissies" or girls. In 1995, however, five-year-old boys happily participated in the game. They also watered plants, swept the floor, and collected garbage, probably because their fathers were engaging in such activities (Gutmann, 1996).

The process of acculturation has become easier than it was in the past, but it still runs a common course. As with African American clients, one of the factors that should be considered when counseling Latinos is their level of acculturation. Ruiz (1990) created a five-stage model that seemed to explain the acculturation process his Latino clients underwent (see Table 3.1). As with the African American models, the first stage (casual stage) involves a denial of the Latino culture and its uniqueness. Negative messages, acts of discrimination, and broadly accepted stereotypes are generally ignored.

As individuals encounter more negative messages, they enter the cognitive stage and face a critical decision. Do they associate with poor Latinos and risk being stereotyped and discriminated against, or do they assimilate into "White" culture to escape stigma or become successful? In the third stage, the consequence stage, Latinos begin to feel ashamed of or embarrassed about their cultural heritage. Either they have chosen to associate only with non-Latinos or they have identified with a group they view as inferior. Either way, they begin to internalize the negative images society has thrust upon them. In reaction, they may abandon cultural customs, attempt to change their name, lighten

TABLE 3.1 *Ruiz's Acculturation Model*

Casual stage	Denial of identification with minority culture and ignorance of institutional racism.
Cognitive stage	The individual chooses whether to blend into the dominant culture or seek to identify with the minority culture.
Consequence stage	Shame regarding their cultural heritage emerges because they have either identified with the dominant culture (which will not completely accept them), or they identify with a group they have long viewed as inferior.
Working-through stage	Components of the minority culture are integrated into one's identity.
Resolution stage	Self-esteem and ethnic pride accompany a growing sense of group/self identity.

their skin, and speak English without an accent. This stage continues until they acknowledge the impossibility of denying their culture—a realization that initiates the fourth stage.

During the fourth stage (working through), the individual realizes that he or she can no longer pretend to identify with an alien ethnic identity. The individual is propelled to reclaim the disowned identity fragments from his or her past life (Sue & Sue, 1999). Although this is a positive process, it can take a toll on the life the individual has attempted to create.

When Marcos entered the working-through stage, he had a lovely European American wife with blond hair and blue eyes. Together they had raised two young children who also looked very European and bore European names. In attempting to assimilate, Marcos has taken a job at his father-in-law's business. Over their six years of marriage, he had been quite successful and was being groomed to run the company when his father-in-law retired. Still, something nagged at him. He did not belong in "their" world, and a growing bitterness arose within him. Sure, he had a wonderful family, great job, and strong prospects for the future, but it came at too high a price. He saw himself as a cardboard figure—a lifeless caricature reflecting what "they" wanted.

He decided to start attending church services at a local Mexican parish to "find himself." His wife said she "understood" and encouraged him to go, though she would not attend herself. After a few months, Marcos "fell in love" with a young Latina. He said, "She makes me feel like a person again—the person I was meant to be." After a few short months, Marcos and his wife filed for divorce and Marcos left his job. He later said he was "happier this way" and finally "felt fulfilled."

Although Marcos left the world that he associated with non-Latino culture, this is simply one man's story—a single interpretation of how an individual can reach fulfillment after completing the fifth stage (resolution). Marcos gained a greater acceptance of his ethnicity and integrated his views into a uni-fied identity. Someone else might have successfully achieved the same level of integration without making any changes in his or her occupation or relation-ships. The central task simply rests with the process of unifying the concept of the self with one's larger ethnic culture. Regardless of the means by which it is achieved, this resolution of self and group identity often leads to enhanced self-esteem and ethnic pride.

Psychological Issues

The close-knit quality of Latino families, while providing many benefits, can also create mental health problems for Latinos. Wasserstein and La Greca (1998) examined the effects of parental conflict on children's stress. After Hurricane Andrew swept through the southeast, they interviewed 89 elemen-tary school students to investigate the factors that contributed to post-trau-matic stress disorder. As Latino families experienced more parental conflict, the children's PTSD symptoms also increased. This pattern was not present for European Americans.

Even when parental bonds are strong, other family-related complications may arise. Acculturated Latino children are expected to adopt an autonomous and independent lifestyle, but this requires children to define themselves as distinctly separate from their parents. Such conceptions of selfhood may dis-rupt the natural flow of the family. I once worked with a family who came to therapy because the parents were unable to make their son finish his chores. When discussing the family dynamics, the parents revealed that the 13-year-old son still shared a bed with them. He had his own room, but when he was four years old, he experienced difficulties sleeping alone and began to share his par-ents' bed. We attempted to discuss some of the problems this might create for the young man and explained how European American culture values autono-my above all other virtues. Throughout the intervention, we explored ways the child could continue to develop his sense of autonomy without attenuating the family bond or cultural lineage.

Beyond daily functioning issues, there are a number of psychological symptoms associated with Latino culture that may appear bizarre to non-Latinos. For example, after the death of a loved one, some Latinos, especially Puerto Ricans, may be "visited" by ghosts for years to come. They may inter-pret these hallucinations as a sign that their loved one is not ready to leave. They may also seek to understand why God has allowed their loved one to die. This blending of spiritualism, Catholicism, and folklore may make it difficult for therapists to know how to assist in the grieving process. When the halluci-nation does not pose a threat to a client's psychological functioning, the metaphor may become a useful component in therapy. The therapist could argue that the ghost would continue to come until the client is ready to let go.

This places responsibility for the apparition on the client, who can use the hallucination as an indication of his or her willingness to let go of the person who has died.

It may take some time for some Latinos to view the ghost as something they are able to control, rather than something external that is haunting them. Latinos often do not hold individuals responsible for their problems. Instead, they believe in fatalism and expect that an emerging problem has a specific purpose. This attitude does not mean, however, that the problem's solution is also viewed as external. Latinos believe they can master the challenges of life by controlling their moods and emotions, particularly anger, anxiety, and depression (Falicov, 1998).

Although they may recognize the need to endure a problem or face their emotions with stoic pride, Latino clients are unlikely to describe the emotion in purely affective terms. Instead, they may internalize the emotion until it is revealed through physical symptoms. Many Latinos, especially women and older individuals, are willing to accept physical symptoms as predictable extensions to emotionally powerful events. For example, at a Latino funeral, especially if it involves the death of a child, attendants may feel physical symptoms, such as gasping for breath, heart palpitations, chest pains, or other such maladies. These are viewed as a natural expression of grief rather than as somatizations, as European Americans might be prone to view them. These physical manifestations are accepted because Latinos do not differentiate between mind and body, as most European Americans do. The heart, mind, body, and soul are all expected to react to one's environment.

Within-Group Differences

The preservation of culture is important to most Latino subgroups, but each ethnic group expresses its history and culture differently. For example, the three largest Latin American groups are Mexicans, Puerto Ricans, and Cubans. Mexican Americans, comprising nearly 64 percent of the Latinos in America, are quite likely to temporarily immigrate to America (Falicov, 1998). Many small Mexican towns virtually lack men between the ages of 15 and 45. They have left for America to earn the funds necessary to support their families, but many return frequently to their "home."

Many European Americans have difficulty understanding why Mexican Americans would remain committed to their homeland. After all, they "chose" to come to America. While they did make the choice, it was also thrust upon them. Many young men see emigration as the only way to escape harrowing life conditions, even though they would prefer to remain near their families. Economic and political hardships often make this preference untenable, so they start to dream about what America might hold for them. They may picture fancy cars, mansions, and other signs of wealth, but the reality is usually less idyllic.

When they arrive on U.S. soil, their initial encounter with Americans is often dis-enchanting. Coyotes (individuals who charge a fee to assist illegal immigrants across the border) often abandon, rob, or abuse their customers. While still dreaming about safety, money, or a home, young immigrants may find them-selves completely alone, penniless, and stranded. They become part of a grow-ing impoverished generation struggling to survive in middle-class America.

Puerto Rican families face an entirely different set of challenges. A fiercely proud people, Puerto Ricans are American citizens. As residents of a common-wealth of America, they are subject to military duty, may benefit from limited social programs and aid, but are unable to vote, collect welfare, or pay taxes. They are stuck between two nations, with two flags, two languages, and two national identities. This dual identity forces them to create a tenuous balance between their two cultures. They want to enjoy the economic benefits that flow from America without losing their Puerto Rican identity. Like their Mexican counterparts, however, they often find the dominant culture in the mainland cold and hostile. Although Puerto Ricans can legally stay in the mainland, they often travel back and forth. They stay long enough to earn a small income before returning home to nourish their cultural roots.

It may seem surprising, but Puerto Ricans suffer higher unemployment than Mexicans (Falicov, 1998). They are generally considered the poorest of all Latino groups. Still, they are considered "transmigrants" because of their abil-ity to sustain family, economic, and social relationships that span geographic and cultural borders (Falicov, 1998).

Puerto Ricans also go to great efforts to pass along values that differ in sig-nificant ways from those of their Anglo counterparts. When ranking a list of values mothers would like to pass on to their children, Puerto Ricans put hon-esty, respect, and responsibility at the top of the list, followed by loyalty to fam-ily, affection, and sharing. Assertiveness, independence, and creativity, which were highly ranked by Anglo parents, were viewed as less important by Puerto Ricans (Gonzalez-Ramos, Zayas, & Cohen, 1998).

While Puerto Ricans are often the poorest Latino "migrants," Cubans tend to be the wealthiest. In the late 1950s, when Fidel Castro took control of Cuba, many of the country's wealthier citizens fled to America. Unlike the Mexicans and Puerto Ricans, many of the Cubans came equipped with financial, politi-cal, and educational resources. These factors contributed to a more favorable reception, and Cuban immigrants were able to establish successful business centers in Miami, New Jersey, and New York (Falicov, 1998).

Although Cubans are generally accepted within American society, many resist Americanization. They may long for a pre-revolutionary Cuba and seek to restore their traditional Spanish values and lifestyles. This anti-American sentiment was clearly displayed in May of 1999 when the Baltimore Orioles hosted the Cuban All-Star baseball team. Anti-Castro protestors made frequent demonstrations, and even interrupted the game by running onto the field. The second base umpire, a Cuban currently residing in America, took offense at the demonstration and body-slammed and punched one activist. He considered it "the right thing to do," because, he explained, "Above all, I am Cuban." Although most Cubans would not consider violence the "right thing to do" when their teammates are derided, it is interesting that the umpire's rationale for his actions stemmed directly from his cultural identity. He did not defend his actions as the "right thing for an umpire to do" or even the "right thing for a man to do." As a Cuban American, he clung to his Cuban identity when he was forced to choose an alliance.

Within each Latino group, acculturation is viewed as a mixed blessing. Parents want their children to succeed in America, and they realize that success will require proficiency in the English language and familiarity with European American social mores. However, they also want to pass down the legacy of their Latin history. The tightrope between these two worlds is often very difficult to walk.

Counseling Issues

Latinos, and especially Latino youths, are less likely to seek counseling than their non-Latino counterparts (Wells et al., 1987). Although this reluctance may be related to lower socioeconomic status and a desire to shield family problems from the outside world (Falicov, 1998), it may also indicate a distrust of non-Latino counselors.

The Latin American history of subjugation and conquest may be reflected in the therapeutic relationship. For example, counselors may mistakenly perceive their Latino clients as passive or overly compliant. However, this appearance could be the result of feeling threatened or dominated by the therapist. A simple way to put Latino clients at ease is to offer them food or drink. In many Latino circles, offering food is a gesture of hospitality and friendship. Another tactic is to introduce various conquest myths into the therapeutic conversation (Falicov, 1998). Rather than view change as a threat to the family's way of life, it can be reframed as an opportunity for transformation or success.

A common therapeutic error involves what Comas-Díaz and Jacobsen (1991) have termed the "clinical anthropologist syndrome." Therapists afflicted by this disorder turn off their clinical training and explore their clientele as if they were unlike any of their other clients. They may relabel dysfunctional family issues as acceptable cultural variations. The therapist inadvertently colludes with the family and perpetuates the disorder. It becomes part of the cultural mask the family is permitted to wear. Falicov (1998) notes that shyness, self-sacrifice, over-dependence, domestic violence, child abuse, alcoholism, or harmful religiosity may be accepted or overlooked in the interest of maintaining cultural homeostasis.

Maria came into therapy because she "needed someone to talk to." As the session progressed, she confessed that the problems in her family were her fault. For many therapists, this admission might seem to make little sense, because the family problems began four months earlier when her husband had an affair with his high-school sweetheart. The affair surfaced, much to the husband's disgust, because his girlfriend was pregnant and wanted to keep the baby. In desperation, the husband told Maria what had happened but added that he wanted to save their marriage. He told Maria he did not "love" his girlfriend and realized that his family must come first.

From Maria's point of view, his act of indiscretion was not enough to destroy their sacred marital vows, but she acted upon her anger by making him move out of the house. During therapy, she pummeled herself with statements of shame. "How could I destroy our family like that?" She moaned. "How could I keep my children from their father?" Unable to forgive herself, she added cultural statements such as, "We were married in the eyes of God, and I broke our covenant." It was her duty, she believed, to stay with her husband, no matter what mistakes he made.

Individual therapy sessions with the husband added another dimension to the problem. He confessed that he intended to continue seeing his lover because he now had familial responsibilities to her as well. He realized that he had made a mistake, but he could not punish his unborn child by depriving "him" [sic] of a father. He intended to have his girlfriend move to Mexico, where he could see her and the baby during frequent business trips. His wife never accompanied him on these trips, so he could maintain the dual family. "This is what Latinos do," he said. He also wanted to continue coming to therapy with his wife, provided that the topic of his girlfriend never arose.

There are several ways to handle a situation like the one described above. Most of them, however, are harmful. The worst option would be to collude with the husband and keep the affair secret. In this case, the situation resolved itself when Maria called the girlfriend and learned about her husband's plan to continue seeing both women. This turn of events forced the husband to stop seeing his girlfriend, and both partners continued to attend marital therapy.

The balance between family stability and individuality is a tenuous one for many Latino families. Therapists who ignore family stability to empower the client's sense of individuality may lose their client's respect. This dilemma requires therapists to proceed slowly. The most important element is to build trust *(confianza)*, which is accomplished by communicating kindness, fairness, respect, and personal interest (Falicov, 1998). This trust is more quickly established when therapists are bicultural, bilingual, or Latino, but therapists from different ethnic or cultural backgrounds can dismantle many multicultural problems by stating their philosophy of therapy and mutually agreeing on a therapeutic course. Sharing ideological positions helps create a collaborative dialogue that builds a working alliance and enhances the therapeutic encounter (Falicov, 1998). Therapists need to ask clients if they have any questions about the therapeutic process, and answer all questions honestly and thoroughly.

In all of these recommendations, family involvement plays a significant role. However, prior experience with family therapy does not guarantee success with Latino families. Bernal and Flores-Ortiz (1982) found that the successful engagement of Latino families requires both skills in family therapy *and* sensitivity to cultural issues. The parents must feel that the therapist understands them and will guide their children accordingly. Therapists need to be cognizant of cultural norms in ways such as acknowledging the father's leadership and allowing the father to dictate the involvement of the other family members. If a successful bond is created, the family can assist the therapeutic process in highly significant ways.

Beyond the use of family, the effective therapist must also display a working knowledge of the client's culture. This may be demonstrated in a number of ways. Yeh, Eastman, and Cheung (1994) found that ethnic differences ceased to predict early dropout rates by Mexican clients when language match was added to the model. Counselors who could communicate with their clients at the most basic of levels were more likely to effectively intervene with clients' struggles. However, language is not the only tool counselors can use to make an effective cultural intervention.

Constantino and Rivera (1994) investigated whether a form of narrative therapy could help reduce children's anxiety and behavior problems. They used five mothers who read Latino folktales (*cuentos*) to their children for an hour. After the readings, therapists ran a group in which they asked the children how the stories made them feel and what the morals of the stories were. In some cases, the mother-child dyad was also asked to create a dramatization of the story to illustrate how a given conflict was resolved. After 20 sessions, the researchers assessed the children's growth across a number of areas. When compared to a control group who received traditional play therapy sessions conducted by a therapist and schoolteacher, the family intervention group had fewer anxiety symptoms, increased IQ scores, and fewer behavioral problems.

A common Latino narrative is the story of the Dying Lady. The tale begins with a woman who decides that it is too much work to cook. "It's such a hassle," the old woman states, "It would be easier not to eat." Days turn to weeks, and weeks drag on until the woman finds herself unable to move or care for herself. People dear to the woman beg her to feed herself, but she refuses. "I'm much too tired to cook now," she laments. "I would need more strength to cook and clean." As her health continues to falter, her family and community grow concerned. "Is there nothing we do to help her?" asked one woman. All the people agree that if she will not nurture herself, nothing they can do will change her fate. With much sadness, the assembly decides that the only action left before them is to carry her to her grave. "She will probably be dead when we reach the tomb," one man states. "At least, if we carry her now, we can share in her final moments on earth."

As they carry the woman up the hill that will soon become her final resting place, a couple approaches bearing all types of food. "Here," the woman states, "You may have these beans and rice—eat them and you may live." Trembling, the woman reaches out to touch the food. The couple waits anxiously as she struggles to feel the beans. "They aren't cooked," the woman sighs. "I don't want them unless they have been cooked." With this announcement, the assembly continues up the hill. The woman has sealed her fate by being too lazy to care for herself and too proud to accept the gifts brought to her.

Using stories such as The Dying Lady in therapy can help clients merge their culture with their identity. In this particular story, the woman refused help from the people closest to her; she allowed her misery to overpower; and she demanded perfection from those who wanted to help. Therapists can help clients realize that they may be acting like "dying people" in their households. They might be allowing themselves to remain "depressed," by refusing the help of those dearest to them. Ultimately, to overcome depression, they will need to reach out to the hands serving them, engage in the exercises, and make allowances when the help provided appears inadequate. With this interpretation, the story becomes a catalyst to psychological issues.

Therapists should realize, however, that they may need to expand their repertoire if they wish to have the same impact an ethnically matched therapist would have. Learning Spanish, or at least becoming familiar with key folk stories, is highly recommended for therapists who work with Latino clients on a regular basis. A good place to start would be to read the following texts:

- de Cortes, O. G., & Zwick, L. Y. (1992). "Hispanic Materials and Programs: Bibliography." In C. D. Hayden (Ed.), *Venture into Cultures*: *A Resource Book of Multicultural Materials and Programs* (pp. 82-99). Chicago: American Library Association.
- Duran, D. F. (1979). *Latino Materials*: *A Multimedia Guide for Children and Young Adults*. New York: Neal Schuman, Publishers.
- Schon, I. (1978). *A Bicultural Heritage*: *Themes for the Exploration of Mexican and Mexican-American Culture in Books for Children and Adolescents*. Metuchen, NJ: The Scarecrow Press, Inc.

In addition to the issues discussed previously, there are other topics that may arise during counseling sessions. When you are reading the following example, consider how you might react to the client's view that the difficulties in his marriage are caused by a cultural misunderstanding.

Alfonso's Story

Let me tell you a little bit about a counseling session Evelyn (my European American wife) and I attended. I had some serious issues with the way Evelyn was taking care of the house. Also, her attitude toward me was (as I perceived it) at times a bit too combative and lacked respect. Evelyn worked full time when we first were married. During our first year and a half of being married, I was very supportive: I did the laundry on the weekends, helped with cooking dinner throughout the week, etc. Evelyn was not happy working, and we decided that we would sacrifice the second income in order for her to stay home and raise our children (Rebecca was over a year old at this time, and Anthony wasn't even in the plans yet). Evelyn promised me that she would take over the care of the home and cook dinner, etc., if I agreed to make the financial sacrifice. I did so knowing that it was best for our child if Evelyn was home raising her.

Well, Evelyn's idea of house cleanliness and mine were not the same. It is not as great a priority for her as it was/is for me. I grew up in a compulsively clean home and expected the same after marriage. Latin people, especially Cubans, are neat freaks. We like things really clean and very well organized. Clutter drives us nuts! For example, when I travel to an indigenous region in Mexico for a mission trip each year, it is not uncommon to see the ladies of the house (or hut) sweeping the area in front of the entry to the house. That's normal, except their entries are nothing but dirt! Nevertheless, it is a very well-swept dirt entry.

This contrast in our ideas of cleanliness led to many arguments. There were other issues we were dealing with as newlyweds and the communication methods we used were poor. Every discussion quickly turned into a fight. The root of it all that caused us to fight was two things. First, being a Latin male, I expected (whether right or wrong) total obedience from my wife and a high level of respect for me as the head of the household. Both these things are traditional Latin expectations in a marriage. I perceived the messy house as a violation of both these expectations. Second, Evelyn grew up in a culture where the emphasis on compulsive neatness was not as strong. Priorities are better balanced. Whenever I would confront her with her "obvious lack of attention to the house," and thus my needs, Evelyn felt a personal attack and would immediately counterattack. She later confessed to feeling as though she could never be as good as my mom and that I was expecting too much out of her. Another Latin dynamic—the men are mama's boys . . . big time.

Okay, so we finally decide that we are lousy at communicating and decide to go to counseling to learn how to better communicate. I express my concerns and Evelyn expresses hers. The counselor then asks me a series of questions:

1. How many days a week does the house issue become an argument?

2. How long do you argue for?

3. Is it always about the same thing?

He then pulls out a calculator and does some math. His answer to our issues was that over a year's time, I would end up arguing over 500 hours about something that could easily be avoided if I would just pick up a vacuum cleaner or pick up whatever it was that was bothering me. Set aside the fact that I believe this was poor counseling, the guy never took into account my cultural background, the Latin's retentive cleaning habits, my issues about respect and the male role in a Latin home. Had he understood these things, he could have much better helped Evelyn understand my core issues. Also, he could have much better helped me understand how my "Latin-based" expectations are not the same as Evelyn's "Anglo-based" expectations. It took us years to understand these things and figure it out on our own. Had the counselor picked up on this rather obvious difference in the way Evelyn and I both approached marriage, he could have saved us years of arguing.

Questions to Consider

1. Labels such as Hispanic, Chicano, and Mexican American reflect different emphases within Latino culture. How would you reconcile a family whose members each referred to themselves with different terms?

2. Darker-skinned Latinos may face increased discrimination. How would you assist such an individual through counseling?

3. How do you feel about the term "colored minority" in reference to African Americans and Latinos? Should such terminology be used? What might be better?

4. How might close family ties affect the counseling process? Do you believe enmeshment issues could make individual therapy difficult?

5. How might the double standard for marital unfaithfulness, found in some cultures, affect your intervention in marital therapy?

6. Poverty appears to be most severe among third-generation Mexican Americans. Why do you think this occurs?

7. How might you intervene with a traditional Latino family in which the husband's salary was insufficient to meet the family's needs? How would you handle his shame? How would you explore the wife's potential anger or frustration?

8. What might you do to change a young Latina's view that doing well in school is "Anglo" or "nerdy"?

9. Trust is a critical factor when therapists from other cultural groups work with Latinos. How might you strive to gain your client's trust?

10. Some Latinos may favor cultural explanations for psychological disturbances. Would you use their terminology or try to help your clients to better understand the descriptive categories in the DSM?

11. Would you diagnose schizophrenia in a Latina who repeatedly saw her dead mother appearing to her? Why or why not?

12. Would you treat a Latino family wrestling with adultery differently from a family of another culture?

4

Asian Americans

INSIGHT EXERCISE Naoki (nah-oh-kee) is an 18-year-old male who was raised in Southern California and had little understanding of his Japanese roots. During his first year of college, he began to study Buddhism, and he found himself mesmerized by the Four Noble Truths:

- *Dukkha* (the existence of impermanence): The first noble truth is the full understanding of suffering, which includes understanding the nonpermanence of pleasure. No object, job, relationship, material possession, or social position will last forever. To live, we must endure hardships, and ultimately, we will die.

- *Samudaya* (the origin of suffering is attachment): Pleasure, prosperity, success, and fame are illusory and cause suffering. The more attached we are to possessions or status, the greater our suffering will be.

- *Nirodha* (the cessation of suffering): The supreme truth and final liberation is nirvana, which is achieved as the cause of suffering is eliminated. The mind experiences complete freedom and liberation. Suffering ceases when attachment to desire ceases.

- *Magga* (the middle way or the path to the end of suffering): The end of suffering can be attained by journeying on the Noble Eightfold Path (see the psychology section for more information).

After a few days of meditation and experimentation, he became convinced that he had misunderstood the purpose of life. He had chosen to attend college because he wanted people to respect him and he hoped to become rich. Now, after meditating on the Four Noble Truths, he realized that it would be better for him to donate all of his time to helping the poor. How would you help him sort out this change in belief?

Asian worldviews differ dramatically from Western views. Asians tend to emphasize circularity over linear progression, self-sacrifice over independence, and corporate honor over individual achievement. These striking differences can confound and bewilder Western thinkers, who may find their intervention strategies incompatible with their client's ideology.

83

Classifying the largest group of human beings into the single category "Asian" seems highly inappropriate, but the term is significantly better than "Oriental," which is considered offensive by many. A typical response to being called Oriental is "I am not a rug." Likewise, the term Asian is often used to classify Pacific Islanders (such as Hawaiians, Samoans, Polynesians, etc.), even though such groups are distinctly different from mainland Asian cultures.

The population of Asian Americans comprises more than 20 separate nationalities, according to the 1980 census data (Lai, 1998). With more than 25 percent of the world's population living in China, Japan, India, Vietnam, Korea, Taiwan, Hong Kong, Malaysia, and other countries, there are thousands of cultural groups, each with distinct characteristics and traditions. Despite their diversity, however, Asians experienced similar prejudice as they immigrated to this country. In some ways, as Sue and Sue (1990) note, racial prejudice against Asian Americans is waning, but new struggles accompany these changes in perceived status.

History of Oppression

When many people today think of Asian Americans, they envision the model minorities who have worked hard to challenge European Americans for economic supremacy. Most people are unaware that Asian Americans have suffered some of the most inhumane treatment of any minority group. Many of these struggles are painstakingly depicted in *Thousand Pieces of Gold*, a novel that is based on the true story of a Chinese woman, Lalu, whose father sold her to bandits who forced her to work in a brothel. Eventually she was taken to America and sold to a bar owner (McCunn, 1981). The author describes the difficulties of a young woman who found herself caught between two cultures. As a poor woman, she worked with the farmhands in order to make ends meet, and the work caused her bound feet to stretch and return to their pre-bound shape. This condition made working as a prostitute difficult. One man said he couldn't sleep with her because the size of her feet made him feel he was making love to a man. Eventually, Lalu married and started her own business. She soon realized that being a Chinese woman in America during the early years of the twentieth century meant that she could never be safe. New laborers would threaten her economic stability, and European Americans would constantly threaten her safety.

Such stories are not uncommon. Sue and Sue (1999) discuss how Chinese Americans were easily scapegoated because of their "strange" customs. They spoke a different language, ate foods that were considered unhealthy, wore their hair in pigtails, and dressed differently. At first, these differences in appearance and culture were tolerated because the expanding West Coast needed Chinese laborers to help with railroad construction and gold mining. However, as more Chinese immigrants moved to the West Coast, European Americans saw their manual labor jobs going to "cheap" Chinese labor.

Tensions between Asian and European settlers continued to mount. In 1870 California passed a law against the importation of Chinese, Japanese, and "Mongolian" women for the purpose of prostitution. In 1871, rival Chinese gangs in Los Angeles shot a European American who was caught in the cross-fire of their skirmish. Shortly after the shooting, hundreds of whites stormed the street called Calle de los Negros ("Nigger Alley"), which had become the city's Chinatown. They broke windows, knocked down doors, and attacked Chinese residents. They killed one man by dragging him over the stones of the street by a rope around his neck. Three were hanged from a wagon on Los Angeles Street, although they were more dead than alive from being beaten and kicked. Four were likewise hanged from the western gateway of Tomlinson's corral on New High Street. Two of the victims were mere boys. The total number of Chinese killed in the attack is uncertain, but the death toll was probably around twenty (Hart, 1978).

Another example of California's systematic intolerance was the ethnic cleansing of Chinese immigrants in the late nineteenth century. Regarded as a "yellow peril," they were physically attacked, some lynched, all humiliated, and driven out of whole regions of the state in the 1880s. The Chinese population in California went from more than 75,000 in 1880 to about 45,000 in 1900, from over 9 percent of the population in 1860 to about 3 percent 40 years later.

California was not the only state spawning anti-Chinese violence. In Rock Springs, Wyoming, a staged attack occurred in 1885 when 600 Chinese employees refused to join a labor union. The European American workers burned down 79 huts belonging to the Chinese. As the Chinese employees fled, 28 were killed and 15 were wounded.

When Japanese, Korean, and Filipino workers entered the United States in successive waves, they also met with similar threats (Lai, 1998). By 1882, organized trade unions secured the Chinese Exclusion Act, which prohibited immigration from China. Chinese women, waiting for their husbands to earn enough to bring them to America, found themselves stranded in China. The legislation followed a slew of violent eruptions against Asians. The wave of violence apparently stemmed from the perception that Asians were stealing so-called "American" jobs. Chinese laborers were forced from their homes in Tacoma and Seattle, Washington because they were considered "undesirable" neighbors. Mass murder, physical attacks, and the destruction of homes and property were common occurrences during this era.

Legislation throughout the 1800s allowed for deportation of Chinese Americans (e.g., the 1891 Immigration Act, 1892 Geary Act, and so on). The Immigration Act of 1965 finally removed national origin as the basis of American immigration policies, but after the passage of this act, Asian Americans still were not given the same rights as other ethnic groups (Chan, 1991). Even after gaining citizenship, Asian Americans faced threats from multiple sources. The most discouraging and painful threat stemmed from an unlikely source: the American government itself.

During the Second World War, America established its own prison camps. President Franklin D. Roosevelt signed Executive Order 9066 on February 19, 1942, which allowed military authorities to detain anyone from anywhere without trial or hearings. Although the order did not identify a specific group of people, it soon became clear that the intention of the command was to restrict the freedom of Japanese Americans. One month after EO 9066, Executive Order 9102 was signed. This order established the War Relocation Authority (WRA) with Milton Eisenhower as director, and it set in motion a series of events that would be unimaginable today.

From 1942 to the beginning of 1946, Japanese Americans were swiftly and injudiciously collected into relocation centers as "war criminals." Many were housed in these camps solely because of their national origin. Others had been transferred from prisons, had refused to fight against Japan in World War II, or were considered threatening.

The internment camps were located at Amache (Granada), Colorado (peak population 7,318), Gila River, Arizona (peak population 13,348), Heart Mountain, Wyoming (peak population 10,767), Jerome, Arkansas (peak population 8,497), Manzanar, California (peak population 10,046), Minidoka, Idaho (peak population 9,397), Poston (aka Colorado River), Arizona (peak population 17,814), Rohwer, Arkansas (peak population 8,475), Topaz (aka Central Utah), Utah (peak population 8,130), and Tule Lake, California (peak population 18,789) (Iritani & Iritani, 1995).

In all, 120,313 people were imprisoned. More than 17,000 people were removed directly from their homes. Almost 6,000 children were born in the camps and forced to remain there, and more than 200 people entered the camps voluntarily, generally because they wanted to be with their spouses. Nearly 2,000 died during imprisonment (Iritani & Iritani, 1995).

One of the only means of escape from the camps was to take up arms against the Japanese. More than two 2,000 Japanese American men joined the armed forces to prove their loyalty to the United States. Some served in the famed 442nd Regimental Combat Team, which was made up entirely of Japanese Americans. On October 27 through 30, 1944, the 442nd Regimental Combat Team rescued an American battalion that had been cut off and surrounded by the enemy. Eight hundred casualties were suffered by the 442nd to rescue 211 men. After this rescue, the 442nd was ordered to continue advancing in the forest; they pushed ahead without relief or rest until November 9. In two years of fighting, they became the most decorated unit in U.S. military history.

Why do you think only Asian men and women were confined to American prison camps? They were being held, primarily, because of their Japanese ancestry. It may also be helpful to know that Representative John Dingell of Michigan suggested to President Roosevelt that the United States incarcerate 10,000 Hawaiian Japanese Americans as hostages to ensure "good behavior" on the part of Japan. The letter was dated August 18, 1941, four months before the attack on

Pearl Harbor. Why should this fear be limited to Japanese Americans? Why not detain German Americans as well? Racial prejudice is the obvious answer. Japanese Americans were singled out because they looked "different." The only charges ever brought against the inmates of American prison camps involved draft evasion. On August 10, 1988, H.R. 442 was signed into law by President Ronald Reagan. It provided individual payments of $20,000 to each surviving internee and established a $1.25 billion education fund for Japanese Americans.

Although the past few decades have led to positive changes in the way other American cultures view Asian Americans, the changes have created new problems as well. Today, the most typical form of oppression against Asians stems from the perception that they represent a "model minority." Asian Americans are frequently portrayed as an American success story: they came to America with nothing and pulled themselves up by their bootstraps. Successful in education and business, they are held up as example to admire and copy. It is a wonderful image, but one that belies the underlying problems within Asian communities. Their unemployment, underemployment, and struggles to survive amidst the prejudices of European American society are often overlooked or ignored (Lai, 1998). We will return to these topics later in this chapter. First, we will examine Asian family structure, which contributes to economic and educational achievement.

Family

The family structure holds special significance in Asian cultures. In fact, Marshall Jung (1998) has stated that for many Asian groups, family therapy should be considered a primary intervention. He advises therapists to assist their Asian clients through Chinese American Family Therapy (CAFT), which is an eclectic, multi-dimensional, comprehensive family therapy model. In this model, "family integration" (achieving a harmonious relationship with one's family by learning to live ethically with family members) is the primary goal of therapy. The model assumes that when Chinese individuals learn and accept their cultural values (including Confucian humanitarianism), they will live ethically and in peace with one another.

According to Jung (1998) family integration requires the following components:

- Family centeredness
- Filial loyalty
- Conformity to role expectations
- Ethnocentrism, which includes respecting cultural traditions and rituals
- Being situation-centered
- Conducting oneself in a prudent and reserved manner

These standards differ greatly from the emphasis on autonomy (i.e., ability to choose one's course of action) and individualism in European American cultures (Kitchener, 1984). This closeness is in evidence from the beginning of life. Most Japanese children sleep in the same bed with their mother at least three times per week, while European American children are expected to sleep independently. Rather than create sleep problems, the Japanese practice of co-sleeping appears to decrease regular bedtime struggles and night waking. However, when European American children sleep with their parents, tensions between parents and children often lead to bedtime struggles, night waking, and overall stressful sleep problems. These findings led Latz, Wolf, and Lozoff (1999) to conclude that differing cultural expectations seem to influence the relationship between sleep practices and sleep problems, and co-sleeping *per se* is not associated with increased sleep problems in early childhood.

The close bond between Asian family members may also influence therapeutic goals. Often, counseling consists of encouraging the client to explore what he or she wants. The ultimate goal of such pursuits is the development of a unique individual who is free from the confines of tradition and family expectations. Such a position contradicts the other-focused philosophy of Asian cultures. In most Asian cultures, the decisions an individual makes, even during adulthood, are strongly influenced by parental wishes. Individuals who seek to fulfill their own desires or act in unbecoming ways can shame their families, which is likely to create conflicts for all involved.

The strong connection to family does not imply that family members exchange ideas intimately. Instead, it addresses a more complex form of communal identity. For example, after analyzing videotapes from 59 families, Martini (1996) concluded that European American families are more likely to use their mealtime for members to describe their experiences, wishes, plans, and perceptions. Parents cued children to focus on distinctive aspects of their realities, to talk about "what's new" or unfamiliar to them. In Japanese American households, half of the families watched television while eating. Some others played games, listened to music, talked on the phone, or played with their pets. The emphasis was on being together without necessarily discussing the events of the day. The focus was on collective action, rather than the accomplishments of individuals. Japanese American families function as a unit, emphasizing a smooth group process.

The responsibility for creating harmony and belonging often falls upon women. Compliance with and acceptance of their position is a highly valued quality for women. Ho (1990) studied differences between Chinese, Vietnamese, Laotian, and Khmer women and found that in all groups, girls were punished more severely than boys and had greater demands placed on their behavior. When these girls became mothers, they felt compelled to train their daughters to become obedient and subservient wives. In some cultures this may lead to a lower status for women (Leeder, 1994) but most Asians affirm the equality of the sexes (Subrahmanyan, 1999). Still, a traditional Asian woman is expected to defer to her father, then her husband, and finally her son (after her husband dies).

The emphasis on group survival and constant social harmony puts low-status individuals at great risk. Families are typically loving and caring, but when violence erupts within the family setting it may not be reported to outside authorities. These impermeable family boundaries place women and the elderly at significant risk for continued violence. Ho (1990) commented on the increased potential of domestic violence in Asian homes, given the hierarchical power structure and the consequences women face when leaving their husbands, such as losing custody of their children. Ho observed that when women married, they were dominated by their husbands, with Vietnamese husbands describing their relationship in terms of ownership. Chinese women were the least accepting of the use of violence against them. Nevertheless, Ho estimated that 20 to 30 percent of Chinese women were hit by their spouses, and women in many Asian cultures may fear rejection from their parents or family if they were to leave their husbands.

In societies whose conditions include group and male primacy and in which wrongdoings are typically kept private, the victims of elder mistreatment, especially female victims, may never be identified (Moon, 1999; Tomita, 1999). Families feel responsible for the care of aging relatives, but they are sometimes ill-equipped to handle the frustration that can stem from attending to the needs of a dependent family member. Families are also less likely to take on the perceived burden of parental care if they are already facing financial strain (Ishii-Kuntz, 1997). Even in these cases, however, older Asian Americans usually live close to at least one of their sons. They will also attempt to support each other, talk on the phone, and share financial resources (Kauh, 1997).

Family structure in India differs from that of other Asian countries. Culturally, Hindu values prevail throughout India. Within this context, the family connotes more than a dyad of parents and their children. An Indian family often comprises several households and may span geographical regions. These diverse members share educational, financial, and interpersonal decisions throughout each member's life (Prathikanti, 1997). Children may move between households to complete their schooling. A young woman may move in with her aunt and uncle in order to find a suitable husband. An elderly woman may live with a great-niece to be closer to medical care. In all of these cases, flexibility and utility govern the options chosen.

Based on the research discussed above, it appears that the cohesion of Asian American families has not been weakened by acculturation. However, acculturation may wreak havoc in other ways. Nguyen, Messe, and Stollak (1999) provided some insights into the complexity of Asian acculturation when they examined a group of Vietnamese youths (aged 10 to 23 years) living in a primarily European American community. As they expected, the youths who were involved with European American culture reported less personal distress, higher self-esteem, and better grades. After all, they were living in a European

American community, and therefore involvement within this group would lead to a sense of belonging and intimacy. Similarly, involvement in the Vietnamese culture predicted positive family relationships. The surprising element of this study was that the youths who were strongly involved solely with the Vietnamese culture were more likely to feel anxiety and distress. They did not know where they belonged and had difficulty reconciling the often conflicting demands of both groups.

Family dynamics play a role in how acculturated an individual may become. Manaster, Rhodes, Marcus, and Chan (1998) explored the relationship between birth order and acculturation among 1,042 Nisei (second-generation Japanese Americans) and 802 Sansei (third-generation Japanese Americans). When grown, first-born Nisei were more likely than their siblings to live in Japanese American neighborhoods, use the Japanese language, have stronger Japanese family values, and maintain a traditional Japanese religion (Buddhist or Shinto). The findings held true for the first-born Sansei, but to a lesser degree. First-born Sansei possessed more knowledge about Japanese values and culture, and they were more likely to champion traditional perspectives. The findings regarding birth order suggest that older children are expected to uphold the family culture and pass it along to succeeding generations.

Age is so highly regarded in some cultures that older siblings are given special titles to designate their position. For example, in the Filipino culture, the oldest brother and oldest sister get special honorifics from the other siblings. For example, if the eldest siblings were named Beth and Edwin, they would be referred to as "Ate Beth" and "Cuya Edwin." The parents and grandparents also get special respect. For example, even the traditional greeting for one's parent is unique. When greeting one's father, the child is expected to take his father's hand and place it upon his own forehead. This is apparently a sign of respect as well as thanks.

The effects created by birth order seem to imply that Asian children raised in non-Asian homes may be at a distinct disadvantage. They may never learn about their cultural roots or how to create a corporate identity. Fortunately, emerging research suggests that Asian children raised by non-Asian parents do not inevitably face identity problems. Kim, Shin, and Carey (1999) examined the psychological differences between Korean American adoptees and biological children of their adoptive parents. At least from the parents' perspective, the adopted children did not have any more adjustment issues than their biological children had. Psychological tests also demonstrated that the adopted children did not have more behavioral problems, but transplanted children did feel more socially incompetent than their stepsiblings and also tended to internalize their problems more often. These difficulties, however, may simply stem from the prejudice and discrimination the dominant society casts upon those who look "different."

Parents of adopted, culturally diverse children should realize that their children will have specialized needs. A client once told me that her previous therapist stated, "Your Chinese daughter will grow up American—she won't know what it means to be Chinese." Such statements are blatantly wrong. Even if the child lacks an understanding of what it means to be Chinese, she still has a cultural history that deserves to be explored. To ignore it is to denigrate the individual's past and may lead the child to push away from her adoptive parents when she reaches adulthood.

Economics

Most traditional Chinese immigrants come to the United States with the intention of improving their economic status. This purpose differs from that of Asian "boat people" who are usually fleeing a hostile environment. Before 1990, such refugees emigrated primarily from South Vietnam, Cambodia, and Laos in connection with the Vietnam War. The number of refugees arriving in America has been declining (Buriel & De Ment, 1997). These differing motives have an effect on the direction each group takes after arriving on American shores. When immigrants from Southeast Asia find that it takes at least five years before they achieve economic self-sufficiency in the United States, depression and anger may set in (Law & Schneiderman, 1992). Immigrants may be surprised to find significant obstacles preventing them from obtaining even the most humble jobs. It simply takes time to learn the nuances of the language and the subtleties of the various American cultures.

What makes Asian Americans unique, however, is how they react to the oppression they face. Asian Americans tend to perceive themselves as being more prepared for college, better motivated, and more likely to achieve career success than European Americans (Wong, Lai, Nagasawa, & Lin, 1998). These positive cognitions develop from their family identity and the belief that hard work coupled with community and family support will yield success. Their religious beliefs, especially Hinduism and Buddhism, also help them to view wealth acquisition as a positive element in a person's life. This emphasis on wealth, however, is never primary. It is a consequence of seeking virtue and experiencing Karma. If people learn to emphasize mental, verbal, and physical virtues, Karma is created that will usually result in wealth. If wealth is emphasized, relationships and personal growth are attenuated and Karma may result in misfortune. In Buddhism, this understanding of Karma is explained in the Third Noble Truth. An emphasis on selfish gain (the experience of "me") causes suffering. When we learn to view personal Karma (i.e., an action or cause that is created or re-created by habitual impulse, volitions, natural energies) as caring for the world around us, the experience of personal being is replaced with the experience of "us." These cultural values lead to a long-term view of investment. Asian Americans emphasize family investment over consumption, and they view wealth, in part, as a means of supporting their families and communities (Jain & Joy, 1997).

Acculturation can have a serious impact on the economic views of Asian Americans. In the dominant American society, workers are told to "do what feels right" or "find the job that's best for you." Asian Americans with lower levels of acculturation tend to choose more conventional occupations (i.e., Realistic and Investigative[1] occupations), because their family effectively guides them toward choosing low-risk occupations that are likely to bring success. Occupations are selected on the basis of what the family considers wise, rather than what might best fit the individual's aptitudes or occupational preferences. As young people become acculturated, they experience stronger feelings of self-efficacy and are more willing to pursue their own occupational desires (Tang, Fouad, & Smith, 1999).

In addition to acculturation, perceptions of self-efficacy are also influenced by the family's income level. Miller, Sung, and Seligman (1999) explored whether Korean Americans' beliefs about responsibility and self-improvement were associated with educational levels, family income, and religious commitment. They found that the participants in their study were more likely to make their own vocational choices if they attended church regularly and came from wealthy families. Church provided a sense of inner strength and the belief that obstacles could be overcome with patience, endurance, and confidence. Similarly, the family's income level provides the parents with a better understanding of what comes about from nontraditional occupations. Children from poorer families may believe that the only way to succeed is to pursue traditional paths, but children from wealthier families are more likely to become acquainted with successful entrepreneurs and other nontraditional wage earners.

The global shift away from corporate occupations and toward self-employed entrepreneurs and wage laborers has also reconfigured gender relations within contemporary Asian American society. Female-intensive industries, such as domestic cleaners and childcare providers, have enhanced women's employability over that of some men. This shift in the economic structure of the Asian American community has challenged the patriarchal authority of Asian immigrant men, particularly among the working class (Estiritu, 1999).

Blumberg (1991) predicted these economic advances for women. Her argument was that Asian women, especially Chinese women, needed to feel that they could control their own income and economic resources if they were ever to create a more balanced division of labor within the household. She believed that women's control of economic resources had to be on an equal level to that of their husbands before women could reach a state of equality. Greater control

---

[1] John Holland's Vocational Types are divided into the following categories:
  (a) **Realistic**: use of athletic or mechanical skills in working with objects, machines, tools, plants, or animals;
  (b) **Investigative**: observation, learning, investigation, analyzing, or problem-solving.
  (c) **Artistic**: artistic, innovating, or intuitive abilities emphasizing imagination and creativity.
  (d) **Social**: enlightening, informing, helping, training, or curing others.
  (e) **Enterprising**: influencing, persuading, performing, leading, or managing for organizational goals or economic gain.
  (f) **Conventional**: data processing or clerical duties, with an emphasis on taking care of details or following instructions.

of economic resources comes at a cost for these women, however. They feel the need to bring honor to their household by handling domestic chores while also earning a salary. The difficulty of managing these divergent roles can cause significant tension and anxiety (True, 1990).

These struggles between work and family roles tend to be particularly difficult for Asian American women. Although the addition of a professional identity causes women from many ethnic backgrounds to redefine their identities, Asian women experience a different level of conflict. As Balagopal (1999) mentions, Asian American mothers face challenges that differ from those of European Americans. These women feel compelled to redefine their sense of self as well as their views of family and culture. While they are growing up, Asian American women are often conditioned to view women's employment outside the home as dishonorable. When they realize that their income contributes to the family's economic well-being, their sense of pride and honor increases, especially when their salary is necessary for the family's survival (Lim, 1999).

Despite the challenges discussed above, the average income of Asian Americans is 15 percent above that of European Americans (Boutte, 1999) and this economic advantage has been attributed to a variety of causes. Probably topping this list of reasons is the mutual support offered within Asian American communities. Even during the Great Depression, few Asian Americans turned to public assistance. Instead, they, like members of the Jewish community, turned to each other. This commitment to the financial needs of their community is still evident today.

It should also be noted that the higher incomes of Asian Americans do not necessarily translate into a higher standard of living. Asian Americans are more likely to live in urban environments where the cost of living is higher (Bell, 1994). They are also likely to have a greater number of family members working and contributing to the household income. Traditionally, Asian Americans are employed within family businesses in which all family members work long hours to help the business succeed (Bell, 1994). Takaki (1998) has argued that Asian Americans, despite their high household incomes, have not reached economic parity with European Americans. Instead, they work very long hours for less pay per hour. This reality stands in contrast with the "model minority" view, which implies that Asian Americans enjoy the same economic advantages as the dominant ethnic group.

Education

Father speaking to a counselor: My son simply isn't working hard enough. We know that he has greater potential than he is showing, and we want you to help him realize this. He received a B in math last term, and I would hate to see him ruin his chances for Stanford by earning another B down the road.

There is no doubt that Asian Americans are the academic envy of all other ethnic groups. Over the last half of the twentieth century, the Asian American community has slowly excelled to the point of passing all other groups in high school grade point averages and scores on national examinations such as SATs. Identifying the reasons for this growth is more difficult than one might imagine. Asian Americans do not appear to spend more time studying or doing homework than members of other groups (Asakawa & Csikszentmihalyi, 1998), nor do they appear significantly more intelligent than European Americans. However, there is a key difference: Asian Americans appear to place a higher value on education.

Asakawa and Csikszentmihalyi (1998) compared the subjective academic experiences of 33 Asian American students with those of 33 European American students. All students were adolescents, between sixth and twelfth grades. The findings revealed that while Asians do not spend more time studying, when they do study, their study experience is more positive. They enjoy the study experience and are able to perceive the relationship between studying and achieving their career goals. The motivation for attaining their goals is also high (Wong, Lai, Nagasawa, & Lin, 1998), and since they see a relationship between studying and reaching their goals, they are willing to study more diligently.

Why do Asian Americans achieve so much? Largely, because families place a high value on education. Sun (1998) examined financial, family, cultural, and other influences to see which played the most significant role in the success of East Asian students. Results of this national study indicated that Asian families invested time, money, and energy in their children's educational lives. They were much more likely to do so than any other racial group, even after social and demographic controls were taken into consideration. This increased emphasis on education means that Asian American children are less likely to participate in organized sports, to earn money through chores or employment, or even to spend time dating. Parents are also likely to reduce their children's household chores the day before a test (Krishnan & Sweeney, 1997).

The role of parents in supporting their children's education, however, is also influenced by the family's occupational and ethnic background. Kim, Rendon, and Valadez (1998) found that, on average, South Asians (i.e., those from Afghanistan, Bangladesh, Bhutan, India, Myanmar, Nepal, Pakistan, and Sri Lanka) tend to express the highest educational aspirations, followed by Koreans, Japanese, Chinese, Filipinos, and Southeast Asians. South Asian parents also tend to have the highest levels of education, followed by Koreans, Japanese, Filipinos, Chinese, and Southeast Asians. Finally, South Asian parents also have the highest occupational status, followed by Japanese, Koreans, Filipinos, Chinese, and Southeast Asians. These trends are reflected in the intensity of the educational demands placed on students by their families.

In addition to family values and expectations, the ethnic community also plays an important role in supporting educational achievement. Hao and Bonstead-Bruns (1998) found that the competition between various peer groups stimulates children's achievement rates. This means that families who reside within communities that value education are more likely to produce high-achieving children. This unremarkable finding implies that when families live in Asian communities, their children are more likely to succeed in school (Fuligni, 1997).

What happens when students are unable to achieve their academic goals? For some, catastrophes can occur. More than any other group, Asian American students turn to drugs when their grades go down (Ellickson, Collins, & Bell, 1999). First-generation Asian students are more likely to have difficulty making friends, and they are concerned about how to interact with American lecturers/teachers. First-generation female students, in particular, appear most reticent about approaching lecturers for help and asking questions in class. Most of these difficulties stem from a limited technical competency in English, but there are also issues regarding philosophies of learning (Beaver & Tuck, 1998). European American teachers, especially at higher levels, tend to maintain a discreet distance with their students. When faculty members form relationships with students, the structure is usually collaborative. The student is treated as a junior peer who is granted privileges but is under the faculty member's leadership. Asian Americans are often more comfortable with frameworks resembling parent/child relationships. They respect the office of the teacher/professor and will display reverence, honor, sincere appreciation, and gratitude (including gifts) for small acts, but they may also expect detailed guidance, which may appear to violate the emphasis on autonomy in American colleges. If faculty members fail to respond to an Asian student's request for guidance, the student may become insecure and confused.

Health

One of the issues that highlights the differences between Asian Americans and European Americans is their understanding of health-related issues. Phipps, Cohen, Sorn, and Braitman (1999) interviewed Cambodian and Vietnamese women living in Philadelphia to explore their knowledge of cancer. Only 29 percent of the participants could effectively define the term *cancer*, and only 26 percent were able to identify a cancer prevention strategy. When educational programs are put into place, however, Asian American women are more likely to have undergone a medical evaluation and a Pap test (Jenkins et al., 1999), and they are likely to believe that the overall quality of services rendered was competent (Harju, Long, & Allred, 1998).

The biggest obstacle to creating effective intervention problems for Asians involves cultural views regarding physical health. Many Asian groups attribute health problems to spiritual causes, rather than viruses, bacteria, or other agents. An imbalance of yin (feminine energies) and yang (masculine energies) is viewed as the source of disturbances in the body and mind. All humans are subject to the same elemental forces that govern the rest of the universe (fire, earth, metal, water, and wood). These elements also correspond to the five visceral organs of humans: the heart creates joy, the lungs create sorrow, the liver creates anger, the kidneys create fear, and the spleen creates compassion.

Although Westerners may scoff at the Asian view of health, there are documented benefits to Asian lifestyles. Rogers et al. (1996) examined the National Health Interview Survey to look at the causes of death for various ethnic groups. Their data set included an enormous amount of information including 394,071 survival records and 4,133 death records. The findings indicated that Asian Americans have death rates far below those of European Americans and other groups, which resulted from a combination of healthy behaviors (including diet and exercise) and socioeconomic advantages.

The idea of healthy behaviors guiding Asian Americans' lifestyle choices is not new. Asian Americans speak of their physical health as one of the most important facets of their lives. They also believe that community expectations for personal behaviors help to shape their physical health (Lang & Torres, 1997–1998). Both physical and psychological health are maintained through proper diet and exercise, mental/spiritual conditioning, and family togetherness.

Viewing physical health as the result of spiritual forces, however, creates some problems that must also be addressed. One of the most serious is a lack of access to Western health care. Jang, Lee, and Woo (1998) looked into the ways income, language, and citizenship status affected the use of health care services by Asian Americans in San Francisco. In their study, 63 percent of Chinese Americans were found to be working poor, often locked out of the health care system. As employees, they are often ineligible for welfare or simply refuse to accept it, and their employers refuse to offer health insurance. Most of these employees are foreign-born and monolingual (i.e., they did not speak English). In such cases, the employees do not even know from whom to seek care.

When a lack of knowledge concerning certain medical ailments is combined with a lack of available care, the problems become tragic. Yi (1998) queried 412 Vietnamese American college students (aged 17 to 48 years) concerning their knowledge about HIV-related problems. The participants in her study were aware of the major modes of HIV transmission, but they still held misconceptions that could prove fatal. One of the most frightening elements of her study was that as individuals became more acculturated, they started engaging in more sexual activity. In addition to this, higher acculturation was actually associated with less knowledge about HIV transmission. So, not only was acculturation promoting sexual activity, but it also led to less investigation into the risks. Even more alarming was the fact that when participants believed they were or could be infected, they were not comfortable discussing their HIV and safe-sex concerns with their sexual partners. These factors have led to an increase in the rate of HIV infection among Asian Americans, especially gay males (Choi, Yep, & Kumekawa, 1998).

In an attempt to decrease the risk of HIV infection among Asian Americans, Choi, Yep, and Kumekawa (1998) examined the prevention efforts targeted towards gay and bisexual Asian Americans. They specifically examined five discrete models: health belief model, theory of reasoned action, social learning theory, diffusion theory, and the AIDS risk reduction model. None of these, however, seemed very effective, and they did not address the environmental issues influencing this population group. They proposed an ecological model for health promotion as a potentially useful theoretical framework. The intent would be to tap into all available resources (such as the family, the general Asian community, and the mainstream gay community) to reduce HIV risk among gay and bisexual Asian men. Although there is currently no research to support it, such an approach seems promising.

Ecological interventions may also be useful in addressing a number of other health-related problems that are quickly spreading throughout the Asian American community. Tuberculosis rates for Asian Americans are nearly six times higher than the national mean. Special attention has also been given to the rise in rickets and thalassemia, but there are still few programs to assist with mainstream conditions such as asthma, diabetes, ischemic heart disease, and skin disorders, which also affect this community in high numbers (Hawthorne, 1994).

Another situation creating increased health concerns is the rising rate of smoking, especially among teens. Voorhees, Yanek, Stillman, and Becker (1998) examined the sociodemographic and cultural factors that play a role in cigarette sales in urban areas. One of the factors associated with increased sales to minors was the hostility of the patrons themselves. Merchants reported hostility (66 percent) and foul language (64 percent) when they requested youth identification. Advertisements, not surprisingly, also led to increased requests for cigarettes from minors. Asian merchants were also the most likely to feature advertisements targeted to children, suggesting that socioethnic factors may be an influential component of underage smoking.

The cultural factors involved in teen smoking have also led researchers to look into other treatment programs for teens. Yuen and Nakano-Matsumoto (1998) argue that effective substance abuse treatment for Asian American adolescents requires the providers to be culturally sensitive. With this population, they interpret this to mean that the best programs will be bicultural and bilingual. The providers should understand Western mental health concepts and substance abuse issues, and they must possess counseling skills that enable them to integrate and interpret these concepts within the framework of clients' ethnic cultures. Outside interventions, however, may be less effective than preserving ethnic morals and identity. Asian youths who retain an Asian identity show a stronger resistance to the use of alcohol, inhalants, or marijuana than do acculturated Asians (Suinn, 1999).

Cultural Uniqueness

Because Asian Americans are sometimes regarded as "adopted Whites" (Sue & Sue, 1990), some people fail to realize the immense differences between Asian and European American values. At times, the cultures even contradict one another, which can create a host of misunderstandings. Consider the following encounter, which took place between a European American professor and a Chinese student.

> I started working with Chin-Lin about six months ago when she began taking classes at my university. Her family was from China, and she seemed very much alone. On one occasion, I invited her over for dinner at my house.
>
> My husband and I greeted her when she came into the house, and we accepted the houseplant she brought as a gift (though we added that it wasn't necessary). She tried to get her shoes off, but we told her that it was not necessary either. Eventually, we made it into the living room and discussed school issues for a few minutes, while my husband continued the preparations for dinner. After about 20 minutes, completely out of the blue, she said, "Aren't you going to offer me some food?" I was a little taken aback by her boldness. I thought Asians were supposed to be meek, but I managed to get out, "Dinner is almost ready."
>
> After our meal, I asked if she would like me to walk her to her car. She looked down and said, "It is not necessary." So we watched as she walked into the darkness and turned off the light after she drove away.
>
> For the next few days, Chin-Lin seemed distant and a little hostile. I asked if everything was all right, and she just said, "Yes—thank you." I don't know how to handle this situation. Please help.

A number of cultural issues arose during this interaction that Mary, the professor, simply did not recognize. Each of these issues could have had a profound impact on the relationship between Mary and Chin-Lin. Let's examine them in order. First, Chin-Lin presented Mary with the houseplant as a token of friendship. Although Mary accepted the gift, she implied that it was unwelcome. Next, Mary and her husband prevented Chin-Lin from removing her shoes. Thus, Chin-Lin's efforts to show respect for her professor's home were compromised. By refusing to disgrace their floors, she wished to demonstrate that she was honored to be in their home.

Next, Chin-Lin expressed frustration over not being fed. In many Asian cultures touch, such as handshakes or hugs, is considered rude. Instead, it is polite to welcome a guest by offering a gift, often food. The food itself is not nearly as important as the guest's acceptance of it. If Mary had gone to Chin-Lin's house and refused the food tokens provided, her actions would have sent an irrefutable message that Chin-Lin's friendship was not desired.

By the time they finished their meal, Chin-Lin was ready to leave. Mary correctly surmised that she should accompany Chin-Lin to her car. When Chin-Lin said, "It is not necessary," Mary thought her duty had ended. In Chinese cultures, however, the visitor is expected to show good will by relieving the host of the obligation of walking her home. However, the truly gracious host will walk the visitor home anyway.

Although the topic was not mentioned by Mary, another misunderstanding could have arisen from the Asian avoidance of "harsh" terms. Had Mary asked if Chin-Lin liked the meatloaf she was serving, Chin-Lin would have replied, "Yes." Chin-Lin's response would not mean that she actually enjoyed the meal, merely that it would have been considered rude to answer otherwise. In most Asian cultures, the expression "no" in any context is considered rude. In Japan, for example, rather than answer so harshly, someone might say, "It would be difficult." Such an answer often means "no" in the strongest sense of the word. This type of cultural boundary would present serious difficulties to someone investigating a topic considered "taboo" (such as sex). The avoidance of such topics can also be extended to mundane matters. Asking a Japanese person what they would like to drink may produce the response, "Anything will be fine." The rationale for this response is to avoid insulting the host by asking for something unavailable. Usually, it is better to provide the guest with a list of possible choices (e.g., coffee or tea).

When Asians immigrate to America, they often must contend with being treated as "adopted Whites" rather than as members of distinct ethnic cultures. Kim (1985) developed an Asian identity development model in which incorporation of White identity is the first of five stages. The model is depicted in Table 4.1, and it includes the following elements: White identification, awakening to social political consciousness, redirection to Asian American consciousness, and incorporation. The key difference between this identity development process and that of other minorities is the initial acceptance by the dominant society. The awakening stage may take longer to come for Asian Americans than it would for African Americans or Latinos.

Although many of the cultural differences between European American society and Asian cultures are subtle, they are also quite pronounced. Consider the issue of gift giving. In many Asian cultures, a gift is considered to have a specific meaning related to its function. Gifts are usually viewed as expressions of purpose or emotion. If, for example, you brought a hospital-bound Japanese person a potted plant, the gift could be interpreted to mean, "You expect me to

TABLE 4.1 *Asian Identity Development Model (Kim, 1985)*

White identification	Incorporation into "white" culture produces a desire to accept European values while rejecting the values of one's ethnic culture.
Awakening to social political consciousness	The ethnic culture is viewed as being oppressed by the dominant culture, rather than being inferior to it.
Redirection of Asian American consciousness	There is a gradual immersion into one's ethnic culture. This may include feelings of anger toward European American culture, but energy is focused mainly on the creation of an ethnic identity.
Incorporation	After learning to identify with their ethnic heritage, the individual is ready to seek out and incorporate elements from other cultures. This process might include adopting traditions and beliefs from other Asian cultures as well as European American values.

be here for a very long time." In such cases, cut flowers are preferable. Similarly, the number and size of gifts is endowed with meaning. In Japan, it is customary to bring a gift to a hosting family but not to the individual family members. Gifts to individuals are reserved for family members or intimate friends. Family gifts should be presented with the saying, *minasan de douzo* (please share amongst yourselves).

When cultural norms are violated, or more significant offense is made, a sense of shame will often ensue. Often shame is felt for dishonoring one's family, occupation, or religion, but what is difficult for many Westerners to understand is that shame is associated with inaction as well as action. Not attending a meeting or failing to perform a duty to the expected level may result in feelings of intense shame. In Japan, the term for "goodbye" *(Shideshimas)* could be translated, "I am rude." Cultural mores are intricate and detailed. Here is a short list:

- Public physical contact is generally inappropriate. Slapping someone's back or giving a hug could be considered an immense dishonor. Touching someone's head, which connotes intense intimacy, would be the most serious violation.

- Asians have special guidelines about feet. Typically, feet are considered unclean. Even discussions about feet could be considered rude. Placing your feet on the furniture or even tapping your foot on the floor might be considered offensive by some groups.

- Eye contact is best kept to a minimal level.

- Closed body language (e.g., crossed arms) is considered coarse.

- The use of hands is quite intricate. Typically, when sitting, hands should rest in the lap. When standing, hands should *not* be hidden in pockets. In many ways, the use of hands conveys openness. If your hands are hidden, you are pulling away from the conversation. For this reason, if you are accepting a gift, business card, or other object, accepting it with both hands conveys respect and honor. In some cultures, such as that of India, you should never touch anything with your left hand, which is considered unclean.

- Boundaries of personal space vary by culture. The Chinese require little personal space, while Indians require nearly three feet.

From this discussion, it should be apparent that some cultural norms appear contradictory. Such cultural incongruities are most apparent regarding rules for meekness. Most Asian cultures value reserved temperaments, but the cultures are also frank and open. Greg Snyder (1998), while teaching English in Japan, found himself in an uncomfortable situation while walking down a crowded street. A Japanese woman approached him and stated, "You are fat. Why?" The question was not intended to be insulting. It simply conveyed the woman's curiosity about a topic that was not considered taboo.

Another difference between Asian and European American culture is the belief in Juni-shi (Chinese Zodiac). The ancient Chinese associated the calendar with 12 animals that were divided by year rather than month. The 12 animals are called Juni-shi. The animals include Ne (mouse or rat), Ushi (bull or ox), Tora (tiger), Usagi (rabbit), Tatsu (dragon), Mi (snake), Uma (horse), Hitsuji (sheep or goat), Saru (monkey), Tori (rooster or chicken), Inu (dog), and Inoshishi (Wild Boar). For example, 2001 was the year of the snake, and 2002 was the year of the horse. This set of 12 animals is the Japanese version of Juni-shi, slightly modified from the original Chinese zodiac. Japanese used this calendar for more than a thousand years. Many Asians believe that their Juni-shi birth year says something about their personality and character. For example, it is said that a man born in Uma-doshi works hard. A woman born under the Ne-doshi is meek. These beliefs are accepted to about the same degree that astrology is accepted in America.

Other superstitions involve the belief that blood type influences personality. Even though there is no research to support this theory, there is still a lingering belief that each blood type has a special function. Blood type A individuals are believed to be diligent, methodical, steady, and nervous. Blood type B individuals are gifted with originality but are also fickle. Blood type AB individuals are both sociable and sensitive. Finally, blood type O individuals are durable and resolute. For example, O-typed men are thought to make good soldiers.

Psychological Issues

Cultural differences also lead to distinctive perspectives regarding mental health. Many Asian Americans believe disorders such as depression, anxiety, confusion, and even posttraumatic stress disorder (PTSD) stem from their physical and spiritual health. Mental illness is attributed to karma (caused by deeds from past lives or punishment from God). Sometimes, the divine element becomes all-important and mental health may be equated with spiritual unrest projected onto the individual from a vengeful spirit (Lee, 1997b). These spiritual elements will likely correspond to physical complaints, with the two working for or against each other. The worse a person's physical functioning, the more severe the affective symptoms may become (Nicholson, 1997). According to Cornwell (1998), Asian Americans are more likely to complain of physical symptoms than European Americans (67.5 percent compared to 22 percent). This corresponds to mental health practices in Asia, where patients are more likely to consult physicians when seeking assistance with mental health problems. To remedy depression or other ailments, Asian physicians or priests may recommend massage, herbal medicine, tea ceremonies, martial arts work, or meditation. This does not imply, however, that Asian Americans will prefer physical interventions such as psychopharmacology. In fact, it appears that Asians are less likely to continue taking antidepressants than are European Americans (Cornwell, 1998).

Kawanishi (1992) writes that this tendency towards somatization is different from what would commonly be found among European Americans. He refers to it as facilitative somatization because it helps people to identify the affective flux in a holistic manner. Krause, Rosser, Khiani, and Lotay (1990) found that somatic and psychological symptoms may accompany each other more consistently for Asians than for those of European descent, but these symptoms were not associated with increased pathology overall. Some depressive symptomatology was noted, but it played a different role for Asians than it did for Europeans.

Why the emphasis on physical functioning? In part, it may stem from Asian religious beliefs and worldviews. Buddhism, the most common religion among many Asian groups, holds that there are four noble truths: (1) suffering exists, (2) suffering arises from attachment to desires, (3) suffering ceases when attachment to desire ceases, and, (4) freedom from suffering is possible by practicing the Eightfold Path (often grouped in the following three sections):

- *Wisdom (panna)*
  Right Understanding (samma ditthi)
  Right Aspiration (samma sankappa)

- *Morality (sila)*
  Right Speech (samma vaca)
  Right Action (samma kammanta)
  Right Livelihood (samma ajiva)

- *Concentration (samadhi)*
  Right Effort (samma vayama)
  Right Mindfulness (samma sati)
  Right Concentration (samma samadhi)

With suffering playing such an important role in the Asian worldview, depressive symptomatology could represent a healthy existential sadness that helps people to move along the path to enlightenment. A certain amount of psychological suffering is consistent with the philosophical orientations of South Asian religions and may not be an indication of psychopathology (Krause, Rosser, Khiani, & Lotay, 1990).

The presence of facilitative somatization or functional depression should not be allowed to mask all symptoms, however. For some unexplained reason, Asians seem to experience seasonal variation in affective illnesses. This means that when Asians suffer from affective disorders, such as bipolar disorder, they are more likely to experience depression in the winter. Their bodies appear less able to adapt to the lack of sunshine. Women with bipolar disorder are more likely to experience manic symptoms in the summer (Suhail & Cochrane, 1998). These tendencies were not found in any other ethnic group.

Family and economic issues also affect levels of depression. Mothers with absent husbands and young people with absent parents also have elevated rates of mental disorder (Abbott et al., 1999). In general, the best predictor for healthy psychological adjustment (as measured by happiness and a lack of demoralization) is a sense that life is comprehensible, manageable, and meaningful. Asian Americans who hold onto traditional values, arrive in America at a younger age, succeed in finding employment, and achieve higher education are the most likely to be well adjusted psychologically (Ying & Akutsu, 1997). They are also likely to have supportive family members or close friends. In fact, as they begin to feel they lack support, their somatization and depression is likely to rise. Generally, the converse is true too. The higher the scores on perceived or received support, the higher the reported happiness. Both perceived and received support showed a buffering effect on somatic complaints and depression (Jou & Fukada, 1997).

When depression becomes significant for Asian clients, talk therapy or traditional psychological interventions appear to be effective. Discussing problems with another person was correlated with lowered rates for anxiety and depression (Nahulu et al., 1996). In a group with a suicide rate three times that of the national average in America, the depressive symptomatology and anxiety are extremely important to address.

Just because we know talk therapy is effective, however, does not mean that Asian Americans are likely to seek out such help. Asian Americans/Pacific Islanders are three times *less* likely than their European American counterparts to use available mental health services (Matsuoka, Breaux, & Ryujin, 1997). They also tend to accept behavioral patterns that, by European American standards, are considered harmful. For example, Chinese Americans are known to have a high rate of pathological gambling addictions (Lee, 1997b), but they seldom seek treatment for this problem.

Within-Group Differences

The differences between these groups are so vast that they cannot be addressed fully in this text. It must be noted that most of the groups mentioned in the preceding sections were from eastern Asia (Japan, China, etc.). There are other groups of Asians, such as Indians.

India dates its history back to 6500 B.C. and has created sophisticated traditions of medicine, astronomy, physical sciences, religion, philosophy, and the arts. India has withstood invasions from the Mongols, Muslims, French, Portuguese, and the British, and won their independence from Britain in 1947 when India became the world's largest democracy. India is the mother of Buddhism, Jainism, Sikhism, and is currently home to myriad religious and cultural leaders. Although most citizens are Hindu and speak Hindi, 14 major Indian languages are also spoken, along with hundreds of rural dialects.

The primary cultural difference between Indian families and other Asians is the *dharma*. The *dharma* addresses the sacredness of all life and encompasses well-defined rules of right conduct, including an elaborate hierarchy that encompasses variables such as age, gender, birth order, marital status, and the role of animals (Kakar, 1978). All life is interconnected and has function and value within the community. According to the Vedas, a collection of Sanskrit verses collected across several Indian regions over a period of millennia, an individual's life is divided into four quarters: study and moral development, marital and family development, the passing of obligations to the next genera-tion, and finally a spiritual inquiry that leads to a union with *atma* or universal self. If an individual fails to pass through any of these stages, the family may use collective guilt, shame, or moral reasoning to bring him or her back to the dharma (Prathikanti, 1997).

Another important cultural difference is the Indian view of women. Women, although often relegated to limited social roles, have enjoyed notable success in India. Indira Gandhi led the country prior to the election of England's first female prime minister. There are nearly equal numbers of female and male medical students, and female lawyers have long been arguing before the courts. The success of women may be due in part to the widespread worship of female deities. If such deities were limited to goddesses of children (such as Befana, Mayavel, and Rumina), their legacy might not be as grand. But their influence extends much farther. The ancient goddess, Ammavaru, was said to have existed before time. It was she who laid the egg that hatched into the divine trinity of Brahma, Vishnu, and Shiva. Even the Hindu Trinity has a feminine counterpart. Shiva-Rudra (beneficent and destructive) is married to Durga (the moon goddess); Vishnu (the omnipresent) is married to Lakhsmi; and Brahma (the creator) was married to Sarasvati (goddess of knowledge, fer-tility, and prosperity). Sarasvati is also considered the originator of speech and of all the arts.

Although these myths have created some advantages for women, they have not cured all the ills. First- and second-generation Indian American women have reported higher levels of domestic violence when married to men of the same ethnicity (Passano, 1995). Bhattacharjee (1999) suggests that this trend is not endemic to Indian culture but stems from the bourgeois separation of private and public life. She suggests that divergent public and private roles can create the foundation for domestic abuse, which may not even be apparent to outsiders. Adding to the problem, Indian men appear to have a double stan-dard for their partners. They will accept the feminist ideals of European American women but expect an Indian wife to accept the traditional submis-sive role (Devji, 1999). Indian American women are slowly attempting to weave biculturality into their relationships and are expanding their power within marital relationships (Gupta, 1999).

In China, Japan, Korea, and many other Asian countries, traditional Eastern religions dominate the spirituality of the people. These include Shintoism (a descendant of ancient animism, mixed with ancestor worship, sun worship, and Buddhism), Jodo Buddhism (the dominant sect of Buddhism in Japan), Esoteric Buddhism (the priests of Esoterics invoke powerful miracles, called *horiki*, through which they can cure diseases, curse a person to death, or see into the future), Zen Buddhism (dominated by the idea that spiritual awakening is attained only by meditation), and Taoism (the Chinese blend of native religions, divination, Confucian courtesy, and ceremony). In many Asian countries, Christianity is relatively uncommon because it does not adapt well to the traditional caste system.

The Philippines, by contrast, is primarily a Catholic nation, which means Filipinos have much in common with Catholics from Mexico or Brazil. For example, Filipinos accept the traditional Catholic use of godparents, who often play an important role in the parenting of children. The similarity between Filipino culture and European American/Latino culture may be responsible for the international explosion of mail-order brides (Ordonez, 1997). The number of Filipinas coming to America as mail-order brides has increased in recent years, and this phenomenon may be associated with the fact that Filipinas have a lower college enrollment rate and a lower self-employment rate than other Asian women. They are, however, also more likely to be employed than other Asian women (Agbayani-Siewert & Revilla, 1995).

Counseling Issues

William Mikulas (2002) argues that Asian cultures tend to shy away from psychology because the notion of separating a person's mind from his or her nutritional status, energy level, family relations, and spiritual practices would be futile. This distinction is often hard for Westerners to grasp, because Western thought has long attempted to compartmentalize everything. These differing worldviews have made talk therapy virtually nonexistent in Asia. The reasons for this trend are complex, but they rest in part on the Asian conceptualization of mental health. In many Asian cultures, the admission that an individual has mental health "problems" can further intensify feelings of shame, and this shame is exacerbated by disclosing problems to someone outside one's immediate family (Lee, 1997b). Typically, Asians will turn to a trusted friend, spiritual leader, or physician when they are unable to resolve mental health issues within the family. It is only after exhausting these resources that they will turn to mental health practitioners, and even then, it is usually at the request of a physician. Even in these cases, the family is likely to feel more comfortable and attend more sessions if the counselor speaks the client's language or belongs to the same ethnic group (Flaskerud & Liu, 1991).

To Westerners, the lack of talk therapy might indicate poor mental health interventions, but many experts view Asian therapies as more integrated and systematic than Western psychology. Even the practice of Buddhism can be viewed as a form of psychotherapy. As the pupil progresses, he or she tries daily to harmonize conflicting inner forces, resolving conflicts by creating an inner sense of calmness. Such a pursuit is called the Sublime Way *(Ariya Magga)* or the Harmonious Way *(Samma Magga)*, and this lifestyle is viewed as a means of achieving mental health *(Arogya)*. The calm mind is able to observe subjective experiences objectively; if someone hurts you, your pain should be no greater than if you witnessed that action committed against someone else.

While it is not a product of Buddhism, Yoga (a precursor to Indian Hinduism) can illustrate how *Arogya* can be achieved. To its adherents, describing yoga as physical exercise (which is how Westerns commonly perceive it) is misleading and offensive—on a par with dismissing mental health interventions as "talking with a friend." Das (2001) refers to yoga as a means of linking oneself with the Supreme (the inner and universal source of life). It is viewed as a process of releasing one's spiritual energy from the worldly realm and rising to a spiritual purity. The mind is trained to avoid all worldly distractions by learning to shun the glitter of material nature. Obviously, it takes time to learn this process, and there are eight stages to yogic development. In the early stages, the focus is upon being in harmony with the principles of life *(yama, niyama)* and on training the body. Once the postures are learned, and the individual has mastered the art of breathing, the student learns to clear the mind of all inner and outer obstacles. As the pupil's skill and knowledge increase, the meditation processes deepen until he or she ceases all disturbing mental activities *(chitta vritti nirodha)*. In Raja Yoga, the *chitta vritti nirodha* is reached by first clearing the mind of all thoughts except one sound or idea. This is practiced in 10–20 second intervals *(Pratyahara)*. When *Pratyahara* is mastered, the student may progress to *Dharana* (holding on to a single mental object for 2 to 4 minutes), *Dhyana* (holding on to a single mental object for 30 to 40 minutes), and finally, Samadhi (holding on to a single mental object for 6 or more hours). With each level, complex physical, emotional, and intellectual tasks are united to create mental health.

Yoga's bridging of mental and physical health is common to many Asian interventions. In the Asian worldview, there are four levels of being (biological, behavioral, personal, and transpersonal), and each must be addressed in a mental health intervention to help the client improve (Mikulas, 2002). Contemporary psychological theories have addressed the personal and behavioral dimensions, but there has been little discussion of the biological and transpersonal areas. One of the contemporary counseling approaches built upon an Asian worldview is conjunctive psychology, which addresses the four dimensions listed above. Within this theoretical orientation, interventions involving the biological dimension could include prescribing medications, as well as understanding the effects of the seasons, color and light, weather, pollution, herbs, and diets. The transpersonal dimension may include meditation, spiritual awakening, progressing beyond personal concerns, or striving for any other form of higher consciousness.

To envision a conjunctive intervention, picture the following scenario. You are working with a Chinese American woman who is feeling depressed and confused about her marriage. Her concerns rest within the personal and behavioral dimensions, and she is trapped within these confines. To free her, steps must be taken beyond the individual, beyond the personal. One of the most important beginning stages is to experience the world as a part of the self. Have the client choose a calming position and have him or her focus on one of the senses (i.e., smell, taste, sight, touch, and hearing). If the sense of touch is chosen, have the client attempt to perceive subtle breezes, the way her feet touch the floor, how her body touches the chair, changes in temperature, or even the sensation of clothes against the body. During most of the day, we are oblivious to these environmental nuances. Instead, we focus on the "problems" of our lives, which can enslave us. If the client can transcend the problems surrounding her, she can awaken to a new way of living. The sensations of the moment can overpower her seemingly insurmountable feelings and circumstances. To reach this point, however, all four dimensions must be investigated. She might spend ten minutes sitting in the afternoon sun, change her diet, or learn to fast. She may also be asked to redefine herself as individual, to view herself as a part of a larger world. To do this, she will need to discover or rediscover meaningful myths and stories. These techniques may fit within the Western therapeutic model, but they are seldom employed.

Another difference between Eastern and Western worldviews involves the role of the family, as already mentioned. The family is extremely important, and a certain structure must be maintained. For this reason, scapegoating may occur and an individual, especially one with a history of physical illness, may be blamed for family problems (Lee, 1997b). The perceived shame of seeking outside help has also led many traditional Asian husbands or fathers to prevent the family from attending therapy. When crises arise with children, and the family is unable to effectively address the critical issues without help, some men will send their wives to therapy sessions rather than lose face by participating in therapy (Lee, 1997a). Such complications require therapists to maintain a flexible structure for family therapy. The therapist should be willing to alter treatment plans if necessary and evaluate therapeutic outcomes. Such an approach will assist in establishing a cooperative therapeutic relationship and maintaining trust (Jung, 1998).

When Asians attend therapy, they will probably be reluctant to voice their deepest concerns. They are more likely to view themselves as being victims of a tragic environmental situation or unable to cope with some physical discomfort (Lee, 1997a). This is probably one of the reasons that Asian Americans are less satisfied with psychotherapy in the early stages of the process. They are also more likely, after four treatment sessions, to report depression, hostility, and anxiety (Zane, Enomoto, Chun, 1994). Rather than focus on the affective dimensions of therapy, Cimmarusti (1999) recommended that counselors avoid action-oriented techniques, such as role-playing, and instead focus on "meaning-oriented techniques." The latter may include interventions such as reframing problems within the client's cultural framework (e.g., viewing depression as a physical or spiritual problem) or engaging in circular questioning (e.g., asking, "When you are tense, you close off your senses; are you experiencing your surroundings now?"). These are more effective ways to help clients fulfill cultural demands for harmony and build a strong boundary around the clan.

Consider the case of Teva Chan, a second-generation Cambodian American, and her husband, Chay Chan, a third-generation Cambodian American. During the initial interview, Chay vocalized their concerns. "We are just having a hard time communicating," he stated. "She is a wonderful person, but I'm not able to give her what she needs." Teva sat silently, her head bowed down and her gaze focused on the ground.

"What would you like to address, Mrs. Chan?" the therapist inquired, careful to use her title as a sign of respect. Teva remained silent. After a few seconds she jerked her head up and quickly looked into her husband's eyes. She then returned to her original position. "I . . . I don't think this is the right place to discuss it," she finally lamented. Chay sighed. "You see what I mean?" he moaned with obvious frustration. "There is something wrong, but I don't know how to get through."

With such hesitance, role-playing is unlikely to produce positive results. Instead, a more profitable course might involve reframing Teva's discomfort within the cultural framework. The therapist could reframe her quiet temperament in the following way:

> Mrs. Chan, I can sense that you value harmony and you try to avoid hurting those close to you, especially your husband. I think Mr. Chan feels the same way. In fact, from what he has stated so far, it seems like he wants to use this time to better understand how he can serve you.

Statements such as these will not create a flow of conversation, as would be expected in European American marital sessions, but they may help both parties feel more comfortable with the intervention. Most of the problems Teva and Chay faced were related to their differing levels of acculturation. Teva believed that confronting her husband about his spending habits would be disrespectful, but Chay had dated only European American women and he did not understand his wife's reluctance to discuss why she felt so uncomfortable around him. Even coming to therapy was forced upon her, and the process left her feeling vulnerable and uncomfortable. Culturally aware therapists will avoid confrontations that could lead to an embarrassing disclosure.

In the case of Teva and Chay, differences in acculturation had led to the conflict. If both partners had been recent immigrants, it is less likely that they would have sought help from outsiders. When such support is sought, it is usually with the intention of ending a particular crisis rather than changing an ongoing family dynamic. When Asian families contact service providers, the contact tends to be crisis-related, brief, and solution-oriented; thus, insight and growth-oriented approaches are not recommended (Berg & Jaya, 1993). A traditional Asian family may expect therapy sessions to last longer than one hour and take place more often than once a week. They desire a quick resolution to an immediate problem (Lee, 1997a). Given this understanding, therapists need to help clients find pragmatic solutions to problems, rather than encourage them to share their feelings. In many cases, clinicians should address the family's needs over the individuals needs so the family can more quickly return to homeostasis.

The family's needs should never supersede an individual's safety, however. Therapists working with Asian clients may expect them to be submissive and quiet, but the therapeutic process can be intense and highly charged. Clients may have suicidal ideation or be extremely angry or argumentative. Complications can be even more serious, depending on the family members' interactional patterns, personalities, and levels of motivation. Each case can present the therapist with new challenges and opportunities for professional and personal growth.

A basic framework for counseling Asian clients can be summarized with the acronym ASIA: acceptance, support, impartiality, and adaptability. Acceptance includes a variety of important dimensions. Therapists must learn to accept and feel comfortable in the roles of authority figure, expert, and educator. Each of these roles is often difficult for therapists to accept, because most schools of thought view the therapist as a co-collaborator in the client's growth. Many Asian clients, however, will expect their therapist to have answers, offer advice, and provide hope. This means that the therapist, not the client, is viewed as the primary change agent. The clients will look to the therapist for direction and leadership. The therapist is viewed as a healer who is expected to provide solutions specific to the problem. Clear guidelines about the nature of therapy should be communicated, including expectations for the therapist and the client.

Support is the second foundational element necessary when working with Asian clients. Therapists must find a way to support the family's hierarchical structure without allowing this structure to threaten an individual's growth or mental health. Consider the case of Lee, who is feeling suicidal. Lee's family wants to keep him at home because hospitalization would cause them to feel embarrassed. In this situation, in which a client's life is in danger, the therapist must give higher priority to the needs of the client than to the family's wishes. It is helpful, however, to support family structure by reframing growth issues. For example, a woman's desire for greater independence could be viewed as something that provides her husband with more free time.

The "I" in our ASIA acronym is impartiality. Counselors need to operate from a neutral vantage point and learn to listen objectively to their clients' statements. Some cultural issues may appear odd or pathological to Western therapists. If a client discusses the healing power of herbs or the connection between a physical symptom and depression, such perceptions should be accepted and then worked through.

The final component is adaptability. Working with Asian clients requires therapists to be flexible enough to adopt different intervention strategies and intervention styles. Basically, anything that helps the client(s) continue to grow while feeling accepted and honored will be successful. Therapists should also help clients use self-reflection as a method of maintaining health (e.g., meditation, self-control of negative thoughts, or other self-discipline tools). The Center for Mental Health Services (2000) recommends the incorporation of alternative approaches to mental health care that emphasize the interrelationship between mind, body, and spirit. For Asian Americans, therapists may solicit the assistance of community resources to provide services such as acupuncture, shiatsu,[2] and reiki.[3] When used along with other forms of mental health therapy, these techniques can address clients' needs on physical and spiritual levels.

When counseling Asian Americans, especially first-generation Asian Americans, counselors may often be unaware of the cultural differences. Often, a client's attempt to acculturate will mask the cultural diversity beneath the surface. For example, consider the case of Suzume, who moved from Taiwan to California at the beginning of high school.

Suzume's Story

I like Americans. They are interesting and different. At first I didn't really know what to make of them. They were so open and talkative—they would talk about anything. The first day I went to lunch with some of my American classmates, they started to talk about things they were afraid of. When they asked me about my fears, I could only look down and hope they would not ask again.

One of the girls asked me later if I was embarrassed by the conversation. I simply asked, "Is this normal American talk?" She nodded and smiled. It's not that the material truly embarrassed me. I could have held such conversations with my family. But with strangers and in public, it did not seem right.

The next day, my friends were much more quiet at lunch, and they continued to look at me. I think they were concerned that they would say something else to offend me. I really didn't know what to do. Finally, I started asking them

---

[2]Shiatsu is a Japanese healing art deeply rooted in the philosophy and practices of traditional Chinese medicine. Incorporating the therapeutic massage of Japan, and more recently embracing its original focus of meditation and self-healing, shiatsu is gaining popularity in the West. The purpose of shiatsu is achieving a balance between practitioner and receiver, in which the healing power of both build upon each other to clear and balance the vital life force known as Qi.

[3]Reiki is a technique for stress reduction and relaxation that allows people to tap into an unlimited supply of "life force energy" to improve health and enhance the quality of life.

about their classes. This seemed to give them all something to talk about, but even this conversation was different. They talked about their teachers as they would discuss television stars. "Oh, I hope you don't get Ms. Tomas, she's the worst." I had never heard students talk about teachers like this. They did not seem to value their teachers or their position. In my country, Taiwan, teachers are revered because of their position. We respect them because they have received positions of honor.

In Taiwan, teachers were almost like parents. We all respected them and would honor them with gifts. Here, teachers were a blend of friends, colleagues, and enemies. I did not understand.

Questions to Consider

1. Asian concepts of identity give priority to the needs of the group. Individuals' actions are seen as bringing shame or honor to their families, and these actions have lasting repercussions. With this orientation in mind, should individual therapy focus on the individual's feelings and personal growth, or on behavioral changes targeted to increase the honor the client brings to the family?

2. If an individual seeks therapy, and therefore implies that the family is not capable of solving conflicts on their own, should family therapy be attempted to mitigate the shame?

3. How would you attempt to measure acculturation during the course of an intake, and how would you use this information in developing a treatment plan?

4. Asian children who are adopted transracially do not appear to face increased psychological difficulties growing up, but there are unique issues that must be addressed. What advice or information would you provide to a European American family who adopted an Asian child?

5. Asian religious principles often diverge from those of Christianity. Should therapists with Christian or secular backgrounds attempt to help a Hindu and Buddhist with spiritual concerns? Would your answer differ if the individual believed his depression stemmed from spiritual pain?

6. How would you intervene with an Asian middle school student who was distraught over earning B's in school? Would it make a difference if the child's grades were significantly above her intelligence score (i.e., she was absorbing more information than most people with similar intelligence scores)?

7. Asian Americans are sometimes referred to as "adopted Whites." What do you think of this terminology, and what implications does this attitude hold for therapeutic interventions with Asian Americans?

8. Asians are more likely to complain of physical symptoms than European Americans. Does this make them more likely to benefit from medical interventions, or is such externalization a problem that should be addressed in psychotherapy?

9. When Asians attend therapy sessions, they are likely to be reluctant to voice their deepest concerns. They are likely to view themselves as being victims of a tragic environmental situation or unable to cope with some physical discomfort. Should deeper concerns be addressed, or should the therapist stay within the client's comfort zone?

5

Native Americans

INSIGHT EXERCISE I've come to realize something about people: we will never understand each other. I recently became engaged to a wonderful man who sincerely loves me and wants to spend his life with me. The problem is, he is White, and my family will not accept him. They even went so far as to suggest that I had wounded the Great Spirit by embracing the enemy of my forefathers. I don't know why my parents can't accept that John is different from other White people. I suppose, though, that they might know more than me.

My grandmother asked me to "test" John by asking him some basic questions about our people, the Pomo. He didn't know anything about us. He didn't know about the Russian onslaught in the eighteenth century, when fur traders attacked villages and kidnapped all the women and children, or that we were forced into slavery just 150 years ago and were hunted by the United States military when we finally escaped. Am I betraying my people by marrying the man I love?

The term "Native American" is often used to describe an ethnically distinct group of American citizens indigenous to North America. This diverse group includes American Indians, Alaska Natives, Eskimos, and Aleuts. Although these latter terms can be used in an ethnologically descriptive sense, they also have legal and political meanings. An "American Indian" has been defined as a person with some amount of Indian blood who is recognized as such by his or her tribe or community (United States Environmental Protection Agency, 1999). Many tribes take this blood history very seriously and may view only "pure-blood" Indians as authentic. This practice is rooted in a long and violent history of interaction between Europeans and Indians, in which Indians were nearly driven to extinction by White aggression and diseases such as smallpox.

Before the Europeans came to North America, Native Americans may have numbered between 20 and 40 million people. By the turn of the twentieth century, the population had been reduced to less than half a million. As they experienced a 98 percent reduction in their population base from 1500 to 1900, Native North Americans experienced a concomitant 97.5 percent reduc-

tion in their land base (Churchill & LaDuke, 1992). Many tribes faced extinction. By the 1980s, the Native American population had recovered slightly and
numbered just over a million throughout the Northern Hemisphere. By the
mid-1990s, the number had grown beyond 2 million, although this number
still represents only 1 percent of the American population (Allen, 1998). These
considerations should be kept in mind when examining the cultures, history,
and psychology of Native Americans. Their experiences have been described
as the American Holocaust.

History of Oppression

> The white people, who are trying to make us over into their image, they
> want us to be what they call "assimilated," bringing the Indians into the
> mainstream and destroying our own way of life and our own cultural pat-
> terns. They believe we should be contented like those whose concept of
> happiness is materialistic and greedy, which is very different from our way.
> We want freedom from the white man rather than to be integrated. We
> don't want any part of the establishment, we want to be free to raise our
> children in our religion, in our ways, to be able to hunt and fish and live in
> peace. We don't want power. We don't want to be congressmen, or bankers.
> We want to be ourselves. We want to have our heritage, because we are the
> owners of this land and because we belong here. The white man says,
> "There is freedom and justice for all." We have had "freedom and justice,"
> and that is why we have been almost exterminated. We shall not forget this.
> (From the 1927 Grand Council of American Indians)

Native Americans may be the most oppressed group in North America.
The facts are so staggering that they are painful to convey. As late as the 1980s,
approximately 25 percent of surviving Native American women and 10 percent
of Native American men had been sterilized without their consent. During the
1990s, their infant mortality rate soared beyond the national average because of
inadequate medical care. The life expectancy for Native Americans hovered
around 55 years of age, approximately 20 years lower than the national average
(Allen, 1998).

Even the process of mass murder had not been eliminated by the twentieth
century, because Native Americans were viewed as a threat to land accumulation. In the 1930s, more than 125,000 Native Americans, from different tribes,
were forced to leave their homes and move to Oklahoma. Thousands of Native
Americans were evicted from their land, which was considered sacred and part
of their corporate identity—sometimes forced to leave through violence and
tortuous means. In many ways, the final stand Native Americans were willing
to take against an oppressive government occurred near the end of the nineteenth century at the battle at Wounded Knee in South Dakota.

The struggle had begun centuries earlier. Soon after Columbus set foot in North America, Native Americans found their very way of life threatened. As Dee Brown (1979) pointed out in *Bury My Heart at Wounded Knee* (pp. 1–2):

> "So tractable, so peaceable, are these people," Columbus wrote to the King and Queen of Spain [referring to the Tainos on the island of San Salvador, which was so named by Columbus], "that I swear to your Majesties there is not in the world a better nation. They love their neighbors as themselves, and their discourse is ever sweet and gentle, and accompanied with a smile; and though it is true that they are naked, yet their manners are decorous and praiseworthy."
>
> All this, of course, was taken as a sign of weakness, if not heathenism, and Columbus being a righteous European was convinced the people should be "made to work, sow and do all that is necessary and to adopt our ways." Over the next four centuries (1492–1890) several million Europeans and their descendants undertook to enforce their ways upon the people of the New World.

Of all the conflicts between the American government and Native American people, perhaps the most pivotal is the battle at Wounded Knee. The story is important because it demonstrates the limited abilities of the two groups to understand each other. To the American government, the battle at Wounded Knee was an important show of strength and an event that would help to end Indian uprisings. To the Native Americans, it meant the loss of their identity, culture, and hope for the future. They were reduced from a proud, independent people to a subordinate group forced to follow the rules of a harsh and dishonest government.

The problems began in 1889 when a young mystic, Wovoka, had a vision that the Whites would be destroyed and the land would be reborn with all the lost souls (including the buffalo) restored. He and his followers started a new dance and a new faith to usher in the new era. The precepts of this new faith called for no fighting, no war, nothing that resembled war, no stealing, no lying, and no cruelty. Wovoka learned the dance during his vision in the Spirit World. Each of the worshippers, painted with sacred red pigment, shuffled counterclockwise in a circle, moving slowly at first but increasing the tempo while singing songs of resurrection.

European Americans eventually called the religion the Ghost Dance Religion because of the emphasis on resurrection and reunion with the dead. When the religion spread to the Sioux, they began dancing in loose shirts, adorned with feathers or other trimmings. The shirts were believed to be sacred and impervious armor against an attacker's bullets. Agent James McLaughlin mistakenly reported that Sioux leader Sitting Bull [Tatanka-Iyotanka (1831–1890)] planned to use the Ghost Dance Religion to reestablish himself in the leadership of the people. This false message led to the deployment of U.S. Army soldiers with orders to eliminate any observed outbreak.

On December 14, 1890, McLaughlin had Sitting Bull arrested. During the apprehension, Sitting Bull protested, and one of his followers fired a rifle at one of the arresting officers, a fellow Sioux named Lt. Bull Head. As the police chief fell, he managed to put a bullet into Sitting Bull. General gunfire erupted, taking the lives of Sitting Bull, six policemen, and eight of Sitting Bull's followers. The killing of the chief exacerbated the turmoil that was already sweeping the reservation lands. Bands of Sioux fled, all frightened, many of them still holding onto the hope of deliverance through the Ghost Dance miracle. Some of Sitting Bull's followers hurried toward the camp of Big Foot, a Miniconjou Sioux chief. They met up with Big Foot while he and his people were on their way to agency headquarters near Fort Bennett to procure rations. When the army found Big Foot, they ordered Big Foot's followers, numbering more than 300, to accompany him to Camp Cheyenne, where they would be kept under watchful eye. The Indians followed, but later fled to the Badlands fearing more troops were coming to force them away from their homes.

The troops pursued and took up surrounding positions around the area known as Wounded Knee Creek. In the morning, the American soldiers prepared to disarm their captives. Four rapid-fire Hotchkiss guns were set into place on a low hill overlooking the camp from the north, to be used in the event of an outburst. When the soldiers approached the camp, they pawed through the tribe's personal belongings and began confiscating guns. Tensions increased until a young Indian pulled a gun out from under his robe and began firing wildly. Instantly, the soldiers retaliated with a point-blank volley, which cut down nearly half of the warriors. The other warriors drew concealed weapons and charged the soldiers.

What happened next is unclear. The Army reported that the Indians fired at them and shot many of their own women and children in the process. The Indians believe that the Hotchkiss guns on the hill fired down on the camp, ripping the civilians apart with explosive shells. When the battle ended, at least 180 Indians had been killed. Their bodies were left unattended for three days. When the burial party reached the scene, four babies were discovered still alive, wrapped in their dead mothers' shawls. Most of the other children had been killed.

Family

"With all things and in all things, we are relatives." (Sioux)

Native Americans, like Latino and Asian groups, are likely to maintain an interconnected web of kin (MacPhee, Fritz, & Miller-Heyl, 1996). Unlike the extended family of other ethnic groups, however, Native Americans receive part of their identity and family belonging from their tribe. Individuals who find unique ways to benefit the tribe are rewarded and given greater community support, which implies that all members are expected to place the needs of the tribe above the needs of the individual. Individuals who leave the tribe often face a threatened sense of identity (Anderson & Ellis, 1995).

The corporate identity of Native Americans keeps people on the reservations. Urban case studies indicate that many Native Americans living in urban areas retain ties to their tribes and hope to move back when they retire. Also, 71 percent of the Native Americans who live outside of reservation areas but still reside in the same county indicated that they would prefer to move back (United States Environmental Protection Agency, 1999). Native Americans are not leaving the reservations in large numbers and, in fact, it is more likely that these communities will develop to accommodate their increasing numbers. Of the nearly 2 million Native Americans counted in the 1990 census, 37 percent lived in tribal areas and 23 percent in surrounding counties. Another 31 percent resided in metropolitan areas in other parts of the country, and 9 percent lived in other nonmetropolitan areas.

The close ties within the tribe help to create a sense of community and encourage interdependence. Even distant tribe members are considered relatives in times of crisis and ceremony, on both happy and sad occasions. One of the clearest examples of group intimacy can be seen in Native Americans' treatment of visitors. Traditionally, when a family saw visitors approaching, the family would automatically begin cooking a full meal for the visitors. The visitors were then expected to sit and eat, and refusing to do so would offend the host family. The tradition has changed somewhat in recent times, and the host family will prepare a meal only if the visitors have not eaten recently (Edmo, 1989).

Another example of tribal unity involves child-rearing practices. The tribe and extended family can act as a basic unit, with children often raised by uncles, aunts, grandparents, or distant cousins. At times, outsiders might misinterpret these collective child-rearing practices as a sign of family unrest. Consider the case of Chris, who decided to live with her maternal aunt because her father was having problems with alcohol. When her teacher, Ms. Anderson, found out that Chris had moved away from her parents, Ms. Anderson contacted social services. Ms. Anderson believed that Chris was in danger and needed protection. The teacher failed to understand that aunts in Native American families typically take maternal roles within the broader family setting. The child's cultural values were not taken into consideration.

Another striking difference between Native Americans and other ethnic groups is the presence of a matriarchal and matrilineal structure. Traditionally, Native American women held great political and economic power within their tribes (Rivers, 1995). Among the Senecas, women owned and cultivated the land, which they had inherited through their mothers. After marriage, the husband moved into the wife's household, where he lived with the wife's female relatives and their spouses and children. Men devoted most of their time to hunting and fighting battles. When the Europeans arrived in America, patriarchal structures were imposed on Native American families and women found themselves stripped of their former power.

The appreciation of womanhood is apparent in the tradition of moontime, a practice still followed by many Native American nations. In ancient times, menstruating women would retreat to a moon lodge where they rested, released their blood to the earth, and harnessed the powerful visionary energy that accompanied moontime. The dreams and visions experienced during these times were viewed as sacred and used as a source of inspiration and prophecy for the entire community. The experience was not simply one of solitary reflection, however. This was a time for storytelling and humor, for counseling and teaching the younger women, for expression through artwork and song, and for experiencing the bonds of sisterhood (Leland, 1992).

A woman's first moontime was celebrated within the tribe. Anne Cameron (1996) tells the story of a village who honored a girl's first moontime through a very special ceremony. The community gathered together, bringing food and gifts for celebration. The grandmothers dressed the girl in the best ceremonial finery, and everyone gathered at the shore of the lake. The grandmothers rowed with the girl out to the middle of the lake. When the girl was stripped down to her skin, she dove into the water while the grandmothers rowed back to shore and waited with the rest of the tribe for her to swim back. When she reached the shore, everyone cheered and the people said, "A girl went out in a boat, and a woman swam back." The drumming, dancing, and feasting went on for days.

As Native Americans were acculturated into the dominant society, they lost many of their matriarchal rituals. The evolution away from matriarchy and toward the European American patriarchal power structure may be responsible for an increased incidence of rape among certain Native American groups. Rape may now be the most frequently committed crime on Navajo reservations. Old Dog Cross (1982) reported that at least 80 percent of the women seeking mental health services (across a five-state area) had experienced some form of sexual assault. She also reported that many Native American women were falling prey to "training," a form of gang rape. Groups of males would band together and "punish" a selected woman for her indiscretions.

Other problems are emerging in Native American families. Generally speaking, there is a high fertility rate and a large percentage of out-of-wedlock births in Native American populations. Berry, Shillington, Peak, and Hohman (2000) studied 5,053 women between the ages of 23 and 31 years and explored risk and protective factors for adolescent pregnancy. Their findings revealed, as expected, that higher self-esteem and a higher level of education are protective factors, while living in poverty as a young teen, engaging in substance abuse, and adolescent marriage are factors associated with an increased risk for teen pregnancy. There is also emerging evidence that Native American girls who become pregnant will receive marginal prenatal care, feel afraid to tell their families, experience loneliness, and face suicidal ideation (Liu, Slap, Kinsman, & Khalid, 1994).

Economics

"Once I was in Victoria, and I saw a very large house. They told me it was a bank and that the white men place their money there to be taken care of, and that by and by they got it back with interest. We are Indians and we have no such bank, but when we have plenty of money or blankets, we give them away to other chiefs and people, and by and by they return them with interest, and our hearts feel good. Our way of giving is our bank." (Chief Maquinna, Nootka)

Teenage pregnancy is only one of the risks associated with poverty, and poverty seems to pervade every sector of Native American life. About 47 percent of the Native American population resides in areas that are remote, sparsely populated, and poor, with little access to employment and other economic opportunities. In some ways, this makes encroachment of larger non–Native American populations beneficial because the growing population could bring new jobs. Unemployment rates range between 60 and 90 percent (Allen, 1998), and when people are able to find employment, there is a high concentration in semiskilled and service positions, with Native Americans doubling the national average for farming or related occupations (Aponte & Crouch, 1995). The high concentration of group members in low-level occupations has a direct bearing on their quality of life and opportunities for increasing family income. Overall, Native Americans (including Eskimos and Aleutian Islanders) have the highest rate of poverty of any ethnic group (U.S. Bureau of Census, 1992). The 1989 rate for Native Americans living below the poverty level was 34 percent, almost twice the rate for non-Indians. Poverty rates were highest in tribal areas, at 36 percent, and somewhat lower in metropolitan areas, nonmetropolitan areas, and surrounding counties (U.S. Environmental Protection Agency, 1984).

Despite the poverty that still permeates many reservations, some tribes have created new sources of wealth by establishing reservation casinos. The income generated from casinos is still unknown, but the interest from major financial backers has been strong. Donald Trump is courting a Native American tribe with the idea of building the world's largest casino in Manhattan. Other major casinos with luxury hotels are springing up around San Diego, San Francisco, and Seattle. The new wealth has left many lawmakers unsure how to address the windfall. In August 2000, the tribes of California sent $34.5 million to the state government. The State Attorney General, Bill Lockyer, the official most responsible for regulating gambling in the state, said he expected considerably less money than was submitted. He planned to begin an investigation into just how much the tribes were making (Morain, 2000).

Whatever the amount earned at the casinos, Native Americans are finding themselves in unfamiliar territory. In California, where Native American casinos have been rapidly expanding, the wealth that has been created has turned

Native Americans into a powerful political force. During the 2000 Democratic National Convention, tribes fielded a record number of delegates, hosting parties at glamorous locations (Tamaki, 2000). They have also contributed to local elections, with California tribes spending more than $100 million on state campaigns during their first two years of casino operations. Bill Lockyer (Morain, 2000) estimates that a casino with 2,000 slot machines could reap $219 million a year from those machines alone. These funds would be in addition to the money made from other forms of gambling, as well as revenues from hotels and restaurants.

The increased wealth of certain tribes has also led to ethical and spiritual introspection. Kathryn Gabriel (1998) writes that gambling has roots in most of the world's religions. She argues that in many archaeological records, dice is associated with the cycle of death and rebirth. In fact, it is even unclear whether game playing predates gambling as a recognized pastime. In the Bible, stories are told of decisions made by casting lots (e.g., Isaiah 34:17), and in Native American history, gambling had been present a thousand years before European contact. This is not to suggest, she cautions, that all Native Americans have historically viewed gambling as positive. The Navajos considered gambling taboo. A thorough examination of Native American beliefs, however, revealed that more than 100 surviving myths address gambling as means of bringing harmony to the cosmos, just as in ancient Hindu Mahabharata, gambling was a metaphor for balance in the continuum of death and rebirth. Gabriel concludes that while gambling creates vices, it should not be viewed as an evil in itself but as a form of spiritual seeking. Addictive gambling is only superficially the act of seeking economic fortune. It is also the process of seeking a personal transformation—a feeling of invincibility and liberation, even if only for a moment.

Regardless of the possible spiritual focus gambling might bring, the wealth created by gambling is likely to change Native Americans' economic status. In some states, provisions have been made for tribes without on-site gambling. In California, the tribes with casinos must pay $1.1 million a year to tribes without casinos. It is hoped that the creation of new jobs and wealth will also translate into higher educational attainment. At the moment, the academic statistics for Native Americans leave much room for improvement.

Education

> "Knowledge that is not used is abused." (Cree)

In the United States, Thanksgiving is traditionally a time to teach schoolchildren about "the Indians." In classrooms across the country, children are busily coloring pictures of Indians dressed in feathers and moccasins; singing "one little, two little, three little Indians," or making "Indian jewelry" out of macaroni and string. Teachers direct pupils to "sit like Indians" or "be quiet as Indians."

Pictures of a headdress-bedecked Indian chief on a pinto horse or of an Indian "squaw" with a "papoose" decorate the walls. It is not uncommon to even see ceilings covered with paper "tomahawks," hung precariously. The aesthetic value of genuine handicrafts is minimized, and students are left with a trivialized impression of Native American culture.

When educational institutions advance artificial views of Native American culture, history, and art, Native American children are likely to view their histories negatively. In part, this might explain some of the pitfalls of the Native American educational experience, but there are additional problems to address. Native American children begin their academic careers well, but they start to fall behind other ethnic groups when they approach the end of elementary/primary school (around the fourth grade). As students progress through school, they begin to believe that education has little to do with their lives (Wood & Clay, 1996). Their grades begin to fall, and they are more likely to drop out of school altogether. Of equal concern, incidents of violence or disruption increase around this time. Native Americans are more likely to receive suspensions and other disciplinary actions than their European American peers (Sue & Sue, 1999).

To keep Native American children from dropping out of school, the educational format may need to be modified. Native American children appear to benefit from different styles of teaching and learning (Guild, 1994). They generally value and develop acute visual discrimination, are skilled in the use of imagery, perceive facts globally, and rely on reflective thinking patterns. To incorporate these findings, effective teaching strategies for Native Americans should include providing quiet time for reflection and adopting an instructional approach that helps children understand the meaning behind a given task. The latter would go beyond teaching children "why" a particular subject is important. Instead, children would be encouraged to explore the topic, derive personalized meaning from it, and learn how to apply the knowledge in a specific context. In tribal environments, children have typically learned by interacting freely with adults. Bonds are established that help determine which individual can best instruct the child, and the activities made available to the child are specifically designed to develop his or her talents (Okakok, 1989).

European American schools do not incorporate these meaning-oriented learning styles. Even at the college level, learning is based on acquiring knowledge, rather than deriving meaning from that knowledge. This approach may be one of the reasons the majority of Native Americans avoid higher education (Boutte, 1999). When they do receive advanced training, it is often confined to the field of education (Lomawaima, 1995). There is a dire lack of Native American scientists.

Lack of accommodation to different learning styles and a failure to incorporate Native American values into the educational system have combined to produce frighteningly high dropout rates. Native Americans have the highest high school dropout rate of all ethnic groups in America (Kasten, 1992). Only half of the students entering kindergarten will complete their high school education. If they attend college, only about 8 percent (half of the national average)

will complete a four-year degree at an established institution of higher education (Lomawaima, 1995). Lack of educational attainment is not due to insufficient parental involvement. Goldenberg (1998) argued that Native American
parents want their children to do well in school and even encourage them to go
as far as possible. Such messages are especially important for Native
Americans, because an intergenerational cycle of poor educational experiences
and poverty may contribute to high rates of suicide and teenage pregnancy
(Keane, Dick, Bechtold, & Manson, 1996).

Recently, there have been signs of improvement. SAT scores for Native
Americans increased an average of 15 points between 1987 and 1997 (Boutte,
1999). This change raised them above African American and many Latino
American groups. These increases may foretell greater educational achievement in the coming decades. Further growth might come if schools and Native
American organizations continue to cooperate. Even the physical location of a
school can assist in this process. When schools are located on reservations,
Native American adolescents tend to form deeper friendships with members of
their own culture (Rice, 2001). Building a strong ethnic identity tends to
increase cultural pride by using the reservation communities as a resource for
classroom activities. Such an association between education and cultural development may lead to increased understanding of traditions, familiarity with cultural history, and feelings of ethnic pride.

Health

Native Americans have significantly higher mortality rates than the general
population. Suicide and homicide rates were especially high in the 1990s, as
were rates of death from tuberculosis, accidents, diabetes, flu, and pneumonia
(U.S. Department of Health and Human Services, 1997). However, two of the
greatest mortality threats for Native Americans are tobacco and alcohol abuse.
A survey commissioned in 1999 by MADD (Mothers Against Drunk Driving)
indicated that Native Americans are significantly more likely to die in alcohol-
related car crashes than their peers. Alcohol-related traffic deaths accounted for
73.2 percent of Native American traffic fatalities. The numbers were considerably lower for other groups. For example, only 27.1 percent of traffic fatalities
among Asian/Pacific Islanders involved alcohol consumption. European
Americans fell in the middle at 44.1 percent, and Latinos varied considerably
according to their countries of origin.

Among the biggest alcohol-related problems have been the effects of
underage drinking. Young Native Americans who abuse alcohol and other
drugs are at higher risk for weak family bonding, poor school adjustment, and
higher dropout rates (Swaim, Oetting, Thurman, Beauvais, & Edwards, 1993).
Such problems appear to be related to weak family sanctions and positive attitudes towards alcohol use within the family structure. Once the abuse occurs,
it will likely continue into adulthood and make it more difficult for a person to

find a job. There is also evidence suggesting that continued occupational problems are associated with the maintenance or exacerbation of substance abuse (Oetting, 1992). This reciprocal relationship between substance abuse and limited economic opportunities also contributes to community problems such as violence and discrimination.

Interventions for these health problems have traditionally been ineffective. Native Americans are likely to reject Western medical interventions and turn instead to healers who focus on the restoration of harmony in all life, including nonhuman spheres (Koss-Chioino, 1995). We will discuss this topic at greater length in the section on counseling issues.

Cultural Uniqueness

"The ground on which we stand is sacred ground. It is the blood of our ancestors." (From *Chief Plenty Coups*, Crow)

"A wee child toddling in a wonder world, I prefer to their dogma my excursions into the natural gardens where the voice of the Great Spirit is heard in the twittering of birds, the rippling of mighty waters, and the sweet breathing of flowers. If this is Paganism, then at present, at least, I am a Pagan." (Zitkala-Sa)

In many ways, the cultural distinctiveness of many Native American groups has been eradicated due to prejudice and intolerance. From the southern plains to the Native Alaskans, there have been systematic, federally funded efforts to sterilize members of Native American groups, remove them from their homelands, and force assimilation (Thurman, Swaim, & Plested, 1995). The hostility against Native Americans has appeared in countless ways, but the political arena is where their culture has been harmed the most. Although they were the original inhabitants of the land, Native Americans did not gain the right to vote as U.S. citizens until 1946 in Arizona and New Mexico, and they were viewed as savages requiring careful guidance from members of an "advanced" civilization.

Despite the animosity between European and Native groups, both sides continued to interact and learn from each other. Unfortunately, with one group having more power than the other, abuses were inevitable. Up until the 1960s, many church-affiliated boarding schools provided scholarships to Native Americans living on reservations. The Native students would interact with their European peers, which was viewed as a means of speeding acculturation. Some Native Americans tell stories of being terrorized by the White students and staff members. School administrators attempted to separate students from their cultural history by punishing them for speaking their own language, forcing them to receive extremely short haircuts, and denigrating their cultural traditions during classroom lessons (Thurman, Swaim, & Plested, 1995). Such experiences had a profound impact on the transmission of Native American culture. Although these institutional practices have been abandoned, they caused many Native Americans to become alienated from their cultural roots.

Native Americans have made some attempts to restructure themselves. After the Indian Reorganization Act of 1934, the federally recognized tribes formed coalitions and elected tribal chairpersons. Each community elects a council and appoints a leader. This leader works in concert with the council but is not technically a chief, which refers to a hereditary position (Kniffen, Gregory, & Stokes, 1987). The structure of the group is egalitarian in nature. The council strives for consensus and cannot act until near-total agreement has been achieved. This emphasis on consensus makes it one of the most democratic forms of government in America, but also one that appears chaotic and poorly managed to outsiders.

The structure of the reorganized tribes incorporates the communal functioning that permeates many Native American cultures. Interdependence is valued more highly than autonomy, and Native Americans are often unfamiliar with the idea of being expected to work autonomously. These communal elements have also been carried over into Native American religious practices, as will be discussed shortly. Two of the dominant religious movements among Native Americans are the Native American Church (a pan-Indian religion based on rituals that connect members with the Great Spirit) and Christian Pentecostalism (Koss-Chioino, 1995). The Native American Church, interestingly, was imported from Mexico in the last decades of the nineteenth century, but it also incorporates many cultural elements from various Native American tribes (Aberle, 1966). The religion involves peyote, pipe, and cigarette smoking to clear the mind. There are also drums, songs, and prayers, which are used to help purify individuals and restore them with their environment (Bergman, 1973). Many tribes perform ceremonies according to instructions given in sacred stories.

Some of the most important ceremonies are conducted at certain places at specific times of the year, such as solstices and equinoxes. There are ceremonies to heal the sick, renew relationships with spiritual beings, initiate people into religious societies, ensure success in hunting and growing crops, pray for rain, mark important life-cycle events in a person's life, and to give thanks for harvests. Some ceremonies are performed in order to ensure survival of the earth and all forms of life. During these rituals, healing techniques are performed to address tribe members' physical, psychological, and spiritual needs, including ailments such as alcohol addiction. One traditional technique involves bringing the needy individual into the center of a ring. The other members sing and pray, attempting to draw out the evil spirits that reside in the needy soul. Other rituals involve conversion experiences or vision quests that occur as the result of taking peyote. In these cases, the individual may experience a revelation and then a physical purging that will remove the individual's sins. Such an experience often creates clear moral injunctions regarding marital fidelity, restraint from vengeance, and abstinence from alcohol (Koss-Chioino, 1995). In all of these activities, the religious transcendence rarely occurs while the individual is alone. It is a group process, often involving family members and significant friends.

The interconnectedness between Native Americans also extends to a perceived bond with the environment. Nowhere was this belief stated more eloquently than when Chief Seattle replied to President Franklin Pierce's request to purchase Indian land. In 1854, the great Chief wrote that the sky and the warmth of the land cannot be purchased, because every shining pine needle, every sandy shore, every mist in the woods, every clearing and humming insect is holy in the memory and experience of Native Americans. The shining water that moves in streams and rivers is not just water but the blood of the ancestors.

The chief added that if the tribe decided to sell the land, the White Americans would have to hold it sacred and teach their children to respect its mysteries. As an example, the rivers are our brothers. They quench our thirst, carry our canoes, and feed our children. As such, they deserve the kindness we would give to any brother. Similarly, the earth is our mother and the ground beneath our feet is the ashes of our grandfathers. For these reasons, the earth does not belong to man; man belongs to the earth. Whatever befalls the earth also befalls the sons of the earth. If men spit upon the ground, they spit upon themselves and their children.

The chief also added that the White man does not understand this position, and views the earth not as his brother but as an enemy. It is simply something to be conquered and discarded. He leaves his father's graves behind, and he does not care. He kidnaps the earth from his children, and he does not care. His father's grave and his children's birthright are forgotten. He treats his mother, the earth, and his brother, the sky, as things to be bought, plundered, and sold like sheep or bright beads. His appetite will devour the earth and leave behind only a desert.

Although these comments are understandable, given what Chief Seattle must have observed, a more accurate view of European Americans might be that they viewed the world in terms of causal connections and linear chronology. Traditional Native American philosophy stresses the idea of continuity and the continuous renewal, by each new generation, of certain values that cannot be made redundant by myths of technological change and material amelioration (Brookeman, 1990). A person is respected not for possessing great wealth, but for giving to others. Value is placed on giving, and a person who tries to accumulate goods is often feared.

Chief Seattle's leadership resulted in the naming of a city after him. A bronze statue has been erected to commemorate this fact, and each year, the Boy Scouts hold a memorial ceremony at his tomb. One of the reasons Chief Seattle gained recognition from White Americans is that he attempted to understand their culture. Missionaries converted him to Catholicism in the 1830s, and his actions made him appear conciliatory. In 1855, he was the first signer of the Port Elliott Treaty, by which the Washington tribes were given a reservation. The Suquamish were allied with several smaller tribes in what is now Washington and Oregon. In many ways, it seems that Seattle knew what it took generations for European Americans to understand—that all people are brothers and sisters.

In many ways, Native Americans who attempted to understand "White" culture have felt that their own values have been overlooked, ignored, or denigrated. Take, for instance, the Native American understanding of time. Sweezy (1967), in his memoirs of the early twentieth century, wrote that the Cheyenne and the Arapaho viewed time differently from the Europeans. Rather than measure the minutes in a day, they would simply enjoy the day. They were more concerned with larger blocks of times such as seasons than with the intricate details of minutes and seconds. In some ways, these trends continue today. Many tribes have no word for time; there is no need to be punctual or "on time" because there is always plenty of time in an individual's life for necessary tasks. To be occupied with things and events too far into the future is to invite trouble and threats to those future plans. These value statements are reflected in the concept of "Indian time," which means that a meeting set for 8:00 may not start until 10:00. Native Americans are more likely to finish an important chore than to arbitrarily shift their attention to a new task simply because an hour has passed.

As in working with members of other cultural groups, discovering the level of acculturation is often essential in knowing when and how to intervene. Sue and Sue (1999) recommend that therapists assess the acculturation of Native Americans across four domains:

- *Cognitive:* What is their understanding of their native culture, languages, and customs?
- *Behavioral:* Do they participate in tribal or European American activities, groups, or clubs?
- *Affective/spiritual:* Are they connected with the spiritual identity of their tribe or with European American churches?
- *Social/environmental:* Do they believe their method of blending in with their environment fits better with traditional or European American values?

The ways in which clients answer these questions will reflect the degree to which they understand and identify with their own culture, as well as the extent to which they incorporate elements of the dominant culture.

One of the ways in which Native American culture is passed down is through the stories told at tribal gatherings. Native American histories, cultural traditions, and laws have been passed on by storytelling. The stories explain how the people first came into being, how the sun, moon, stars, rainbows, sunsets, sky, thunder, lakes, mountains, and other natural occurrences came about. Tribal stories explain the origin of landmarks, plants, and animals. Some stories tell about the hazards of greed, selfishness, or boastfulness. The stories often give practical advice such as techniques for hunting or fishing, and some include recipes for healing potions, or describe how to find the right root or herb. They teach laws and the consequences for violating them. Some stories are so sacred and powerful that they are treated with special respect: for example, creation stories are often recited in a ritual way and told in a serious manner. They have been passed on for hundreds of years or more, and their continuation is threatened by encroachments of the dominant culture (Hirschfelder, 2000).

The Chipewyan tell a story of a primordial woman who lived alone in a cave. One night, a mysterious being in the shape of a dog crept into the cave and lay down beside her. Gradually the creature began to change form. His limbs grew straight, his skin became smooth, and he was soon transformed into a handsome youth. Nine months later a child was born. The child was the first Chipewyan. The story is told to explain why the Chipewyan should treat dogs with special respect.

Most cultures also tell stories linked to daily living experiences and the dangers that stem from certain desires. The Ojibway of Northern Minnesota have a story about two foolish girls who longed to sleep outside of the lodge under the stars. One night, they crept outside and began to imagine what it might be like to make love to a star. "They must be good lovers," one girl said to the other. They fell asleep, and when they awoke they found themselves in the sky surrounded by stars, male stars. One of the stars spoke, saying, "You wanted us—well, here we are." After a while the girls realized that star husbands were not as much fun as they had imagined. All the husbands did was eat star food, make love, and shine. The girls could peer down at earth and watch their friends from the tribe playing games, so they asked their husbands to help them go home by letting them down on long ropes made from plants. The two girls swore never to sleep outside the lodge again.

Psychological Issues

One of the problems that Native Americans face is the pressure to conform to the European American view of reality. Consider Black Bird, who believes that a spirit appeared in the form of a vulture that perched on her window. She views the bird's arrival as a warning to avoid traveling outside for the rest of the day. Her therapist, a European American, asks for more details about the nature of these visions and whether she sees them on a regular basis. Black Bird explains that in her youth, she was closed to the wisdom of the spirits, but after using her dream catcher she was able to bring some of the images into her awakened mind. Her therapist diagnosed her visions as an emerging thought disorder and recommended her for psychiatric treatment. The assumption was made that Black Bird's hallucinations were a sign of mental illness.

Many Native Americans have suffered because they have been misunderstood and wrongly diagnosed. The standard categories of depression, anxiety, and personality problems may not fit Native Americans because of their strong corporate identity. There is, however, one psychological issue that overshadows all others: suicide. The suicide rate among American Indians is double the national average, and alcohol is involved in more than 90 percent of successful suicides (Johnson, 1994). Additionally, the culture of individualism brought by the Europeans is positively associated with Native American suicide rates (Lester, 1997), which supports other data suggesting that suicide rates are positively associated with acculturation stress and negatively associated with ethnic pride (Lester, 1999).

Marlene EchoHawk (1997) suggested that forced education and legislative acts concerning territory have weakened and fragmented tribal unity by erecting language barriers, undermining parental influence, introducing nontraditional religions, and uprooting tribes from their lands. Such factors have robbed young Native Americans of tribal mechanisms for coping with adversities such as the death of a loved one. Instead of drawing strength from tradition, they are forced to seek understanding on their own, without a foundational belief structure or support group. Communities that have taken active steps to preserve and rehabilitate their own cultures have dramatically lowered youth suicide rates (Chandler & Lalonde, 1998).

Economic hardship also leads to suicidality, but here, the correlation is more complex. Lester (1996) argues that American Indian suicide and homicide rates were not associated with unemployment rates, and some Native American groups with the highest poverty rates (especially the Navajo) have the lowest suicide rates (Young, 1990). But this is not the whole story. Young and French (1996) found that "absolute poverty" and suicide were highly significant, but "relative poverty" did not have a significant effect on suicide rates. Similarly, data collected from the 48 contiguous states in 1980 showed that the suicide rate among Native Americans was higher in states where a greater percentage of the population was Native American and impoverished (Lester, 1994). The effect of this communal abject poverty is profound. In fact, when groups of urban, middle-class Native Americans are studied, there is no difference between their suicide rates and those of other ethnic groups (Shiang, 1998).

Within-Group Differences

> "All birds, even those of the same species, are not alike, and it is the same with animals and with human beings." (Sioux)

Most Native Americans identify themselves according to tribal membership. Within the United States, however, we have generally used the terms "Indian," "American Indian," and "Alaska Native" to designate the original inhabitants of this continent. The diversity among various tribes is vast, with populations ranging from large groups such as the Navajos of Arizona and New Mexico who number more than 160,000, to communities of less than 100, like the Chumash of California and the Modocs of Oklahoma (Brookeman, 1990). Typically, the tribal groups are clustered together geographically, creating five major groups: the tribes of the eastern woodlands, the tribes of the plains, the tribes of the southwest, the tribes of the northwest, and the peoples of the far north (which includes all of Canada and Alaska).

Tribes vary in aspects such as appearance, clothing, customs, ceremonies, family roles, child-rearing practices, beliefs, and attitudes (Thurman, Swaim, & Plested, 1995). There are currently 500 federally recognized tribes, each with practices so diverse that it would be impossible to address them all adequately here. There are key differences, however, that can help students understand some of the subtle distinctions between groups. For example, within the peoples of the far north, language differences tend to create problems for outsiders. The word Eskimo, as used by Northern Indians, means "eaters of raw meat" (Axelson, 1999). Instead of this term, Northern Indians call themselves Inuit, while Siberian Eskimos call themselves Yuit. There are also Aleuts, who live in Alaska but have a distinctly different culture and language system. The Aleuts also have a distinct history of abuse, as they were exploited by Russian traders during World War II and sent to prison by the Japanese who invaded portions of the Aleutian Islands. Table 5.1 provides a list of some of the different Native American groups, but it should be clear that a comprehensive list would be quite massive, with overlaps between the various categories.

Alvin Josephy (1973) identified four factors that determined a tribe's home, clothing, food, and customs:

- *Climate:* If the climate was cold, the home needed to be sturdy and clothing needed to be heavy, such as animal fur or hide. Warm climates led to well-ventilated houses and lightweight clothing.

- *Availability of materials:* In the southwest, where trees were not available, the Indians became skilled in using mud, brush, and sod in the construction of their homes. Also, the Indians of the Great Basin lived in a very dry area that did not permit farming, so they gathered wild plants and hunted for their food.

- *Length of time a group would stay in an area:* The Indians of the northeast were farmers and there was plenty of game for hunting. Consequently, their homes were sturdy longhouses made of wood, and often 100 or more houses were built together and surrounded by a stockade. Nomadic tribes of the plains lived in homes made of poles and animal hides because they were easy to put up, take down, and carry.

- *Customs:* Some Plains Indians wore feathers to indicate position, bravery, and respect. In some tribes acquiring wealth was important. Shells were strung on a cord and worn around the neck or waist by members of tribes of the northeast. Such adornment, called wampum, was used as

TABLE 5.1 *Tribes of the Americas*

Area	*Groups/Tribes*	*Belief Systems*
Peoples of the far north	The groups include the Alaskan Eskimos, Aleuts (who live mostly in Alaska and the Aleutian Islands), and Yuit (Siberian Eskimos).	All animals and objects in nature have spirits and should be revered for their life-giving qualities. Each object in nature has a specific purpose; e.g., bears can possess a spirit and help lead a person to food. These groups also have a history of training shamans (healers) who are believed to have the ability to predict the future.
Tribes of the eastern woodlands	The Iroquois Nation (a cluster of five tribes formed in the 1500s), Cherokee, Chickasaw, Choctaw, Creek, Natchez, Seminole, Fox, Illinois, Menominee, Miami, Potawatomi, Sauk, Shawnee, and Winnebago tribes.	This was the first group to encounter the Europeans. Their area spans from the Northeastern coast of America to the Southeast. They operated from a highly organized and systematic theology. It included a struggle between light and dark, good and ill fortune. These spiritual forces guided the universe and led their followers to survival.
Tribes of the plains	From the Mississippi River on the east to the Rocky Mountains on the west, and from the U.S./Canadian border to Mexico, these groups flourished with the introduction of horses by the Spaniards. Groups include the Arapaho, Blackfoot, Cheyenne, Comanche, Crow, Pawnee, and various Sioux.	Despite being characterized in movies as aggressive hunters, most of these tribes were agrarian. When they did hunt, they usually hunted the buffalo, who was provided by the Earth Mother as food for believers. Many of the tribes were nearly forced into extinction when European settlers brought smallpox and cholera to their areas. Most of these tribes were later relocated to Nebraska and Oklahoma. These groups are also the ones responsible for the famous "Ghost Dance."
Tribes of the Pacific Northwest and the Great Basin Area	These tribes survived on the West Coast for more than a thousand years. War with the U.S. government, smallpox, starvation, and overdependence on the Spaniards destroyed most of these tribes.	Wealth and social status were measured by material possessions (such as blankets, canoes, tools, etc.). Today, the homeland of these tribes is governed by some of the wealthiest citizens in America.
Tribes of the Southwest	This is a semi-desert region that includes Arizona, Colorado, New Mexico, Utah, and northern Mexico. Tribes include the Apache, Cochimi, Navajo, Papago, Pima, Pueblo, Yaqui, and Yuma.	The prevalent beliefs and rituals of these groups include the Pueblo rain festivals, which reflect a strong association between human action and nature. The Navajos were also known for their shamans or medicine men/women.

Note: Table 5.1 was created using information from J. A. Axelson (1999), *Counseling and Development in a Multicultural Society*. Pacific Grove, CA: Brooks/Cole Publishing Company.

money or as a symbol of a promise made to another person. The Zuni and Hopi of the southwest built a kiva in their pueblos for religious ceremonies. Homes of the Great Basin were small because only a single family lived in each one, whereas a pueblo was large enough to house many families.

The stereotype of American Indians as warriors wearing feathers and riding horses can be applied to only a very small group living in the Midwestern United States. Even among these groups, the horse became part of the culture only after it was introduced by Spanish immigrants.

The existing Native American groups are less diverse today than they were a hundred years ago. When young Native Americans were forced into boarding schools and prohibited from speaking their native languages, many lost part of their corporate identity. Today, only about 20 of the 175 existing Native American languages spoken in the United States are being passed down from mother to child, and about 300 to 400 languages have already been lost forever (Brooke, 1998). For some tribes, traditional knowledge can be fully communicated only in the tribal language, because there is no easy way to translate it into English. The loss of language has a profound effect on the maintenance of Native American culture.

Counseling Issues

Little is known about building effective mental health interventions for Native Americans, because most of the literature addresses treatment programs for drug and alcohol abuse rather than individual psychotherapy (Sue, Chun, & Gee, 1995). This literature indicates that prevention programs have greater demonstrated efficacy than treatment programs (LaFromboise, Trimble, & Mohatt, 1990). A fact that is known, but often hard to accept among non-Native therapists, is that Native American attitudes toward people are not usually contingent upon a person's role or status in the community. An individual's title, power, authority, or influence in a private or governmental organization does not determine the respect Native Americans will bestow. The character traits of the individual, rather than the prestige of the entity that the person represents, are instrumental in establishing rapport and cooperation. Building rapport will take time and patience, but the bonds created are likely to be stronger. The relationship is also more likely to be sustained if the therapist shows a desire to involve the client's family.

Among Hopi and Navajo groups, multigenerational interventions may require special skills and knowledge. In many cases, the services of a skilled translator will be needed (Aponte & Morrow, 1995). With Native American families, it is also important to include community resources. The therapist may want to involve traditional healers, clan leaders, village chiefs, or other tribal leaders.

Dexheimer-Pharris, Resnick, and Blum (1997) examined information collected on 13,923 Native American children. They wanted to learn how to help sexually abused youths recover from feelings of hopelessness and depression. Their discriminant function analysis revealed that different factors were helpful for girls and boys. Family attention, positive feelings toward school, parental expectations, and caring exhibited by family, adults, and tribal leaders were associated with absence of suicidality and hopelessness in girls. For suicidality in boys, significant protective factors for suicide (but not for hopelessness) were enjoyment of school, involvement in traditional activities, strong academic performance, and caring exhibited by family, adults, teachers, school administrators, and tribal leaders.

The efficacy of bonding with tribal leaders in preventing suicide and assisting recovery implies that community interventions should be explored. Native American healing practices such as the sweat lodge and talking circles operate under the notion that wellness involves maintaining a balance between the spiritual, physical, and mental/emotional "selves." The sweat lodge ceremony is an example of how these three forces can be melded into a single treatment process.

For the Ojibway, the sweat lodge ritual became popularized after alcoholism threatened their way of life. Drunkenness, unknown to Native groups prior to the influx of Europeans, brought about abusive behaviors that had never before been seen in native cultures. Wife and child abuse became rampant, and the Ojibway desperately needed to find their way back to traditional ways of living. In the sweat lodge, not only could tribe members draw out the poison of alcohol but they could also address the behaviors associated with drunkenness. By means of intense heat and steam, toxins were physically sweated out of the body. Medicine Men and Women also helped to repair the damage done to people's spirits. The lodge was not only a place of refuge and healing but also a mechanism to obtain answers and guidance from spiritual entities, totem helpers, the Creator, and Mother Earth.

The sweat lodge, like most Native American traditions, involves a sense of community and belonging. Such practices de-emphasize the presence of personal or individual guilt and instead address the notion of a corporate sense of shame. Statements such as, "You did not act like a Paiute" are commonly used to help redirect the individual toward behaving in a way that matches the values of the group. Disciplinary practices among Native American groups often include shaming an individual, but this is a temporary process. Once the shaming punishment is executed, the individual releases the guilt and the group forgets the transgression.

Therapists focusing on their client's shame must provide a mechanism for release. In many cases, this requires an intervention from a community agency (e.g., a medicine man). It should also be noted that Native Americans tend to view healing as a long-term process. Time is the great friend of Native Americans, and there is no need to rush the cycle. In generating a healing process, Lewis, Duran, and Woodis (1999) argue for the use of rituals and prayer in the therapeutic encounter, as well as the therapeutic use of synchronous events.

Thier (1999) has integrated vision quests and counseling into what he calls a "Dream Quest." This hybrid technique provides a forum for modern encounters with the Great Spirit. Rather than requiring the participant to spend days alone in the wilderness with little or no shelter, clothing or food, this approach can be carried out in the comfort of home. The practice involves a form of narrative exploration. The individual thinks of himself or herself as a spiritual warrior battling the demons and encountering the angels inside the soul or psyche. The sacred or holy place, according to this model, is not necessarily outside the body, but can be a place within the innermost corners of the mind.

Although the dream quest may be a symbolic exercise in survival, it still requires the individual to focus on the outside world. The questor must create a highly sensitive state of bodily awareness and feel the connection he or she shares with nature and all living things. Bodily states of emptiness and weakness often give rise to issues about personal survival, and moving through these fears reveals unexpected sources of strength and power.

Focusing on restorative or healing interventions is usually preferred to solving diagnostic problems, especially early in the therapeutic process. In some ways, clinical interventions, wrought with diagnoses and labeling, can push clients away from the cultural healing processes. Winona Simms (1999) tells the story of Alita, a 27-year-old Native American woman who sought out guidance from her university counseling center. Late in her childhood, Alita had moved in with loving, European American foster parents, but her bicultural background and growing lack of self-confidence eventually led to social and academic problems.

The therapists attempted to merge contemporary psychotherapy (cognitive behavioral approach) with traditional Native healing. Alita's problems appeared to stem from alcohol dependence, but the initial focus was not on diagnosis or pathology. Instead, Alita was given information about depression, alcoholism, and meditation. She also engaged in "cultural strengthening," which involved participation in the talking circle and sweats. As her participation in these forums increased, she expressed a greater sense of spiritual awareness and felt more in touch with her American Indian identity. With her self-concept improving, Alita was referred to support groups in her community for people dealing with alcohol abuse. Simms argues that the delayed focus on diagnostic issues helped Alita build a new lifestyle that made it easier for her to cope with her alcoholism. Had her therapists emphasized diagnostic concerns at the outset of treatment, Alita would have lacked the necessary skills to create lasting change.

Culturally sensitive interventions, such as the one used for Alita, appear to have the best success rates. Integrating tactics such as a sweat lodge with traditional psychotherapeutic interventions also has yielded success for Native Americans wrestling with substance abuse (Gutierres & Todd, 1997). The success of such programs depends upon the creation of a nonaccusatory format, together with an emphasis on ideas over feelings. The latter element led Trimble and LaFromboise (1987) to argue that person-centered approaches are typically ill advised for Native American clients. Instead, other nondirective approaches, such as those involving cultural activities, the telling of myths, and psychodrama may be more appropriate. For example, with Alita we could follow up the tribal intervention with a psychological exploration, as illustrated below.

Therapist:	Let's talk about the last vision you had in the sweat lodge.
Alita:	Okay, I was lying on my back, and I looked up and saw a bear in the clouds. I remember thinking, "This is cool." I waited for a few seconds, and the bear started to move. It sailed toward another cloud, I think it looked like a fish, or something. Soon, they became one cloud and then joined the rest of the sky.
Therapist:	Wow, you haven't talked about anything like this before. I would imagine the images had a huge effect on you. The bear is often a symbol of power, maternal cunning, healing, gentle strength, and dreaming. Do you think your vision fit into one of these categories?
Alita:	Well, I thought it seemed strange, but it did seem like a gentle strength. It moved so slowly but it never wavered.
Therapist:	I would imagine that is how you have started to see yourself and your progress with drinking and depression. You are moving slowly and steadily, like the young bear cloud. You know, sometimes a fish is viewed as a symbol of persistence and determination. The salmon must swim for great distances to reach its final destination. Maybe the gentle strength and determination have been merging in you?
Alita:	I don't know. Maybe. I would like to believe that. If nothing else, it is something to hope for.

No matter what approach is attempted, the intervention is not likely to be successful until trust has been sufficiently developed (Sue & Sue, 1999). Developing trust might require therapists to change their tactics. Early in the intervention, therapists should be slow to speak and careful not to interrupt the client. Putting pressure on the client to reveal information too quickly may be viewed as reflecting a lack of respect or an attempt to dominate or control the client. For some clients, there may also be problems operating within the confines of an hour. It may help the client, at least in the early phases of therapy, to meet with the therapist until the topic has been sufficiently addressed, within reason. Providing an extra five or ten minutes may help to strengthen the working alliance and increase client commitment.

If you decide to integrate a specific ceremony into your session, remember that many Native American ceremonies follow a consistent pattern. Lonegren

(1996) argued that Native American ceremonies are intrinsically flexible and vary to meet the needs of the Spirit. But there is a beginning, middle, and end to the events. The process usually contains the following:

- *Purification:* This is a good beginning because of its focus on removing impurities and other spiritual elements that could hamper successful connection with an individual's or group's goals. In some ceremonies, a feather is used to brush down the aura and to sweep away bits of psychological or spiritual trash. Incense may also be used to cleanse the aura. Even one's sitting posture may have an effect on the cleansing process. Some Native Americans honor the four directions east, south, west, and north with burning sage. Another possibility is to have a guided meditation where each participant imagines a ball of light expanding outward until it sweeps away all impurities.
- *Invocation:* At this stage, the individual asks the Creator for help. Often, there is a ritual associated with this request, such as lighting a candle in the center of a circle.
- *Receiving:* As the divine elements enter the group or individual, there is a time of slowly receiving spiritual power. A time of slowly building the energy is often evidenced through chanting, moving in place, simple repetitive songs, dancing, clapping, or playing instruments such as drums, pipes, or rattles. There is a cycle involved in this process as well. Usually, the slow pace builds until it reaches a certain pitch, then it falls, only to be rebuilt to a higher level the second time. This is repeated several times, each time reaching higher levels to symbolize rising toward a spiritual climax.
- *Giving:* When the spiritual energy has been internalized, it can then be used for healing, not just for the self but for the world. The energy is believed to be so great that thoughts of peace can help heal a troubled world. Creating visions of healing light can surround and assist friends in need. In a less metaphysical sense, the energy can be given back to the Earth and Sky, which grounds the individual and helps the process occur more easily the next time. Gardening, hunting, painting, sewing, or working with one's hands can help heal the body and the soul.

Although some of these elements would be impractical as part of a counseling session, therapists can use the structure of the ceremony to harmonize therapy with cultural rituals. The ideas of purification, healing, acceptance, and giving are all valid psychological constructs that, when specifically associated with ritual, may help Native Americans view the therapeutic process more positively.

Spirituality is seldom brought into the counseling environment, but a basic understanding of the earthly, cyclical elements of Native American religions can help therapists understand the issues that are fundamentally important for many clients. These issues are readily apparent in the case of Little Dove, whose pride, sensitivity, and longing for her people are obvious. Such issues are common themes among Native Americans. Even though she had lived in poverty as a child, she speaks fondly of being with the land. Living within White society, she prays her children will one day understand their heritage. Such views suggest the importance of therapist sensitivity to Indian pride.

Little Dove's Story

I have been living among the White people for almost 20 years now. My husband, a White man, fell in love with me and lived on the reservation for three years to win my heart. I could not deny him. Most people think of my children as White, but I hope my daughter and son will one day look beneath their skin to the spirit inside. I still long for the land of my grandparents.

When I was growing up, I used to play under a tree behind my parents' house. We had fastened an old tire to it, and I would swing for hours, just feeling the spirit of the breeze on my cheek. My grandfather once came out and told me that the tree I loved was partly responsible for my birth.

"Why, grandfather?" I asked with curiosity.

"Because it was under this tree that your grandmother's spirit first spoke to me." He rubbed his cheek, as if feeling the warmth of her spirit around him. "Years ago, I made a bench and placed it right here. It is the bench we now use for our meals. When your grandmother and I were very young, we would sit on the bench and feel the spirits, just as you have been doing today. Sometimes, we would talk. Sometimes, we would only feel each other's presence and our love for this land. So, you see, Little Dove, your love for this place has a reason and a purpose."

Whenever my family journeys out to the reservation with me, I always spend time under my grandfather's tree. To the chagrin of my children, I sometimes sit for an hour gazing at the beauty of the desert and remembering the love of my grandfather. I could stay longer, but usually *my* children come to me complaining of being bored. "There is nothing to do here," they protest. By that, I'm sure they mean there is no electricity for boom boxes, no television for video games, no computer for surfing the Net. Usually, I can't respond to their sadness. I just sigh and motion for them to sit with me, which they never do. Hopefully, my grandfather's spirit will speak to them one day and they will appreciate the history under their feet. It is what made them.

Questions to Consider

1. The treatment of Native Americans has been referred to as "the American holocaust." Is this statement accurate? If so, what role might the government take in compensating Native Americans for their losses?

2. Does the Battle of Wounded Knee represent an American massacre, or do both groups simply misunderstand the events that took place?

3. Native Americans traditionally held women in high regard. How does the practice of the moon lodge reflect women's status? How do you think the dominant American society would view this practice?

4. Many Native American tribes stand to earn considerable income through tribal casinos. Given this fact, is their view regarding the spirituality of gambling most likely rationalization, or does the act of gambling hold secrets to self-development?

5. Native American children generally value and develop acute visual discrimination and imagery skills, perceive facts globally, and use reflective thinking patterns. How could the curriculum in America's schools be changed to emphasize these strengths? Should such changes be implemented?

6. Young Native Americans who abuse drugs and alcohol are at higher risk for weak family bonding, poor school adjustment, and higher dropout rates. What can be done to reverse this trend?

7. During some religious rituals, tribal members receive healing for physical, psychological, and spiritual needs, including ailments such as alcoholism. One traditional technique involves bringing the needy individual into the center of a ring. The other members sing and pray, attempting to draw out the evil spirits that reside in the needy soul. Would such a practice be wise to incorporate into group counseling? Why or why not?

8. Many tribes have no word for time. They see no need to be punctual or "on time" because they believe there is always plenty of time in an individual's life for necessary tasks. How would you demonstrate cultural sensitivity to a client who was making genuine progress during a counseling session? Would you end the session on time or continue into the next hour?

9. The suicide epidemic among Native Americans has been attributed to alcohol abuse, poverty, boredom, and family breakdown. Which of these factors do you believe to be the most salient? What interventions should be made to reverse the trend?

10. The sweat lodge, along with most Native American traditions, involves a sense of community and belonging. What do you believe are the most healing elements of the ritual?

11. No matter what approach is attempted, none is likely to be successful until trust has been sufficiently developed. What therapeutic tactics might need to be altered in order to establish trust with Native American clients?

6

European Americans

INSIGHT EXERCISE All my life, I wanted to be a fireman. When I was young, I used to run around with the garden hose and put out pretend fires on the grass. I still have the junior fireman's badge I earned in third grade. It just seemed like the perfect life for me.

I am a fireman now, but I'm not sure I will ever make captain, as my father did. Maybe I should have been born ten years ago. I think my skills would have been better appreciated then. In 1993, I was told that I was not going to be promoted because 11 African American and four Latino candidates were scheduled to be promoted ahead of me. Now, they did not score higher on the exam. They were being promoted because there weren't enough minority captains in the Chicago Fire Department. I remember feeling stunned and thinking, "Surely this can't happen in America!"

I rallied with some of the other White candidates, and we took our case all the way to the Supreme Court. But on November 9, 1998, the Supreme Court refused to hear our appeal. No comment was offered. Our request was simply and quietly denied. I don't think I should be given anything just because I'm White, but neither does it seem fair to punish me because my skin is light.

Should we protect White employees from reverse discrimination, or must we first allow minorities to obtain managerial positions in order to level the playing field?

A number of problems arise when discussing the cultural group commonly referred to as "White." Like Asians, Latinos, and other groups, "White" Americans are a diverse group whose origins may be Western European, Eastern European, Arab, Jewish, South American, Australian, or other nationalities. A total of 53 categories of ethnic groups are identified by the term "White." With a group this diverse, any collective term is likely to lose the cultural distinctiveness of the various facets represented. Nevertheless, some terms are more accurate than others.

One of the terms that has been used to identify White Americans is "Anglo-Saxon." This term technically refers to a culture that began in fifth-century England. It was during this time that the fragmented kingdoms of England united to fight the invading Germanic tribes. These events paved the way for the emergence of a common language (Old English), which is represented in such documents as the *Anglo-Saxon Chronicle* and *Beowulf*. Even the term "England" comes from the union of the Old English word "Engla" (Angles) and land, meaning "land of the Angles." For obvious reasons, referring to all White Americans as Anglo or Anglo-Saxon could be considered offensive by those who are not of English descent. The term Anglo American should be reserved for those who speak English as a primary language and adhere to a cultural heritage that is primarily English in nature.

In this text, we use the term "European American" in reference to the broad category of "White" Americans. Although this term excludes Arab and Jewish individuals, it includes those Americans whose descendants emigrated from any European nation. Thus, it permits categorization on the basis of ancestry rather than skin color. Even with this arbitrary construct, members of this group have the privilege of identifying with a specific ancestry (e.g., English) or simply referring to themselves as "White" or "American" (Waters, 1998). It is this latter impulse that often leaves European Americans confused about diversity training. They may say, "Why do we need all of these terms? Why can't we all just be Americans?" The answer rests with the connection between European Americans and the dominant culture. They can call themselves "American" without any prefix because they wrongly believe that they have the same culture as an Asian American, African American, or Latino. European Americans find it easy to blend into a variety of settings because they are part of the dominant group, not necessarily because their culture is "American."

If the culture of European Americans differs from that of other groups, what constitutes European American culture? In answering this question, it is important to realize that European Americans have not been immune to persecution.

History of Oppression

Of all the "White" groups who have suffered oppression, no persecution has been greater than that of the Jews and Gypsies (members of a dark Caucasoid people originating in northern India but living principally in Europe). The Holocaust of the Second World War testifies to humanity's ability to dehumanize a cultural group. But even more importantly, it serves as a reminder that similarities in ethnicity can be overlooked if certain differences are highlighted.

Adolf Hitler's persecution of the Jews in Germany began a month after he became chancellor at the beginning of 1933. Jewish businesses were boycotted and soon vandalized, and Jewish personnel were dismissed from local governments, law courts, and universities. Between 1933 and 1938, Hitler succeeded in undermining the political and economic foundations of German Jewry. His attack focused not on the religious beliefs of individuals but on their ethnic origins. Nazi definitions of Jewry included thousands of German Christians with Jewish ancestry. The 1935 Nuremberg laws robbed Jews of their citizenship and forbade them to intermarry with other Germans. By 1939, as World War II began, Jews had lost their citizenship. They were no longer permitted to attend public schools, engage in many businesses, own land, associate with non-Jews, or frequent parks, libraries, or museums.

At the notorious Wannsee Conference, on January 20, 1942, Nazi bureaucrats met to discuss the "final solution of the Jewish question." They decided to systematically evacuate Jews from the countries in occupied Europe to camps in the East, where they would be "treated accordingly." Some would be exterminated outright (although the word *extermination* was not used officially), and others would be organized into huge labor battalions. Exhausting work, poor living conditions, and meager food would ultimately lead to the death of survivors or their selection for extermination. The total number of Jews killed by the Nazis during the war is estimated at 5,700,000. This figure includes some 2,950,000 Jews who lived in Poland, about 1,050,000 in the Soviet Union, and approximately 560,000 in Hungary. In addition to Jews, as many as 400,000 Gypsies perished in the Holocaust.

The memory of the Holocaust has faded for many Americans, and anti-Semitism continues to permeate our culture. Even groups who are struggling under oppression from the dominant society can become instigators of hostile acts against other minority groups. A poignant example of this attitude occurred in 1994 when a group of minority high school students in Oakland, California, watched Steven Spielberg's epic film, *Schindler's List*. As the movie depicted Jews being slaughtered, raped, starved, and tortured, members of the young audience began to laugh and cheer (Britt, 1994). Demonstrations of this nature are nearly as tragic as the Holocaust itself, and they dampen the optimistic view that humanity has risen above such behaviors.

While travesties of justice have occurred (and continue to occur) to Jews, Bosnians, Czechoslovakians, and other groups, European Americans are often considered to be free from oppression because they are members of the dominant group. Such a perspective, however, is incorrect. In America, European Americans were the first immigrants, and they were able to influence the way later groups of immigrants were treated. In 1820, 80 percent of the 9.2 million immigrants to America were of European descent. Scandinavians, English, French, Italians, Scots, Germans, Poles, Czechs, and Dutch made their way to the New World, and each wave of immigrants brought something of their culture with them. As other cultures were assimilated into American society, a new, pluralistic culture was created. The immigrants from Europe often belonged to the lower class in their homelands, but America provided them with opportunities to form a new identity. They proudly called themselves

"Americans," but many found that the New World did not offer economic prosperity to all.

Prior to the Civil War, a great disparity began to appear between various groups of European immigrants. German workers were often recruited to come to America because of their fine craftsmanship. These workers included silversmiths, clockmakers, and other tradesmen who quickly found employment. The Irish, however, during the same time period often moved to America to escape poverty and famine. Many lacked professional skills and were forced to take the lowest-paying jobs available, working as ditch diggers, railroad laborers, or servants (McFadden, 1999). The economic successes or failures of first-generation immigrants were often passed down to members of succeeding generations, creating a hierarchy that would continue for more than a hundred years.

Family

Although the violence perpetrated on certain groups of European Americans should not be overlooked, neither should we ignore the privileged status this group enjoys in American and European societies. In many ways, the treatment of European Americans as a group determines or at least predicts their functioning within subgroups such as the family. For instance, the role of physical discipline tends to differ between European Americans and members of other cultures, especially African Americans. Whaley (2000) reviewed the literature related to the developmental consequences of the use of physical discipline during childhood for European Americans and African Americans. As mentioned in Chapter 2, the use of physical discipline was associated with an increased incidence of disruptive disorders in children within European American families, but research on African American families found a negative association or none at all (Larzelere, 2000). Moreover, a review of the literature indicates that the positive association between spanking and children's behavioral problems is bidirectional for White families. This means that if a child is caught doing something wrong, and spanked for that wrongdoing, he or she is more likely to increase the negative behavior, which will in turn result in more spankings.

Why would children from various ethnic groups respond differently to corporal punishment? In part, the difference may stem from what we have already revealed about the two groups. European American mothers place greater emphasis on socialization goals and childrearing strategies consonant with a more individualistic orientation (Harwood, Schoelmerich, Schulze, & Gonzalez, 1999). African Americans tend to view the world as an unfair system that will steal their ability to be judged for their actions. As such, European Americans are unlikely to benefit from punishments that restrict their freedom, while African Americans are likely to heed discipline designed to make their actions socially acceptable.

The need for autonomy is something that follows European Americans throughout their lives. Hornung et al. (1998) examined the relationship between ethnicity and decision making among geriatric patients. They retrospectively examined the charts of 1,193 participants in a program for frail geriatric patients, paying attention to demographic characteristics and the presence or absence of an alternative decision maker. Nearly all of the White patients (91 percent) expressed their own health care preferences, a proportion that was considerably higher than any of the other ethnic groups. Additionally, only about 8 percent of Whites had an alternative decision maker assigned in case something happened to impair their judgment. When such a person was given the right to make health care decisions, it was usually a spouse, which was directly contrary to the trends from other ethnic groups. African American and Latino patients were most likely to place a daughter in this role, and Asians were most likely to have a son as an alternative decision maker. All of the non-White patients were significantly more likely to have a family member assigned to this role.

In European American families, instilling autonomy is one of the family's primary tasks. The emphasis on independence creates a tenuous balance between family relationships and peer relationships, and it gives peers a greater influence in determining the individual's life goals. Chen, Greenberger, Lester, Dong, and Guo (1998) examined causes of misconduct among European American, Chinese American, and native Chinese adolescents. They found that 51 to 62 percent of the variance for misconduct was explained by family and peer relationships in the European American group. However, the same variables contributed to only 15 to 24 percent of the Chinese group's misconduct. The most interesting finding of the study was the effect of peers. As Chinese adolescents became more acculturated, peer relationships had a greater impact on their misconduct.

Despite an emphasis on individualism and mutual respect, European American families are less egalitarian than some other ethnic groups. For example, African American couples are more egalitarian in their performance of household tasks. European American men tend to offer little domestic support and instead strive to increase the family's income (Kamo & Cohen, 1998). It is also interesting to note that rising levels of employment among women in Austria, Germany, England, Hungary, Ireland, Italy, the Netherlands, and the United States have not produced more egalitarian gender roles (Hoellinger, 1991).

Economics

Given the economic differences between European Americans and other cultures, it is not surprising to find differing attitudes toward income. In an interesting study, Chadiha, Veroff, and Leber (1998) asked African American and

European American newlyweds to describe the meaning of their first year of marriage. This broad topic created a huge narrative, which was then analyzed. After controlling for the couple's education, household income, years of living together before marriage, premarital parental status, and length of the narrative, the authors found some important differences. European American newlyweds were more likely than their counterparts to emphasize achievement and work-related themes in their narratives. In contrast, African American newlyweds were more likely to discuss relationship issues and religion.

The emphasis on work and achievement appears to affect every area of European American culture. Williams, Takeuchi, and Adair (1992) examined the relationship between socioeconomic status (SES) and lifetime rates of psychiatric disorders among 4,287 Blacks and Whites. Among African Americans, the rates for depression were unrelated to SES. Among European Americans, however, lower SES was associated with higher rates of depression. Even more alarming, European American males of lower SES had higher rates of psychiatric illness than did their Black peers. The study suggests that income plays a significantly larger role in the mental health of European Americans than it does for members of minority groups.

Why is income so important to European Americans? The answer may involve access to certain privileges. In the African American section of this text, we discussed the erroneous stereotype that African American women were always stronger and less emotional than European American women. Such perceptions have become integrated into the occupational structure of American society. Caputo (2000) surveyed 2,030 females (aged 14 to 24 years) between 1968 and 1995. He wanted to find out if European American women received "family-friendly" benefits more often than African American women. Such benefits would include flexible work schedules, access to childcare, time off to take children to appointments, and so on. His findings suggest that African American women, regardless of how many years they had worked, were less likely than their European American peers to find family-friendly employment. Such differences may help explain why income plays a role in European Americans' mental health. European Americans may come to expect "special" treatment, and when this treatment is not available, their mental health may suffer. African Americans may be more likely to accept mistreatment as part of life.

Ethnic privilege not only affects the quality of employment found, but it can determine whether an individual is hired. Cook and Jordan (1997) found that 37 percent of the households headed by single White mothers lived in poverty, whereas 55 percent of those headed by mothers of Hispanic origin were poor. The difference, from their study of nearly 100,000 workers, was that disadvantaged Latina mothers had poorer English skills and they were less likely to be citizens. Clearly, citizenship and knowing the lingua franca would assist in finding employment, but the results of this study hint at a broader problem. When do factors associated with ethnicity interfere with the ability to find a job? Could having a Spanish accent or being dark-skinned hamper one's ability to gain employment? If so, such differences might explain why European American workers have a broader range of occupational interests in adulthood (Kaufman & McLean, 1996), but, during childhood, ethnic minorities and European Americans have similar interest levels (Davison-Aviles & Spokane, 1999). As they start high school, minority students may begin to sense the reality of prejudice, which could cause them to abandon some of their previously held ideals. White students, however, are free to continue reaching for their dreams. Such ambitions are largely rooted in the educational system.

Education

After Asian Americans, European Americans have the highest levels of educational achievement. Although there is some evidence of educational ambitions developing prior to junior high school, the most important factors leading to educational success appear to originate in high school. Kao and Tienda (1998) used data from the National Education Longitudinal Study of 1988 to analyze how educational aspirations are formed and maintained. After examining a nationally representative sample of 24,599 students from 1,052 randomly selected schools, their results suggest that the socioeconomic status of family members not only had an effect on the aspirations of eighth graders but, more importantly, created higher aspirations that lasted throughout the high school years. The reason why Asian and European American families appear to maintain higher educational aspirations seems to be related to higher socioeconomic status.

This finding is not surprising in light of established educational models. Belsky's (Baharudin & Luster, 1998) model assumed that mothers with better education, higher intelligence, and greater self-esteem would nurture the same qualities in their children. Although this theory does not address ethnicity, Baharudin and Luster (1998) found that the most supportive mothers had higher family incomes, fewer children, and higher marital stability (Foss, 1996; Fracasso, Lamb, Schoelmerich, & Leyendecker, 1997). All of these components are associated with higher socioeconomic status, which is also associated with European American ethnicity.

There is also some evidence that European American children are aware of their ethnic identity while they attend school. For many years, it was believed that European American school children were unlikely to be aware of ethnicity while attending predominantly White schools. However, Dutton, Singer, and Devlin (1998) disproved this theory. When using the Draw-A-Person test to examine the racial attitudes of fourth-graders, they found that children in nonintegrated schools were more likely to dislike children of other ethnicities. They also found that children, regardless of their ethnicity, who attended predominantly White schools produced drawings that depicted their ethnicity more obviously than did children from predominantly non-White schools.

Regardless of their cultural identity, White children appear to have learning styles that differ from those of minority children. Mainstream White Americans are typically described as valuing independence, analytical thinking, objectivity, and accuracy (Boutte, 1999). These are the facets that have led to classroom experiences that focus on competition, acquisition of abstract information, objective tests, and linear logic. These are also typically the skills and learning styles that will be emphasized in European American work environments, which implies that learning these skills is essential to working in the "White" world. As such, the 20 percent of European Americans who fail to earn a high school degree (Huang & Oei, 1996) are at a disadvantage for lack of skills and failure to acculturate into the dominant occupational structure.

Health

Smoking is a significant health risk among European Americans. European American teenagers are more likely than African Americans or Latinos to start smoking (Gritz et al., 1998) and they tend to consume more cigarettes over the course of their lifetimes (Griesler & Kandel, 1998). Although all European Americans are at risk for smoking, teenagers are at the greatest risk. Rates for adults appear to be falling, but rates among teenagers continue to rise. There has been some debate as to possible causes for the increase, but advertising seems to be one of the primary agents. During the early 1990s, more than 90 percent of six-year-olds were able to match Joe Camel with a picture of a cigarette, making him as well known as Mickey Mouse (by comparison, only 67 percent of adults recognized Joe Camel) (Fischer et al., 1991). The recent bans on cigarette advertisements targeting children, however, appear to be having an effect, and the rates for teen smoking started to fall at the beginning of the new millennium (National Institutes of Health, 2001).

In addition to their susceptibility to influence by advertisements, European Americans appear less able than other groups to avoid becoming addicted to cigarettes. Smoking rates for European Americans tend to be relatively stable as they age. In 1983, 35.0 percent of European American adults smoked, in comparison to 32.6 percent of their African American peers. In 1993, 28.9 percent of European Americans continued to smoke, compared to only 13.9 percent of their African American peers (Flint, Yamada, & Novotny, 1998). To some extent, these differences are explained by parents' and peers' attitudes toward smoking, religious practices, and risk-taking tendencies (Flint, Yamada, & Novotny, 1998), but there are still a number of factors yet to be discovered.

High rates of smoking are associated with high rates of cancer. It is in this domain that the looser family ties of European Americans seem to create additional health consequences. Social support has been linked to better prognosis, strengthening of the immune system, and possibly longer survival for cancer patients, and White cancer patients appear to have less adequate social support networks than Latinos. Further, African Americans are more willing to spend time with family members who are sick (Suinn, 1999).

In contrast to smoking, European Americans appear to have fewer problems with alcohol than do their peers. Their rate of abuse is slightly lower than that of their non–European American peers (Caetano & Clark, 1998), and they may learn to control their drinking at earlier ages than their peers do. Neff and Dassori (1998) conducted a cross-sectional study of 164 European Americans, 168 African Americans, and 149 Mexican Americans. All of these participants were males from 20 to 50 years of age who drank alcoholic beverages regularly. When analyzing the group's drinking history, the researchers found that European Americans were more likely to grow out of heavy drinking patterns than were other ethnic groups.

> *An rud nach leigheasann im ná uisce beatha níl aon leigheas air.*
> Translation: What butter or whiskey does not cure cannot be cured.
> (Irish Proverb)

One group of European Americans, the Irish, has often been stereotyped as being prone to use alcohol to excess. Greenslade, Pearson, and Madden (1995) traced the historical origins of these stereotypes and evaluated their accuracy. They found an interesting dichotomy. The Irish rates of abstinence were higher than those of the British. At the same time, rates of alcoholism in Ireland were higher than those among Jews and Italians. Why the dichotomy? One reason may be the age at which children are introduced to alcohol. In Jewish and Italian families, alcohol is introduced to children at an early age. It is associated with family and religious events, and is not stigmatized. These cultures judge individuals negatively only if they drink too much. By contrast, the Irish seldom introduce alcohol into the family until the child reaches the age of consent. At this time, drinking is introduced as a rite of passage to adulthood.

The differences in drinking rates between Irish and other European/ Scandinavian groups correspond with earlier studies done on religious groups. Barbara Lorch and Robert Hughes (1988) compared the prevention techniques of several organized religions to determine if proscriptive churches were more effective in deterring adolescents from alcohol and drug abuse than prescriptive ones. This study yielded mixed results, but its findings were significant. In churches (such as Presbyterians and Lutherans) where alcohol was viewed as an acceptable drink, within moderation, practitioners were more likely to use alcohol but less likely to become alcoholics. In churches (such as the Mormons) that either condemned alcohol or failed to discuss the topic at all, abstinence rates were higher, but so were alcoholism rates.

Cultural Uniqueness

The English language binds together most European Americans. For those who have emigrated from countries where other languages were spoken, there is often a sense of pride associated with mastering English (McFadden, 1999). However, the process of changing one's primary language often involves loss as well as triumph. The language of one's birth country is closely connected with one's memories and culture, and much of that culture is lost with the removal of the language from the family. Nora, an 88-year-old resident of a skilled care center, recalls,

> When I first entered the nursing home, I thought my family had deserted me. My son never came to visit, my husband had died, and I think my children just wanted me to leave the earth as well. I didn't realize how alone I felt until I heard someone speak German. The speaker was our new chaplain, who was born in Italy but spoke five languages fluently. He was quoting a line from a Friedrich Conrad Dietrich Wyneken sermon, and I could feel a tear in my eye after just one sentence. He must have seen me crying, because he came over, put his arm around me and asked, "What's the matter?" I could only reply, "Ich bin glücklich" (I am happy). He just smiled and I felt my soul stir within me again. For a brief time, I thought it had left me.

Nora needed to hear her native tongue, even though English had been her primary language for most of her life. Something about the culture of her past, her heritage, helped her to feel alive again. Language is often an essential component of cultural identity and the development of the self.

Beyond language, though, there is little that unifies European Americans in a cultural sense. Ting-Toomey et al. (2000) noted that European Americans have a weaker ethnic identity than members of other groups, but this is not to say that there are no ethnic remnants. For example, the Puritan work ethic still permeates much of "White" culture. The Puritans believed that honest toil produced spiritual and material rewards. This belief led to two assumptions that continue to affect American society:

(i)   Hard work leads to material wealth.
(ii) Hard work builds character and is morally good.

Although such cultural beliefs have created wealth for many European Americans, this prosperity has also come at a price. The popular notion of "no pain, no gain" has left its mark on leisure-time recreation. Adventure travel, involving intense and sometimes grueling activities, is quickly becoming the vacation of choice for young European Americans. It provides the opportunity to work at a dude ranch, canoe on white-water rivers, climb a glacier, or risk life and limb in some other way. All of these activities drain the body and give participants the "right" to relax.

The Puritan work ethic is deeply rooted in European American culture and can be traced to a variety of social and religious influences. Prior to the 1800s, about 62 percent of the U.S. population consisted of Congregationalists, Anglicans, and Presbyterians. About 14 percent comprised Dutch Reformed, Lutherans, German Reformed, Society of Friends (Quakers), Baptists, or Methodists. Nearly 23 percent were considered "unchurched slaves," and only 1.1 percent were Catholics (Axelson, 1999). The latter statistic implies that the Anglo influence was dominant early in the development of the European American culture. It is for this reason that the Puritan work ethic, which was based primarily on the Anglo religions, especially Calvinism, continues to influence upper-middle-class European Americans today.

Although it is still influential, the Puritan work ethic has begun to fall from favor, in part because of the need to adapt to other cultural norms. To fully develop one's own ethnic identity, it is necessary to develop an understanding and appreciation of other cultures. Helms (1990) argues that European Americans are likely to find themselves at one of six stages in a process of White identity development, described in Table 6.1.

Out of all these stages, the movement to pseudoindependence seems the most difficult. Something must force the White individual to recognize that the world is not as it appears. This is the first step towards forming a nonracist identity, but it often comes with much pain. It is here that the individual may start to realize subtleties in his or her interaction with minorities: e.g., "I don't have a problem with Blacks, but I was nervous when that dark-skinned man sat next to me at the restaurant."

If the individual can successfully make it through the pseudoindependence stage, another, more subtle difficulty must be overcome. During immersion/emersion, the individual must come to realize his or her role in accepting or encouraging "White privilege." As shown in the following incident, privilege can take many forms. Jan, an African American speech instructor at a college, threw a party for her students. Most of the speech students were European Americans, but Jan also invited some of her African American colleagues. After discussing politics, religion, and school issues, the conversation turned to ethnicity. The African Americans began to talk about the difficulties of being on a "White" campus and having to fight for their freedom and independence. Marsha, a young European American student, attempted to jump into the discussion.

"Yeah, I know what you mean." Marsha's sincerity was obvious, but her light hair and blue eyes caused some of the African American faculty to smile. "When I started here," she continued, "I never thought I would be accepted. It's like everyone expects you to have the right clothes, perfect hair, and expensive cars."

"Oh, you think you have it so hard?" Jan said to the European American student with an undercurrent of resentment in her voice. "You don't know the first thing about hardship."

Marsha, having grown up in abject poverty and attending college on an academic scholarship, felt cruelly attacked. She reacted fiercely, summarizing her life story and stating that her life was as difficult as it could be. The professor responded by saying, "No matter how difficult your life may have been, you have never been judged by the color of your skin. You have never watched

TABLE 6.1 *Helms's White Identity Model*

Stage	*Description*
Contact	The White individual encounters one or more members of a minority ethnic group, especially African Americans, and forms an attitude about at least one of these people. Depending on the White individual's family history, the encounter could be viewed with trepidation or naïve curiosity. During this stage, the White individual is likely to view the condition of minority groups simplistically. Common statements may include, "I'm glad we can help the Blacks with welfare money."
Disintegration	As the White individual continues to learn about the plight facing minority groups, a serious conflict develops. There is a conscious awareness that African and European Americans are not treated equally, and this new knowledge creates dissonance. The White individual wonders, "Why does this difference exist?"
Reintegration	In seeking answers to questions raised during the disintegration stage, the White individual will likely retreat into White culture. The dominant culture will create reasons for why minority groups are not entitled to share in the privileges bestowed on Whites, such as the idea that Blacks lack social, moral, or intellectual status, which is why their lives are more difficult. Many White Americans will remain in this stage indefinitely. It takes a jarring event or shock to transport them to the fourth stage.
Pseudoindependence	If the White individual comes to a realization that members of minority groups are not innately inferior to Whites, he or she is ready to build a healthy White identity. Events such as the Civil Rights Movement could spawn such a change, but the process will not be easy. Whites in the reintegration stage may regard this individual as confused or traitorous. Blacks are likely to regard this individual with suspicion.
Immersion-Emersion	If the individual continues along the path of development, he or she may begin to discard the myths and stereotypes passed down through the dominant society. At this stage, there is an active attempt to participate in White consciousness groups and fight to create community or social change. Racist and prejudiced attitudes that have been repressed or denied are actively rejected, and the individual will want to help end the oppression caused by White culture and create more positive definitions of White identity.
Autonomy	In the final stage, which is ongoing throughout the remainder of life, the individual seeks to participate in minority events while not forsaking his or her cultural roots. There is an active appreciation of minority cultures as well as the dominant culture. This appreciation is combined with activism for equality and a resistance to racist forces in the White culture.

people leave a store because you entered, or realized that everyone in a restaurant was talking about you. You have only known one type of poverty and, as hard as it might have been for you, there are worse kinds to face."

There are "White" cultural groups, however, who do understand the effects of racism and discrimination. We have already mentioned the Jews and the horrors they faced during the Holocaust. Similarly, Arab Americans often find themselves falling into either "Asian" or "European" cultural categories, but they are a unique group with a unique culture. Often, the cultural differences in religion alone are difficult for Westerners to fully understand or appreciate, and the shared symbols and language between, for example, Christianity and Islam further complicate matters.

Muslims believe they are the chosen people of God and the true followers of YHWH and Jesus. They view the Jews as children of Isaac and the Arabs as children of Ishmael (the firstborn son of Abraham). Following this line of reasoning, the Arabs and Jews are brother cultures, but they have followed different paths. Abraham married Sarah, but she was childless for many years. So she gave Abraham her Egyptian maid, Hagar, to be his second wife, in accordance with the customs of the day. Hagar gave birth to a son, Ishmael. With the birth of Ishmael, Sarah's wish for a full inheritance was granted. But then God caused Sarah to conceive, and she gave birth to a son, Isaac (Genesis, Chapter 21). Now she could have her full inheritance through her own "flesh and blood." Without delay, she demanded that Hagar, and Ishmael with her, be cast out of the house. Abraham loved Ishmael, and Sarah's request grieved him greatly. But the voice of God told him to consent to Sarah's wishes, and he did so. He "took bread and a bottle of water, and gave them unto Hagar, put the child on her shoulder, and sent her away" (Genesis 21:14). On that day, according to Muslim beliefs, the religion known as "Islam" was born.

Hagar and Ishmael wandered through the wilderness, and Hagar began to fear for her life. As they neared death, God brought forth water from the earth, and saved the two of them. This spring of water is identified by Muslims as the well of Zamzam, located today within the al-Haram Mosque in Mecca, and part of the Hajj (obligatory pilgrimage to Mecca). As recounted in Genesis 16:10, Hagar was later visited by the angel, who said to her "I will multiply thy seed exceedingly, that it shall not be numbered for multitude." And, as for Ishmael, Genesis 17:20 stated "I have blessed him, and will make him fruitful, and will multiply him exceedingly; twelve princes shall he beget, and I will make him a great nation." The great nation is Islam.

In Islam, the person of Jesus Christ also plays a critical role, but the Muslim view of Jesus differs from that of most Christian sects. See Table 6.2.

The key differences between Islamic and Christian beliefs involve the role and divinity of Jesus. Muslims believe Jesus was a great prophet and a person worthy of homage (Muslims add the phrase "peace be upon him"[1] after they say the name "Jesus" or "Mohammad"), but they do not view Jesus as God or

---

[1]When greeting a fellow Muslim, it is customary to say, "As-salamo 'alaikum" (Peace be upon you!). The response to this greeting is, "Wa 'alai-komus-salaam" (And upon you be peace!).

TABLE 6.2 *Comparison of Islamic and Christian Beliefs*

	Islam (Meaning Submission or Peace)	***Christianity*** *(Christian* Means "Disciple of Jesus Christ"; Literally, "Christ one")*
Other prophets	God's messengers are evidenced through a chain of prophets starting with Adam and including Noah, Abraham, Ishmael, Isaac, Jacob, Joseph, Job, Moses, Aaron, David, Solomon, Elias, Jonah, John the Baptist, and Jesus, peace be upon them. But God's final message to man, a reconfirmation of the eternal message and a summing-up of all that has gone before was revealed to the Prophet Muhammad (pbuh) through Gabriel.	The Jewish prophets foretold the coming of Jesus. The apostles spread Jesus' message to the rest of the world.
Beliefs about Jesus	• Jesus (pbuh)[2] was born human (iii, 45: 47; xix, 22–33) and remained sinless (iii, 59). • Jesus (pbuh) was a righteous prophet (vi, 85). • Jesus (pbuh) is not the son of God (ix, 30). Allah is one. He has no children. There is no other God like him. • He was not crucified (iv, 157). The Jews did not crucify him, but it was made to appear so. They actually crucified Judas while believing it to be Jesus (pbuh) (Sura 4, Verses 157 and 158). • Jesus (pbuh) will descend at the end of time and judge all people with justice, according to the Law of our Prophet Muhammad (pbuh) (an-Nisa, 4:159).	• Jesus was born human (Matthew 1:23) and remained sinless (Romans 5:14). • Jesus was a righteous prophet and high priest of the faith (Hebrews 3:1). • Jesus is the only son of the Supreme God, born of Mary, begotten by the Holy Spirit (the power and presence of God). He descended from Heaven, became human and died for all people to demonstrate God's love for humanity. • Jesus was crucified, killed, and buried (Matthew 27, Mark 15, Luke 23, Acts 2:36). • Jesus will come down from Heaven, bring believers with him into the clouds, raise the dead, and judge the wicked (1 Thessalonians 4:16).
The paraclete	Jesus' mission was to be completed by another (n. 1861 to xiii, 38). He prophesied the coming of Muhammad (pbuh) (the paracletos) (lxi, 6).	In the book of Luke 24: 47–49, Jesus tells his disciples to wait in Jerusalem until he sent the Paraclete (often translated as counselor or advocate). Christians regard the paraclete as "the Holy Spirit" (Acts 1:8), the third person of the Trinitarian Godhead.
Trinity	There is no Trinity. There is only one God, Allah, and the prophets (v, 19, 75).	The early church "father" Tertullian (A.D. 145–220) was the first to use the word "Trinity" in reference to God. It was Bishop Augustine of Hippo ("St. Augustine") who fully developed the idea in his book "De Trinitate" (400 A.D.). It was established as "official" teaching at the Councils of Nicea (325 A.D.) and Constantinople (381 A.D.). There are few Biblical passages referring to the Trinity (e.g., I John 5:7[3], Matthew 28:19; John 1:1). *continued*

[2]Muslims use the phrase "peace be upon him" whenever they utter or write the name of a prophet. This is especially important when using the names of Jesus or Mohammad (peace be upon them). The practice, however, becomes cumbersome so the acronym pbuh is often used. Please note that the practice is followed only in Islam. Christians do not have such a custom.

[3]The earliest and most reliable Greek texts do not include this passage. It was likely inserted into the Christian text well after the second century.

TABLE 6.2 *Comparison of Islamic and Christian Beliefs (continued)*

	Islam *(Meaning Submission or Peace)*	Christianity *(Christian Means "Disciple of Jesus Christ"; Literally, "Christ one")*
Scriptures	Moses' "Torah" David's "Zaboor" (Psalms) Jesus's "Injeel" (Gospel) Mohamed's Qur'an Muslims are told that the previous scriptures were tampered with by mankind and the Bible should only be accepted insofar as it is confirmed by Arabic version of the Qur'an.	The Bible, consisting of 66 Old Testament books in Hebrew and Aramaic and 29 New Testament books in Greek, were composed by numerous authors across many centuries under the guidance of the Holy Spirit and written in the dialect of the common people.
Sin and forgiveness	Every person is born free from sin. When a person reaches the age of maturity, and if he is mentally competent, he becomes accountable for all his deeds and intentions.	"For all have sinned and fallen short of the glory of God" (Romans 3:23). The grace of God and the gift of His Holy Spirit imbue humans with the ability to turn from their sinful nature and become holy.
Life after death	At the Resurrection, the righteous will be sent to the Garden of God, but they will not see God. The wicked will be sent to an eternal fire. Those who are especially righteous, such as martyrs, may enter the garden at death.	All will be resurrected. The righteous will rule with Jesus in God's eternal kingdom when the dwelling of God will be with men. Those who reject God's way will be sent to hell.
Enemies	"Fight in the way of Allah against those who fight against you, but begin not hostilities. Lo! Allah loveth not aggressors. And slay them wherever ye find them" (2:190). "O ye who believe! Fight those of the disbelievers who are near you, and let them find harshness in you" (9:123).	"But I say unto you, Love your enemies, bless them that curse you, do good to them that hate you, and pray for them which despitefully use you, and persecute you" (Matt. 5:4). "Jesus answered, My kingdom is not of this world: if my kingdom were of this world, then would my servants fight" (John 18:36).
Prayers	Five prayers [i.e., times of prayer]—the Almighty Allah made them obligatory. "When the call is heard for the prayer of the day of congregation, haste unto remembrance of Allah" (62:9).	"But thou, when thou prayest, enter into thy closet, and when thou hast shut thy door, pray to thy Father which is in secret; and thy Father which seeth in secret shall reward thee openly" (Matt. 6:6).
Modesty for women	". . . they (believing women) should not display their beauty and ornaments except what (must ordinarily) appear thereof; that they should draw their veils over their bosoms and not display their beauty except to their husbands, their fathers, their husbands' fathers, their sons, their husbands' sons, their brothers or their brothers' sons, or their sisters' sons, or their women . . . or small children who have no sense of the shame of sex" (24:31[4]).	"In like manner also, that women adorn themselves in modest apparel, with shame facedness and sobriety; not with broided hair, or gold, or pearls, or costly array" (1 Tim. 2:9). "But every woman that prayeth or prophesieth with her head uncovered dishonoureth her head: for that is even all one as if she were shaven" (1 Cor. 11:5).

[4]Neither of these passages actually prescribe head coverings. Only the Christian texts, which are not usually followed, offer such a command. The traditional head coverings found in conservative Islamic nations have more to do with culture than religion.

the son of God. Muslims respect and revere Jesus and await his Second Coming. He is viewed as one of God's greatest messengers to mankind, but Muslims believe his message was limited and he did not rise from the dead. Islam is so adamant about these points that Muslims view people holding contrary views as heretics and blasphemers. For the Muslim, worshipping (rather than respecting) Jesus is equivalent to polytheism and is therefore anathema. Instead, true followers, they argue, should be following Mohammad, whose coming, they believe, was prophesied by Jesus.

Christians tend to emphasize an atonement theory (i.e., the concept that having faith in Jesus is sufficient for salvation), but Muslims view this belief with disdain. They argue that it overlooks the importance of conforming to God's laws, which are highly prized by Islam. They accept the idea that no one can enter heaven by works alone, but they view obedience and action as key components. Muslims who are seeking to please Allah strive to follow the five pillars listed below:

1. *Shahadah:* This Arabic word meaning "witness" refers to the declaration that there is no God but Allah and that Muhammad is the divine messenger. This declaration occurs often in prayer, in association with life-cycle events, and in a person's conversion to Islam.

2. *Salat:* This Arabic term meaning "prayer" most often refers to the five statutory prayers required daily. These prayers, recited while facing toward Mecca, include cycles of postures called "rak'a" which vary depending on which prayer service is recited. There are special prayer times in the early morning, noon, mid-afternoon, sunset, and evening.

3. *Sawm:* This Arabic term refers to the fast during the month of Ramadan. Since the Muslims follow a lunar calendar, the month of fasting occurs in different seasons from year to year. The fast has historical references to Muhammad as well as personal and social implications.

4. *Zakat:* This term refers to the statutory tax required of every Muslim adult, although in non-Muslim countries Zakat has become a matter of personal choice. Several Muslim observances are invalidated unless they are paid for by assets on which Zakat has been paid. Usually, a Zakat is 2.5 percent of one's annual savings, but there are complicated rules for calculating what is owed. A Zakat is 20 percent on resources such as oil or precious metals (i.e., gold, silver). You would pay 20 percent on what you produced in one year. There are also different Zakats. Zakat-ul-Fitr is for fasting Muslims to give food or money on behalf of fasting people. The food or money is equal to one day's meals for one person. The money is given to the poor (Fuqara), the needy (Masakin), and employees of the Zakah.

5. *Hajj:* This term refers to the obligatory pilgrimage to Mecca, which every Muslim must perform at least once in a lifetime. It consists of several actions that recall the life of Abraham, his wife Hagar, and their son Ishmael. The Hajj is a life-transforming experience for participants.

The commitment of Muslims to follow a holy life stands in marked contrast to the violence spawned by some Muslim extremists. The terrorist attack on the World Trade Center on September 11, 2001, introduced many Americans to a side of Islam that should be viewed as anomalous. Instead, some Americans began to think of all Muslims as terrorists. In a sense, anti-Islamic prejudice became an act of terror in itself. In the days immediately following the attack on America, a backlash against Muslims and Arab Americans occurred. Shots were fired at mosques; women in traditional Islamic garments were shunned; a Molotov cocktail was thrown at an Arab American community center; and windows were shattered in many homes. But the greatest assault may simply be the tacit change in American views of Muslims. Sincere followers of Islam had to endure bomb threats, graffiti, chat-room abuse, being spat upon, or simply receiving sideways glances when carrying out their daily chores. The end of the prejudice and terrorism is hard to predict, but it is clear that the battle has been costly for both sides.

Psychological Issues

The conflict between Muslims and Christians parallels the one between Jan, the African American speech instructor, and Marsha, the European American student. One of the reasons Marsha did not understand Jan's position was that the two of them were operating within different sets of rules. Jan's access to educational and employment opportunities was restricted by racial discrimination, while Marsha's progress had been unimpeded by her ethnicity. Marsha had worked hard, been admitted to an exclusive college, and was looking forward to a successful career. However, even in cases where hard work produces results, a number of psychological side-effects can arise. The strictest elements of the Puritan work ethic involve self-denial. Hard work, productive leisure-time activities, and avoidance of personal pleasure are interwoven into European American culture. In order to achieve success through hard work, the physical self was downgraded to secondary consideration. Sometimes this deemphasis on physical pleasures results in the suppression of the sexual self. Such tendencies can result in sexual dysfunction, especially among middle-class European Americans (Axelson, 1999).

The rejection of the physical self and the guilt associated with personal pleasure may also be associated with the "White women's disorder," bulimia nervosa. It is interesting to note that obesity is not the best predictor of the severity of eating disorders among European American clients. Fitzgibbon et al. (1998) examined 351 women (55 European American, 179 African American, and 117 Latina) for factors associated with binge eating. Across all ethnic groups, women who binged more were heavier, more depressed, and idealized a slimmer body build. However, binge-eating severity was most accurately predicted by the presence of depression and shame in European Americans.

It is possible that European American women may be susceptible to eating disorders because of the pressure they feel to be attractive. When evaluating the importance placed on attractiveness by young women, Murray (1996) found that African American girls considered attractiveness only mildly important, Latina girls considered it very important, and European American girls reached near-obsessive levels concerning their looks. This anxiety over their looks significantly affects European American girls' self-esteem. They are largely dissatisfied with their appearance, which leaves them with lower levels of self-worth than girls of other ethnic groups (Ogden & Elder, 1998). In fact, when rating photographs of heavy White women, European American women rated them lower on attractiveness, intelligence, job success, relationship success, happiness, and popularity than they did average-weight or thin women (Hebl & Heatherton, 1998).

Although eating disorders can lead to death, they are not intended as suicidal acts. The anorexic does not wish to die; she wants to maintain control of her life. There are unique signs, however, of suicidality among European Americans. Kung, Liu, and Juon (1998) compared the lifestyles of European Americans who died of natural causes and those who committed suicide. Their study revealed that suicidal European Americans were more likely to have a high school education, to work in blue-collar jobs, and to have used mental health services. Of these findings, the latter is the most disconcerting. It implies that European Americans attend therapy when they feel depressed, but therapy does not renew their sense of hope.

Within-Group Differences

How do we identify the differences between specific European American groups and the dominant American culture as a whole? Probably the best place to start is to discuss the Anglo influence, which is a primary element in the dominant American culture.

English traditions strongly influence European American culture, but there are elements of English society that are not readily apparent in the dominant European American culture. For example, traditional European American psychotherapy focuses on an expression of affect and catharsis, but such practices may be unproductive with English clients. The English are likely to resist discussions of personal issues, viewing the airing of emotions as roughly equivalent to taking a bath in public. The discussion of emotions is even avoided within the confines of the home. Instead, there is an emphasis on external (e.g., political, religious, etc.) or community issues, which are considered safer topics.

Anglo Americans are apt to view any show of emotion as evidence of a lack of personal strength. In particular, showing aggression is a sign of weakness. Typically, the first person to show any sign of aggression is viewed as demonstrating a loss of control and poor planning. Such differences in culture have led to a number of conflicts between African Americans and Anglos. In many Black cultures, showing emotion is an indication of passion and motivation. Neither side is apt to understand or appreciate the speaking style of the other.

The British are also more likely to emphasize speech over appearance. Class differences, bounded by language and birth, are more critical to earning respect than the color of one's skin. It is possible that a middle-class African American woman would be better accepted in England than a White male with a Cockney accent. Prior to the American Civil Rights initiative, many African American entertainers preferred to live in Europe where they were respected for their abilities. In England, provided one had acceptable manners, speech, and skills, one was likely to be accepted.

In discussing manners, it is also important to note that English manners are different from European American manners. The English are likely to require a larger personal space than Americans. They will also downplay their power by putting their hands in their pockets, walking with small, quiet, subtle steps, and deemphasizing showiness. Such meekness and distance often makes the formation of friendships arduous. Although intimate friendships are likely to be more difficult to form, however, they are likely to last a lifetime.

The following dialogue depicts a clash between British and American cultures:

White American:	John! How are you doing? I haven't seen you for some time!
Englishman:	(understated) Things are fine, I've just been away for a few weeks.
White American:	Really, what have you been up to?
Englishman:	Oh (pause) . . . nothing really, I just had some issues with my family.
White American:	Oh, I hope everything is all right.
Englishman:	It will be for most, but not for all. My mother died.
White American:	I'm very sorry to hear that. Were you close to her?

At this point, the conversation could go nowhere. The Englishman, by not volunteering information, was making it clear that this was not a topic to be explored. He did not explicitly state, "I don't want to talk about this." It was simply supposed to be understood. The White American, unaware of this cultural element, probed for more information and potentially damaged the relationship.

The English are just as likely, however, to misunderstand other European cultures. Throughout history, the English held the Italians and Australians in great disdain. After all, Australia was an open prison for the British Empire. As for the Italians, the English tended to regard them as uncouth and overexpressive. With this history firmly established, when Italians immigrated to the Americas during the nineteenth century, they faced strong prejudice from the

Anglo community. The majority were unskilled, illiterate workers who were exploited by their employers. They coped by maintaining strong family ties and living in interdependent neighborhoods. Their Catholicism (more than 80 percent of Italian Americans consider themselves Catholic) also helped them maintain their cultural uniqueness and prevent absorption into the mainstream culture. These strong values guided them toward economic and educational success. Today, Italian Americans have reached the point where their college attendance is approximately the same as the rates for other European American groups (Axelson, 1999). Belfiglio (1986) in his study of fourth-generation Italian Americans, found that maintaining cultural traits includes possession of an Italian birth name, membership in the Catholic church, preference for Italian folk music and Italian cuisine, and pride in Italian music and art.

Polish Americans were also mostly unskilled when they came to America. They worked in the automobile factories of Detroit, the stockyards of Chicago, and the mines of Ohio. Their cultural values encouraged them to work hard at these jobs, and even today, many work at two places of employment (Axelson, 1999). They tend to value frugality, careful saving, and the wise use of financial resources. They are also likely to have strict household rules that children are expected to obey without question, and women are in charge of managing domestic matters. This family structure has led to a below-average crime rate among this cultural group. Polish Americans are also likely to face intense guilt and shame if resorting to divorce.

Irish Americans came from backgrounds similar to Polish Americans, but there were also differences between the two groups. Irish American women have traditionally dominated family life, defined their social life through their church, and enjoy more independence than women from other European American cultures. Although Irish American women might define their gender roles and social freedoms, in part, from their religion, Catholicism takes many forms. Portuguese Americans, who are also influenced by Catholicism, structure their household relationships differently. They tend to follow Latino cultural norms in which the husband is obeyed and the wife seeks virtue and purity. In a sense, culture interprets religion, rather than the other way around.

Jewish people often came to America not for economic opportunities but to escape persecution. In some ways, the immigration process has been easier for Jews than for Irish and Italian immigrants. The reason for this is the underlying beliefs of Zionism. A significant belief for Zionist Jews is that each Jew has an innate bond with other Jews around the world. This belief structure helped Jewish immigrants find a supportive Jewish community when they arrived in the states, even though they still faced prejudice and opposition from the dominant society.

In addition to Zionism, there are a number of other Jewish factions. Post-Zionist Jews advocate the importance of belief or identity over ethnicity. They continue to live by the Torah and Talmud, but they are typically characterized by Jewish "liberalism." Rather than provide support to their Jewish peers, they emphasize responsibility to all poor people, widows, and orphans. In either case, Jewish values place a strong emphasis on formal learning and scholarship (Axelson, 1999), and the efforts of Jews in academia have produced numerous advances, including several psychological theories. It is no coincidence that psychoanalysis was created within the Jewish culture. Langman (1997) argued that the influence of Jewish culture on the origin and development of psychotherapy has been profound and unique. Jewish mysticism appears to have influenced psychoanalysis and Gestalt psychology. Both of these approaches contrast sharply with the behavioral psychology of European theorists.

Counseling Issues

Contemporary psychotherapy traditionally falls into traditions spawned by psychoanalysis, behaviorism, and humanistic existentialism. Most of these theories and their variants were created by European Americans, and practiced by White, middle-class therapists. As such, most counselors are likely to feel well trained to intervene with troubled European American clients. However, there are important cultural considerations unique to this group.

Shame and guilt are especially important for European American clients. Thandeka (1999) defined "White shame" as the conscious experience of feeling indelibly flawed because one is not meeting the expectations of a cultural community. Thandeka argues that this state includes feeling too sinful, bad, or unproductive to be loved for oneself. Feelings of unworthiness may lead children to seek group support and attempt to bury the feelings deep within themselves. Shame, seen in this context, becomes a social event: the environment fails to provide the message that the individual is intrinsically lovable.

Although guilt and shame are common to all ethnic groups, the condition is different for European Americans. Lutwak, Razzino, and Ferrari (1998) examined how various ethnic groups reported their experiences of guilt and shame. They found that guilt-proneness was not significantly related to any self-report variable across cultural groups. However, shame—the state of feeling unworthy—was culturally mitigated. The best predictor of shame among African Americans was a fear of intimacy, which makes sense considering the lack of trust they face from the dominant society. For Latinos, shame was associated with a sense of inauthenticity and failing to lead the life they felt called to live. For Asian and European Americans, shame was predicted by feelings of self-deprecation.

Although self-deprecation appears to predict shame for both Asian and European Americans, there are differences in the way shame is experienced by these groups. Liem (1997) argues that shame among first-generation Asian Americans is often embedded in a triadic structure comprising the actor, a shamed other, and an audience. This corresponds to the community element commonly melded into the Asian identity. For European Americans, however, shame experiences typically conform to a dyadic structure of actor and audience. This is the Shakespearean figure who wrestles with the horror of having followed a path he knows to be wrong. He is not held guilty by anyone except God and himself, but believes that all observers can see the shame in his heart.

This sense of unworthiness can be seen in the anorexic who strives for physical or academic perfection but knows that she will fall short. It is apparent in the depressed middle-aged man who is unable to accept the fact that he will not reach the lofty ambitions of his youth. For nearly all European American clients, shame propels them into some actions and prohibits them from others. Consider the case of Tom, who was struggling to overcome a compulsion to expose his genitals to children.

> I don't know how to stop it. It's like something just comes over me and forces me to do this. I think there is something biologically wrong with me. Could that be the case? I know I don't have control over it. I don't seem to have much control over anything in my life. I can't handle my work, my family is out of control, and I know it's because of this one problem.

When Tom was able to realize that he felt unsure about himself, his world changed. He needed to learn that his exhibitionism increased when he felt he could not control his environment. When he had a fight with his wife, an argument with his boss, or lost an important sale, his shame increased and he felt completely unworthy. When he reached this low point, his desire to expose himself increased. Perhaps he felt, "I can't do anything else right, so I might as well give in to these other bad feelings."

After facing his insecurities and accepting his weaknesses, Tom learned how feelings of failure and inadequacy triggered his fears and created "out-of-control" impulses. The more content he became, the less he desired exhibitionism. In a way, Tom's success had more to do with gaining personal insight than changing his behavior. When he attempted to change his exhibitionism directly, he found himself overwhelmed by the impulses. When he focused on accepting himself and keeping himself busy with healthy activities, his exhibitionism no longer controlled him. Similar processes have been effective for European Americans struggling with other compulsive disorders. They come to therapy seeking help with a given problem. They usually report feeling overwhelmed and out of control, but they fail to realize how their feelings reinforce their compulsion. In most cases, they feel intensely guilty whenever they have a compulsive thought. When they acknowledge the thought, they become guiltier. When they feel guilty, they feel like bad people. As bad people, nothing prevents them from acting out in negative ways. Picture a man coming to therapy for compulsive use of pornography. He is likely to express an "uncontrollable" urge to purchase pornographic material, and believes he is too weak to act otherwise. In a very real way, such a person is usually addicted to guilt at least as much as pornography. If he learns to purchase pornography without feeling guilty, his compulsion will likely decrease. If he can replace the time he spends reading pornography with other, more productive tasks, his mental health will likely increase further.

Guilt plays a special role for European Americans, but other groups have similar feelings. It is important to realize, however, that our perception of mental health varies according to our culture. Because of these differences, European American clients working with minority therapists may doubt their therapists' ability to understand them. Ayonrinde (1999) concludes that ethnic minority therapists are often placed in a unique position. They are viewed as neither "Black" nor "White" but something in between. The therapist is set apart from the client because of race, but the therapist's education and status connect him or her with the dominant culture. When merging these two elements, the therapist often is placed in a cultural vacuum—neither wholly White nor wholly Black.

When minority therapists attempt to help European American clients, they need to realize that European Americans are more likely to encounter discrimination than in the past. Clients are more likely to reach their therapeutic goals when their therapist acknowledges injustice and provides ways to cope with discrimination. For example, in John's story, described below, the discrimination suffered was genuine. Had his therapist slighted his experience, it is unlikely John would have continued in therapy. Instead, he probably would have become skeptical of minority therapists.

John's Story

Okay, I admit it. When I was in college, I didn't have a clue what it meant to be "White." I just thought the world was a treasure chest waiting for anyone to uncover its secrets. I honestly felt people from all ethnic groups had the same opportunities.

It wasn't until my senior year of college that reality struck me. A friend of mine was applying for a mortgage loan. My friend happened to be Black, and the bank turned him down flat. He had much better credentials than anyone else in my class, and the rejected loan scared me to death. I pictured myself living in a tiny dorm room for the rest of my life after investing so much time and money into my education.

I decided to conduct an experiment, and I applied for the same loan. Sure enough, the bank approved my application. I didn't have the heart to tell my friend.

This is not to say that being White is always favorable. In fact, my first job out of college was a disaster (the bank would have been wiser accepting my friend's application!). It was at a small but prestigious university in a culturally varied department. Personally, the diversity of the group excited me, because it seemed to add depth to our global strategy. Even when I learned that I was the only White faculty member, I never thought twice about the consequences.

Yep, you guessed it. Less than five weeks into the semester, I was asked to leave the department because we were a "poor fit" for each other. To this day, I have no doubt that the "poor fit" was the color of my skin (they hired an African American male to take my place). The experience devastated me. I sought counseling under a minority therapist and asked her point blank if she thought I was a racist. She just smiled warmly and said, "You've been hurt, and you're trying to grow—why don't we start from there?" She was absolutely right—that's where we needed to start. Had I attempted to confront my prejudices then, I might not have ever recovered from my pain.

Two universities later, I started working in a mostly White department. Early on, I made some serious mistakes; let me just say they were ten times worse than the very mild errors made at the first college. I kept waiting for the dean to call me into his office for the "poor fit" talk. It never came. Instead, I was greeted with affirmations and encouragement. They realized how difficult adjusting to a new environment could be. They gave me the time I needed to adapt and grow.

I often wonder how many times minorities get the "poor fit" talk when they honestly don't deserve it. I'm sure it is more often than White employees hear it. Still, it seems like more and more of my White friends have stories like mine. Maybe that is how the playing field is being leveled: making it unfair for everyone. Too bad. It would be great if we could somehow figure out how to look for the treasure chest together.

Questions to Consider

1. Why do we need so many terms to describe various American ethnic groups? Why can't we all just be Americans?

2. As discussed in this chapter, a group of minority high school students in California laughed and cheered as they watched Jews being tortured in Steven Spielberg's epic masterpiece, *Schindler's List*. Why do you think this reaction occurred? What could be done to foster a greater sense of compassion toward the suffering of other oppressed groups?

3. Why would children from various ethnic groups respond differently to corporal punishment?

4. One study suggests that income plays a significantly larger role in the mental health of European Americans than it does for minority groups. Why is this the case?

5. Are European Americans who fail to graduate from high school likely to experience greater disadvantage than those from other cultures?

6. Far from the stereotypical image of the Irish embodied in the ubiquitous drunk male laborer, rates of abstinence from alcohol are higher in Ireland than in England. Why does the stereotype continue?

7. Helms (1984, 1995) argues that European Americans are likely find themselves following a six-stage process of racial development: Contact, Disintegration, Reintegration, Pseudoindependence, Immersion-Emersion, and Autonomy. Of all these stages, the movement to pseudoindependence seems the most difficult. Do you know people who seem to be "stuck" at a particular stage? What might need to happen before they move to the next level?

8. Eating disorders may be more prevalent among European American women because of the pressure they feel to be attractive. Why do these pressures seem to be greater for European American women than minority women?

9. British culture is the foundation to European American culture, but there are elements of English society that are not shared by the dominant European American culture. What are the more salient differences?

10. It is no coincidence that psychoanalysis was created within the Jewish culture. Langman (1997) argued that the influence of Jewish culture on the origin and development of psychotherapy was profound and unique. What makes psychoanalysis more Jewish than European?

11. For European Americans, feelings of shame typically involve a dyadic structure of actor and audience. This is the Shakespearean figure who wrestles with the horror of having followed a path he knows to be wrong. He is not held guilty by anyone except God and himself, but all who observe (or so he believes) can see the shame in his heart. How might this orientation interfere with mental well-being?

PART III

Gender and Sexuality

Why do we need to discuss gender and sexual orientation in the context of multicultural counseling? This question is being asked in a variety of circles, and there are still no conclusive answers. However, there is a trend toward inclusion based, in part, on Pope's (1995) impassioned argument for the inclusion of gays and lesbians. Pope offered the following points for consideration:

- Sexual minorities must face identity-formation tasks similar to those of racial and ethnic minorities.
- Multicultural skills are useful and helpful when dealing with sexual minorities.
- A lesbian and gay culture exists.
- People are oppressed because of their sexual orientation.

It would be hard to deny these points, but they create more questions than answers. There are dozens of groups that might satisfy similar criteria, and the difficulty lies not in finding groups to include but in deciding where to end the process.

Let's examine the limitations of sexual orientation as a cultural category. The easiest place to start is to examine the differences between gender identity and sexual desires. A man, for example, can feel perfectly content with his male identity while being physically and sexually attracted to other men. His *gay orientation* does not interfere with his *male core identity*. Similarly, a male transvestite, who enjoys wearing women's clothing, may feel that he has a feminine or female *secondary identity*, but most transvestites are sexually attracted to the opposite sex. His *secondary female identity* does not affect his *heterosexual orientation*. These issues can become extremely complex. Imagine you are working with a male-to-female transsexual. She was born male but has recently completed a sex change operation, because, she explains, she has "always been female on the inside and wanted the outside to match." From her earliest awareness, she had been attracted to women. When she lived in the body of a male, people viewed her as heterosexual, but she always viewed herself as a woman and therefore considered herself a lesbian. Some people may never accept her as female, and their perceptions will interfere with how they view her sexual orientation. From a therapeutic point of view, however, it is important to let the client determine and express her sexual and gender orientations.

From this discussion of gender, it should be clear that gender identity is not equivalent with biological sex. The term *sex* usually indicates an individual's biological or chromosomal sex, and the term *gender* denotes the individual's perception, interpretation, or expressed identification of his or her sex. By age three, most children have a firmly established gender identity. By age five, most children are remarkably adept at identifying the genders of other children (Feinbloom, 1976). For most individuals, their sex and gender are congruent, but for some, conflicts arise from an early age. This leads to the rather confusing issue of defining male and female issues in counseling. For example, is an intersexual (someone born with physiological characteristics of both sexes) a real woman? Is a lesbian (a female who is primarily attracted to members of her sex) a real woman? Is a male-to-female transsexual (someone who is born with XY chromosomes, who takes female hormones to grow breasts, and has his penis surgically reconstructed into a vagina) a real woman?

As a young therapist beginning a job at a college counseling center, I remember looking forward to working with my first client. I sat in my office and imagined what he or she would be like. When he arrived, I was surprised at how closely he fit my ideal image. He was an honor student, student body president, and looking forward to a promising career. He presented with his head high, made excellent eye contact, and displayed remarkable confidence. After briefly reciting his accomplishments, he added, "Oh, and I'm gay." Without pausing, he continued, "How do you feel about this?"

A little surprised by his approach, I replied with some incoherent psychobabble such as "I think we're here to talk about you." I was ready to work with him as a client, but I wasn't prepared to answer questions about my own beliefs. As the session progressed, he began to explain his goals for counseling. For the past six months, he had dated a fellow college student. They had recently drifted apart and seemed to have lost interest in one another. He wanted to end the relationship, and he was seeking counseling to deal with his fear of saying the "wrong thing." It was a common story. I had heard it many times before from men conflicted about their relationships. The only difference in this case was that the client was dating another man.

To some degree, social bias against gays and lesbians is understandable. Our family members, friends, coworkers, and the media drop both subtle and blunt statements about why some people are not acceptable. Some of these images are bound to stay with us.

In saying this, I am not implying that counselors and psychologists should refrain from holding moral convictions. Instead, we should learn to recognize when our moral convictions preclude us from working within a client's framework. If you do not feel comfortable helping a client with his presenting problem of "accepting his homosexuality," you should not attempt to do so. Know your limitations, and refer the client to another counselor. Problems arise when we attempt to impose our moral, racial, or ethnic worldview on someone else.

7

Gays and Lesbians

Have you ever wondered what it would be like to live in a society where it was illegal to be physically attracted to someone? Let's say you are attracted to a member of the opposite sex. You aren't thinking about being attracted, but your body reacts when you notice this person. As soon as your body reacts, your mind starts reeling. "I can't be attracted to this person—it's illegal." You glance at the other person, hoping to find some flaw that might convince your body to quell its desires. As you look toward the person's face, your eyes meet. You stare at each other for an instant, and you realize that the other person is thinking the same thing you are. Is it safe to say something to this person? The police may be watching—not the police you are used to, but ones who will respond with violent force and crippling blows. This person could be a spy who may attack (verbally or otherwise) if propositioned. It's a frightening world, and a struggle between mind and body.

Would you choose to deny your bodily desire for love or to face the consequences of acting on an "illegal" desire?

Sexual orientation, perhaps more than any other topic related to gender or sexuality, elicits strong opinions. Staunch opponents of gay and lesbian behavior view it as a "manifestation of a depraved nature and a perversion of divine standards" (Ontario Consultants on Religious Tolerance, 1998a). On the other hand, those who advocate social tolerance of gays and lesbians have likened American homophobia to the "wholesale torture and extermination of innocent people during the 'witch'-burning times" (Ontario Consultants on Religious Tolerance, 1998b). Battle lines are sharply drawn, and movement from one camp to the other seems unlikely.

History of Oppression

The battle over the morality or appropriateness of same-sex relationships is fought in political, occupational, and religious arenas. Sometimes the attacks leveled against gays and lesbians come from the most unpredictable sources. For example, consider the following remark:

> I can't really warm up to homosexuals. . . . As long as they leave me alone, I'll let them be. But if my kid ever said, "I'm gay, Daddy," I think I'd die. I still think of homosexuals as fags, queers, and fruits (Feinbloom, 1976).

You may be surprised to learn that a male transvestite uttered the above comment. Many people wrongly consider all men who dress in women's clothing to be homosexual. This misunderstanding stems from problems dissociating gender from sexual issues. If other "divergent" groups comment on the inappropriateness of the gay or lesbian lifestyle, it is not surprising that the larger society has also conveyed animosity toward them. Throughout recorded history, gays and lesbians have faced oppression from heterosexuals. Even the terminology applied to this group has a frightening origin. For example, the pejorative term *faggot* (literally, a bundle of twigs used for kindling) was originally applied to homosexuals because, in the Middle Ages, people would literally burn gays as they did kindling (Stoller, 1997). Such acts of violence are not limited to the Middle Ages. Although we would like to believe contemporary society is beyond such horrors, the past century has witnessed similar tragedies.

Many people are aware of the persecution the Jews experienced during the Nazi Holocaust, but fewer realize how gays and lesbians were treated. In Germany, gays and lesbians were forced to wear pink triangles or a patch marked "175" on their clothes. The virulent homophobia that underlay the Nazi desire to annihilate Germany's gays and lesbians led to many strategies for their degradation, imprisonment, enslavement, and extermination. During the Nazis' 12-year rule, they convicted nearly 50,000 gays and lesbians of criminal homosexuality. Most ended up in concentration camps (Kogon, 1950) where they were brutalized by both the guards and other inmates. While in the camps, they were assigned to the dirtiest jobs: they worked in the clay pits and the quarries, shoveled snow with their bare hands, and were used as living targets on the firing range. Some were told, near the end of the war, that they would be released if they allowed themselves to be castrated. Instead of being set free, they were shipped to the infamous Dirlwanger penal division on the Russian front (Rector, 1981). It is now known that at least 500,000 gays and lesbians died in the Holocaust (Rector, 1981). Even when liberation came, those wearing the pink triangle remained in German prisons to serve out the remainder of their sentences.

In the United States, the plight of gays, lesbians, and bisexuals followed a different path. Prior to the 1970s, psychological and psychiatric organizations considered homosexuality a "mental illness." Gay men and lesbians had to fight to preserve their civil rights. When their sexual orientation was known, they were denied jobs, housing, and even volunteer leadership positions. Unlike all other Americans, they were forced to prove their competence, reliability, and mental stability (Stoller, 1997).

With the publication of the DSM-II in 1972, the status of homosexuality changed. The American Psychiatric Association listed it as a disorder only if it was considered "ego-dystonic." Ego-dystonic clients were those who refused to accept their sexual orientation and continued to wrestle with guilt and shame regarding sexual behaviors, while ego-syntonic clients accepted their homosexuality and viewed themselves as gay. Although this change may seem minor, its effect on the status of homosexuality was enormous. The revised perspective has been traced to Marmor's (1965) assertion that gay and lesbian people could be happy with their lives and contribute to the development of a new minority group in our society. This finding was enough to support the APA's conclusion that homosexuality did not represent an inherent disadvantage in all cultures or subcultures (American Psychological Association, 1997). Homosexuality, in and of itself, did not promote mental instability. Only the *belief* that one's sexual orientation was wrong made a client unstable.

By the late 1980s, the entire notion of ego-dystonic homosexuality was being questioned. Many of the arguments followed a simple line of reasoning: "Being uncomfortable with one's sexuality does not necessarily mean that a person is mentally ill." Discomfort or denial of one's sexual orientation may stem from the negative images projected by society, rather than the mental health status of the gay individual. Arguments such as these led to dramatic changes in the DSM-III-R, in which the categorization of homosexuality as pathology was removed entirely (American Psychological Association, 1997). Homosexuality could no longer be associated with mental illness because almost all people who are homosexual initially go through a phase in which their homosexuality is ego-dystonic. Whether individuals are straight or gay, they may have difficulties clarifying their sexual orientation, but this difficulty involves the anxiety of social emergence rather than sexual confusion.

In the 1990s, the American Psychological Association strengthened its position. Douglas Haldeman (chair of the APA's Committee on Lesbian, Gay, and Bisexual Issues) stated, "Gay men and lesbians do not differ from other populations in such areas as decision-making, intimate relationships, self-esteem and vocational adjustment" (Sleek, 1996). Statements like these have affected society's views about gays and lesbians, but new dangers have emerged to hinder the integration of gays and lesbians into the larger society.

Polls show more acceptance of gays and lesbians in the United States today than in the past, but there has been a concurrent rise in anti-gay bias. A recent Gallup Poll (Newport, 2001) demonstrates that more people than ever before consider homosexuality an acceptable alternative lifestyle (52 percent of those surveyed in 2001, compared to 34 percent in 1982), and roughly the same proportion believe homosexuality should be legal. Although these trends may seem to indicate greater acceptance of gays and lesbians, most of the change comes from a decrease in the "no opinion" category (4 percent in 2001 compared to 14 percent in 1977). In 1977, 43 percent of Americans thought homosexuality should be illegal, and in 2001, 42 percent felt the same way. In a sense, the American populace has polarized on the topic, with few people being converted to either camp. The ideological struggle has left gays and lesbians vulnerable to assault. Freiberg (1995) notes that gay and lesbians are significantly overrepresented among victims of violence. Herek, Gillis, Cogan, and Glunt (1997) interviewed 74 bisexual females and 73 bisexual males living in Sacramento and found that 41 percent of them reported having been criminally victimized at least once since the age of 16. The assaults were perceived as bias-related and were generally perpetrated by European American males. The victims of such crimes were more likely to experience depression, anxiety, anger, and post-traumatic stress syndrome than were their peers who had not been assaulted.

To counter such attacks, legislation has been introduced to increase the penalties for acts of violence and other forms of discrimination based on a person's membership in a group. In 1996, the state of Washington adopted Initiative Measure No. 669 (Munro, 1996). The act promoted equal rights for gays and lesbians without providing them special status. The difference between equal treatment and special rights was clearly delineated: "The people find that equal protection of the law, not special rights, is a fundamental principle of constitutional government and is essential to the well-being and perpetuation of a free society." The rights extended to gays, lesbians, bisexuals, transsexuals, or transvestites encompassed matters related to status, preference, orientation, conduct, act, practice, or relationships. This act also sought to protect the rights of those who opposed such lifestyles, and it prohibited teachers from acting against sincerely held views of parents on the subject. It also prohibited state organizations from promoting or approving of these lifestyles as positive, healthy, or appropriate behaviors.

Etiology

The increased acceptance of homosexuality is due in part to a broader understanding of its origins. Homosexuality exists in virtually every culture on earth, and in some, it is a highly respected lifestyle (Herdt, 1982). The question theorists have tried to answer is "Why are some persons attracted to members of the same sex?" Freud (1905) traced homosexuality to an unresolved Oedipus complex, in which a young boy who failed to identify with his father was more likely to adopt the sexual orientation of his mother. Freud believed that all people were born bisexual with latent homosexual impulses. Over the course of childhood, according to Freud, a person's sexual orientation was "determined" through early interaction with his or her parents.

Stoller's (1968) early work reestablished the psychoanalytic components of homosexuality. He admitted that boys raised with domineering mothers and distant fathers were more likely to demonstrate some form of sexual confusion, but he also noted that it was difficult to predict the form such an orientation would take. He believed that the same processes are at work for the transsexual and homosexual child. However, in the transsexual child, the mother completely overwhelms her son and motivates him to believe in the superiority of womanhood. The homosexual child merely adopts the mother's sexual attraction toward males.

Despite Stoller's continued arguments in favor of his position, later researchers have focused more on genetic etiologies. Günter Dörner et al. (1980, 1982) offered the strongest argument in this vein, stating that homosexuality results from abnormal levels of testosterone exposure during a critical stage of prenatal brain development. Gay males, he argued, had been exposed in utero to lower than normal levels of testosterone, while lesbians had been exposed to higher than normal levels.

Dörner et al. (1980) hypothesized that lower levels of maternal testosterone might be caused by environmental stress. To test his theory, Dörner located 794 German gay males born shortly before, during, and after World War II. Based on research linking stress with decreased levels of testosterone during pregnancy. Dörner, Götz, and Docke (1982) hypothesized that the stress of wartime or postwar experiences would have depleted the mother's testosterone levels. The results showed that significantly higher numbers of gay males had been born between 1942 and 1947 than in the years before and after this period (Figure 7.1).

FIGURE 7.1 *Relative Frequency of Homosexual Males Born in Germany (or GDR) Before, During, and After WWII (n = 794)*

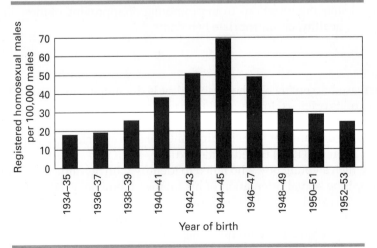

TABLE 7.1 *Variations in Sexual Orientation*

		ATTRACTION TO SAME SEX	
		Low	*High*
ATTRACTION	*High*	Heterosexual	Bisexual
TO OPPOSITE SEX	*Low*	Asexual	Gay or Lesbian

Animal studies provide some support for this theory. Hernandez-Tristan, Arevalo, and Canals (1999) found that male offspring of many animal species acted in typically feminine ways when their mother's testosterone levels were depleted during pregnancy. Newly emerging evidence also suggests that many of the differences between male and female behavior that were previously thought to be genetic may actually be hormonally based. Even sexual arousal may have more to do with controllable hormonal levels than neuroanatomy (Azar, 1998). These supporting studies have kept Dörner's theory alive, but most contemporary researchers have been looking for genetic causes.

The latest hypothesis involves the "gay gene" (the suspected gene for homosexuality may lie in a pseudoautosomal region of the X and Y chromosomes: Xq28/Yq11), which is believed to foster a predisposition towards homosexuality (Turner, 1995). The presence of such a gene would not predict a homosexual lifestyle, but it would identify children who were more likely to become homosexual. This distinction is important for several reasons. We can predict that from a group of children with the "gay gene," more would grow up homosexual than would children in a comparable group without the gene. In either case, learning and environment play a role in actualizing a child's sexual orientation.

With a continued emphasis on environmental components that shape sexual orientation, it is becoming increasingly unlikely that sexuality exists in a purely dichotomous form. Rather than classifying people as either homosexual or heterosexual, it may be more realistic to acknowledge that sexual orientation has several variations based on the relative strength of attraction a person feels toward members of the same sex and the opposite sex (see Table 7.1).

From this perspective, some people have a greater predisposition toward a heterosexual lifestyle, while others are more likely to be homosexual, bisexual, or asexual. This model, unlike the dichotomous model, suggests that some people would find it easier than others to change their orientation. Individuals who have strong sexual attraction for members of the same sex but weak attraction for members of the opposite sex (or vice versa) are unlikely to change their dominant orientation under any circumstances. Others, born with more neutral predispositions, can change but are less likely to do so after they immerse themselves in a particular lifestyle. It should be noted that lasting changes in sexual orientation are rare. A *Newsweek* poll (Leland & Miller, 1998) showed that only 33 percent of the general population believed sexual orientation is something a person is born with, but 75 percent of gay respondents believed

FIGURE 7.2 *The Continuum of Sexual Orientation as Indicated Through the Texual Orientation Dot*

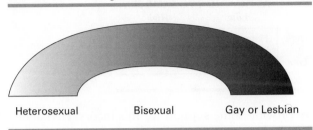

Heterosexual   Bisexual   Gay or Lesbian

their sexuality was innate. Similarly, 56 percent of the overall population believes gays and lesbians can change their orientation, but only 11 percent of gays believe this. If sexual orientation can change, it is likely to happen for only a small number of people.

Another way to think of orientation is to picture it as a continuum. Imagine we had a test for sexual orientation that resembled a mood dot (i.e., a small piece of material that, when placed on your body, turns colors to indicate your present mood). When this imaginary dot is placed on heterosexuals, it turns white. When it is placed on a person who is gay or lesbian, it turns blue. The process seems simple enough until we start viewing the results. In real life, few people would have purely white or purely blue dots. Most would have some shade of blue, ranging from faint to dark, as indicated in Figure 7.2. The closer the color is to blue or white, however, the less likely an individual would be to identify with the opposite end of the continuum.

Family

The 1990s witnessed a movement that questioned the effect families have on children. What role do parents play in the formation of their children's personalities? In regard to sexuality, it appears that biology may play a more important role than environment. Children raised in gay or lesbian households are *not* more likely to become homosexual than are children raised by heterosexual parents (Golombok & Tasker, 1996). In fact, the children of gays or lesbians do not differ from other groups of children with respect to intelligence, psychological adjustment, social adjustment, popularity with friends, development of social sex role identity, or development of sexual orientation (American Psychological Association, 1997), although those from lesbian families were somewhat more likely to explore same-sex relationships, particularly if their childhood family environment was characterized by an openness and acceptance of lesbian and gay relationships (Golombok & Tasker, 1996).

Another stereotype is the notion that gay men have a tendency to molest children. In 1977, when Anita Bryant successfully campaigned to repeal a Dade

County (FL) ordinance prohibiting anti-gay discrimination, she called her organization "Save Our Children." In a campaign fueled by fear, she warned, "A particularly deviant-minded [gay] teacher could sexually molest children" (Bryant, 1977, p. 114). What studies actually show is that healthy homosexual men are less likely than any other group to molest children.

Part of the problem with studying the incidence of homosexual molestation of children rests in the terminology surrounding it. If a "homosexual relationship" includes all same-sex relationships, then most child molestation would be homosexual. However, this includes men who are predominantly heterosexual and whose only homosexual contact is with children. It also includes gays and lesbians who have never had an adult homosexual relationship. In a study of 175 convicted child molesters, Groth and Birnbaum (1978) found that none of the adult males in their sample had an exclusively homosexual adult sexual orientation. The greatest proportion (47 percent) of the men had never had a healthy adult relationship. Of those in adult relationships, most (40 percent) were heterosexuals. The remaining 13 percent were classified as adult bisexuals. "None of the men in their study were primarily sexually attracted to other adult males" (p. 180). In a separate archival study, Jenny, Roesler, and Poyer (1994) reviewed 352 medical charts from either the emergency room or child abuse clinic of a Denver children's hospital. In these records, gay or lesbian adults were responsible for less than 1 percent of the total number of abuse cases.

Societal stereotypes depicting gay men as child abusers may be one of the reasons gay men are less likely to raise children. In 1993, a survey was conducted by the Voters News Service comparing the composition of heterosexual households to that of households headed by gays or lesbians. Lesbian and heterosexual couples were equally likely to have children living in their homes. Gay men, however, were half as likely as heterosexual men to have minors living with them (DeAngelis, 1996a). A gay man in his twenties provided some support for the latter finding:

> At this point of my life, I don't want kids. I see my friends struggling to adopt, and that's okay, but society already has a hard time with me as I am. I don't think I want to raise a child in this environment.

Even when gay males wish to raise children, they may face considerable obstacles to parenthood. Lesbians may be inseminated with donor sperm and become pregnant, but gay men have fewer options available to them. Some gay couples have teamed up with lesbian couples to raise children together, but such arrangements are intrinsically complicated. Who will care for the children? What happens if one couple breaks up? (DeAngelis, 1996a). Such complications add to the inherent pressures of child rearing and family development.

Another difficult family constellation involves a heterosexual couple raising a child with gay or lesbian impulses. In my practice, parents have brought children as young as six years old for counseling because they were worried about "inappropriate" behaviors. This usually means that their son has been playing with dolls or their daughter will not wear dresses. These innocuous behaviors are viewed as signs of a problematic sexual orientation. Although the children I have seen rarely express sexual ambiguity, their parents have sent a clear message: "It is wrong to be gay." The consequences of this message, while well intentioned, may be dire. Children may fear their parents' rejection, and they may seek other avenues of support. Such alternative support groups are rarely optimal, and therefore most therapists will find a way of involving the parents, if possible. Tom Sauerman (1995), in discussing the coming-out process for teens and young adults, suggests that the first step in speaking to one's parents about sexual orientation is preparing for possible outcomes. Before raising the issue, it is important for clients to ask themselves the following questions:

- Am I ready for the consequences?
- Am I comfortable with gay sexuality?
- Do I have the support of friends and other family members?
- Am I knowledgeable about gay and lesbian culture?
- Can I be patient?
- What is my motive for coming out now?
- Am I financially dependent on my parents?
- Are my parents emotionally equipped to handle this announcement?

The answers to these questions reflect the maturity and empathy of the client. If the client is still wrestling with guilt or periods of depression, announcing a homosexual orientation will simply drain him or her of any remaining strength. In working with these clients, role-plays should include highly negative scenarios. Even liberal or open parents may react with extreme hostility. They may banish the client from the family or attack the child's character or soul. In preparing for these unwanted possibilities, every client should have a friend, relative, or group to turn to for support. This support is valuable even when parents simply require time to process the information. If the information comes as a surprise, parents may need several months or years to process it.

The likelihood of a positive resolution will also depend on the client's motive for coming out. Clients who desire to tear down the wall of secrecy between themselves and their parents are in the best position. If animosity has already developed, and the client hopes to hurt his or her parents, this revelation could cause irreparable damage. The client should honestly examine the reason for discussing this topic with his or her parents. The client must acknowledge the risks involved and carefully consider each step.

In response to the coming-out of their son or daughter, most parents will follow six stages: shock, denial, guilt, expression of feelings, personal decision making, and true acceptance (Sauerman, 1995). Of course, no two families are alike, and some parents will fail to reach the true acceptance phase. Parental rejection presents a serious threat to the mental health of gay children, who, like all children, desire their parents' love and support. Telljohann and Price (1993) administered an open-ended questionnaire to 89 males and 31 females (aged 14 to 21 years), which explored how they felt about themselves and their parents. Approximately 42 percent of the females and 30 percent of the males believed their families treated them negatively because of their sexual orientation, and less than one in five of the participants could identify someone who had been supportive of them.

With acceptance from nongay family and friends hard to find, gay and lesbian couples face unique challenges. When gay or lesbian couples learn to accept their orientation and build a life together, they must attempt to work through a number of social difficulties. Not the least of these involves what term to use in referring to the person with whom they have chosen to spend their life. "Hi. I'd like you to meet my partner—no, that sounds like we own a business together. Really, this is my lover—but sex is only a small part of our relationship." What other options are there? "Spouse" sounds as if the other person has no gender. The terms "husband" and "wife" may seem forced and contrived. "Life partner" has a pretentious tone. The phrase "long-time companion" and words like "friend" or "roommate" often don't fully explain the relationship. "Mate" is often misunderstood. Some couples use the term "co-husband" or "co-wife" to stress the equality of their relationship. There is no perfect solution to this dilemma, because straight couples have difficulty understanding the meaning of the relationship and there are no titles in the heterosexual world that apply to same-sex intimate relationships. The word "partner," which is often used in reference to nonmarried heterosexual relationships, is the most commonly used term. It should be clear, however, that the American culture does not yet have a place for gay and lesbian relationships in the mainstream of society.

When gay or lesbian partnerships end, the couple is also likely to face unique difficulties. Susan Morton (1998) argued that divorcing lesbians share many experiences with their heterosexual counterparts, but unlike heterosexual women, lesbians often feel society devalued their relationship, which makes it difficult for them to find emotional support and understanding. Even their family members may be thinking, "I'm glad *that* is finally over," leaving the woman feeling isolated and alone. Therapists who are equivocal about their feelings regarding gays and lesbians may share this ambivalence. Such an approach is unlikely to produce positive results.

Another rarely explored but equally distressing component of some gay and lesbian relationships is the possibility of domestic violence. Rates of domestic violence in gay and lesbian households are slightly higher than in heterosexual families (Burke & Follingstad, 1999), but there is little guidance concerning how to effectively intervene with violence in these relationships (Miller,

Bobner, & Zarski, 2000). For gay men, violence in relationships may be especially difficult to address, because men are trained be independent, strong, and autonomous. They may underreport abuse or feel intense shame regarding their inability to prevent the violence.

Economics

With gays and lesbians struggling to find respect and support, it seems reasonable that they may turn to financial success as a means of gaining society's blessing. Unfortunately, employers continue to present obstacles to gays and lesbians. A General Social Survey (these surveys are conducted periodically by the National Opinion Research Center to collect data about social attitudes and demographic information), found that gay males and lesbians tend to earn less than their heterosexual counterparts (DeAngelis, 1996a). In 1995, homosexual men earned an average income of $26,000 compared to $28,000 for heterosexual men, and lesbians earned an average income of $15,000 a year compared to $18,000 for heterosexual women. These economic difficulties add to the many struggles lesbian women face, and the elevated risk of poverty also increases the level of prejudice they experience. The reasons for these trends are unclear, but it seems reasonable to assume that society continues to limit the occupational options of people who are openly gay or lesbian.

Earlier, we discussed Anita Bryant's campaign against the hiring of homosexual teachers. When she published her ideas in 1977, only 27 percent of Americans said they would accept gay people as elementary school teachers (Colasanto, 1989). In 1992, a Gallup poll revealed that this number had increased to 41 percent (Herek, 1998). While this change is significant, most of the people surveyed still believed homosexual teachers posed a threat to their children's well-being. Such perceptions, if widespread, would have an impact on wages and job availability. Any man applying for work in a female-dominated industry may be regarded as "suspect." Co-workers or bosses may not openly regard such people as gay, but they are likely to view this person negatively. Back in the 1980s, Draper and Gordon (1984) investigated how people viewed male childcare workers. Not only did the participants in this study view the workers as "homosexual," but they also viewed them as "lazy." It's possible that gay workers may be regarded negatively simply because they are males and gay.

When occupational difficulties arise, there are probable mental health effects as well. Ross (1990) found that changes in employment or income were strongly related to clinical depression and anxiety. Such changes were also associated with the development of acquired immune deficiency syndrome (AIDS) in HIV-infected patients. The impact of work and economic related variables, according to Ross, was amplified when the individual was stigmatized as gay or psychologically unsound.

Education

Occupational discrimination is not the only way in which gays and lesbians are treated unfairly. Long before they find their first job, most gays and lesbians have encountered prejudice. Gay and lesbian youths are regarded as being an invisible minority—a small group actively discriminates against them, but most of their friends are unaware of their struggles. Young people who are confused about their gender and sexual orientation are reported to compose 10 percent of our youth population (Little, 2001). If this statistic is correct, there is a huge body of students facing unique challenges who are often overlooked by teachers and school personnel. In many ways, the struggles of gay children are unparalleled. When other minority groups are harmed, there are usually advocates fighting for their equality. When gay youths are assaulted, most teachers are unaware of the reasons. They may assume the children had an innocuous argument that escalated out of control. They might even believe one boy stole something from another but was unwilling to confess. Myriad possibilities are likely to be explored before the child's sexual orientation is addressed. This puts gay and lesbian children at particular risk for physical, emotional, and social problems in the school setting (Thomas & Larrabee, 2002). When examining a sample of 3,054 students in grades nine through twelve, Faulkner and Cranston (1998) found that students who had reported having a gay or lesbian experience were more likely to report fighting and victimization, frequent use of alcohol or drugs, and recent suicidal behaviors. The frequency of these behaviors seems to be related to social taboos associated with this topic.

The tendency to assume that all children are heterosexual is often regarded as "heterosexism." Herr (1997) notes that heterosexism and homophobia contribute to the likelihood of school "failure" among gays and lesbians. At a time when adolescents are struggling to understand themselves, homosexual students face the added challenges posed by hate crimes, risk of disease, poor self-esteem, isolation, and deciding whether to come out to their friends. Attitudes of teachers may create additional problems. Half of the students surveyed by Telljohann and Price (1993) claimed that homosexuality had been discussed in their classes. However, 50 percent of the females and 37 percent of the males claimed it was handled negatively. These added pressures have led many gay and lesbian teenagers to develop poor coping mechanisms.

Teachers and administrators aren't the only ones exhibiting heterosexist behaviors. Many clients even have difficulty discussing their sexuality with professional counselors. Telljohann and Price (1993) investigated the support gays and lesbians received from others and found that only about one-fourth of students felt comfortable talking with their school counselor about the issue. In fact, less than 20 percent of those surveyed could identify a supportive person in their life.

Despite the lack of support gays and lesbians receive from school counselors, most professionals in this setting regularly deal with sexual orientation issues. Fontaine (1998) investigated the extent to which school counselors work with adolescents who are questioning their sexual identity or who clearly identify themselves as gay or lesbian. At the middle school (junior high) level, 93 percent of the counselors surveyed by Fontaine reported working with students who were dealing with sexual identity issues. Puberty, to some degree, can explain part of this number, but it is important to note that sexual identity surfaces before sexual activity has taken place. Try to think back to your tenth birthday. Puberty had not yet begun to cause changes in your body, but you had vague and unexplainable reactions to certain people. Such thoughts, when they involve members of the same sex, can be disconcerting and frightening, which explains why 21 percent of elementary school counselors in Fontaine's study had seen students with these concerns. These younger students are presenting with issues related to identity and a growing understanding of self. Even prior to age 12, gay and lesbian students are often riddled with self-doubt, depression, poor self-esteem, social isolation, and fear of negative reactions from family and friends (Fontaine, 1998). These problems often mount until the child feels there is no escape.

Mark, who experienced his academic problems well after elementary school, provided a "typical" story regarding society's treatment of gay and lesbian children:

> People kept coming up to me and calling me horrible names. I think they enjoyed watching me cry, which I did often. Some people put letters in my locker saying how I was going to hell and how my parents probably hate me. Kids from the football team would follow me home and throw things at me along the way. After awhile, I just didn't feel like living any more. I thought it would probably be better to drop out of school than kill myself.

Mark's solution to the harassment is not uncommon. About 28 percent of gay and lesbian high school students fail to graduate from high school. They usually report that their decision was predominantly influenced by ongoing verbal and physical harassment related to their sexual orientation (Snider, 1998). Snider argued that the risk was so great that special measures should be taken to protect lesbian and gay students, but there is no clear way to accomplish this goal. The Toronto Board of Education designed a "Triangle Program" that targeted lesbian and gay youth who were at risk of dropping out of high school. Snider argued that the program backfired because it further marginalized and isolated lesbian and gay students by removing them from mainstream education. If homophobia remains unchallenged, workable solutions may be slow in coming.

When gays and lesbians enter college, their struggles continue. Rey and Gibson (1997) studied abuse of gays and lesbians perpetrated by college students. The most likely perpetrators were found to be males with anti-homosexual attitudes and low grade point averages. These were the only predictable variables found for abuse against gays and lesbians. Neither age, membership on an intercollegiate athletic team, political ideology, religiosity, nor even the number of interactions an individual had with gays and lesbians had a predictable impact on the likelihood of abuse. Abuse against gays and lesbians crosses all of these dimensions. Of the 226 college students Rey and Gibson surveyed, 94.9 percent had perpetrated some form of discriminatory act against gays and lesbians. Even more alarming, nearly a third of those surveyed (32.7 percent) had committed an act that was rated as "moderately harmful or higher."

Health

With little protection from harassment, gays and lesbians face physical danger throughout much of their lives. Many attempt to "go straight," but achieving a permanent change of sexual orientation may be impossible for most of those who try. As they begin to accept the permanent nature of their sexual orientation, they often enter a period of despair. Although victimization does not appear to be directly linked to suicide attempts (Freiberg, 1995), it may play a role in self-hatred among lesbians and gays. The National Institutes of Health report that about 30 percent of all youth suicides are committed by gays and lesbians who realize that they cannot change their sexual orientation (Chandler, 1996; Remafedi, 1999). Approximately 24 percent of teenage lesbians and 30 percent of gay adolescent males reported having attempted suicide (Bradford & Ryan, 1994; Fontaine, 1998), indicating that sexual orientation is one of the highest risk factors for teen suicide. Add to this the increased incidence of alcohol and drug abuse and trouble maintaining long-term, monogamous relationships, and the vulnerability of lesbian and gay adolescents reaches staggering proportions (Edwards, 1996).

Suicide and alcoholism are serious health risks, yet they are overshadowed by the threat posed by HIV (human immunodeficiency virus) and AIDS (acquired immune deficiency syndrome). Between 1985, when AIDS was still relatively rare, and 1999, more than 729,000 people, including 8,400 children, were reported with AIDS in the United States, according to the Centers for Disease Control and Prevention (2001). Worldwide, AIDS has become the most devastating communicable disease in human history. More than 60 million people have been infected with the virus. The disease is the leading cause of death in sub-Saharan Africa, and it is the fourth biggest killer worldwide (World Health Organization, 2001).

Over the past two decades, bisexuals have received the stigma of being viewed as the prime spreaders of AIDS (Highleyman, 1993). They were believed to be responsible for turning what was once a "homosexual problem" into a "national problem" (Highleyman, 1993), but bisexuals have probably played a smaller role than the combination of unsafe sex with intravenous drug use. Sharing hypodermic needles is a very efficient way of spreading HIV, making prevention programs among injecting drug user populations another top priority. Upwards of 50 percent of injecting drug users have acquired the virus in Myanmar, Nepal, Thailand, China's Yunan Province, and Manipur in India (World Health Organization, 2001).

Intravenous drug use is only one of the behaviors associated with HIV exposure. When addressing the role of behavior in the spread of sexually transmitted diseases, it is the lack of protection, such as failure to use a condom, that best predicts HIV exposure. In studying the factors associated with unprotected anal intercourse among nonmonogamous gay and bisexual men, Folkman, Chesney, Pollack, and Phillips (1992) found that an individual's ability to cope with stress had a substantial effect on whether they would engage in unprotected intercourse. Although stress, by itself, did not predict unsafe practice, many individuals in their study used sex as a means to help cope with stressful situations. Such individuals attempted to keep their emotions to themselves and tried to deal with their feelings primarily through sexual activity. In contrast, individuals who found solace in religious faith or emotional support from others were less likely to engage in sexually risky behaviors.

When bisexuals practice unsafe sex, they are also unlikely to disclose this information to their partners. Data are reported from 745 male respondents (aged 16 to 73 years). Roughly a third of the respondents in a study of 745 bisexuals by Weatherburn et al. (1998) disclosed their homosexual activity to their female partners. That means that most bisexuals may keep their homosexual relationships secret, which may decrease their fears and increase the spread of sexually transmitted diseases. These trends are even more alarming when the shifting attitudes of bisexuals are considered. Although most gays and bisexuals believe safe sex precautions are still needed, somewhere between 6 and 8 percent stated in 1998 that they were less likely to practice safe sex because they believed that new medical interventions made AIDS and other sexually transmitted diseases less threatening (Kelly, Hoffmann, Rompa, & Gray, 1998)

When AIDS was first identified, the diagnosis required that the patient evidenced at least one serious illness resulting from a severely impaired immune system. Today, however, a person can be diagnosed with AIDS based solely on his or her T-helper blood count. A person whose blood test shows less than 200 T-helper cells in his or her blood count can be diagnosed with AIDS even before experiencing a serious illness (Kalichman, 1998). The process of testing for HIV antibodies is among the most accurate diagnostic tools in medicine. The procedures used for HIV antibody testing detect antibodies 99 percent of the time that they are present, and confirmatory tests are 99 percent correct at pinpointing which antibodies have been produced (Kalichman, 1998). However, before submitting themselves for HIV testing, clients must wait for their body to react against the virus by producing antibodies. Tests done shortly after HIV exposure are not always accurate because the body takes time to begin producing antibodies. Some people develop antibodies in as little as two weeks after becoming infected, whereas other people may take months. Most people exposed to HIV will have developed antibodies within three to six months after being infected.

Until recently, the only populations seeking HIV testing were gay males and IV drug users. In America, gay men still account for 51 percent of the total number of AIDS cases, and people who inject illicit drugs account for another 25. This leaves 24 percent accounted for by heterosexual sex, receiving HIV-tainted blood products, birth to an HIV infected mother, or some other rare cause. With heterosexual intercourse, women are more vulnerable to infection than men are because the soft tissue of the vagina is more likely to tear (Kalichman, 1998).

During the mid-1990s, the AIDS epidemic in the United States appeared to wane among certain groups. For example, in the Northeast, where AIDS rates were highest, fewer than 2 of every 1,000 young women were infected with the AIDS virus in 1996, and the numbers were falling sharply (Mental Health Net, 1996). However, there has since been a resurgence in the rate of infection. A survey from the U.S. Centers for Disease Control and Prevention (2001) found that 4.4 percent of gay and bisexual men between the ages of 23 and 29 are newly infected each year with HIV. For Blacks in that group, the figures are staggering: one in seven becomes HIV positive per year—roughly the same infection rate currently found among adults in South Africa (McClain, 2001). African American women are 17 times more likely to contract HIV through heterosexual contact than European American women, and African American men now comprise 33 percent of all new AIDS cases among gay and bisexual men (Cooper, 2000). Additionally, young people, regardless of ethnicity, remain at high risk for HIV infection across the United States, Europe, and Canada (Mental Health Net, 1996) because they are less likely to use condoms and more likely to have multiple sexual partners (Kalichman, 1998). This age group also tends to believe they are invulnerable to disease, which also elevates their risk by decreasing the likelihood that they will follow safe-sex precautions.

Cultural Uniqueness

Before looking at the ways in which specific ethnic groups approach homosexuality, it is important to realize that the gay culture has a history of its own, independent of ethnicity. During the early part of the twentieth century, repressive anti-sodomy laws were passed in New York and other areas with substantial proportions of homosexual residents. Police crackdowns ensued, raids were made on homosexual bars, and homosexuals were subject to arrest and imprisonment. In order to survive, homosexual men and women had to find code words to avoid entrapment by police. One such word was the term "gay," which probably derives from London slang. In the seventeenth century, the term "gay" was expanded from its earlier meaning of cheerful and came also to refer to men with a reputation for being playboys. Its expansion to include male homosexual activity seemed a natural extension. The term "lesbian" stems from the ancient Greek poet Sappho who lived on the island of Lesbos. As Sappho became known for her poems celebrating love between women, the term lesbian changed its primary meaning from "one who lives on Lesbos" to "a woman like Sappho and her followers."

The terms "gay" and "lesbian," however, were too well known to be used safely. Other terms and expressions were developed to throw off the police. One such term was "a friend of Dorothy." This expression referred to the *Wizard of Oz* heroine played by Judy Garland, whose musical ability and tragic life story were popular with gay audiences. Saying you were a friend of Dorothy meant you were gay. In some gay circles, myths are told how police would enter bars and begin their inquisitions with "Where is Dorothy?" The stories are told to indicate the cleverness of the gay community and the stubborn ignorance of the police.

Gays and lesbians also have derogatory terms for each other and outsiders. A "bungie boy" is a straight acting but gay or bisexual man. "Pansy" refers to an effeminate gay man. A "chicken" is anyone under the legal age of consent. A "femme" can refer to either a lesbian or gay man who acts and dresses effeminately. "Laddie" or "Lassie" refers to children with gay parents. The term began with a negative connotation, assuming that the child would also be gay or lesbian. It has been reclaimed as an affectionate term and a way for children of gays or lesbians to identify each other in public.

Learning the codes associated with the culture of sexual orientation takes place over a long process. Substantial research has been conducted over the years regarding the development of gay and lesbian identities, with possibly the clearest model being advanced by McCarn and Fassinger (1996). See Table 7.2.

TABLE 7.2 *Sexual Minority Identity Formation*

	Internal Affect	*Feelings About Minority Group*
Stage 1: Awareness	Feels "different" or "odd" but is not willing to acknowledge anything else.	Knows very little about different sexual orientations.
Stage 2: Exploration	Strong, erotic feelings emerge for members of the same sex.	There is a growing awareness of the existence of "gay culture" but little exploration into this group.
Stage 3: Deepening/ Commitment	The individual begins to gain a sense of self-knowledge and self-fulfillment. Choices about how to act out on sexual orientation begin to crystalize.	A commitment begins to form with gay and lesbian groups. There is an awareness of oppression and the consequences of group choices.
Stage 4: Internalization/ Synthesis	Love for same-sex partner spills over into an overall identity for self.	Across a variety of contexts, there is openness about being a member of the gay/lesbian community.

Beyond the culture of the gay world, there are ethnic differences in the treatment of gays and lesbians. In some Native American cultures, where homosexuality is positively associated with "having two spirits" and shamanism, members of the community have adopted the negative views of the dominant culture. Doyle Robertson (1997) encountered a Dakota woman who explained that the term for gays *(winkte)* had a verb form *(iwinkte)* which meant, "To glory in or be proud of." She added, however, that the verb form was no longer in use. For Robertson, the loss of the positive verb reflected the adoption of negative views of homosexuality.

Cultural biases have created new challenges for gays and lesbians. As they strive to form a corporate identity, they have encountered pressure from existing cultural institutions. One of the more challenging components of this developing culture involves religion. Gay rights activists and liberal clergy have criticized the Christian Coalition and other conservative groups for running an advertisement concerning a lesbian woman who had been "healed" of her plight. The woman was transformed from lesbian life and later married and had children. The criticism rested on the notion that such positions would drive "a wedge between gays and God" (Goldwyn, 1998).

In attempting to find a place within traditional religions, gays and lesbians have attempted to redefine the essential components of religion. When Chris Paige, a lesbian Presbyterian minister, was asked if gays and lesbians could be Christians, she replied, "I've been a Christian all my life... God wants integrity more than anything else" (Goldwyn, 1998). Others, such as Rich Yates, a celibate gay male who works with Harvest USA, believe the homosexual lifestyle is harmful to one's spirituality.

The debate over acceptance of the homosexual lifestyle has intensified of late within both the United Methodist and Protestant Episcopal denominations. In the summer of 1998, the subject of homosexuality nearly split the Lambeth Conference of 735 Anglican bishops. One delegate likened homosexuality to bestiality and child abuse. Many delegates expressed surprise at the ferocity of the debate. What transpired was similar to what we have seen in many other organizations. Conservative evangelicals from the United States, Australia, Asia, and England insisted that the Bible forbids homosexuality, while others expressed a willingness to accept homosexuals without question. The Episcopal denomination had to admit that attempts to reach a compromise seemed unlikely (Scripps Howard News Service, 1998). Others are likely to reach the same conclusion in time.

In the aftermath of such struggles, some gay and lesbian groups are turning to individual churches that are willing to break from their organizations' official positions. In the summer of 1998, a group of 100 San Francisco area clergy signed a statement saying they had officiated or were willing to officiate at religious marriages of same-gender couples. The signers comprised leaders from Baptist, Episcopal, Zen Buddhist, Jewish (Reform, Reconstructionist, and

Renewal), Presbyterian, Lutheran, UMC, Unitarian Universalist, UCC, and nondenominational Christian churches (Interfaith Working Group, 1998).

As promising as this movement may seem, finding a minister who will officiate at a wedding does not provide gays and lesbians with legal access to marriage. Without legal marriages, many same-sex couples find themselves unsure about how to identify themselves. For example, medical history forms and hospital admission data banks typically ask if a patient is single, married, divorced, or widowed. There is no category provided for those living with same-sex partners, but responses on these forms may determine power of attorney should the patient become disabled or unable to communicate (Lynch & Ferri, 1997). Gays find themselves wondering whether they should make their relationship known and risk negative repercussions from their employers, or downplay the relationship and leave their partners without any legal standing if they were to become disabled.

Some clients ask their therapists for advice on the morality of their sexual orientation. In most cases, even if someone is well acquainted with the literature, it is best to refer the client to a pastor, rabbi, or other religious leader. Still, therapists should become familiar with the religious teachings regarding homosexuality and understand how these teachings may affect their client's well being. Although a thorough review of the major religious teachings is outside the scope of this text, an introduction to the prevailing Judeo-Christian perspective should provide some insight into the depth of the problem (see Table 7.3). In the Christian Bible, five texts condemn homosexuality.

These passages are subject to many different interpretations, and the difficulty is compounded by the arbitrary nature with which Biblical instructions are accepted and followed today. For example, Leviticus 23 commands followers to adhere to "complete rest" on the Sabbath day and demands that animal sacrifices be carried out according to exact instructions. Leviticus 18:19 forbids a husband from having sex with his wife during, or soon after, her menstrual period. Leviticus 19:19 forbids mixed breeding of various kinds of cattle, sowing various kinds of seeds in your field or wearing a garment made from two kinds of material mixed together. Leviticus 19:27 demands that "you shall not round off the side-growth of your heads, nor harm the edges of your beard." The next verse forbids "tattoo marks on yourself." Leviticus 11:1–12 forbids eating unclean animals as food, including rabbits, pigs, and shellfish. Near the end of Leviticus, a condemnation is rendered for those failing to follow *all* of the laws. Pastors and religious scholars will need to help the client understand which, if any, of these verses apply to the client's religious worldview and identity, but it may be helpful for clients to realize that interpretation of the Bible is more complicated than it seems. Faith and discernment appear to play a considerable role in how a specific passage is understood.

For couples who keep their relationship secret, other difficulties arise. When a gay relationship ends, the trauma can be equivalent to becoming divorced or widowed. When the bereaved person is unable to express grief, the

TABLE 7.3 *Varying Interpretations of Biblical Passages on Homosexuality*

	Conservative Interpretation	*Liberal Interpretation*
Leviticus 18:22: "You shall not lie with a man as with a woman."	Homosexuality is specifically mentioned as a sinful lifestyle.	The passage directly precedes a discussion of the problems with neighboring pagan societies. The condemnation appears to be related to pagan rituals rather than loving gay relationships. It might be better to interpret this line as, "Do not engage in temple sexual practices."
Leviticus 20:13: "If a man lies with a male as those who lie with a woman, both of them have committed an abomination and they shall surely be put to death."	Gay relationships should never be condoned, and were once viewed as grounds for capital punishment.	This verse refers to those taking part in the Ba'al fertility rituals. The word "abomination" in Leviticus was used for anything that was considered to be religiously unclean or associated with idol worship.
I Corinthians 6:9: "The unrighteous shall not inherit the kingdom of God. So do not be deceived; neither fornicators, nor idolaters, nor adulterers, nor effeminate, nor homosexuals, nor thieves, nor covetous, nor drunkards, nor revilers, nor swindlers, shall inherit the realm of God."	Homosexuality is listed with some of the most vile and dangerous sins. People practicing these behaviors will be kept out of heaven.	The Greek word *arsenokoites*, translated as homosexual, was formed from two words meaning "male" and "bed." This word is not found anywhere else in the Bible and has not been found anywhere in the contemporary Greek of Paul's time. We do not know what it means. It probably refers to male prostitutes with female customers, which was a common practice in the Roman world.
Romans 1:26-27: "For this reason God gave them over to degrading passions: for their women exchanged the natural use for that which is against nature. And in the same way also the men abandoned the natural use of the woman and burned in their desire toward one another, men with men committing indecent acts and receiving in their own persons the due penalty for their error."	Homosexuality is a sexual perversion that is as vile as idolatry.	This passage refers to idolatrous religious practices that were common in the time of Paul. Verse 25 is clearly a denunciation of idol worship, "For they exchanged the truth of God for a lie and worshiped and served the creature and not the Creator, who is blessed forever. Amen." This passage stands in contrast to loving homosexual couples who are acting upon their "natural" gay desires.

process of healing may be obstructed (Slater, 1995). Grief may be further compounded if the bereaved person is closeted or isolated and thus lacking in social supports. When a lesbian or gay man sustains a personal loss, the traditional family structure is often unwilling to provide assistance. Many gay people have created alternative family networks, and effective counselors can help clients tap into these networks for support (Lynch & Ferri, 1997).

Surprisingly, an individual's ethnic background plays only a minor role in openness concerning sexual orientation. Mays, Chatters, Cochran, and Mackness (1998) surveyed 506 lesbians and 673 gay men (both groups were African American) and discovered that most had disclosed their sexual orientation to at least one immediate family member (e.g., father, mother, or sibling), but fewer had opened up to other relatives. These statistics are similar to those reported for other ethnic groups.

Ethnicity does play a role in the way sexual orientation is evidenced. At the 1996 APA Annual Convention, Joseph Stokes, Peter Vanable, and David McKirnan (DeAngelis, 1996b) compared the sexual behaviors, attitudes and perceptions of 313 African American and European American bisexual men. They found that there were more similarities than differences between the two groups, but they also observed some noteworthy differences. For example, African American men were less likely to engage in oral sex than bisexual European American men, and European American men had more male partners and engaged in casual and anonymous sex more often than African American respondents. Why might this be important information? In part, because it demonstrates differences in beliefs about sexual orientation.

In a very real sense, gays and lesbians of color are a double minority, facing challenges from both ethnic and gender prejudices. This dual existence, in some ways, forces them to choose between cultural identities: for example, are they gay or Native American? European Americans are less likely to face this dilemma. As we have already discussed, many European Americans never consider their ethnicity to be a primary component of their cultural makeup. This means that for many European American lesbians, gay men, and bisexuals, sexual orientation becomes the primary basis for identity, while for members of minority ethnic groups the primary basis for identity may remain ethnicity (Cabaj, 1996).

Psychological Issues

With so many gender, ethnic, and social issues raised by the topic of sexual orientation, many still wonder whether being gay is psychologically damaging to an individual. In 1957, Evelyn Hooker offered the first concrete evidence that sexual orientation does not appear to cause psychopathology. She found 30 gay men who were not in therapy, matched them with 30 heterosexual men by age, education, and IQ, and gave each of the men a battery of psychological tests.

She also obtained a life history of each man and provided the results of the testing and the survey to several clinical colleagues. Her colleagues were unable to identify which of the tests and surveys were from the gay men. This implies that there are no *essential* differences between the psychological adjustment of gay and heterosexual males, and there does not appear to be a "homosexual" profile apart from sexual orientation issues.

Although gays and heterosexuals do not differ on psychological profiles, there are unique psychological elements for homosexuals. Gay men, especially, are at risk for certain mental health problems (Meyer, 1995) and emotional distress (Ross, 1990). Meyer proposed that these problems arise from the stress placed on gay men from discrimination and negative experiences in society. This is often referred to as the minority stress hypothesis. At present, there is not enough information to know whether the same pattern exists for women, but there is evidence to suggest that lesbian and bisexual women may be coping with stressors resulting from their multiple minority status in maladaptive and unhealthy ways (DiPlacido, 1998).

It may be difficult to tell which comes first. Are certain mental health problems associated with being gay or lesbian, or does the experience of living a gay or lesbian lifestyle create stress that becomes a type of mental fatigue? If the former were true, then there should be some evidence of problems with psychological well-being or self-esteem. A variety of studies indicate that such pathologies do not exist (Coyle, 1993; Fox, 1996; Herek, 1991). So how can social stressors create certain mental problems? Consider, for the moment, Alice and Mary. While the two women were having breakfast together, Mary began to evidence symptoms of a cardiac arrest. Alice rushed her partner to the hospital and tightly held her hand as the two rushed into the emergency room of the local hospital. As Mary struggled to survive, the hospital administrators informed Alice that she was not allowed into the ER, which was reserved for "family members" only. A few hours later, Mary died. There should be no doubt that such an incident would be associated with feelings of helplessness, depression, and disruption of normative grief processes (Berger & Kelly, 1996; Slater, 1995).

Let's try a more complicated illustration of how difficult diagnosis can be with a gay or lesbian client. Take, for example, the case of a 16-year-old male who presented with depression and suicidality. His physician started him on paroxetine, and he attended outpatient group psychotherapy to help cope with his depression. Six months later, his family physician sent him to a psychologist to rule out bipolar disorder. During this session, the client revealed that he was struggling with his sexual orientation and having difficulty coping. When these areas were addressed directly, his complaints of mood disturbances disappeared (Hussain & Roberts, 1998).

It may seem odd that clients would be more willing to discuss suicidality and depression than their sexual orientation, but sexuality is an extremely sensitive topic. Clients fear rejection or exposure and seek only resolution to their immediate concerns. They expect practitioners to help them with traditional "mental health" topics, such as depression or anxiety. In a study of depression among gay youth, researchers found that depression strikes homosexual youth four to five times more severely than their nongay peers (Hammelman, 1993).

When issues of homosexuality are addressed, other complications may arise. Gay male partners, for example, frequently struggle with issues of competition and hierarchy, because both partners have been socialized to confirm their self-worth in this way (Scrivner & Eldridge, 1995). They may also struggle with methods of overcoming conflict. Domestic violence, or battering, within the lesbian and gay communities is thought to be underreported. When such behaviors occur in gay and lesbian couples, a "conspiracy of silence" results. These couples neither wish to discuss the violence nor expose their relationship. As difficult as it is for heterosexual couples to merge their divergent sexual identities, gay couples often experience extreme difficulty merging *matched* sexual identities. This struggle is made all the more problematic when the gay relationship is not sanctioned by society as a whole. Gay couples require a sensitive assessment, permitting disclosure in a safe, nonjudgmental setting (Lynch & Ferri, 1997).

Within-Group Differences

Gays and lesbians are often classified as a single unit, but these two groups are quite distinct from each other. From the dawn of the gay rights movement, the two genders sought different results. During the early years of lesbian feminism, lesbians sought to define themselves apart from men and reject male definitions of how they should feel, act, look, and live (Bunch, 1972). To be a lesbian, Bunch argued, was to love oneself as a woman. This definition views lesbianism not simply as a sexual act but as a woman's attempt to define her sense of self and energies, including sexual energies, around women. Women are important to her. She is important to herself. Lesbians must become feminists and fight against oppression of women, just as feminists must become lesbians if they hope to end male supremacy (Bunch, 1972).

Today, the feminist lesbian movement focuses primarily on achieving social acceptance rather than bringing about sweeping changes in society. Lesbians struggle to receive the recognition, validation, and support that are commonly given to heterosexual relationships (Kitzinger, 2001). They may even find validation of relationships to be lacking within their own community. Often lesbians will view other lesbians as available, even when in a relationship. This makes sustaining long-lasting partnerships even more difficult (Siegel, 1985). When relationships are sustained, they face additional cultural threats. Nearly half of all women will become victims of a sexually coercive act during their lifetimes (Murphy, 1992), and lesbian couples are more likely than other couples to express fears about their physical safety. Lesbians also face a great deal of difficulty with boundary setting and individuation within the relationship because both partners have been socialized to put the needs of others before their own (Scrivner & Eldridge, 1995). In contrast to men, who tend to experience themselves according to their deeds, women experience themselves relationally. In lesbian relationships, the tendency for increased intimacy and fusion (enmeshment) is multiplied (Siegel, 1985). These women often have difficulties confronting each other because they fear offending their partner.

Gay men face different struggles. Intimacy can present special difficulties for gay males. In European American culture, men are not socialized to foster intimate relationships (Harrison, 1987). They are expected to seek sexual gratification rather than emotional closeness, which may lead to additional difficulties with the risk of HIV infection. This risk is especially high among younger men (Harrison, 1987). Early in counseling, gay couples may need help with communication, courting skills, and safe sex practices. This may entail more of a psychoeducational approach than is commonly employed, but later sessions can help the couple use these skills during the session. Role plays of courting practices, expressing feelings, and discussing dating boundaries can help the partners better understand each other.

Bisexuals of either gender face an entirely different set of problems. Although it may be possible, as Freud (1905) theorized, to consider that this orientation is common to all people, such a position is untenable to most heterosexuals or gays. Many gay and lesbian organizations consider bisexuals "closet homosexuals," and believe they are attempting to hide their sexual orientation under the guise of also being attracted to members of the opposite sex. Still others argue that bisexuals are simply going through a phase and have yet to realize their "true" sexuality (McDonald & Steinhorn, 1990). They posit that bisexuals are close to achieving a healthy "straight" relationship but are trapped within the ideology of the gay world.

Even the concept of bisexuality is sometimes difficult to define. Typically, bisexuality refers to people who are "attracted emotionally and sexually to people of either gender" (McDonald & Steinhorn, 1990, p. 30), but this is not always the case. There are many self-identified bisexual women who have not had sex with men, while some self-identified lesbians have had sexual relationships with men (Highleyman, 1993). The true definition belongs to the individual. A woman who believes herself to be a lesbian but is married to a man is stating that she is primarily attracted to women. From the point of view of those around her, she is likely to be described as bisexual or straight, but sexual orientation is inherently internal. It requires self-attribution.

Counseling Issues

Although learning about gay culture can help counselors understand their clients, such understanding is useless if the counselor harbors feelings of disgust or discomfort. Counselors who believe homosexuality is sinful or wrong should not work with gay clients unless the client wishes to change his or her orientation, which we will discuss in more detail later. Therapists who cannot comfortably interact with their clients should be honest and disqualify themselves from therapy. For example, do you find yourself asking questions that would not be appropriate to ask a heterosexual client? Can you ask sexual questions without passing judgment? Your answers to these questions may reveal limitations to your ability to counsel such clients.

Male counselors who find themselves hostile to homosexuality face additional difficulties in therapy. A University of Georgia study found that men who scored high on homophobia measures appeared more aroused by homoerotic stimuli than those with lower homophobia scores (Adams, Wright, & Lohr, 1998). The arousal was measured using penile plethysmography, which measures penile engorgement. Both homophobic and nonhomophobic men were equally aroused when watching a video depicting either a man or a woman having sex or a tape showing lesbian sex scenes. Homophobic men showed a significant increase (54 percent) in penile circumference when viewing the male-male video compared to the nonhomophobic men (24 percent), but they were also more likely to underreport their arousal. If this arousal can be interpreted as sexual attraction, homophobic counselors may find themselves both attracted to and resentful of their clients. This condition is not conducive to effective therapy.

When counselors have adequately examined themselves and feel comfortable with gay clients, they should then prepare for their interventions. Sometimes, counselors focus upon issues related to the origin of the client's sexual orientation. For example, it is not uncommon for counselors to ask, "How long have you known you were gay?" Even worse, counselors could ask, "How do you and your partner have sex?" In general, it is better to address only those questions you would ask heterosexual clients. Questions concerning sexuality could be discussed from a more neutral point of view. For example, the counselor could inquire, "How did you adapt to your early sexual feelings?" As we discussed, many gay clients are uncomfortable discussing their sexual orientation. Asking inappropriate questions only decreases the likelihood of an effective intervention.

In addition to the danger of inappropriate counselor questions, a number of other challenges involve the openness of gay clients regarding their sexuality. Gary Hollander and Ariel Shidlo (Sleek, 1996) found that some homosexuals may have "internalized homophobia." These clients are less likely to reveal anything about their sexuality. An example of such feelings is illustrated by the following quote:

> I was very unhappy. I was drinking far too much and really hating my life. I was not being honest about who I was. I came to realize how internalized my homophobia was, how much I felt inferior because I was gay . . . I would second-guess myself when the partners would ask me what I thought about a case. I would never say what I was thinking. I would think, "What does he want me to think?"

Admittedly, that concern is there for everyone, but it is an extra burden for closeted gays and lesbians because we spend all our time dealing with that pressure . . . Hiding takes energy on a constant basis. It's stressful—there's always the fear of discovery or slipping up, substituting pronouns, using "my friend"-type language, "sanitizing" the nature of events (Shime, 1992).

In the past, homosexuals who had difficulty accepting their orientation were referred to as ego-dystonic, which means they could not accept themselves because of their sexual orientation. Their sexuality clashes with the other ways they conceptualize themselves. People who are more open about their homosexuality include the following:

- Those who have discussed their sexuality with friends and acquaintances, particularly with heterosexuals.
- Women who have told their parents about their sexual orientation.
- People who have strong support both within and outside the gay or lesbian community.
- Gay and bisexual men who have told their mothers about their sexual orientation.

When homosexual clients appear unwilling to discuss their sexuality or believe their sexuality is wrong, counselors must proceed with care. As we discussed, young homosexual clients are most vulnerable to suicidal ideation when they believe their sexuality is wrong but cannot be changed. When counselors encourage their clients to "overcome" or "cure" themselves of their sexual orientation, the counselor may unwittingly increase the client's feelings of despair.

There are clinicians who believe that homosexuals can adopt a heterosexual lifestyle. Joseph Nicolosi (1991, 1997) believes political ideology interferes with the scientific discourse of conversion therapy. Nicolosi believes that if homosexual clients wish to have a heterosexual relationship, he should be allowed to help them. He admits that such approaches require extensive psychotherapy (Sleek, 1996). Therapists following his model seek to help patients realize the origins of their sexual feelings, understand their relationships with their parents, and overcome their fear of heterosexual contact.

The American Psychological Association and the American Psychiatric Association, however, have challenged Nicolosi's approach. In December 1998, the American Psychiatric Association Board of Trustees voted unanimously to oppose any psychiatric treatment designed to convert homosexuals to heterosexuality (Katz, 1998). The American Academy of Pediatrics, the American Counseling Association, the American Psychiatric Association, the American Psychological Association, the National Association of School Psychologists, and the National Association of Social Workers, together representing more than 477,000 health and mental health professionals, have all taken the position that being gay or lesbian is not associated with any mental disorder, and thus there is no need for a "cure."

The united stance taken by mental health organizations against conversion therapies has stemmed from the effect such interventions have had on clients. The process of conversion often leads to depression, anxiety and self-destructive behavior. Many clients have internalized the prevailing societal prejudices against homosexuals, and conversion therapy reinforces the self-hatred they already feel. It should also be noted that the research demonstrating the effectiveness of conversion therapy is scant.

In 1990, the American Psychological Association (American Psychological Association, 1997) stated that there was little scientific evidence demonstrating the effectiveness of conversion therapy and that attempting such therapies may do more harm than good. Encouraging clients to change their immediate sexual behavior would not be very difficult, but changing a client's orientation would include altering emotional, romantic, and sexual feelings, and restructuring self-concept and social identity. Such statements have not ended the debate, however, and Columbia University professor Robert Spitzer, a psychiatrist who helped remove homosexuality from the DSM-II, has started a crusade in favor of reparative therapy. During the 2001 American Psychiatric Convention in New Orleans, he announced the results of a 200-person survey of persons reporting their experiences with reparative therapy. He conducted 45-minute telephone interviews with 143 men and 57 women who claimed they had changed their orientation from gay to heterosexual. Spitzer concluded that 66 percent of the men and 44 percent of the women had arrived at what he called good heterosexual functioning.

The American Psychiatric Association issued a statement distancing itself from Spitzer's findings, saying there was no "publishable scientific evidence" showing that therapy could change a person's sexual orientation. In the second study, also released at the 2001 APA convention, New York City psychologists Ariel Shidlo and Michael Schroeder said just 6 of 202 gay men and lesbians they interviewed had reported changing their orientation from homosexual to heterosexual after counseling. Of the rest, 178 said they had not changed, and 18 reported becoming asexual or sexually confused. Schroeder called for long-term research to determine the efficacy of counseling, which he said can leave patients depressed and suicidal if it does not change them (Depp, 2001).

Unfortunately, conversion therapists tend to view sexuality as a dichotomous state rather than something operating on multiple dimensions. Although there is still no research on this topic, it is reasonable to assume that successful conversion is a function of how engrossed someone is in their given lifestyle. People spending years actively involved in heterosexual relationships are generally unlikely to be "converted" to a gay lifestyle, just as those actively involved in gay relationships are less likely to feel completely comfortable in heterosexual marriages. The difficulty rests in identifying those clients who have only marginal tendencies one way or another. At present, there are no tests for assessing such predispositions. Counselors who attempt to follow conversion therapy should warn their clients that such approaches might not work. They should also find mechanisms to support their clients emotionally if their conversion attempts fail.

Probably the most important consideration when working with clients who wish to change their sexual orientation is answering the question "Why am I gay?" It is not uncommon for clients to use the Bible to support their contention that they are wicked and evil. This dimension often rests outside a counselor's range of expertise. Instead of turning a session into a theological debate, counselors should focus on the shame and guilt associated with such positions. Consider the following discussion:

Client: I was at church this week and the sermon was on homosexuality. The pastor spoke with such anger and fear. He read passages from the Old and New Testaments that referred to homosexuals as "depraved." He also said that homosexuals could never enter the kingdom of heaven. I left feeling so dirty and sad. I feel really bad right now.

Therapist: I can tell your church and your beliefs are important to you. How can you reconcile your beliefs with your sexual feelings?

Client: I'm not sure I can.

Therapist: It must be very painful to be in that type of bind.

Client: Yes, it is. I'm not sure I can take it any more.

Therapist: (pause)

Client: I'm not sure I can live like this any more.

Therapist: You almost sound like you're ready to give up.

Client: I just can't live like this.

Therapist: Let's explore your options. How might you be able to end this pain?

Client: Well, (laughs) I could kill myself! (laughs again)

Therapist: (sigh) Yes, that would end the conflict, but I will do everything in my power to keep you from that option. You have no idea how much you can contribute to this world and how much you mean to your family, friends, and me. What other options do you have?

Client: I guess I could become celibate or change my religion?

Therapist: Both of those sound like better options than death. How can you explore those possibilities this week?

The above session could have deteriorated into a theological debate, which would have served little purpose. At the moment, saving the client's life was of utmost importance. Most clinicians have moral views regarding homosexual celibacy or religious conversion. By advocating celibacy, an assumption is made that monogamous homosexual relationships are inferior to heterosexual relationships. This presumption can increase the client's shame and lead to future complications. By advocating a change in religion, the clients may lose a critical component of their identity and feel isolated, depressed, and alone. However, therapists can help clients work through these issues if the client continues to work with them. Considering both options provided this client with a sense of hope, which is invaluable to someone who feels completely hopeless.

Not all gays and lesbians who seek therapy want to change their sexual orientation. Gays and lesbians may seek counseling for much more mundane reasons. For example, they may seek psychological help to "come out" or to deal with prejudice, discrimination, and violence. When therapy focuses on these or other clinical issues, the client's sexual orientation may still play a role in the therapeutic process but the secondary issues are usually more important. For example, consider a young gay male who harbors beliefs about hierarchy in relationships, how men express vulnerability or tenderness, and how to use work as a means of achieving identity. If others have identified him as gay during his childhood, he may hold these masculine ideals to an extreme. His counselor may need to challenge his assumptions or beliefs about gender roles.

In addition to complex cultural issues, homosexual couples face several other difficult life issues requiring special attention from their counselors. Many counselors do not feel prepared to deal with clients who are currently married to members of the opposite sex or seeking help in disclosing their sexuality to their children. However, such cases are quite common (McDonald & Steinhorn, 1990). They are also some of the most challenging cases a therapist can face.

Counselors are often surprised when they discover that one of their married clients is gay. Even when clients make this announcement, counselors should not presume to know what they expect out of therapy. Some people will decide to keep their lifestyle secret, which often leads to increased shame and hardship, but is a decision that the client should make. Others may wish to use therapy as a means of telling their spouse. When the spouse does not suspect the client's sexual orientation, such sessions can be painful for all involved. Sometimes the unsuspecting spouse will become angry at the therapist, who is seen as a co-conspirator. Others may direct their anger toward the client, becoming violent. Therapists, caught in the middle, often feel trapped. Consider the following interaction:

> *Therapist:* Kathy, I'm glad you could join us here today. Mark had some things he wanted to discuss with you and thought this might be the best way to do it. This must be a little scary for you. Do you have any idea what this is about?
>
> *Kathy:* I have an idea. I think—well, I think he's having an affair with his secretary.
>
> (Later in the session)
>
> *Mark:* Kathy, I really love you but I feel like I'm living a lie. I can't keep this up. Honey (pause), I'm gay.

Kathy:	Can't keep what up? Your marriage? Your commitment to love and honor until death? I can't believe you're doing this! Why didn't you tell me before we had children! You f****** jerk!
Mark:	Hell, I wasn't sure. I do love you. I . . .
Kathy:	Don't you dare talk to me about love.
Therapist:	(deep sigh) (softly) There's so much pain in this room. (pause) Kathy clearly feels betrayed, hurt, and scared. Mark wants to make everything better and doesn't know how to help.
Kathy:	(to the therapist) How can you pretend to care about me? You probably put this idea in his mind anyway.
Mark:	(to his wife) Hey, this is me. Nobody made me like this.
Kathy:	(sobbing and quiet)
Therapist:	You both have some very difficult decisions to make. After today, your relationship has changed. Mark, I think you want a quick resolution, but, as we discussed before, it will take time to heal these wounds. Let's try to figure out some options.

Throughout a session of this type, counselors should help their clients express their feelings and discuss their plans. If the counselor has seen one client individually, his or her partner may view the therapist as a co-conspirator, which is what happened in the above example. Even when such blaming occurs, the counselor can help direct the flow of the discussion by helping the couple work through their pain and anger. If these issues are avoided, the couple will attempt to solve their problems on their own, which may lead them to lash out at each other through their pain. The gay client's shame and guilt could lead to suicide, while the spouse's anger could lead to physical, financial, or emotional harm.

Parents seeking to announce their sexuality to their children face similar conflicts. Children desire the love and respect of their parents, but they also expect their parents to stay together. Disillusionment with a relationship is difficult for children to understand. Similarly, gay and lesbian parents fear their children's rejection when they are told about their parent's sexual orientation. They may attempt to hide their relationships from their children even if they are "out" with everyone else. It may help your client to learn that children are relatively indifferent to the sexual orientation of their parents (DeAngelis, 1996a). Instead, they are more concerned about the quality of the relationship they have with their parents (Miller, 1979).

In addition to dreading their children's reaction, many gays and lesbians fear rejection from employers, spouses, friends, and others. These fears are often justified. In order to gain a better understanding of the potential benefits and complications related to coming out, all homosexual clients should contact a local gay or lesbian organization. These groups often hold monthly meetings or regular activities that can assist clients to increase their self-acceptance. Some examples of regional organizations include the Hetrick Martin Institute in New York (212-633-8920); Sexual Minority Youth Assistance League in Washington,

D.C. (202-296-0221); Horizons in Chicago (312-472-6469); and the Gay and Lesbian Community Service Center in Hollywood (213-464-7400). These organizations are usually well prepared to help clients address their sexuality and explore it in a safe and positive fashion.

Heterosexual therapists can also benefit by participating in these organizations. In order to understand lesbian and gay culture, it is necessary to interact with and enjoy the environment you may recommend to your clients. It may also help you to better understand the struggles and pressures homosexuals face. In addition to attending such groups, reading narratives about gay and lesbian life can benefit therapists and clients alike.

The following story, although not written from a first-person perspective, provides important insights into the counseling process. Gabi Clayton tells the tragic story of her bisexual son, Bill. Her passionate tale clearly portrays the pain and frustration of raising a gay child in a heterosexist society.

Bill's Story

(by G. Clayton and S. Schalchlin)
Bill came out to us as bisexual when he was 14. He was afraid to tell us, because he knew that other kids had told their parents and that their parents had disowned them or reacted in other ways that were frightening. He had read a book I had loaned him, *Changing Bodies, Changing Lives*, and there were coming-out stories in the book. Finally he worked up the courage to tell us, and we assured him that we loved him and accepted him. He was so happy that he wanted to tell the whole world. We recommended a support group out at the college, which I had just graduated from. Bill went to that group three times and stopped—he said he really liked it but that he was fine and didn't need to go any more.

The Kid I Knew and Loved

Bill was the child who came home from school the first week in first grade so excited because his teacher had let him go to a special room! Turns out he finished a project early and decided to make animal noises to entertain the other children. As discipline he was sent to the coatroom off the classroom. He enjoyed swinging on the closet bar so much that he wondered if the teacher would let him do it again the next day.

He was a gifted student who didn't always get the best of grades because he was always doing 20 things at the same time, and homework wasn't always on the top of the list.

Shy? Well, he told me that he was shy, but it was really hard to tell. His friends always loved him—when he wasn't driving them crazy.

He wanted to be a sculptor, a teacher, an architect, a counselor. . .

An Assault

So, he told us he went to that support group three times, and we didn't question it. Over the next year he had a hard time in school, but seemed basically OK—sometimes somewhat withdrawn or moody. We were worried, but thought it was just typical teen emotional ups and downs. We were wrong.

On the way to the third support group meeting, he had met a man from the group who was 20 years old and who told Bill he was a member of another support group for gay/lesbian/bisexual/transgendered youth. He talked Bill into getting off the bus to go to his house "to borrow a book." When they got there he made Bill have sex with him. Bill was only a 14-year-old kid who didn't expect this, didn't know what to do, and he was unable to stop it. He came home that day and pretended he had gone to that meeting because he didn't want to admit to anyone—especially himself—what had happened. Ironically perhaps, at the time I was doing a graduate internship at a counseling center that specializes in sexual abuse.

Bill finally told Sam, his best friend. He told Sam that the memories of that sexual assault were overwhelming him and that he was suicidal. He asked Sam not to tell anyone, but Sam put the friendship on the line and told me, because he didn't want to lose his friend. Bill was relieved once we knew, and we reported it to the police and got Bill started with a therapist.

It took the police a long time to find the man. When they finally questioned him he confessed to exactly what Bill had said. Then he got a lawyer, pled not guilty at his arraignment, and managed to avoid jail and court until a month after Bill died. (He finally went to prison for 13 months.) So, Bill would see him around town—which aggravated the post-traumatic stress he was in counseling for. There were times when Bill would suddenly take a nose-dive into severe depression for no apparent reason. Later we would find out that it was because he had seen this man on the bus or at the movies. Bill was so depressed and suicidal at one point that he spent some time in the hospital.

He stayed in counseling, and finally was getting back to being his old, impish self again. His mental health improved tremendously. He had a summer job doing computer and office stuff, and he loved it. He started looking forward to school again (after two rough years), and he felt like he had a future. Yes, he was back! He and his counselor agreed that he was done with therapy, and she closed his case with Crime Victims Compensation on April 5, 1995.

The Beginning of the End

The Activist Club at Olympia High School had invited Colonel Margarethe Cammermeyer to speak at a school assembly in honor of Women's History Month. (She is the highest-ranking person to have challenged the military's ban of gays, and was the subject of the TV movie *Serving in Silence*.)

Controversy erupted when a group of homophobic parents and community members—mostly people who object to homosexuality on "religious grounds"—found out that she had accepted the invitation and that the assembly was scheduled. We (supporters) found out that there was going to be a hullabaloo at the next school board meeting, and that these people were going to attend in large numbers to complain and ask the school board to cancel the assembly. Bill was out at school, and he was one of a group of kids who put up flyers about the assembly and promoted people attending the school board meeting to support the speech.

Catherine (our housemate and our kid's second mom) and I and Bill and many others attended. All in all there were about 300 people there, and the meeting lasted for about two and a half hours. I think there were a few more supporters than objectors who spoke—I was one of the supporters. The school board decided to remain firm in their decision to let her speak, and she did— on March 21, 1995. But the climate in the community was not good during this time. There were some awful, hateful letters to the editor in our daily newspaper, and in general a lot of anti-gay feelings were stirred up.

April 6, 1995

On April 6, 1995, Sam and his girlfriend, Jenny, were walking with Bill near their high school to Jenny's house to watch a video they had rented. Four guys—one of whom knew Bill and Sam because he was in the same high school (and had gone to their middle school before that)—followed them in a car and yelled things I will not repeat, related to sexual orientation. Bill and his friends ignored them and decided to walk through the high school campus, thinking it would be safer because the gate was closed. The four guys drove off, but they parked the car nearby, because the next thing Bill and his friends knew, they came up on foot and surrounded them. They said, "You wanna fight?" Bill, Sam and Jenny tried to walk away—they didn't want to fight at all.

The four then brutally assaulted Bill and Sam, kicking and beating them both into unconsciousness, while Jenny screamed at them to stop. It was broad daylight during spring break.

When they regained consciousness a minute after the attackers left, Bill, Sam and Jenny ran to the school custodian's office and called the police and then their families. They were taken to the emergency room where we met them. Bill had abrasions and bruises. They thought he might have kidney damage, but he didn't. Sam was a mess too, with a broken nose and many bruises.

While we were in the emergency room, one of the guys who did the assault came casually walking through with two other friends, to visit a friend who had just had a baby. Sam saw him, and Sam's parents called the police. When they found him, he confessed and told the police who the other guys were— they were all under 18 years old. The police treated it as a hate crime from the very beginning.

A Rally Against Hate

A lot of wonderful people in Olympia responded quickly and supported Bill (and us all) and held an incredible anti-hate-crime rally on April 14, a few days after the assault. Many people spoke there, including Colonel Cammermeyer, who returned to support the kids. At the rally, Bill spoke from his heart. He said,

> In all likelihood, my friends Sam and Jenny will never have to tolerate this—or never have to endure this type of hate crime or any other type in their lives—and I hope that's true. But as an openly bisexual person in Olympia, I'm probably—or may be—the victim of this sort of thing again. Hate crimes, especially those against homosexuals and bisexuals and transgendered people, are on the rise in this area. And that is why now—more than ever—we, the gay community, need to come out and band together and fight for our civil rights and our right to be safe in our homes and on the streets. Thank you for coming.

I spoke to Bill, and to all the people who were there in Sylvester Park that day. I stood at the microphone (voice and hands shaking—I am not comfortable with making speeches), and I said,

> First of all, I felt it was important as Bill's mom for me to stand up here and tell Bill how very much I love him and how incredibly proud I am of him. And I'm incredibly proud of him not just for the courage he's showing tonight and since this happened, but because of who he is as a person—and that means every bit of him, including the fact that he is bisexual. I think it's important for parents to do that. . . .
>
> My father was a German Jewish refugee, and the hate he faced as a child in Germany is the same hate that my son and these kids faced on that street by that school. And hate doesn't grow in a vacuum. It can't grow unless we allow it to. It grows on fear, and it grows on silence.

Alec (my husband and Bill's dad, who had always been the one of us who handled public speaking with more ease) stepped up to the microphone and said,

> I had a speech planned, but this outpouring of sympathy and support has got me all choked up. I can't talk—thank you for coming.

Alec was in tears as he left the podium.

I will never forget the events of these past weeks. I intend to fight, and I ask you all to join me, until no one has to walk the streets afraid, until no one has to live in fear of persecution or assault no matter what their race, religion or sexuality.

The Consequences of Hate

We thought he was going to make it—he seemed to handle things really well until after the rally, and then he crashed back into depression. He was suicidal again—it was too much. The assault sent him right back into the place he had fought so hard to get out of. He suddenly became depressed and suicidal, and we had to put him in the hospital again. While he was in the hospital, he heard that a friend of his was gay-bashed at school in a nearby town.

After about ten days he came home. We, and his doctors in the hospital, thought he had gotten past being suicidal. But Bill took a massive overdose on May 8. Alec found him unconscious on the kitchen floor and had him rushed to the hospital, but they couldn't save him.

He didn't leave a suicide note, but he had said to me before he was hospitalized after the rally that he was just tired of coping. It was the constant knowledge that at any time he could be attacked again simply because of who he was, that at any time his friends could be attacked for the same reason, that despite the love of his family and friends all he could see ahead was a lifetime of facing a world filled with hate and violence, going from one assault to another. He was 17 years old—an age when kids are supposed to be excited about moving out into the world as adults. The only place he felt safe was at home. He saw no hope, so he chose to end his life.

The memorial service we held for Bill was an incredible part of our healing process. It was a big job to put it all together. We felt it had to be something Bill would have wanted, and he had considered himself a pagan. We felt so strongly that he had to be respected in this last thing. It was an incredible ceremony. So many people helped, and so many friends and strangers came. We had let it be known that anyone in the community who wanted to come was invited. There was music and drumming and ceremony and people who wished to were given a chance to speak.

Everyone there had been asked to bring a candle, and was given a prayer stick (a small twig) to hold during the memorial and asked to think of good wishes for Bill. After the ceremony we stood at the door and lit each person's candle. Each person took their candle over to Sylvester Park (which was just across the street) in silent vigil, and there we collected the sticks. Later that night the family and a few close friends took the baskets of sticks to the land behind Sam's house and placed each stick in a beautiful bonfire to release the wishes for Bill so that they would travel with him. It was wonderful. Not at all "traditional"—but then we have never been known for being that . . .

The boys who assaulted Bill and Sam were finally sentenced to 20 to 30 days in juvenile detention followed by probation and community service and 4 hours of diversity training focusing on sexual orientation.

Missed He Will Be, But Not Forgotten . . .

Bill's life and death have touched perhaps thousands of people. There was an outpouring of support for us here, both from friends and from people we had never met. Throughout the time of the hate crime and Bill's suicide, I have never felt so supported and connected to a community.

At the memorial for Bill, I was given a letter written by Gery Gers, Bill's history teacher at Olympia High School that year, who was unable to attend. In his letter, he wrote:

> Bill was such a caring person, a sharer. He gave so much to me during lunch or before school. In class he shared insights that no one else did; what a big heart, gentle man, probing mind . . . in the time he was to be on this earth he touched so many lives in so many positive ways, especially mine. I want to tell you parents that both your sons have been kind, caring, giving, and considerate to me and I value that so much. In this world that is a tremendous legacy.
>
> Clearly, as you can see by the turnout of support at Sylvester Park and now, Bill was and is loved. Fear not that he will be forgotten. Missed he will be, but not forgotten . . .
>
> I'd like to write to Bill, now, what I would have written in his annual:
> Bill, you have impressed me with your keen insights into history, government, and people. Your insight comes from deep caring and feeling, the result of being tested of character and perseverance. The world is lucky to have such as you, for your demeanor is gentle and your dedication to truth and learning is exemplary. My class won't be the same without your original additions to discussions and your sharings with me after class. Your brain was always working, and so was your heart. Thanks for help with "the" assembly and for your trust and confidence in me, not to mention your smile that showed you cared. You are going to be missed, but the door's always open . . . drop by some time and know your time this year was valued.

Nothing will bring Bill back. I am sharing his story in the hope that it can help in some way to put an end to the hate and homophobia. This world cannot remain so hard to live in and to have hope in—not for all the "Bills" who are out there now, and all who are yet to come.

Alec read Bill's Story and asked me to include this:

> After Bill's death I found in one of his notebooks where he had drawn the gay symbol, a pink triangle. Across it he had written, "This is not my choice. This is not forced upon me. This just is."
>
> We wanted to create some kind of memorial to Bill, and without making a conscious decision we realized that the best memorial we could create would be our own lives—working towards the elimination of the senseless and destructive hatred that is all too prevalent in our society. Of those who may be touched by Bill's story, we ask one thing: join us.

© 1996 by Gabi Clayton, http://members.tripod.com/~claytoly/Bills_Story
Used with permission.

Questions to Consider

1. Does heterosexism exist? If so, what steps should be taken in schools and businesses to help gays and lesbians feel more comfortable in these environments?

2. Is homosexuality learned, biological, or some combination?

3. Families often have difficulty accepting the nontraditional sexual orientation of their children. How should they be equipped to handle such news? When is the best time to tell them?

4. Many lesbians have great difficulty with economic issues. Should these issues be addressed in a counseling setting? How should it be done?

5. What responsibilities or ethical obligations does a therapist have when working with a client who has AIDS?

6. How would you begin a conjoint (marital) therapy session with a man attempting to tell his wife that he is gay?

7. Jim is a 16-year-old male who seems to be doing well in life. He is a captain of the football team, earns A's and B's, and has a host of friends. He comes to counseling because he is "scared" that he is bisexual. His first sexual experience happened earlier this year. He just earned his driver's license and had intercourse with a cheerleader. Since that time, he has been fantasizing about a fellow football player. He still finds women attractive but feels "consumed" by his passion for this boy. How would you counsel Jim? Would you discourage the exploration of his homoerotic feelings?

8. Alice, a 17-year-old female, was raised Baptist and believes that the Bible is the inspired Word of God. She is troubled by a repeated dream in which she caresses the naked body of another woman. The woman in the dream is a friend of hers and she fears she will act on these impulses. "How can I do that?" she asks. "Fondling another woman is a sin." In working with Alice, how would you address these theological issues?

9. Tom is a middle-aged man with three children (ages seven, five, and two). He has been married for 20 years and considers his wife the "most important person" in his life. Still, he believes that he has lied to her for their entire marriage because he is not attracted to her. He loves her as the mother of his children, but has only been attracted to men. Last month, he had his first extra-marital affair. It was with a man at his office, and he is contemplating moving in with him. "I don't want to hurt my wife," he said, "but I want to have just one passionate relationship during my lifetime." How would you respond to Tom? Would your bias in this situation come across?

10. Sam and Sue have brought their 12-year-old son, Scott, in for therapy. During the intake session, Sam states that they believe Scott is "gay," and they want you to help Scott become "normal" again. They are willing to have therapy continue for "as long as it takes," because they realize how much pain he will experience if he "chooses" a gay lifestyle. Would you continue to work with this family? Would you work with the parents and child separately?

8

Transgendered Persons

INSIGHT EXERCISE In Tom's diversity awareness class, the discussion eventually turned to the topic of gender issues. A female classmate leaned over to him and whispered, "Can you imagine how messed up someone must be to think he is a girl on the inside?" Tom shook his head but said nothing. He was still wondering if he really was "messed up" for having the feelings his classmate condemned.

Tom, who from all outward appearances was comfortable in his male persona, had always struggled to "be" male. It was a role he could play; he had been practicing it most of his life. He just never felt natural being masculine. When women would confide in him and involve him in their conversations, he felt great satisfaction. He relished simply being able to interconnect, on an emotional level, with women, but he was constantly aware that he did not "fit in" and would be rejected for being different.

He had joined a few transgendered groups, hoping to establish "feminine" relationships with others who felt the same way, but none of these efforts seemed to help. He always felt the others were men trying to act like women, which was not the type of relationship he craved. There were a few times when he would find a sympathetic woman who would accept him as a friend or he would meet a fellow male who had a similar feminine soul, but such encounters were few and far between. In his dreams, he would imagine that he was transformed into the opposite sex and magically accepted in this role as if he had been born female. Everything about him was the same, with the exception of his body, and only he was aware that anything had changed. Of course, this was just a fantasy, and he knew it would never happen. Even if he had a sex change operation, some people would always know about his past life—or worse, they might suspect his past by his large hands or body.

How can Tom find satisfaction? Should he simply learn to enjoy talking about football and hunting? Should he strive to realize his dream and accept his feminine nature? Is there a way to choose between these two options?

*T*he television show *M*A*S*H* began each episode with a dramatic introduction of the characters. Hawkeye and his fellow physicians would be shown running to the helicopter carrying wounded soldiers, and the rest of the camp would play their part in saving lives. During this musical prologue, the nurses ran to ambulances wearing khaki pants and shirts and regulation Army hats. Basically, they wore the same clothes as their male counterparts. In several episodes Jamie Farr (Klinger) would appear wearing the traditional white uniform of a nurse. Apparently, a nurse dressing the same as a male soldier was acceptable and possibly admirable, but a soldier dressing as a female nurse was humorous.

Clothing designates how others see us. Simply from a person's clothes, an observer may guess at the individual's sex, occupation (e.g., uniforms), rank (e.g., military or medical), socioeconomic status, destination (e.g., party or office clothes), activity (yard work or playing sports), or even prison status (Feinbloom, 1976). For transgendered people (i.e., those whose gender identities do not conform to their anatomy), the frequently unconscious nature of these symbols becomes conscious, and the images associated with attire become a passageway to another aspect of the self.

Few mental health practitioners regularly counsel transgendered clients, but the topic warrants discussion as an introduction to gender issues. The construct of *gender* differs from that of *sex*. The latter usually corresponds to an individual's biological or chromosomal identity. Gender, while usually associated with sex, involves social construction as well as biology. Individuals grow up with parental, peer, and social gender training. They come to view themselves on the basis of their sex, and by the gender roles they choose to accept. Gender is a pervasive belief about one's identity as a male or female. It is largely influenced by membership within a social group and strongly reinforced from birth. Money and Ehrhardt (1972) defined gender identity as the private expression of one's gender role. They noted that a gender role is anything we do with the intention of displaying the degree to which we are male, female, or ambivalent. Sometimes we act to convince others of our gender, and sometimes we act to convince ourselves. The key aspect is the extent of our intentionality. We may view ourselves as masculine or feminine, but this conception may not be how others see us. For this reason, a man might view himself as a woman and choose to wear feminine clothes, work in a feminine industry, and adopt feminine mannerisms. Based solely on physical appearance, this man might still be regarded as masculine. In this case, his sex is male, but his gender is female. He may view himself as a "masculine woman," which may confuse people whose sex and gender match.

The potential conflict between sex and gender is only one topic requiring exploration. In some cases, an individual's biological sex is ambiguous. Plato viewed all substances as having a perfect form that existed only in the world of ideas. If such a perfect form existed for sex, there would be only two kinds of people: males, with an X and a Y chromosome, testes, and a penis; and females, with two X chromosomes, ovaries, a womb, and recognizable secondary sexual characteristics (e.g., breasts). Fausto-Sterling (2000) advocates recognition of five sexes: males, females, herms (i.e., those born with a testis and an ovary); merms (i.e., male pseudohermaphrodites, who are born with testes and some aspect of female genitalia); and ferms (i.e., female pseudohermaphrodites, who have ovaries combined with some aspect of male genitalia). Fausto-Sterling estimated that between 1.7 and 4 percent of all births fit into an intersexed category. Until recently, the method of dealing with such people was relatively predictable and based on research developed in the 1950s. Money and Ehrhardt (1972) believed gender identity was completely malleable for about eighteen months after birth. This hypothesis implied that a medical team could surgically assign the gender of an infant who was born with ambiguous genitalia. Corrective genital surgeries were performed within the first year of life, and medicine was used to help correct nature's "mistake."

Creighton and Minto (2001) argue that Money's theories were ill conceived and require updating. Rather than keep intersexed conditions hidden from patients, they argue for full disclosure. They advise physicians to avoid irreversible assignments, such as surgical removal or modification of gonads or genitalia. Instead, counseling and psychological interventions are recommended in order to give the individual time to identify his or her sex.

Because gender identity is formed within the first two years of life, counseling of intersexed persons needs to begin very early. Even before the child can speak, therapists can help the child's parents to explore the medical and surgical options open to the intersexual and to examine their own feelings about same-sex arousal patterns. Given the amount of knowledge needed to work with intersexed clients, therapists require extensive training before assisting this population. A competent therapist in this area should specialize in sex therapy and sexological theory. Topics of study include androgen insensitivity syndrome (AIS) (a genetic condition in which the body is unable to respond to androgen), progestin-induced virilization (progestin becomes virilized, which leads to a masculine appearance at birth but a feminization during puberty), adrenal hyperplasia (an XX person has an abnormal adrenal function that causes masculinizing effects before and after birth), Klinefelter's syndrome (XXY chromosomal structure), hypospadias (the urethral meatus, or "pee-hole," is located along the underside of the penis, rather than at the tip), and gonadal tumors (sometimes common in intersexed children with a Y chromosome). Numerous other conditions exist, which should indicate the level of research and study necessary to become an expert in this field.

Another important consideration is how to treat individuals with unambiguous chromosomes and genitalia who, for a variety of reasons, view their gender as corresponding to the opposite sex. In some cases, these persons may seek hormonal or surgical procedures to help their sex match their gender. These are transsexuals, who have been largely misunderstood, and the confusion associated with their gender has caused them great pain.

History of Oppression

In some cultures, transgendered individuals have received special regard. In more than 150 North American Indian tribes, there is evidence of "two-spirit" roles in which males dressed as females and took on women's duties, or women dressed and behaved as warriors (Roscoe, 1987). Even in the annals of western Europe, transgendered roles were frequently interwoven into religious practices prior to the dawn of Christianity (Roscoe, 1994). Christians felt compelled to emphasis differences in gender clothing styles because of Biblical passages such as Deuteronomy 22:5, which reads,

> 22:4 You shall not see your brother's donkey or his ox fallen down by the way, and hide yourself from them: you shall surely help him to lift them up again. 22:5 A woman shall not wear men's clothing, neither shall a man put on women's clothing; for whoever does these things is an abomination to Yahweh your God. 22:6 If a bird's nest chance to be before you in the way, in any tree or on the ground, with young ones or eggs, and the hen sitting on the young, or on the eggs, you shall not take the hen with the young . . . (American Standard Version)

The passage is confusing, in part, because it is surrounded by instructions regarding the treatment of animals. The passage appears to imply that certain social duties are required by men and women. Wearing clothing associated with the opposite gender might be seen as a way to *hide* from these duties. Also of interest is the amount of attention paid to verse five. The same chapter also condemns wearing clothes made of mixed fabrics, and it advocates killing women whose honeymoon night does not indicate the traumatic tearing of the hymen. Most Christian and Jewish sects ignore these instructions. It is also interesting to note that the contemporary condemnation against cross-dressing is unidirectional. Men are prohibited from dressing as women, but few restrictions are placed on women. In fact, during the beginning of the Christian era, women who acted like men were much admired. There are more than 30 female saints who, while they were alive, were thought to be men.

The passage has also been debated in Jewish circles. In the Talmud, Rabbi Eliezer ben Jacob uses this verse to show that women should not be allowed to go to war because doing so would require them to wear the armor of a man (B. Naz. 59a). Another Talmudic interpretation is that women should not be allowed to pose as men in order to enter areas restricted to men (e.g., temple chambers). If you saw the movie *Yentl*, you can probably imagine how this prohibition would have been observed. Men and women did not interact in social groups. Their clothing was gender-specific to prevent intermixing. If this explanation captures the intent of the law, the Bible's admonitions would not apply to most transgendered people.

For whatever reason, gender dysphoria still evokes negative reactions in our society. In some ways, federal and state laws have institutionalized society's discrimination against transgendered individuals. A number of courts have found that transsexuals and cross-dressers are not protected by Title VII of the Civil Rights Act of 1963 (cf. *Kirkpatrick v. Seligman & Latz, Inc., et al., 1979*), and transsexuals and cross-dressers are specifically excluded from coverage by the Americans with Disabilities Act (Howard, 1991). Even personal relationships fall under the jurisdiction of the government because after a person changes gender through surgery, the marital contract is rendered null and void by regulations forbidding homosexual marriages.

Despite the continued legal barriers in some states to cross-dressing, the most glaring form of oppression lies in the dominant culture's unwillingness to understand these groups. Transgendered individuals are not a unified group, and each subgroup has its own history, culture, and psychology. For example, transvestites appear to be the most common group, but there are also transsexuals, drag queens, female impersonators, and variants of each of these. Although none of these groups are still classified as mental disorders in the DSM-IV, which lists only Transvestic Fetishism, Gender Identity Disorder, and Gender Dysphoria, each subgroup of the transgendered community is distinct and requires classification.

A common misperception regarding transgendered individuals is that they are gay and have chosen an unorthodox way to express their sexuality. This is seldom the case. In fact, the emergence of transvestism as a field of interest came about because Magnus Hirschfeld (who coined the term in 1910) was surprised to find that most cross-dressers were heterosexual. It is true that some gay men who dress as women do so in a mocking style or with the intent of attracting men. Gay transgendered individuals are either *drag queens* (who are often male prostitutes) or *female impersonators* (male actors, dancers, or singers who impersonate women). In both cases, there is an intent to seduce men (Bornstein, 1994). Most transgendered people have spent their lives trying to fit into their assigned sex role, which includes learning how to interpret sexual cues from members of the opposite sex. When they suddenly find members of their own sex attracted to them, they lack the experience and training to interpret these cues. This lack of knowledge could leave a transgendered male vulnerable to sexual assault; he lacks the ability to distinguish flirtation from more serious advances. In a very real sense, an adult male who is transitioning into a woman is going through adolescence, but unlike most adolescents, she is surrounded by men who expect her to understand adult sexual cues (Carroll & Gilroy, 2002).

The complexity of transvestism rests in the fact that the individual harbors elements of both genders. If the core gender identity of a male transvestite remains masculine, the cross-dressing behavior is usually a fetish or a mechanism of coping with anxiety. If, however, there is confusion regarding one's core gender identity, or the core gender identity contrasts with that of the individual's biological sex, issues of gender dysphoria arise. In some cases, gender dysphoria may create a desire to transform one's physical body to correspond to one's gender identity. This condition is sometimes referred to as transsexualism and may lead to sexual reassignment surgery (SRS), which will be discussed in more detail later. It is not uncommon to hear a transsexual claim to be living in the wrong body (Feinbloom, 1976). This is not a delusion about having the sexual characteristics of the opposite sex—it is simply a statement that the individual's core gender identity differs from his or her sex.

Unlike male transvestites, who have a masculine core gender identity, male-to-female transsexuals have a feminine gender identity and often grow up with cognitions similar to those of girls. Devor (1989, p. 20) provides a succinct and helpful definition: "a transsexual is a person whose physical sex is unambiguous, and whose gender identity is unambiguous, but whose sex and gender do not concur." However, even this definition is being questioned because the notion of gender is less clearly defined than was once thought. The difficulty, as should be apparent by now, is that the term "transsexualism" is too specific and the term "gender dysphoria" is too general. Ekins and King (1997) noted that saying a patient suffers from gender dysphoria is about as noncommittal as saying a patient suffers from back pain or headaches. Still, it is a beginning, and at least it provides a classification that applies to transvestites and transsexuals alike.

All of the issues addressed so far involve gender identity, which is markedly different from sexual orientation. The various categories are listed in Table 8.1. A man with a female gender identity is often sexually attracted to women. In such cases, he may view himself as lesbian in order to combine his gender identity with his sexual orientation. It is important to note, as will be discussed in more detail in the family section, that most individuals with gender identities that differ from their sex are attracted to individuals of the opposite sex. Such issues are important considerations both from a counseling standpoint and for expanding our understanding of sexuality as a whole.

Regardless of an individual's intersexed or gender dysphoric identity, he or she is likely to be misunderstood. Society seems to have difficulty accepting transgendered individuals, and mental health workers should be prepared to deal with crises caused by self-questioning, harassment, physical attack, hate crimes, rape, persecution, employment and housing discrimination, denial of social services, and even murder (Feinberg, 1996). Conflicts are especially likely when a client is still in school, as access to restrooms, dormitories, and other gender-segregated areas poses challenges that will require special attention.

Some therapists may feel better about the idea of a biological male using a women's restroom if that individual is "transgendered." The problem stems from defining what *transgendered* means. Does it include people who are taking sex-opposite hormones and have the secondary (but not primary) characteristics of their gender? Does it include a chromosomally unambiguous female who has a penis? If you find yourself confused by these questions, your reaction is not unique. The complexity of defining the term *transgendered* has led to its removal from the DSM-IV. The primary reason for the change was the

TABLE 8.1 *Gender Identity Models*

	Gender Identity	View of Gendered Self	Typical Goals
Male Transvestites	Male	Two personalities: feminine and masculine	Be involved in a marriage with an accepting wife; regular and frequent opportunities to be feminine.
Female Transvestites	This is not an identified group and may not exist.		
Male-to-Female Transsexuals	Female	Highly feminine	At the minimum, live as a woman while transforming body with estrogens (which is unlikely to be completely effective if started after puberty). For some, undergo sexual reassignment surgery.
Female-to-Male Transsexuals	Male	Highly masculine	At the minimum, live as a man while transforming body with androgens and, possibly, surgery. Testosterone is extremely effective in masculinization. Transition for these individuals is often faster and easier than for M to F transsexuals.
Hermaphrodites (i.e., those born with a testis and an ovary) *Male pseudohermaphrodites (born with testes and some aspect of female genitalia)* *Female pseudohermaphrodites (born with ovaries combined with some aspect of male genitalia)*	For intersexed individuals, gender identity will be revealed with time. In past years, the primary medical treatment was to create female genitalia (which is simpler in design, though complex in function) and raise the child as a girl. We now realize that this approach is harmful, and that it is better to wait to discern the child's core gender identity and perform corrective surgery to match the perceived gender. The only time restriction is to ensure that the surgery is started prior to puberty, especially if the child has testes.		

increasing difficulty of distinguishing between relatively mild gender identity issues and a more extreme form of desire to change sex. However, the transsexual community continues to view mental health professionals with some skepticism, and their response is quite rational. The American Educational Gender Information Service (AEGIS), beginning in 1991, condemned the practice of requiring individuals to live as the other gender before surgical intervention. This is not a condemnation of counseling or a denial of intrapsychic confusion. They simply noted how disruptive and dangerous it can be for clients to have their gender differ from their sex. Transitioning their bodies to their desired sex makes them less vulnerable to hate crimes and social ostracism (Cole et al., 2000).

Etiology

There is still no clear consensus regarding the origins of transvestism and transsexualism. The most commonly cited cause is psychological, although support
for this premise is incomplete. Robert Stoller champions the psychological etiology, and Pauline Kernberg (Stoller, 1985, p. 31) conceptualizes this position well:

> My suggestion is that the mother of these boys does not consider the child as a
> narcissistic object, but as an idealized version of themselves or of the child they
> believe the maternal grandmother would have liked. Hence, the support for
> the various interests and subliminatory activities and the mother's apparent
> unawareness of any problem in the children. The mother in turn would reen-
> act an O-R [object relations] in which she herself plays the role of her own
> mother, this time enchanted with her daughter-boy; namely, her feminine son.
> The boy submits to mother's need while enjoying his own importance in ful-
> filling mother's needs.

Such stories are quite common throughout the transgendered community, and
they have been recorded throughout history. Transvestism has been reported in
many cultures over thousands of years. In the late nineteenth century, Samuel
Beeton, editor of the London-based publication *The Englishwoman's Domestic
Magazine*, began publishing letters from men who enjoyed wearing women's
corsets. By 1870, he included a letter advocating the punishment of boys by
shaming them. Beeton provided an example of how his governess dressed him
in his sister's clothes to accomplish this purpose (Farrer, 1996). Other than anecdotal evidence, however, support for the "petticoat punishment" theory of
transvestism is lacking.

Most mental health professionals have traditionally favored such environmental theories, and they appear to accept them even today (McFalls, Halluska,
& Gallagher, 1996). There are several problems with such theories, however.
The first two "mother-blame" theories (Stoller, 1968) fell prey to the same problems as early gay theories. They assumed psychoanalytic principles that are not
universal in such clients. For example, transsexuals do not necessarily hate
their genitals (Bornstein, 1994), and reassignment surgery candidates in fact
need the tissues to reconstruct new ones.

Even with strong anecdotal evidence for environmental causes, however,
researchers are continuing to explore other possible reasons for gender migration. One of the most promising theories involves both physiological and hormonal factors. Zhou, Hofman, Gooren, and Swaab (1997) investigated these
factors based on what has been learned from animal studies. In experimental
animals, the gonadal hormones that prenatally determine the morphology of
the genitalia also dramatically influence the morphology and function of the
brain (Swaab & Hofman, 1995). This discovery led to the hypothesis that sexual differentiation of the brain in transsexuals follows a pattern that differs from

what a person's appearance might imply. Prior to this point, all physiological explanations failed to provide any evidence for gender migration.

Zhou et al. (1997) found that the volume of the central subdivision of the bed nucleus of the stria terminalis (BSTc), a part of the brain that is commonly associated with sexual behavior, is larger in men than in women. Male-to-female transsexuals had a BSTc the size of genetic women. This finding is important because it indicates that the size of the BSTc was not influenced by sex hormones in adulthood and was independent of sexual orientation. To date, this is the only study depicting a possible nonenvironmental cause for gender dysphoria. It supports the hypothesis that gender identity develops as a result of an interaction between the developing brain and sex hormones. It is important to note, however, that the evidence for environmental factors (parental rearing) is strong. The contradictory findings regarding etiology, psychopathology, and success of SRS seem to be related to the fact that certain subtypes of transsexuals follow different developmental routes (Cohen-Kettenis & Gooren, 1999).

Family

Most theorists assume transvestites and transsexuals are raised in families in which the child has an intimate, unhealthy relationship with the mother and a distant or nonexistent relationship with the father (Stoller, 1985). Stoller makes his case by noting a common behavior among all of the mothers in his study. Each mother commented on her son's beautiful eyes. Many of the mothers claimed to be drawn to gaze constantly into their son's eyes. As most lovers and mothers know, staring into another's eyes is an inherently intimate experience. Mothers of transgendered children appear to engage in this intimate behavior more often than other mothers. However, since Stoller's anecdotal studies were published, empirical evidence has not supported his hypothesis. Croughan, Saghir, Cohen, and Robins (1980) confirmed the now dominant hypothesis that cross-dressing lacks a familial component either with respect to cross-dressing itself or in association with another disorder.

Despite the lack of discernible childhood patterns, by the time transgendered people start building families of their own, patterns do emerge. Most transvestites are heterosexual, married, and have children (Prince, 1976). They describe themselves as masculine except when expressing their feminine self. Money (1974) described it as a dissociative-like dual personality—a description that is sometimes endorsed by clients. Most transvestites have a feminine name, wardrobe, and identity distinct from their male identity, but they maintain their masculine core personality. When gender-dysphoric men maintain a dominant masculine gender identity, their sexual relationships may create unique conflicts. As adolescents, male transvestites often appear reluctant to date women and may experience a fear of intimacy with women. When these individuals find a partner, they may be likely to seek a conventional, stable woman who is sensitive to social mores. This woman is likely to be perceived more as a motherly type than a sex symbol. The female transvestite, similarly, is likely to be looking for a man who is a conventional, controlled, and cautious individual who will be a good provider. She seeks a man who will not be too demanding a sex partner, but she is usually *not* looking for someone with feminine characteristics. These expectations often create conflicts between the spouses, especially if the husband desires his wife to treat him as a woman. Such potent conflicts have led women married to transgendered men to create the following Bill of Rights (modified from Thomas, 1991):

1. *Disclosure:* Disclosure of transgendered behaviors and feelings should be made early in the relationship, preferably before marriage, but definitely before joining a support group or attending clubs.

2. *Communication:* Open communication between husband and wife is essential, especially regarding the allocation of family resources and when or if to tell the children about a partner's transgendered identity.

3. *Tolerance:* Husbands cannot force their wives/partners to accept their lifestyle.

4. *Femininity:* Women have the right to explore their own femininity, independently from their husband. This may include time to meditate, shop, or work on creative projects.

5. *Masculinity:* Most wives appreciate the masculine elements of their partners. They have the right to spend time with and make love to their masculine husband.

6. *Mutual Ownership:* A woman has the right to her husband's masculine body. A husband exploring his femininity should never begin hormonal therapy or seek surgical alterations without first discussing the matter with his wife.

7. *Support:* Women with transgendered husbands have the right to seek their own support groups, which promote personal growth and well-being.

8. *Support Groups:*
   • Women have the right to attend support groups with their husbands, if they so desire. Groups allowing wives should accept them as full members on an equal basis with their husbands and fully support relationship commitments.
   • If women feel uncomfortable attending public meetings, nightclubs, or rallies, they have the right to abstain from attending. They also have the right to voice concerns for their husband's membership of any group that poses security or exposure risks.

- Support groups should not mock or demean women through sexually explicit or otherwise offensive conversation, dress, or behavior.
- Women have the right to voice concern about any group, especially if that group denigrates healthy masculinity.

9. *Ownership:* A woman's clothing and personal items are hers alone. Makeup, clothing, jewelry, and other items should never be borrowed without consent.

10. *Compliance:* Wives should expect local, regional, and national gender organizations and conventions to support these rights in their programs and policies.

Even when the above conditions are met, however, the couple can face significant struggles. Transgendered individuals, especially transvestites, are likely to marry and father children. This fact contradicts the stereotypical notion that transgendered individuals are "gay," and it helps to distinguish between sexual orientation and gender identity. A man can feel feminine but still be attracted to women, just as a woman can feel masculine and still be attracted to men. Nevertheless, the idea that a man feels feminine can create substantial marital difficulties. For some men, the movement toward femininity may be limited to a simple fetish. An article of clothing may sexually arouse them, and that piece may stimulate them for the rest of their lives. For others, a subtle shift takes place that often leaves the spouse confused and frustrated. If the motivation to experience femininity continues to the point where the husband desires a sex change, the emotions for everyone involved are often overwhelming.

Consider the case of "Anne" (based on letters published on Internet support sites). She could not remember how her husband's cross-dressing began, but instead recalled the fear associated with the progression.

> When I first met Tim, I knew he loved me. At first, he seemed a little "different," but I knew he was a man. He loved sports, competitions, and cars. His mannerisms were rough, bold, and assertive. I just had to accept that he enjoyed wearing a nightgown to bed. I had to transform my love into an unconditional love. I convinced myself I could handle whatever came our way.
>
> After we were married, I approached my husband's cross-dressing with a positive attitude. I avowed, "If you can't beat 'em, join 'em." Tim joined a support group, and he learned how to dress and act feminine. He would sometimes work on his nails, hair, and clothing styles. At times, I would teach him new approaches or let him wear my clothes. It was uncomfortable, but it almost seemed like an infrequent hobby. It was a small part of who he was. But the more he attended the meetings, the worse things became. He started obsessing over his appearance and pulling away from me. Even our sex life suffered as his feminine desires grew. At times, I felt like I really was with a woman, and it bothered me. I was losing my husband.

As my discomfort and anxiety grew, Tim focused more on himself. I tried to bury my feelings and help him through his trials, but it tore me apart. Every time I helped him *dress*, a piece of me was lost. Sometimes he wanted me to play masculine roles in bed, and I would have to fight against nausea, but the worst part was my fear that our boys would find out that their father was a cross-dresser.

Shortly before our tenth year of marriage, Tim started taking more liberties with his clothing. He would leave clear polish on his nails and traces of mascara on his eyes. I begged him to hide his problem from our children. They were the one pure thing left in our marriage. I would live with his femininity as our secret, but if anyone else, especially our children, were to discover Tim's issues, it would crush me. Finally one day, he approached me and announced that he was a woman trapped in a man's body. He couldn't fight back the tears, but I didn't have anything left for him. I had given him my very soul, but it was not enough for him. I felt like a failure as a woman, wife, and mother. I wallowed in self-pity for a few days, until I found the courage to release my anger. He had betrayed our children and me. He had allowed his self-centered fixation to ruin everything I held dear.

I still feel anger now that Tim is officially Tina. When he spends time with the boys, I feel an intense urge to protect them from this freak of a man, but they have accepted him (or her). I'm just left to wonder what went wrong. Was there something wrong with me that I would choose a man with such tendencies? Did I harbor some type of feelings that drew such a man to me? I'll probably always question myself, but I'm trying to move on. I've remarried, and I love my husband. But the pit of my stomach still shakes when I think of having an ex-wife.

Some readers may believe that women wanting a masculine husband will naturally leave such a marriage or will be less likely to have children than those whose husbands are not transgendered. Neither of these assumptions is true. When a woman discovers that her husband enjoys wearing women's clothing (i.e., is a transvestite), she is likely to react with anxiety. However, after the shock fades, she is likely to be supportive and hope that he will "get over it" (Woodhouse, 1985). When she realizes that the "problem" is unlikely to be resolved, she is forced to look inside herself and decide what the behaviors mean. Weinberg and Bullough (1988) found that women with low self-esteem were more likely to rate such relationships as poor than those who thought more highly of themselves, and women with low self-esteem were more likely to feel they had failed as wives and to fear exposure.

Participation of both spouses in marital therapy may help to lower divorce rates (Croughan et al., 1980), and when divorce occurs, it is often for reasons unrelated to the gender dysphoria. Still, feelings of betrayal are commonly experienced by the nontransgendered partner, especially when the dysphoria extends to the point of seeking surgical correction. The nontranssexual partner is likely to feel abandoned and angry. These sentiments have led some to argue that transgendered persons are unfit to be parents. In part, there is a fear that children will become confused about their own gender identity (Green, 1998). The nontransgendered parent may also create negative images of the TG parent, who is often not present after conversion and who may be blamed for all of the family's problems (Gardner, 1998).

Green (1998) noted that the transsexuals he worked with at Charing Cross Hospital in London had not seen their children for years. In part, they avoided their children because they accepted the argument that their presence could harm their children's development. Others feared reprisal from their former spouse because they realized that any additional legal complications would further complicate their situation.

There is no direct evidence indicating that contact with a TG parent adversely affects children. Green's (1998) case studies demonstrate that gender identity confusion does not occur and that any teasing is no more problematic than the teasing children get for a myriad of other reasons. Most of the harm to a family appears to come when the TG parent is removed. Such loss intensifies children's confusion and often leaves them wondering if they caused conflict between their parents. When children do experience problems, counseling interventions have been proven to be effective in helping them adjust to the changes in their lives (Sales, 1995). The best way for the family to adjust is to undergo counseling as a unit prior to or at least during the transformation. Even if the parents are unwilling to involve their children, marital counseling early in the transition process may mitigate the hostility of the nontranssexual parent and this helps the children to adjust (Green, 1998).

Green (1998) explored the stability of families coping with gender-dysphoric parents and examined the long-term effects on children. He interviewed the children twenty years ago and then followed up to see if their opinions remained the same. His findings demonstrate that transsexual persons can be effective parents and that children can understand and empathize with their transsexual parents. Children's best interests are not served by one parent's bullying opposition to the children's continuing contact with the other parent. Divorce may be inevitable between the parents, but separation need not be inevitable between parent and child.

Economics

When a man chooses to live as a woman, her financial prowess often suffers. Alice, a 33-year-old male-to-female transsexual, stated, "The only thing I miss about being a man is male privilege." It is important to note, however, that our operational definition of gender involves self-perception or identity. As such, it is logical to assume that gender-dysphoric males would be likely to pursue professions typically associated with femininity. This would mean that they would be more likely to earn lower wages than their masculine peers simply on the basis of their occupational interests. At present, however, there is no evidence to support this hypothesis. Sellers, Satcher, and Comas (1999) studied 103 children ranging in age from 8 to 11, categorizing them according to the Children's Sex Role Inventory, which measures comfort in gender roles rather than gender identity. Most of their participants were classified as androgynous, but gender identity did not predict differences in occupational desires. A year earlier, Kulik (1998) had reported similar findings. Despite one's comfort in masculine or feminine activities, occupations are chosen based on other criteria.

One reason why gender may play a small role in occupational identity is basic economics. Generally, women tend to earn less than men, which may lead male-to-female transsexuals to pursue masculine occupations. When they begin their careers, they may choose masculine professions to *prove* their manhood. By the time they transition into womanhood, they may already be well accepted in their fields. Lombardi (1999) points out another important consideration. Male-to-female transsexuals who are politically active and involved in TG social organizations are likely to be college-educated, married, employed full-time in a professional occupation, and have a family income between $35,000 and $50,000. Such wages are above the national average, implying that for many transgendered individuals, financial hardship is not inevitable. Clients should realize, however, that the early transitioning phase is more likely to entail financial hardship than the latter phases.

Social factors may play a part in determining the income levels of transsexuals. Barrett (1998) found virtually no differences between the rates of employment for transsexuals pre- and post-SRS, although mean incomes were higher post-SRS. This implies that individuals find greater social acceptance as women than they received as men wearing women's clothing. This trend has been very stable, and Berrett's findings closely approximate those by Hunt and Hampson (1980) twenty years earlier.

Given the relative inelasticity of wages for transgendered individuals, it is not surprising to find that when their dysphoria interferes with their occupation, they are more likely to seek help. Croughan et al. (1980) interviewed 70 male members of cross-dressing clubs, mostly in Los Angeles, Chicago, and Denver. They split the participants into two groups: those seeking psychological treatment and those who did not seek such interventions. Although the two groups were more similar than dissimilar, there were important key differences. More than 95 percent had experienced financial hardship or relationship problems due to their cross-dressing, but individuals who had sought treatment were significantly more likely to have experienced relatively severe financial and social consequences ($P < 0.05$). With regard to occupation, 24 percent of those who sought treatment had experienced adverse consequences from their gender-related behavior, as compared to only 8 percent of those who did not seek treatment.

Education

As with occupational issues, Croughan et al. (1980) found that individuals were more likely to seek therapy when their gender dysphoria affected their education. Of those who sought therapy, 18 percent had experienced negative consequences in school, compared to only 3 percent of the group that did not seek therapy. However, given the secrecy of cross-dressing, it is difficult to ascertain what educational difficulties, if any, are encountered by this population. When a person is identified as transgendered, he or she can face extreme prejudice ranging from verbal abuse to physical violence, but most members of the transgendered population effectively hide their dysphoria. This concealment may lead some to believe that they do not exist or that they do not require special care.

School counselors can assist transgendered students in working through issues of denial, guilt, and shame, helping them to identify ways to act upon their feelings withoug jeopardizing their well-being. If a student has a desire to cross-dress, for instance, but does not want this behavior to be observed by others, the counselor can point out that cross-dressing would be difficult to conceal in a dorm or in the parents' home, but might be indulged with little risk in the privacy of a motel room, at a support group meeting, or at one of the many transgender conventions held across the country. If the student wishes to appear in public cross-dressed, the counselor can discuss the potential for being recognized in one's home town or on campus and suggest ways the student can dress and behave in public to minimize the risk of exposure. Support groups can be especially useful in providing suggestions of this nature.

Health

When a transgendered male decides to take estrogens, he often looks forward to developing large breasts and living as a woman. Many transsexuals fail to realize that the introduction of these hormones into their bodies will cause permanent changes and have serious health consequences. For example, taking estrogens will increase the risk of developing cancers of the breast, liver, and gall bladder (Ayerst Laboratories, 1988). The increased breast development actually makes the transsexual as susceptible to breast cancer as a genetic female. Estrogens also increase the risk of blood clotting in various parts of the body, leading to a higher incidence of stroke, angina (narrowing of a coronary blood vessel), or pulmonary embolus (a clot that forms in the legs or pelvis, then breaks off and travels to the lungs). Even when the hormones do not produce life-threatening consequences, their use often leads to nausea, vomiting, depression, breast tenderness, and fluid retention. Estrogens may also increase or worsen existing medical conditions such as asthma, epilepsy, migraines, heart disease, or kidney disease.

In addition to all of the above health problems, the results of the treatment may be less dramatic than the transgendered individual anticipates. Breast development is usually about one size smaller than the breast size of genetic women in their family of origin, although results are difficult to accurately predict for any given individual. Some transsexuals choose to receive implants and then find their breasts continuing to grow. As many women have come to realize, large breasts can cause discomfort, backaches, and mobility problems. In addition to problems with excessive growth, some GID individuals change their minds as their bodies change. Consider "Angela's" note to a transgendered newsgroup:

> After almost five months, I knew it [hormone treatment] was not what I wanted. The changes were too drastic, too all enveloping. And while my soft skin disappeared and my thighs lost their newly found thickness, what breasts I had developed barely shrunk. They aren't so large, maybe a cup and a half, but they are there. Large nipples, my areola grew wider and is much darker. The breasts have begun to sag just a bit. I am now going to have surgery to have them removed. And even then, there will always be an extra fold of flesh there. So, everyone, until you know for sure, hold back.

Other common expectations for hormone treatment may include a reduction in facial hair, but estrogens have no impact on facial hair. The treatment may actually make electrolysis more painful by making the skin softer and more sensitive. Beyond all these problems, however, there is also a loss or elimination of the masculine sex drive. As the hormones continue to affect receptor sites throughout the body, the penis can become very tender and erections may actually become painful. The penis may atrophy as well, which can cause problems for sexual reassignment surgery because the penile wall is used to create the vagina. In addition to all of these consequences, after a period of time (two to eight months) on hormones, permanent sterility results.

Cessation of hormone treatments does not restore fertility. Instead, estrogen withdrawal produces a number of additional painful consequences. Initially, when a male ceases taking estrogens, the resulting hormone vacuum causes depression, lethargy, and irritability. When the male hormones start to be produced again, the client is likely to experience sudden, intense periods of aggression, belligerence, and compulsive behavior.

For female-to-male transsexuals, the results of hormonal treatment vary depending on how long it has been since the onset of puberty. For example, the results are considerably more dramatic in an 18-year-old than a 28-year-old, but results usually are not dramatically different between a 38-year-old and a 48-year-old (Savina dot com, 1998).

With effective and continuous dosages of male hormones, a number of irreversible changes begin to occur. The vocal cords thicken, which deepens the voice, although not necessarily all the way down to the register of an average male. Fertility decreases as the menstrual cycle becomes irregular and then stops. Sex drive increases, hair on the face and body begins to grow more quickly and becomes thicker. Male-pattern baldness may set in, and oil and sweat glands become more active. Muscle mass increases with light exercise. Fat is redistributed, with the face becoming more typically male in shape and fat from the hips moving upward to the waist.

Masculinizing hormones fail to change the size of the individual's breasts, although they may change in shape. Breast removal must be done surgically. There is also little change in the shape or size of bone structure, although bone density may change slightly (Savina dot com, 1998).

If an individual continues the process to the point of seeking surgical reassignment surgery, the procedure is elaborate. Male-to-female genital surgery is widely available for about $10,000 and is done in one or two stages. The result can be cosmetically very good, and orgasmic ability may be retained. The operation is elaborate and beyond the scope of this text, but briefly, the penis is partially flayed and pushed inside out into a newly created body cavity. Lifelong dilation is required to keep the cavity large enough to receive a penis during sex. For female-to-male surgery, the process is significantly more difficult. Sometimes hormonal interventions can enlarge the clitoris, which, with surgery, may resemble a small penis. If a hysterectomy has been performed, the vaginal opening can be closed, and a scrotum fashioned around prosthetic testes. Complication rates are much higher if there is an attempt to create a urinary conduit through the neophallus (Barrett, 1998). Such a procedure can eliminate orgasmic ability and create potentially serious health risks. Obtaining sufficient tissue to create a neophallus or neoscrotum may also pose problems. Some surgeons use tissue from co-incidental vulvectomy or mastectomy, after previous stretching of the skin with subcutaneous tissue expanders. There are also significant costs involved. Breast reduction, hysterectomy, and genital surgery can cost upwards of $100,000.

Cultural Uniqueness

A cursory overview of transgendered culture might leave a spectator to conclude that this is a unified group. It might take a few visits to clubs catering to the transgendered community before one begins to appreciate the diversity. One of the most obvious cultural issues involves the terms transgendered people use to identify themselves and their communities. Self-referents such as "gender variant," "gender-bender," "gender outlaw," "gendertrash," "genderqueer," and "trans person" each connote significant differences (Carroll & Gilroy, 2002). In terms of a cultural practice, it is possible to view transgendered individuals as having gender mobility (Hirschauer, 1997). The notion of gender mobility addresses a continuum of gender identity. It may apply to an intersexed individual who is raised as a girl but later decides he is male. Gender mobility may lead to a medical reshaping into the desired gender, although the extent of this reshaping will depend on the individual's gender identity.

Many transgendered individuals attempt to convince themselves that immersion into the stereotypical behavior of their chromosomal sex will cause their desire for transformation to dissipate. For example, genetic males may join the military, play rough sports, or become involved in other masculine rituals. Usually, these efforts fail to establish a greater sense of masculinity. Instead, after cross-dressing in isolation for a few years, the desire to be accepted as a member of their alternate sex may lead them to expand their activities (Buhrich, 1978). These activities usually involve going outside the home, which poses significant risks to the transvestite.

For cross-dressers, but less so with transsexuals, the skills involved in attempting to pass for a member of the opposite sex tend to be self-taught. Makeup may appear overdone, gait may be more masculine than feminine, and the individual may be unaware of how easily others can guess his true sex. The failure to fit into society as a woman may lead to social withdrawal, or, if he is fortunate, contacts with a local association of cross-dressers. The association can provide a safe location for cross-dressing, instruction on how to pass for a woman in public, and opportunities to role-play feminine roles. One of the most important aids for the cross-dresser is the opportunity to be photographed in his feminine attire. These pictures hold special value for the transvestite (Feinbloom, 1976).

For male-to-female transsexuals, or individuals diagnosed with gender identity disorder, there is often less difficulty passing in the female world. From early childhood, these individuals have viewed themselves as females. From their earliest memories, they have played with feminine toys and dolls, preferred feminine clothes, drawn pictures of attractive women, played fantasy games in which they took on feminine roles, and avoided masculine activities. Many of these children express a desire to grow up as a woman and have difficulty accepting they will not become women without medical interventions. A joke that is sometimes told in transgendered circles may help to illuminate this point. "How do you tell if a transvestite has been in the ladies' room?" There is often a pause for effect. "The seat is left up." Any transgendered individual would never commit such a faux pas. They are more likely to be hyperfeminine in their presentation and go to great lengths to remove any indication of their "maleness."

In some Native American cultures, the term "two-spirit" is applied to gay and transgendered individuals. The term refers to a blending of masculine and feminine spirits. Historically, especially among tribal peoples of the northern West Coast, there have been two-spirit cross-dressers who were dubbed shamen with special healing powers (Pilling, 1997). Typically, these have been individuals who viewed themselves as neither women nor men, but members of some other gender, as is common in non-Western cultures (and is becoming increasingly recognized in the West as well) (Eyler & Wright, 1997). They may regard themselves as either ungendered or bi-gendered. In either case, their classification is different from the traditional Western dichotomous view of sex and gender.

European American perceptions of transgendered people have historically been less positive than those of Native Americans. Political and social condemnation led transvestites to pursue their activities in solitude or in safe, private venues (Bolin, 1994; MacKenzie, 1994). During the 1990s, transgendered individuals began to view themselves differently. Rather than striving to slip invisibly into the other gender, or assimilate, transsexuals began to view themselves as a distinct cultural group. Similarly, today's transvestites are less likely to request a "cure" and may instead seek psychotherapy to help integrate their gender identity into all areas of their lives (Ekins & King, 1997). These attitudinal changes, together with the increased visibility of transgendered people, have led to the emergence of a "third sex."

The International Bill of Gender Rights (1995) asserts that transgendered people are entitled to a wide array of civil rights, including access to gendered spaces such as public toilets or publicly available locker rooms at gyms and swimming pools, protection against employment discrimination, and the right to marry people of the opposite gender but same sex. It is difficult to predict whether such cultural goals will ever be achieved in America or abroad.

Psychological Issues

> "The guy could be a crackhead, a psychopath, a flasher, a junkie, a transvestite, a chain-saw murderer, or someone really sick, like Rick." Becky, from the 1992 movie *Sleepless in Seattle*, by Jeff Arch.

The psychological status of transgendered individuals has been misunderstood and misrepresented. The psychological classification of transgendered individuals varied considerably over the twentieth century. Transsexuality has been labeled a psychotic condition, a neuroendocrinopathy, a borderline syndrome, and a creative defense mechanism (Hirschauer, 1997). Clearly, the range of these nosological classifications implies the existence of a political agenda. In most cases, individuals with "gender identity disorder" and "transvestic fetishism" have been perceived as maladjusted men and women who can be "treated" and made better by the medical community (Denny, 1997). Such conceptualizations provide a treatment framework that has helped many transgendered people in crisis, but it has also contributed to an atmosphere of shame and guilt by establishing certain gender identities as illnesses (Bolin, 1988). Therapists will experience greater success if they focus on the secondary psychological issues to the gender dysphoria; i.e., fetishisms; inability to perform at work; and physical abuse from family members (Denny & Green, 1996).

Although there are political implications for keeping gender identity in the DSM-IV while removing homosexuality, the fact remains that gender identity issues remain diagnosable. With this in mind, it is important to discuss what the psychological ramifications of these "disorders" are. Defining the differences between transvestites and transsexuals is a more daunting task than it appears. The DSM-IV describes Transvestic Fetishism as follows:

A. Over a period of at least 6 months, in a heterosexual male, recurrent, intense sexually arousing fantasies, sexual urges, or behaviors involving cross-dressing.

B. The fantasies, sexual urges, or behaviors cause clinically significant distress or impairment in social, occupational, or other important areas of functioning.

Specify if: With Gender-Dysphoria: if the person has persistent discomfort with gender role or identity.

Criterion A is said to change over time. If an individual begins to cross-dress while sexually aroused, it does not mean that he will always be aroused by the activity. The DSM-IV notes that the progression of the "disorder" may lead to nonsexual behaviors. The individual may use the dressing as a means of relaxation, excitement, or anxiety release. In such cases, if the "condition" continues to cause distress or impairment, the diagnosis is applied.

Diagnostic complications also exist for Gender Identity Disorder (GID). For adults, such a classification is relatively easy, but diagnosis during childhood is more complicated. The DSM-IV defines GID as being manifested by symptoms such as preoccupation with getting rid of primary and secondary sex characteristics (e.g., request for hormones, surgery, or other procedures to physically alter sexual characteristics and thereby simulate the other sex) or belief that he or she was born the wrong sex. It is also contrasted with a physical intersexed condition in which the individual has sexual characteristics of both sexes. Intersexuals (sometimes known as hermaphrodites) are unfortunately forced into living one role or the other, but this confusion is not associated with GID.

Of primary importance when defining GID is the presence of a marked level of distress or impairment in social, occupational, or other important areas of functioning.[1] One of the areas that could cause distress is the existence of self-abusive behaviors. The actual rate of suicidality among GID teens is unknown, but it is likely to resemble the rates among gay and lesbian teens, who share similar guilt and shame traits (Denny, 1997). A retrospective study of mortality

---

[1]It is interesting to note that sexual orientation is included in the diagnosis of sexually mature GID individuals. Although homosexuality is no longer considered diagnosable, it is clinically relevant when the client is transgendered.

and morbidity in a cohort of 425 transsexual patients given hormonal therapy found five times more deaths in male-to-female persons than expected (Asscheman, Gooren, & Eklund, 1989). Other studies have indicated that up to 50 percent of post-operative transsexuals may consider suicide (Denny, 1997).

Mutilation of the genitalia also occurs with some frequency in transgendered persons (Haberman & Michael, 1979). This self-mutilation can consist of self-castration, penectomy, or both. In some cases, the individual prepares carefully. Lowy & Kolivakis (1971), reported that one individual, after repeatedly being denied hormonal treatment by the medical community, became a nurse and took a course in urological nursing so that he could do a more competent job of castrating himself. However, self-mutilation is most likely to occur during times of extreme frustration and in association with substance abuse.

If there is a psychological issue separating transgendered individuals from nontransgendered people, it would involve an attempt to salvage a fragile sense of self. Hartmann, Becker, and Rueffer-Hesse (1997) found a modest but significant narcissistic pathology in most of their transgendered clients. They argued that this narcissism served the purpose of attempting to stabilize a fragmented self. This is not to say that other psychological issues may not be present for transgendered clients. It has been well documented that transgendered individuals often report problems with mood, anxiety, and abuse of alcohol or other drugs (Denny & Green, 1996).

Substance Abuse

In general, cross-dressing is infrequently associated with sadomasochism and not at all with exhibitionism, but there are psychological issues associated with transgendered behavioral patterns. Although alcohol and cigarette use do not appear to increase after corrective sexual surgery (Barrett, 1998), substance abuse is common with this population.

Because transgendered young people are often desperate to change their bodies, they are easy prey for unscrupulous "practitioners" who perform quasi-medical services in exchange for money. In addition to all of the substances that are traditionally considered when one thinks of substance abuse (alcohol, tobacco, marijuana, cocaine, heroin, amphetamines, and barbiturates), transgendered youth seek to feminize or masculinize their bodies by injection of hormones and liquid silicone.

Hormones are obtained from other transgendered persons (or from nontransgendered persons), or by forging prescriptions, or are purchased in Mexico. They are injected, often without proper attention to safety precautions, often in large quantities, and in unorthodox areas of the body such as the breasts and genitals, using the street logic that "more is better" and that the hormones will somehow be more effective if administered directly to the genital and breast areas. Hormone pills are abused, as well.

Hormones are potent substances, and their administration is associated with a variety of risks, including thromboembolic events (i.e., deep vein thrombosis, pulmonary embolism, or both) and elevation of liver enzymes for estrogens (the female hormones), and liver damage for androgens (the male hormones). Their use requires periodic medical monitoring, which includes blood tests, but transgendered youth who use hormones procured on the street receive no monitoring or other procedural safeguards such as counseling (Walker et al., 1984).

Medical-grade silicone was once obtained by cannibalizing breast implant sacs, but this source (which was probably rarely used, anyway) dried up after the FDA's ban (*San Francisco Chronicle*, January 8, 1992). The most commonly used silicone, both before and after the FDA ban, is an industrial grade purchased in hardware stores or automotive supply houses (*Oakland Tribune*, February 18, 1993). It is injected subcutaneously into cheeks, lips, chins, foreheads, breasts, thighs, hips and almost any other imaginable part of the body by nontrained, unlicensed lay "practitioners" who travel across the country, charging large sums for such "treatments." Eventually, the bodies of the "patients" may contain large quantities (up to 3 liters) of liquid silicone. Once injected, the substance is impossible to remove without extensive plastic surgery, and scarring is almost inevitable (Ohtake, Itoh, & Shioya, 1992). Some patients have experienced ruptures in their silicone implants. The silicone leaks into their system and migrates, leaving the breasts asymmetrical. If the surgical removal of the silicone is less then complete, the patient may be left with joint pain, muscle aches, swelling, and memory loss.

In addition to the potential physiological problems directly associated with TG individuals, there is some evidence of concomitant psychological features. Hartmann et al. (1997) compared the scores that men and women with gender dysphoria received in their MMPI-2 profiles with the scores obtained by members of a control group. Men with gender dysphoria scored higher on the so-called "neurotic triad" of Hypochondria, Depression, and Hysteria, while women with gender dysphoria scored lower on these scales than the control group. Similar findings were revealed on the scale for paranoia (scale 6). The male dysphoric group was significantly more trusting than the control group, while the women had an increased tendency for paranoia.

Within-Group Differences

Clarice: (puzzled) Dr. Lecter, there's no correlation in the literature between transsexualism and violence. Transsexuals are very passive.

Dr. Lecter: Clever girl. You're so close to the way you're going to catch him—do you realize that?

The Silence of the Lambs, by Ted Tally (1989).

In the 1991 film *The Silence of the Lambs*, the serial killer stole the skins of women to clothe himself. The movie script briefly commented on the poor correlation between violence and transgendered individuals, but the association between transsexualism and violence likely stayed with many moviegoers. It is unfortunate that such images are presented in connection with transgendered individuals. In addition to transvestites and transsexuals, there are also various intersexed conditions that fit into the large category of transgendered. Klinefelter Syndrome is a genetic abnormality involving XXY chromosomes. These individuals may develop gynecomastia (female-appearing breasts), wide hips, and narrow shoulders, but appear otherwise masculine. In Turner's Syndrome, the individual is missing a second chromosome (XO). These people develop anatomically as females but have no gonads to produce sex hormones.

In addition to chromosomal anomalies, there are other important physiological conditions that cause feminization. Complete androgen insensitivity affects some XY males and prevents their bodies from absorbing the testosterone produced by the testes or introduced through medication. While these individuals lack internal reproductive organs (e.g., ovaries, uterus, and vagina), they appear feminine. Temporal lobe disorder (paraoxysmal) appears to produce cross-gender behavior in males. With the remission of the brain disorder, the aberrant behavior immediately stops. Other conditions can cause masculinization. Otherwise normal females who received large doses of progesterone (a female hormone biologically similar to androgens) in utero have masculinized genitals and are likely to be described as tomboys. All of these conditions are relatively rare, however, and are unlikely to be encountered by most counselors.

With regard to the two primary groups discussed in this chapter, cross-dressers and transsexuals, cultural differences abound. For example, consider the meaning associated with clothing. Male transvestites, unlike transsexuals, usually view their core gender as masculine but often believe they have a second self or a feminine identity. This other self may be distinct from the core gender. Transvestites, who are almost exclusively male, range from fetishistic, intermittent cross-dressers to cross-dressers who wear traditional feminine or exaggeratedly feminine clothing on a regular basis. In any case, while *dressed* as women, they desire to appear feminine or to experience femininity, but their appearance, occupation, vocation, and other life components are strictly masculine (Feinbloom, 1976).

For most transvestites, the pattern of feminine dressing begins as a fetish. A piece of clothing becomes a symbol of sexuality and is used as an erotic tool. Often, these behaviors begin around puberty. In adolescence or early adulthood, the transvestite may begin experimenting with entire outfits and attempt to pass as a woman in public. If these behaviors continue through adulthood, they may lose their sexual power and become a way of escaping from stress.

Stoller (1985) claims the erotic element may cool down but is unlikely to disappear. Sexual motivation may be displaced by gender dysphoria in the aging transvestite when the cross-sexed clothes are viewed as a mode of personal expression. When this transition occurs, some transvestites may express interest in living as a member of the opposite sex. The presence of gender dysphoria is also associated with a desire to seek hormonal or surgical sexual reassignment. Few transvestites, however, will seek sexual reassignment. Instead, they tend to view their dressing as a hobby (Feinbloom, 1976), but, as we will discuss, a hobby that can cause great pain.

Transsexualism is considered to be the extreme end of the spectrum of gender identity disorders. This condition is characterized by, among other things, a pursuit of sexual reassignment surgery (SRS) (Cohen-Kettenis & Gooren, 1999). Transsexuals experience a sustained desire to match their anatomy to their core identity. In many cases, they will seek to surgically alter their genitals, take female hormones, undergo electrolysis, or endure plastic surgery.

The above definitions are oversimplified, but it must be said that none of the terms applied to transgendered persons are easily defined. Stoller (1985) argued for two types of transsexual classifications: primary and secondary.

For example, consider the case of Terry, an individual somewhere along the way of gender migration. Terry was born male and appeared unremarkably masculine throughout his childhood. Just prior to puberty, however, he developed a fetish, as described below.

> I started dressing in women's clothing during childhood. At first, I just wore my mother's panties. When I reached adolescence, I found my desire had extended to wearing an entire outfit. By the end of high school, I was wearing makeup and venturing outside for evening drives. During college, I realized that I wanted to feel more feminine. I started taking progesterone and estrogen that I stole from my mother who was taking them to help with menopause. After a few months, I started growing breasts and I got scared. I tried stopping the treatment, but I couldn't handle the emotional swings. I convinced myself that I needed the treatment, but I didn't want to become a woman. Now, I have small breasts and I take the estrogen in very small amounts. I'm happy with myself this way, and I don't want to go any further.

Terry did not seek corrective surgery to become a woman, and he still derives satisfaction from being male. Struggles to define such individuals have led to a distinction between *primary* and *secondary* transsexuals. The former are typically children who, from an early age, felt that they were members of the other sex. Their appearance and behavior are indistinguishable from that of the opposite sex, and they are likely to request SRS at an early age. Secondary transsexuals, by contrast, do not enter gender dysphoria until later in life. Although Terry could be considered a secondary transsexual, even this term is problematic because he ended his feminization prior to surgical correction.

When an individual continues to the point of SRS, a number of unique cultural elements arise. In addition to changing the information on birth certificates, Social Security cards, driver's licenses, college records, and other important documents, there are issues associated with a new identity that can take years to sort out. Previous employers may refuse to provide references for someone who changed genders, or the transgendered individual may feel uncomfortable providing documents with the previous name.

Counseling Issues

Counselors with limited exposure to transgendered communities sometimes exhibit a voyeuristic curiosity with transgendered clients (Ettner, 1996). The topics can be stimulating and intellectually provocative. For these reasons, counselors should establish ties with both local and national support organizations prior to beginning work with such clients (Carroll & Gilroy, 2002). Such ties will not only benefit the counselor and provide insight into a unique cultural group, but an increased knowledge of these groups can help clients connect with such support groups. Transgendered clients who belong to local support groups are significantly more likely to feel better about themselves and their gender issues (Lombardi, 1999).

Although the Harry Benjamin International Gender Dysphoria Association's Standards of Care still recommend ongoing psychotherapy for transgendered individuals (Meyer et al., 2001), counselors should understand the purpose of these interventions. Croughan et al. (1980) found that, in their small study, all but two of the subjects had tried to stop cross-dressing on at least one occasion. These efforts are not surprising, considering the social stigma associated with this behavior. What is surprising is that more than half of the study's participants made only one attempt to quit cross-dressing. Fewer than 30 percent tried three or more times to quit. Attending therapy made no significant difference in the number of attempts to quit or the rate of abstinence from cross-dressing. The longest average period of abstinence for those who were surveyed was only about one year.

With the exception of isolated cases associated with episodes of psychosis (Lukianowicz, 1959; Ward, 1975) the course of cross-dressing is consistently described as chronic and unremitting. This characteristic was certainly evident in the present study, where, on the average, subjects had been cross-dressing on at least a weekly basis for more than two decades, with occasional brief periods of remission usually lasting from a few months to a few years. A comparison with Buhrich's data (1978) reveals that 54 percent of transvestites in his study attempted to discard permanently all of their women's clothes, with 40 percent discarding them on more than one occasion.

The act of attempting to quit gender-dysphoric behaviors often involves "purging." For cross-dressers, but less so with transsexuals, there may be a recurring cycle of buying and throwing away or destroying expensive clothing, cosmetics, and reading materials. This "binge-purge" syndrome is quite common.

Individuals who purge are likely to swear they will never cross-dress again and to divest themselves of everything that reminds them of the behavior.

Material purged may include contact information that they will need when they once again begin to acknowledge and deal with their issues. Purging may be primarily emotional, with the individual swearing he or she will never again engage in transgendered behavior. In a purge phase, she or he may stop attending counseling sessions and refuse to return phone calls from the counseling center; this may be the counselor's only indication that a purge has occurred. Inevitably, the individual will once again begin to accumulate clothing, sometimes in an almost manic fashion. The inability to abide by the decision to purge can lead to additional guilt.

These issues of shame and guilt can often lead to distorted self images, self-hatred, confusion, and self-defeating behaviors. It is important for clients to realize that gender conceptions are stable and unlikely to change. Effective interventions can help clients to accept their feelings and prevent the gender dysphoria from hampering their social, occupational, or educational lives. One method of helping may be to discuss whether the problem is "avoiding acting female" (in the case of the male transvestite) or "having to act male." For many, there is just as much pressure involved in feeling trapped into playing the male role as there is excitement in transforming into a feminine character. In some ways, the dilemma is similar to the plight of a person who is employed as a construction worker while feeling better suited to be a librarian. Eventually, such a person would probably sneak some books to the work site and read in a corner where the other workers would be unlikely to notice.

Children with Gender Dysphoria

With children, therapists and parents alike may feel a need to effectively instill a stable and sex-congruent gender identity. It is important to realize that most young children who experience gender dysphoria will not seek sexual reassignment surgery as adults (Green, 1987). Green studied 50 feminine boys over a period of 15 years. The boys were decidedly feminine as toddlers and consistently cross-dressed (94 percent by age six). They chose to play with dolls, preferred female playmates, and expected to grow into women. An unusual aspect of Green's study was its outcome. Three out of four feminine boys became homosexual as adults, and only one could be considered transgendered. This appears to contradict the conceptual separation between gender and sexual orientation, but these constructs are separate only in adults. Among children, transgendering and sexuality may often be mixed. The process is not linear, and it is often difficult to predict how childhood behavior will evolve.

It was once believed, largely because of the case of John/Joan, that gender could be assigned at birth. In this case, John, while only eight months old, had complications during a botched circumcision. During the operation, his penis was accidentally burned to ablation. The physicians involved decided John could be raised female and convinced his parents to rename him Joan. "Joan" was given estrogens and treated as if he had always been female. The procedure was considered a success until "Joan" rejected hormonal treatment at age 12. Throughout this time, nearly everyone who knew her regarded Joan as masculine. She wore masculine clothes (against her parent's wishes), urinated standing up, and played masculine games. By age 14, she had completely rejected the feminine role thrust upon her, but she had no knowledge of her male past. She simply did not feel feminine. When she refused her final feminizing surgery, her father told her about the surgery she had received as an infant. She immediately requested a mastectomy and phallus reconstruction (which was completed one month prior to his sixteenth birthday) and changed his name back to John. He is currently married, and his second phalloplasty has allowed him to have intercourse with his wife. He is the adoptive father of three children (Colapinto, 1997; Conlon, 1997).

Such cases have forced theorists to realize that gender is not simply a learned behavior. In all likelihood, we are not gender neutral at birth and are strongly influenced by the prenatal environment (Diamond, 1996). If a child's gender is ambiguous, it has been argued that the individual should be allowed to make this decision, because it affects every element of functioning.

By the time an individual reaches adolescence, the decision regarding surgical reassignment is no less daunting than for younger children. There is limited research in this area, but adolescents who undergo sexual reassignment surgery appear to resolve their gender dysphoria (Cohen-Kettins & van Goozen, 1997).

The decision to pursue sexual reassignment is permanent and requires painstaking consideration. On the one hand, if no action is taken, puberty will introduce natural hormones, androgens (male hormones) and estrogens, and quickly curtail the effectiveness of transformation later in life. These considerations are made more complicated by the increase in false positives when initially diagnosing gender dysphoria. There is no simple method for diagnosing the disorder, and there are several risk factors that complicate the process. For example, stress-related late onset of the gender conflict, fetishistic cross-dressing, psychological instability, or social isolation appear to confound the diagnostic process (Kuiper & Cohen-Kettenis, 1998). Kuiper and Cohen-Kettenis also recommend using a multidisciplinary team to lessen the risk of personal biases or insufficient information.

An important first step, in the diagnostic process and treatment plan phase, is to recognize that transgendered issues are not static. This is especially true for children and adolescents, who are constantly creating and discovering themselves. Ekins and King (2001) recommend using the gerund of transgender, namely "transgendering," to highlight the process elements. The active form of the word not only addresses an individual's process of change, but it addresses a societal movement as well. For transgendering clients, the psychological elements of change are always connected with sociological perspectives. The individual's perception of gender and gender roles will continue to evolve within their broader culture.

Transsexuals

When an individual is effectively diagnosed, sexual reassignment surgery (SRS) is an effective method to treat the most extreme form of gender dysphoria. Overall satisfactory post-operative results have been reported for 87 percent of male-to-female transsexuals (MtFs) and for 97 percent of female-to-male transsexuals (FtMs) (Green and Fleming, 1990).

Despite such positive predictions, Robert Stoller, arguably the leading expert on transgendered clients, had argued that little good has come from the social experiment of "sex change" (Stoller, 1985). He believes that primary transsexuals would feel trapped without the option of surgical correction, but most transsexuals seeking sex changes are secondary transsexuals who are less likely to benefit from the procedure.

Research on postoperative functioning of transsexuals does not allow for unequivocal conclusions, but there is little doubt that sexual reassignment substantially alleviates the suffering of transsexuals. However, SRS is no panacea. Psychotherapy may be needed to help transsexuals adapt to the new situation or deal with issues that could not be addressed before treatment (Cohen-Kettenis & Gooren, 1999). How will an individual's friends, relatives, or co-workers react to her new gender identity? What happens if she comes to the conclusion that the decision was a mistake? Can she accept the fact that she will become sterile after SRS? Can she face the prejudice and discrimination that will inevitably follow? These are important considerations that should be thoroughly explored in therapy.

The hormones themselves are also likely to affect the individual's emotional lability. Slabbekoorn, Van Goozen, Gooren, and Cohen-Kettenis (2001) identified differences in the ways male-to-female and female-to-male transsexuals responded to hormonal treatments. MtFs experienced negative emotions more intensely than FtMs both before and after hormone treatment. This finding was not new. Buchanan, Eccles, and Becker (1992) concluded that adolescents' emotional swings were associated with the hormonal changes in their bodies. It is important to realize that anti-androgen and estrogen treatment will increase emotional intensity, while testosterone treatment in FtMs will likely reduce emotional intensity, with the exception of aggression and sexual excitement. These chemical changes are especially important considering suicidality. Males, unaccustomed to intense emotional fluctuations, may find themselves at greater risk.

If clients follow the standards of care and undergo a "real-life" test prior to receiving SRS, therapists should use this time to help them adjust to their internal and external changes. This waiting period provides the transsexual with an opportunity to determine whether the new gender role is congruent with his or her goals and plans. The answer to this question may not be as obvious as it first appears (Barrett, 1998). Counseling can help the individual explore any issues that arise and ensure that the transition goes as smoothly as possible.

Transvestites

When transvestites present for treatment, it is usually because they want help in salvaging their marriages (Bullough & Bullough, 1993). They usually have little or no desire to change their cross-dressing behavior, but the behavior offends the client's wife. Honestly confronting the situation is the best place to start. Both partners need to realize that the cross-dressing is likely to continue but that the cross-dresser has the ability to curtail the compulsions.

If the cross-dressing is so frequent and intense that it interferes with daily activities, obsessive-compulsive tendencies may be present. Lithium, fluoxetine (Prozac), buspirone (BuSpar), and colmipramine (Anafranil) have been used in such cases (Bullough & Bullough, 1993), but it should be noted that transvestites are reluctant to seek help for their condition. In fact, when they seek assistance, it is usually for depression, family conflicts, or some other problem.

As mentioned earlier, successful treatment will address self-acceptance and overcoming the shame associated with the cross-dressing behavior. The therapeutic process is more difficult when the individual's significant others lack the necessary understanding. Consider the following case.

Marsha: This is hard to talk about, but Kyle's sexual desires make me uncomfortable.

(Kyle looks down in shame.)

Therapist: Can either of you tell me more?

Marsha: He wants to dress up in women's clothing when he makes love to me.

(silence)

Therapist: Kyle, you have been very quiet during all of this. Do you feel comfortable talking about this topic?

Kyle: I know it sounds bad, but it's not just a sexual thing for me. I just enjoy wearing nighties.

Marsha: When we were first married, there wasn't a problem. Then one night, he asked if he could wear one of my nightgowns to bed. He said he was just curious what it would be like. He never told me that he had worn them for years. Slowly, he started asking more and more often until it seemed like it was every night.

Kyle's discomfort is readily apparent, and it is clear that there are issues to work out with regard to his behavior. Kyle will need to identify what benefit he obtains from his cross-dressing and to learn to behave in a way that does not harm his relationship. The process may seem difficult for many cross-dressers. They may state that they "cannot control the impulses," and believe that their desires only get worse when abstinence is attempted.

Kyle: I can't control it. If I try, I find myself dressing even more often. I need to do this for reasons I do not understand.

Therapist: When you are at work, what do you do when you get these impulses?

Kyle: Well (pause) I can put them off until I get home, but that's different.

Therapist: We've already discussed that cross-dressing rarely just disappears. The trick is to train your mind so that you will be able to dress in a manner appropriate to your situation. When you decide what you want, we will need to set a routine that is appropriate for all involved.

Kyle is experiencing compulsions specifically associated with cross-dressing. An effective therapist will help the client focus on the emotions accompanying the behaviors, rather than on the compulsive behaviors themselves. Often the compulsion to cross-dress increases when anxiety, boredom, fear, or sexual frustration is present. Clients will need to learn to cope with such feelings and view their transvestism as only one means of coping.

Bonnie's Story

The following letter was written by a transvestite who sought counseling for depression. He wrote the letter about two years prior to undergoing treatment, and he offered it as evidence that he had "come to grips" with his femininity and believed his depression originated from other (biological) sources. As you read the note, imagine how you would counsel such an individual. Try to decide whether you would focus on the gender issues or the depression. Are they necessarily linked? If they are, would it be wise to link them together if the client views them as unrelated?

Dear Andria,

I know that you probably gave up hope on me quite some time ago, and while my temporal knife was not meant to slash any hearts, I can understand if you are harvesting any malicious (or apathetic) feelings against me.

This long-winded introduction is simply attempting to convey my humblest apologies for taking so long to write back to you. Actually, you wrote to me at a terrible time. I had just "purged" myself of my feminine self, Bonnie, and I was attempting to go back to just being Mark again.

As with my other three purging attempts, the process failed miserably.

Now I am [cross] dressing again (although not on a regular basis), and I am attempting to find some good out of this whole situation. If you are wondering why your letter did not get "purged" with all the rest of my stuff, it is because your letter, and one other, were hidden in my desk at work. I had planned on writing back before my "manly" feelings overpowered Bonnie, but the feelings attacked without mercy, and I was left a mindless bowl of mush.

I am not sure why my purging emotions emerged when they did. Maybe my body had just had enough of trying to be both male and female at the same time. Nevertheless, I am now cross-dressing again, and I am constantly attempting to deal with these emotions in a way that won't put me in some asylum.

In fact, last night I dressed up and went to the library to study. I was not sure how this was going to go over, but everything worked out fine. I walked around for a while, picked up some interesting books, visited the ladies' room, and left. Nothing special or out of the ordinary happened, and I think that Bonnie finally had a chance to just be a normal part of my life.

Another event, however, dramatically changed my life and was probably part of the reason for my latest purge. It happened last summer when I decided to go shopping. I specifically sought to try on a dress in a women's clothing store. To make a very long story short, I tried on my dress (and liked it very much), but during the process I was "picked-up-on" by three different men. They each used stereotypical lines, and they all greatly disgusted me.

I did feel like a woman through the whole process. However, my feelings were not right. I am not a woman, and I do not want to be a woman in some make-believe world. I don't mind pretending to be a woman for small amounts of time, but I do not want to be a woman. I think this frightened me out of dressing, and it left me very confused and hurt.

A few months later I decided to be Bonnie for our Halloween party at work. In contrast to my previous experience, I do not think that this could have gone any better. I walked around the office, and was constantly being talked about by every clique. Some of my closest friends were walking up to me and introducing themselves because they did not recognize me. The whole experience left me very excited about dressing up.

Nevertheless, feelings come and go, and I found myself trying to suppress my womanly passions in order to please my wife and my conscience.

I realize now that no matter how hard I try, I won't be able to completely eliminate these feelings, so I'm just hoping to keep them under control, shield them from all outsiders, and continue some correspondence with people in similar situations. Therefore, I am now ready to correspond on a regular basis with you (if you desire), and I am interested in finding out what is going on in your life.

Questions to Consider

1. What is the difference between sex and gender?

2. How would you define the difference between a pre-operative transsexual and a transvestite?

3. Why do you believe the term transsexual was removed from the DSM-IV?

4. In your opinion, what are the causes of gender identity problems?

5. What advice would you give to a woman married to a male transvestite?

6. What is likely to pose the greatest threat to gender-dysphoric individuals in the workplace?

7. Should children with gender identity conflicts be allowed to attend school as a member of their perceived gender?

8. What are the primary effects of ingesting sex-contrary hormones?

9. The act of attempting to quit gender-dysphoric behaviors often leads to "purging." Should counselors recommend such an action?

10. How should the compulsiveness of transgendered clients be addressed?

9

Women and Feminism

I tried to imagine what it would be like if all the men in the world suddenly disappeared. How would things change? My first impression was that the change would be marvelous. No more wars, spousal abuse, or social denigration of women. The image was peaceful and refreshing, but it was not real. I started to think about the sensitive men and aggressive women I know. I began to wonder if women would fill the voided roles once occupied by men. They might; it's hard to say.

I turned to my daughter and wondered how her life might change without men in the world. She would never have to question her competence in so-called masculine occupations. She would never have to fear walking to a park alone or wonder if her outfit was too provocative. The world, even if just for her, would probably seem safer and possibly more caring.

Is this assessment fair? I'm not really sure, but it is interesting that the first thought that came to my mind regarding "living as a woman" involved "men." Maybe this is the deeper issue at hand. Can we define womanhood without contrasting it with manhood?

Women's roles, identities, and occupations changed dramatically during the twentieth century. Within a single century, American women won the right to vote, challenged men in traditionally masculine jobs, were elected to office at the national level, and sought to become "superwomen" who could work outside the home, manage a household, and raise children—doing all of these things easily and well. These changing roles have led to new understanding of the sexes and new psychotherapeutic approaches for women.

During the 1960s and 1970s, at the apex of the feminist movement, biological differences between the sexes were downplayed. This trend reversed a previous overemphasis on the supposed gentleness and meekness of the "fairer sex," but it may have swung the pendulum too far in the other direction. Sociobiologists and evolutionary psychologists noted that differences between the sexes had an evolutionary origin, but few considered how, or even if, those differences continued to affect contemporary behavior (Ehrenreich, 1999).

In addition to the obvious physical differences between the sexes, there are more subtle distinctions that are generally accepted by researchers. For example, women are more likely to be right-handed and less likely to be color-blind than men. Their brains are smaller, as befits their smaller body size, but more densely packed with neurons. Women have more immunoglobulins in their blood, while men have more hemoglobin. Men are more tuned in to their internal aches and pains, while more regions of women's brains are devoted to sadness. These are just a few of the proven differences between the sexes, and these differences affect many aspects of life. Nevertheless, it should be noted that the similarities are more numerous than the differences. An anonymous joke spreading across the Internet advises: "Men are from Earth. Women are from Earth. Deal with it." The fact that women and men are more similar than they are different is often considered unworthy of media attention or even the attention of researchers (Unger, 1990).

Although women and men share many of the same strengths and weaknesses and today's women are more independent, self-sufficient, and economically stable than ever before, they still must contend with discrimination and prejudices. Their newfound freedoms and responsibilities have also created a series of new challenges that are likely to remain for some time. Before examining the lives of contemporary women, however, it is important to review what women have had to endure throughout the ages.

History of Oppression

"Men are not the enemy, but the fellow victims. The real enemy is women's denigration of themselves." (Betty Friedan)

Women have been part of every culture and every ethnicity throughout history, yet they have been oppressed in most of these groups. One helpful introduction to this topic comes from evolutionary psychologists Daly and Wilson (1990). They researched the economic arrangements surrounding marriage rituals in more than 1,000 cross-cultural settings and found that women were devalued in many of these societies. In 580 societies, the groom or his family pays the bride's family. The woman is viewed as a commodity to be sold. Marriage arrangements in many other cultures are not much better. In 27 societies, women are exchanged between family groups (e.g., daughter for daughter). In 53 societies, bride prices are set, and in 27 societies, dowries are offered to lure wealthy husbands. More equitable arrangements are significantly less common: in 205 societies there is no formal exchange of goods, and in 53 societies both parties exchange gifts.

Treating brides like chattel stems from a systematic, multicultural mistreatment of women, but there have been cultures that have exalted femininity. Prior to the rise of Judaism, goddess-based religions and cults thrived in Europe and Asia. Many of these religions were based on matriarchal power structures in which women were revered as spiritual beings who could create new life. Women have been valued in Egyptian dynasties and pre-classical Greece matriarchies, as well as some Native American Indian Navajo tribes. As the male role in procreation became more apparent, patriarchies began to arise. Reverence for the womb gave way to various forms of phallus worship.

As social power structures became predominantly masculine, mistreatment of women became more prevalent. Consider the historical role of women in China. For millennia the feudal patriarchal system restricted the political, economic, cultural, social, and familial power of women. During most of China's history, women had no political power, were economically dependent on their husbands or families, had no inheritance rights, and possessed no independent source of income. They were banned from formal education, could not participate in most social activities, and were completely subservient to their husbands. Women's lives were so restricted that they were even forbidden to remarry if their spouse died. Given these circumstances, it should not be surprising to learn that infant girls' feet were routinely broken and bound, and many women were subjected to other forms of physical and mental torture. In 1898, a small group of dissidents started the Reform Movement, whose advocates urged the government to ban foot binding and establish schools for women. Little else changed for women until the People's Republic of China was formed in the latter half of the twentieth century.

Eastern countries were not the only ones who mistreated women. Throughout the ages, women in many different societies have faced considerable tyranny at the hands of men. During the Middle Ages in Europe, Friar Cherubino (Martin, 1987, p. 23) wrote a book entitled *Rules of Marriage*, in which he stated that if a husband's verbal correction of his wife was not effective, then he was "obligated to beat her with a stick." The purpose of the beating was to "strike his wife out of concern for her soul." Beating was viewed as the only way to restore her to spiritual health. Another "marriage enrichment" manual of the time stated the control of women should extend not only to wives but also to daughters. Women were viewed as "an empty thing, easily swayed," and at great risk when away from their husbands or fathers (O'Faolin & Matines, 1973, p. 169). A good father and husband was one who ruled his household the same way a king would rule over his subjects. Fathers were instructed to keep their daughters busy with domestic chores, such as cooking and sewing. Reading and other intellectual pursuits were considered appropriate only for women who intended to become nuns.

Without access to gainful employment or education, most women were expected to marry a man and raise his children. Augustine argued that marriage served three purposes: to procreate the race, as a metaphor of fidelity, and as a sacrament before God (Cole, 1877). From this point of view, sex was viewed only as a means to an end: procreation. Augustine described sexuality in the following way: "A man can direct the wild horse of lust into the bridle path of domesticity if he will exert all of his strength and allow it to run only when intent upon the carnal generation of children" (Cole, 1877, p. 52). The issue of women's sexual enjoyment was not even addressed. Women were simply required to perform their wifely duties.

Clearly women were treated more as possessions than as equal partners. Women served an important function but were also viewed with suspicion by men. The view of woman as the ruin of man reached its apogee in the medieval theory of witchcraft. The alleged malevolent magic of women was said to emanate from a compact with the devil. Women toppled men from their devotion to God by using their powers to engage men's passions.

These feminine powers came to be associated with demonic forces and spawned a legacy of genocide that has often been overlooked. The practice of identifying and convicting women as witches began in the 1400s and spread through much of Europe and the Americas. The most recently recorded conviction and execution for witchcraft took place in 1792 in Poland, although it is possible that the Jesuits were burning heretics as late as the 1830s in South America. The organized practice of burning witches, then, lasted for more than 300 years, constituting a female Holocaust during which 487 "witches" per year were tortured and murdered (Ontario Consultants on Religious Tolerance, 1998b). Nearly 150,000 women died in this fashion.

During the Romantic Era of the late eighteenth century, a subtle shift occurred concerning the objectification of women. The Romantics turned away from the debasing objectification of women and replaced it with a diametrically opposite image. Women were now depicted as goddesses rather than sinners. A woman was seen as virtuous, pure, and innocent. By raising the Western, White female to a goddesslike status, European men effectively removed the stigma imposed on women during the Middle Ages.

> "Women's virtue is man's greatest invention." (Cornelia Otis Skinner)

During the so-called Age of Reason, women were viewed as porcelain dolls requiring men to nourish and sustain them. Physicians of the nineteenth century focused on the physiology of menstruation to explain why women were inferior and weaker than their male counterparts. They asserted the importance of menstruation in defining a woman's overall health (Owen, 1993) and recommended that women rest during this time of the month. They also argued that women's regular loss of blood was associated with their weakened condition and fainting spells. In reality, both problems most likely were caused by tightly laced corsets.

The development of the silk industry in Italy and Spain created fabrics that needed a more severe treatment to reveal the body's form. Italy is credited with the first artificial support to the body, called the coche, later accepted by Europe as the busk. It gave a smooth, straight line when the garment was laced. The earliest known corset was made of iron in 1556. Between the sixteenth and twentieth centuries, women's undergarments compressed their bodies so tightly that they could literally faint from lack of oxygen. They even ran the risk of having their lungs punctured by their rib cages, which would change shape as a result of constant pressure during adolescence. As to their weakened condition, the corset eventually caused the muscles around the spine to atrophy, leaving women physically weak and less mobile. Meals had to be much smaller and more frequent, because the corset compressed the intestines leading to severe pain from once "normal" meals. Some corset designs, such as the wasp-waist or S-Curve corset, put significant pressure on the spine and bent it at severe angles. To properly wear a wasp-waist corset, women had to begin training in adolescence to prevent the rib cage from growing normally. The corset literally raised the position of the waist on the torso.

Women's traditional social roles were almost as restrictive as their undergarments, contributing to an image of female frailty. Many feminists, including Donna Jeffe (1995) argue that women continue to be viewed as the weaker sex, even in relationships in which equality is supposedly honored. In many ways, Haaken (1995) believes this devaluation of the feminine has limited women's abilities to shape their lives. Many women allow their life choices to be made for them by others. Pleasing their fathers, lovers, husbands, or defining themselves through their families, become ways of achieving justification at different stages of women's lives (Haaken, 1990). For women (and many ethnic minority groups), a fundamental problem has been that others have controlled the power to define their existence. Social control seems to be a significant aspect of the way women are treated in many societies (Chafe, 1977).

In many contemporary cultures, femininity is still undervalued or misused. Philpot, Brooks, Lusterman, and Nutt (1997) recount a story in which a Greek grandmother threw her newborn granddaughter out of a two-story window because she wasn't a boy. They argue that such stories help to explain why more girls express a desire to be male than boys express a wish to be female. Girls internalize their society's devaluation of femininity and come to believe that domination by males is natural and acceptable.

Psychological theory, too, has contributed to the oppression of women by objectifying them and encouraging conformity to socially assigned roles. Worell and Remer (1992) argued that traditional theories of psychology have typically advanced the following misogynistic ideas:

- Androcentrism: Conclusions about human nature are based upon the experiences of men.
- Gendercentric theories: When ideas involving women are discussed, they are seen as separate paths from those of men.

- Ethnocentricity: Little or no understanding of cultural diversity has been incorporated into psychological theories.
- Heterosexism: Same-sex relationships are often devalued.
- Intrapsychic orientation: All problems are thought to originate from the individual's mental process, without regard to social environment, sexism, or racism.
- Determinism: Personalities are fixed early in life and must simply be accepted.

Psychological techniques have been devised to assist female clients more effectively. These new approaches will be discussed in the section on psychology.

Family

> "A woman without a man is like a fish without a bicycle." (Gloria Steinem)

The feminist movement of the 1970s targeted the traditional family structure as one of the most important barriers to equal rights for women. Hare-Mustin (1978) asserted that the family was the principal arena for the exploitation of women. Although it would be difficult to argue with this statement, it overlooks the importance women attach to familial ties. Even during the 1970s, when feminism made significant inroads on traditional ways of thinking, researchers found that the majority of women continued to take responsibility for maintaining their intimate relationships and to view divorce as a personal failure (Chodorow, 1978). As more people studied women's familial roles, there was a growing understanding that, regardless of ethnicity, women undergo significant strain. Married women begin to question what it means to be a woman (e.g., must one be a mother?), they suffer with problems such as depression, and they often feel they have limited social support when traumas occur (Levant & Philpot, 2002).

Why is family life often difficult for women? There is no clear answer to this question, and some of the answers in the literature contradict each other. Brooks (2000) argues that women tend to experience discomfort in marriage when they conform to stereotypically female behaviors and personality styles (e.g., meekness, unassertiveness, and deference to their husbands). To improve marital quality, Brooks posited, women and men should enter marriage with similar perspectives, skills, and insights. Schell and Weisfeld (1999) offered a completely different perspective. They found that marital satisfaction, for both sexes, was correlated with male leadership in decision making. If the couples said that the husband made more decisions, or if dominance was reflected in his nonverbal signaling, the couple tended to be happier. Their actual behavior was unrelated to marital satisfaction.

So who is right? What helps women feel empowered and happy in their relationships? The answer is complex. Xu and Burleson (2001) studied marital satisfaction in American and Chinese marital relationships. They began with the idea that most modern marriages operate under a "support gap" in which wives receive less spousal support than husbands. Surprisingly, they found that the men and women in their study reported similar levels of support from their spouses, but women reported desiring significantly higher levels of support from spouses than did men. The trend held true for all of the support variables and for both ethnic groups. Specifically, women wanted their husbands to provide more emotional and esteem support (Xu & Burleson, 2001). When a relationship starts to degrade, it is usually not for a lack of love. Spouses who reported poor marital satisfaction early in their marriages cited problems such as low dependability of spouse, dysfunctional beliefs regarding relationships, low emotional expressiveness, and psychological distress (Kurdek, 1999). It seems logical to assume that spouses can still love each other when conflicts arise, but they may begin to feel insecure and unsupported. In a sense, women are less likely to leave a relationship because they feel unloved than if they believe they are unlikely to receive increased love and support over time (Sprecher, 1999). If supportiveness and satisfaction are lacking, the relationship is likely to degrade, leading to increased friction and fewer expressions of affection (Coyne, 2002).

The levels of violence and aggression in a family also affect supportiveness and satisfaction, especially in transitional periods such as pregnancy. Between 7 and 10 percent of pregnant women are beaten by their partners. Violence against women increases during pregnancy, with at least 1 percent of all women with no history of abuse facing it for the first time during pregnancy (Straus, Gelles, & Steinmetz, 1980). Pregnant women may require more attention from their husbands, and hormonal fluctuations may change the family dynamic. Husbands who lack adequate coping skills may find themselves overwhelmed during this time (Svare, Betteridge, Katz, & Samuels, 1981).

In an attempt to find ways to reduce the threat of domestic violence to pregnant women, McFarlane and Wiist (1997) studied a program involving mentor mothers. The mentors were provided to pregnant women who had been identified as abused through routine screening of new prenatal patients at three public health clinics. Mentoring activities consisted of weekly social support visits, education about pregnancy and violence, and referrals when intervention was needed. Pregnant women who participated in the program believed that the mentors' intervention was helpful across all the areas studied. Mentor involvement was not proven to decrease abuse, but it prevented the women from becoming isolated.

Social involvement may play a role in decreasing violence. We already know that culture can play a part in reducing aggressiveness. Torres et al. (2000) found that Latinos tended to experience rates of abuse similar to European Americans during pregnancy, but Cuban American and Central American fathers-to-be were significantly less likely to abuse their pregnant partners. Also, women who spoke only Spanish were less likely to report physical abuse from their partners both before and during pregnancy, which implies that cultural norms can play a role in reducing the problem. Other factors, such as educational attainment, being married, and bearing the biological offspring of the husband can help reduce the risk of abuse.

Levinson's (1989) worldwide study of spousal abuse indicates that the women who are least likely to be abused are active members of supportive communities. He defined an active member as one who would, for example, work within a group when gathering water, tending crops, or selling goods in the marketplace. Levinson also noted that in intimate relationships, equality in domestic decision making, having access to divorce (but using it infrequently), engaging in monogamous marriages, sleeping together in the same bed with their spouse, and living near close friends or family members all contributed to the safety of women.

After the baby arrives, the threat of domestic violence does not disappear. Arguments over the management of children often precipitate violent outbursts and may put the children at risk of physical abuse. Children are more likely to be abused in households where spouses use physical violence against each other (Martin, 1987). With abusive husbands, the probability of child abuse by a violent husband increases from 5 percent with one act of marital violence to near certainty with 50 or more acts of marital violence. With violent wives, the predicted probability of child abuse by a violent wife increases from 5 percent with one act of marital violence to 30 percent with 50 or more acts of marital violence (Ross, 1996). Spousal abuse is a significantly better predictor of child abuse than the abuser's occupational status, income, or class level (McCloskey, 1996).

Even when children are not victims of physical abuse, witnessing the abuse of a parent may have severe consequences. Children who witness violence are more likely to externalize problems (Jouriles et al., 1996). This effect is greater for boys, which may be partly due to the increased abuse they face (Jouriles & Norwood, 1995). However, there is some evidence that girls are affected more than boys by witnessing violence, and boys are more likely to be harmed as a result of concurrent problems such as alcohol use by the parent (Mihalic & Elliott, 1997).

Regardless of their gender, children who witness violence between their parents are more likely to have behavioral problems. Smith, Berthelsen, and O'Connor (1997) found that 42 percent of children aged three to six who had witnessed domestic violence exhibited behavioral problems that warranted clinical intervention. The amount of violence that the child witnessed, the child's responses when the violence occurred, and whether or not the child copied the violent partner's behavior were associated with the child's behavioral adjustment scores. Once these processes have occurred, the family is often unable to correct the behavioral outbursts. Children are likely to act out in school, engage in inappropriate and violent behaviors with other children, and to appear withdrawn and depressed. Unfortunately, if one parent is abusive, the other parent cannot offset the effects through nurturing and compassion (Smith, Berthelsen, & O'Connor, 1997). The only clearly effective intervention is to prevent the abuse from occurring.

Even without violence, the presence of children can have a negative effect on marital satisfaction. Kurdek (1999) found that couples with children reported poorer marital satisfaction levels than their childless peers. Not only did couples with children have poorer relationships, but their relationships tended to deteriorate faster than those of childless couples. Apparently, parents are likely to put considerable emphasis on their children's well being, and their marriage may suffer as a consequence. This is not to say that parents who neglect their children will be happier. Wallerstein (1995) found that among couples who have children, marital satisfaction depends on both partners' willingness to embrace the challenges of parenthood. The secret, Wallerstein believes, is learning how to become full-time parents without abandoning privacy and a healthy sex life. Apparently, given the decreasing marital satisfaction identified by Kurdek's study, many couples with children have difficulty putting equal emphasis into parenting and marriage.

The commitment to raising children is one that both sexes take seriously. Fathers and mothers are likely to invest similar amounts of time in their children's lives, but mothers are more likely to participate in and be knowledgeable about adolescents' friendships than are fathers (Updegraff et al., 2001). Mothers reported more involvement in daughters' friendships, and both mothers and fathers spent more time with same-sex offspring and their peers. Mothers also have higher expectations of their daughters, especially if the mothers are employed in a time-demanding occupation. Expectations of daughters are most likely to involve household tasks (Crouter et al., 2001).

Not all women, however, want children or are ready to become mothers. Epiro (1995) has argued that for many women, unplanned pregnancy decisions are made rashly to escape a situation as quickly as possible, and are often made under coercion from the woman's parents or partner. It is important to note that when a woman terminates a pregnancy for the sake of a relationship, the relationships end about 80 percent of the time. In such cases, Cook (Epiro, 1995) argues that for some women, pregnancy termination can lead to Post Abortion Syndrome (PAS) in which the woman experiences an inability to process her feelings of grief, fear, guilt, and anger. The woman who is most likely to suffer from this condition, according to Cook, believes she has destroyed her baby and not simply a blob of cells. The emergence of the disorder can precipitate self-destructive behaviors, such as eating disorders, drug abuse, and suicide.

Although few contest the potential pitfalls of abortion, new research is addressing who is most likely to face problems with the procedure. Russo and Dabul (1997) found that even religiosity and the belief that abortion was wrong did not necessarily lead to psychological complications with the procedure.

Instead, the patient's pre-existing self-esteem played the most important role. In general, non-Catholic women with high church attendance and one abortion had the highest self-esteem. Their self-esteem ratings were actually higher than low-church-attendance Catholic women who had never had an abortion. These findings have led researchers to assume that while highly religious Catholic women were slightly more likely to exhibit PAS symptoms, their distress may stem from their pre-abortion levels of self-esteem and not their convictions about the procedure. Legal abortion *per se* does not increase a woman's risk of negative well-being. Nevertheless, the experience can be very traumatic.

Other women continue their pregnancies but put their developing children at great risk by using drugs and alcohol. Kaplan-Sanoff and Leib (1995) researched the impact of maternal substance abuse, particularly cocaine, on child development. The longitudinal studies they reviewed demonstrated that children prenatally exposed to cocaine tend to be of low-average to average intelligence and to suffer from distractibility, impulsivity, poor self-regulation, low levels of play, inappropriate peer relations, and speech and language delays. It has been proven that smoking or exposure to second-hand smoke causes a reduction in oxygen to the fetus through the increase in the neuro-transmitters epinephrine and norepinephrine, which results in brain abnormalities, reduced head circumference, cleft palate, and low birth weight. Similarly, women who consume alcohol while pregnant are at risk of having children born with fetal alcohol effects (FAEs). Symptoms of FAE include low birth weight, lack of responsiveness and arousability, irregular heart rate, and respiratory abnormalities. Delayed cognitive development and learning disabilities are also common. Fetal Alcohol Syndrome (FAS), a result of severe and chronic alcohol abuse, damages the central nervous system, causes heart defects, and results in physical deformities such as a small head, distortions of joints, and abnormal facial features. Mental retardation and behavioral disorders such as hyperactivity and poor impulse control are also common. Women who are chronic alcoholics have a 50 to 75 percent chance of giving birth to a child with FAS.

Some women opt to remain single and childless, while others feel unfulfilled until they become wives and mothers. Rybicki (1997) laments that many women still feel they need a husband and family to be complete. Women are bombarded with messages such as "if you don't have a mate you'd better sacrifice everything you have to get one." These messages are difficult to ignore, even if a woman enjoys success in a career. Some women elevate work and career aspirations above creating a family, but they may find themselves questioning their decision later in life. Sylvia Ann Hewlett (2002) found that 42 percent of women in corporate America are childless at age 40 (compared to 25 percent of men), but only 14 percent had planned not to have children. The more a woman succeeds in her career, the less likely it is that she will have a partner or a baby. For men, the opposite is true: the more successful a man is professionally, the more likely he is to be married with children. This double standard can leave career women feeling cheated. The growing number of women who have postponed pregnancy until their mid-thirties or older has also led to a booming infertility treatment market.

Approximately 18 percent of women attempting to bear children will either have difficulty conceiving or will lose a pregnancy. After a year of attempting to conceive, the couple can be classified as infertile. Among this group, only about 50 percent will bear children with the help of modern infertility treatments (Daniluk, 1996). Therapists should realize that even the prospect of infertility is intensely painful for many women. To avoid the pain, those who have abandoned their efforts to bear a child often consider themselves "not yet pregnant" rather than biologically childless. It was only after attempting all possible interventions and realizing that there were no more answers to their questions that the women in Daniluk's study began the painful process of relinquishing or revising their hopes and dreams.

Infertility is just one of the familial struggles women can face. When women reach mid-life, they may be taking care of elderly parents as well as growing children. Some women cope with these demands more successfully than others, often for attitudinal reasons. Atienza, Stephens, and Townsend (2002) explored the effects of dispositional optimism (DO) on the well-being of women caring for elderly parents. These 296 women simultaneously occupied multiple roles as mother, wife, and employee while also acting as the primary caregiver to a parent (aged 50 to 94 years). The researchers found that optimism, regardless of the level of stress experienced by the caregiver, reduced depressive symptoms and increased life satisfaction. The effects remained even after controlling for household income and physical health.

Sometimes, however, optimism is insufficient to help women bear the burden of caring for aging parents. If their parent's condition degrades to include dementia, daughters are unlikely to be prepared for the resulting role reversal, which could undermine their sense of identity. Role reversal tends to be difficult for both parties, with both mother and daughter feeling disempowered. Cecchin (2001) advocates discussing mother/daughter roles while both persons are healthy. Regarding dependency as a predictable aspect of aging can normalize changes in the mother-daughter relationship and increase opportunities for reciprocity. For example, an elderly mother who needs help bathing can still demonstrate support for the family by cleaning or performing other household chores. What must be avoided is the notion that cognitive decline equals worthlessness.

Eventually, no matter how well a family has prepared, death will come. Edelman's (1995) heart-wrenching study of the effect of a mother's death on her daughter was based on interviews with 246 women (aged 17 to 82 years) who lost their mothers between the ages of 1 and 40. The results were stable and profound. Regardless of their age, women viewed the death of their mother as an irrevocably life-changing event. In an instant, a woman loses her caregiver, teacher, adversary, role model, and guide to being a woman. This loss is especially significant as a woman moves through transitional phases, such as leaving home, getting married, or having a child. These are the times when women want to turn to their mothers for guidance and company. When this relationship is missing, a woman's identity, personality, family, and life choices can be threatened. New supportive relationships must be formed, and new coping skills must be created.

Economics

Family relationships and childhood experiences strongly influence the economic status of women. Women who enjoy working in higher-paying, male-dominated fields are more likely to have played competitive sports during childhood and to have had more male playmates and fewer female playmates than women employed in typically feminine professions (Coats & Overman, 1992). Many people, however, continue to view women in nontraditional fields negatively. Even though women have successfully found employment in even the most stereotypically masculine jobs, they are still likely to face intense discrimination. To combat such psychological obstacles, women who feel that they are underappreciated or mistreated may benefit from joining a support group or a stress-management program to help them cope with pressures at home and at the workplace.

Despite the increased career options available to women today, social pressure continues to nudge girls toward traditionally feminine occupations. Yoder and Schleicher (1996) found that women who excelled in currently female-incongruent fields were rated by undergraduates as having personal problems and being unfeminine. These sentiments appear to stem from the continued media campaign directed toward girls and women. Peirce (1993) analyzed the fictional stories in the magazine *Seventeen*, which is directed toward adolescent girls. She found that in the stories written between 1987 and 1991, more than 95 percent of the occupations attributed to female characters were either stereotypically feminine or gender-neutral. Basically, the message is clear: either stay within the confines of the existing female roles or run the risk of being labeled unfeminine. Similarly, Mueller and Yoder (1997) investigated stereotypes involving women's family size, employment, and occupation. They solicited 400 college undergraduates (aged 18 to 49 years) to categorize a hypothetical married woman. The woman was described as voluntarily child-free or the mother of one, two, or eight children, and as unemployed or employed either part- or full-time in either a gender-typical or atypical occupation. They found that the women with any number of children were viewed favorably, but women without children were considered rigid and selfish. Similarly, the women employed in gender-atypical occupations were viewed as unemotional, cold, and unfriendly.

More women are employed today than ever before, but income disparity continues. Over the past 30 years, job growth for women has been unprecedented. The U.S. Department of Labor, Women's Bureau (2001) reported that more than 70 million jobs were created between 1960 and 2000, which more than doubled the jobs available in 1960. Of these jobs, 43 million went to women and 28 million to men. Despite increased job opportunities, American women earn 76 cents for every dollar a man earns, the equivalent of working one week without pay per month (U.S. Department of Labor, Bureau of Statistics, 2001). This is a dramatic improvement from the 58.3 cents to the dollar women earned in 1979, but it still a long way from equality. The pay gap results in a lower standard of living for independent women and may create considerable anxiety. According to a recent Gallup Poll (Saad, 2001), two-thirds of American women believe men and women lack equal job opportunities, while the majority of men (53 percent) believe women already have equal job rights.

Holden (2001) surveyed nearly 20,000 life scientists (from the American Association for the Advancement of Science) and found that salaries for women averaged about $72,000 compared with $94,000 for men. This 31 percent gap is still present, despite the fact that women are strongly represented in the life sciences—approaching 50 percent in some fields. The continued disparity in incomes, however, is only part of the story. Holden also found that two-thirds of female scientists said their careers had been limited "at least a little" by the career demands of a spouse or domestic partner. In contrast, only 7 percent of the male scientists said their careers had been limited significantly by the careers of their spouses. How can these patterns continue in a world with growing economic resources and enlightened views? A Worldwatch (DeAngelis, 1997) study suggests that discrimination against women is responsible for the continuing discrepancy. Single women, who often have faced the most intense levels of discrimination, live a quality of life below that of many other women. In the gravest of circumstances, such women grew up believing that they would be financially supported by men. Instead, they found themselves either having to increase their education in order to improve their wage-earning ability, or learning to cope with the stress of ongoing financial hardship.

Research by Bylsma and Major (1992) indicates that women eventually view the privileges offered to European American males as normative. A self-fulfilling prophecy occurs in which women accept lower wages because they feel they deserve less than men. In this specific study, undergraduate students were asked how much a woman should earn for performing a given job. The 99 undergraduate women and 104 undergraduate men were asked to read and imagine themselves in one of nine employment scenarios. After reading the case, they were then asked to rate how much they should earn for the given job. When giving an immediate reply, women paid themselves less than the men paid themselves. However, when women were told how much the men paid themselves and were told that their performance was equivalent to that of the men, they matched their income to the level specified by the men.

From a global perspective, limiting women's economic potential due to gender bias has the effect of increasing population growth rates. Women in many parts of the world view childbearing as their only form of economic security. In fact, rising female literacy rates have been linked to declining birth rates. But girls are less likely to attend school than boys. Worldwatch (DeAngelis, 1997) suggests that ending hunger, malnutrition, illness, and loss of economic productivity requires the elimination of gender biases. When women receive better access to education, opportunities for business ownership, and supplies, the global population will stabilize and Third World countries will increase their economic strength. In subsistence economies, which include more than half of the world's population, women are often the primary economic providers, but even in these economies they face legal barriers to owning land, the threat of violence by men, difficulty obtaining child care, and educational barriers. Such biases not only limit women's ability to succeed but also force many Third World Nations to remain in poverty (Jacobson, 1991).

As society continues to devalue women and attempts to confine them within rigid gender roles, it is not surprising that female workers face frequent and consistent gender harassment. Piotrkowski (1998) found that 70 percent of women, regardless of ethnicity, face gender harassment in their respective occupations. Furthermore, although many women do not see themselves as victims of harassment, they are likely to experience negative psychological and job-related outcomes. A national Gallup Poll shows that little has changed in the new millennium. Asked about their own experiences, only 37 percent of women reported never having felt discriminated against in public life or employment because they were women. At the other extreme, 22 percent reported having felt victimized by gender discrimination on a fairly frequent basis (Saad, 2001).

Schneider, Fitzgerald, and Swan (1997) interviewed 447 private-sector women and 300 female university employees about how often they experienced uninvited sexually oriented behavior. Such behaviors included crude sexual jokes, physical touching, hugging, stroking, or repeated pressure for dates or sexual favors. They found that, regardless of the intensity of the abuse, even relatively mild forms of harassment have negative outcomes. Women who undergo such attacks reported decreased job satisfaction and increased psychological stress, including somatic complaints and alcohol consumption (Piotrkowski, 1998). In light of these findings, managers need to take all sexual harassment protests seriously, even if they do not appear serious to an outsider.

Gender harassment is only one of the difficulties working women face. Although women have made remarkable progress in traditionally male-dominated jobs, their success has created new problems as well. Women who work in male-dominated industries may face increased risks of physical injury. In a ten-year study of 47 Swedish women who worked in the automobile industry, those in departments in which they thought their sex was a barrier to success were more likely to report joint and muscle pain than women who viewed their surroundings as offering equal opportunities to both sexes (Mann, 1996). Physical symptoms, psychological distress, diminished quality of living and other such problems seem to be related to these struggles against gender bias.

In addition to discriminatory practices, McCloskey (1996) found that women face pressures at home related to their economic status. When women earn more than men do, they are significantly more likely to become victims of abuse. Asymmetrical incomes favoring women are better predictors of the frequency and severity of a husband's abuse toward his wife than total family income. It may be true that members of lower-income families are at greater risk of violence, but this appears to be related to the fact that in these families both partners must work to survive. In some cases, earning less than his wife may increase a husband's insecurity and, consequently, his tendency to use violence to assert his authority.

Male partners' attempts to maintain control of the household income may compromise a woman's security. Many abused women are expected to stay at home, or at least earn less than their husbands. This financial dependence leaves female victims of spousal abuse less prepared to support themselves (Wolf, 1991), which is one of the reasons women are more likely to remain in abusive relationships. Rusbult and Martz (1995) also found that women were more likely to remain in an abusive situation when they were more heavily invested in their relationships (e.g., were married) and experienced less dissatisfaction (e.g., reported less severe abuse).

The ability to invest in a relationship can have positive outcomes for women. Barbara Gutek (Mann, 1996), a professor of management and policy at the University of Arizona in Tucson, noted that if women lose their jobs or retire, they have a variety of other roles available to them. Men, she argues, find their identities linked to their paid work roles. Combining career and family allows women to use their work as a form of self-expression while still finding satisfaction in family relationships (Kirschenbaum & Reis, 1997). Today's girls seem to recognize the value of professional employment and are more concerned with their future careers and financial responsibilities than previous generations had been. An APA task force asked 733 adolescent girls to write down six questions that they would like to ask an expert. Rather than inquire about marital or family issues, the girls were likely to request information about economic topics. They wanted to know how to find the right career and how to access adult mentors to help them (Murray, 1998).

As mentioned in the family section, striving for a career and maintaining a family is often harder for women than for men. Philpot, Brooks, Lusterman, and Nutt (1997) discussed the problem of role overload that comes from attempting to be full-time parents and full-time career women. Balancing these two roles can be even more difficult than working two full-time jobs, because family roles and career roles often require very different skills, and sometimes the skills required by one may run completely contrary to the skills required for the other.

Women who pursue female-dominated jobs may find the demands of child care and vocation less overwhelming. Olson, Frieze, and Detlefsen (1990) examined the differences between women with master's degrees in library science and those with MBAs. Women in both groups felt that their careers had taken time away from their families, and both groups were about equally likely to feel that family duties interrupted their jobs. However, women with MBAs found that the more their family life intruded on their career (e.g., needing to leave early to pick up children from school, taking children to doctors visits, etc.), the greater the impact on their salary. Women with the library science degree simply restructured their days or opted for part-time work. Both of these options allowed women in the female-dominated profession of library science to more easily combine family responsibilities with a career.

The complications of balancing family and work are more difficult for many women because of the expectations held by their partners. In 1996, Levinson updated his classic study on male vocational development by interviewing 45 women (15 homemakers, 15 businesswomen, and 15 academics). In general, he found that unlike men, women's vocational "dreams" were split between achievement and relationships. Only 18 percent were focused on achievement alone, and only 15 percent focused on relationships alone. The women in this study were also more likely to reinterpret their dreams of achievement within the context of their husbands' goals, and their husbands were more likely to expect help with their goals than to help their partners with theirs. Lack of assistance from their partners can make the demands of child care all the more difficult for working women. Riley (2002) noted that most working women (53 percent) would prefer that their children be cared for by their husbands, but only a minority of couples (23 percent) actually used the baby's father as the primarily caregiver.

It should also be noted that women's perceptions of their jobs are affected by the quality and structure of family life. Sinacore-Guinn, Akcali, and Fledderus (1999) surveyed and tested 173 employed women to determine how their family experiences predicted their job satisfaction. They found that women who perceived their families as structured and organized were more satisfied with their pay. Their relationship with their supervisor corresponded with their perceived family cohesion. They even felt better about their jobs, overall, when their family was open to competition, participated in political and cultural activities, expressed feelings readily, and operated within a clear set of rules and procedures.

Education

For decades, we have known that boys and girls do not differ in basic mathematical abilities (Orenstein, 2000). Throughout elementary school and middle school, girls tend to outperform their male peers and express interest in math. In high school, girls continue to earn better grades in math classes than boys, but they appear to lose their competitive advantage on standardized tests (Eccles, 1989). Males score an average of 41 points higher than females on math aptitude tests (Shea, 1994), a gap that is considerably smaller than in previous years (Crawford & Unger, 2000). What could be continuing to cause the difference in math aptitude scores, and does the difference indicate anything meaningful?

Jones and Jacka (1995) argue that the attention given to girls' lower math and science test scores has wrongly overshadowed the success of girls' academic performance. It gives the impression that girls lack intelligence. This perception, they argue, while attempting to provide increased resources to girls, paradoxically leads to a societal impression that girls need more help and are somehow less capable than boys. Girls tend to underestimate their ability to succeed in mathematics and science and to view these fields as masculine.

Rather than focus on educational deficits, Heller and Ziegler (1996) argue that parents and educators should be addressing the cognitive and attributional issues that create girls' apparent antipathy towards math and science. Even when they are intellectually gifted, girls may start to experience the "imposter phenomenon" in which high-achieving women believe themselves to be intellectual frauds. No matter how hard they work to achieve their goals or how talented they may be, they are unable to take credit for their accomplishments (Miller & Kastberg, 1995). European American girls, more than any other group, have lower self-esteem than boys. This trend begins as they enter puberty. During adolescence, girls tend to feel worse about themselves (Blakes, 1994). Heller and Ziegler developed attributional retraining techniques that appear to help girls view their skills more realistically. Rather than view their failures as inevitable and attribute their successes to luck, the girls undergoing their intervention program learned to take ownership of their successes and to attribute their failures to a correctable lack of knowledge.

Efforts to encourage positive attributions, however, are offset by many social ills. Elementary school teachers, who themselves were socialized to emphasize the success of men, may actively resist efforts to promote gender-inclusive science education (McGinnis & Pearsall, 1998). Such differences in academic treatment may leave girls with the impression that they simply cannot compete in masculine domains.

> I have a teacher who calls me "airhead" and "ditz." I used to think I was smart, but now I don't know. Maybe I'm not. What if he's right? The more he treats me like an airhead, the more I think maybe I am (Sadker & Sadker, 1994, p. 135).

This young woman is likely to doubt her own abilities because of her teacher's dismissive attitude. Some might argue that girls' lack of confidence stems from a decreased ability to succeed, but the self-devaluation appears to start during junior high school when girls are still outperforming boys in math ability (Crawford & Unger, 2000). A more reasonable hypothesis would be that their lack of confidence seriously limits their continued achievement.

There are a variety of legal and social reforms designed to promote equal rights in school settings. Without a doubt, Title IX of the Education

Amendments of 1972 (Title 20 U.S.C. Sections 1681–1688) had the greatest impact on sex equity in education. The law mandated equality in all educational activities, including sports. It required schools to allocate finances based on the total number of male and female athletes, with equal amounts going to male and female athletes. The regulation is so specific that it examines the number of athletes; quality, suitability, quantity, availability, and maintenance of equipment and supplies; number of competitive events per sport; modes of transportation; opportunities to receive academic tutoring; opportunities to receive coaching, assignment, and compensation; quality of locker rooms and facilities; medical and training facilities and services; expenses for publicity; support services for each sporting discipline; and recruitment of student-athletes. These changes have dramatically increased the number of female athletes, but there have been costs as well. Gavora (2001) believes Title IX was well intentioned but misguided. She notes that some of the most prestigious men's sports programs have been eliminated in the name of "gender equity." Providence College's baseball team, Princeton's wrestling squad, Boston University's football team, and the UCLA men's swimming program are among the hundreds of men's sports teams eliminated. Given the recent negative attention Title IX has received, the program's future may be in jeopardy.

There is no doubt that Title IX and other programs have helped women, even though they may have harmed men. During the past three decades women have significantly increased their presence in most college programs. It may seem reasonable to expect that attending college would help women feel they were capable of whatever they desired to accomplish, but even college does not overcome these deep-seated prejudices. Henderson-King and Stewart (1999) sought to discover whether women's studies classes were more likely to create a feminist consciousness than other college courses. Participants were tested at the beginning and end of the semester. Sixty-two students enrolled in women's studies were compared with 41 students who had expressed interest, but not enrolled, in women's studies. The students enrolled in women's studies showed an increase on several aspects of feminist consciousness, whereas the control group did not. Even worse, the students who had not taken women's studies courses became desensitized to sexism, a finding with frightening implications for the university system.

The desensitization of university students to women's issues is apparent in the following quote by an anonymous student teacher:

> I really do not feel like there needs to be changes in education for females. This may sound harsh, but if females truly want to be treated like males then they should learn to work and function in the system that exists. Having said that, I really do not believe that education is differentiated between the sexes. I have yet to discriminate or see discrimination aimed at a girl solely based on gender. Seems like many people just look for things to gripe about.

This male student believed that women wish to be treated "like males" instead of being treated like human beings. He failed to realize that the prejudices women face within school settings are subtle and covert. Boys do not block the doors to prevent girls from entering the classrooms. Teachers do not force girls to sit in the back of the class and remain quiet. However, the discrimination that this student teacher did not see is just as real as these examples and in some ways can be even more detrimental. Teachers can convey prejudice in tones of voice, minimal eye contact, or decreased expectations.

Subtle forms of discrimination can follow women throughout their academic careers. Mary Berry (1995) studied the experiences of 169 female students at an urban British university. Fewer than 10 percent of the women interviewed stated that they were content with their financial situation, and several were considering dropping out because of cost. For those who found the financial means to continue, other problems arose that similarly threatened their achievement. The most severe of these alternative problems involved sexual harassment.

While Berry noted that most of the women offered favorable assessments of their academic experiences, they also reported disappointment regarding the gender bias they encountered. In general, their fellow students provided a safe and positive environment, but more than half of the students feared for their personal security when traveling between home and the university. These situations caused acute anxiety and led more than 70 percent to state they were suffering from "stress."

Even women going into mental-health-related fields have not been free from harmful gender bias. Miller and Larrabee (1995) surveyed 315 female members of the Association for Counselor Education and Supervision. They found that 6 percent of the women reported sexual contacts with supervisors or educators while enrolled in counselor training programs. When a relationship developed, many of the women did not view it as harmful, but in retrospect, they realized that the sexual relationship negatively affected their working relationships.

Health

In general, women are more likely than men to seek out health care, and they visit a physician almost three times as often as men. Even though women realize the importance of annual physicals, healthy diets, and exercise, other health issues remain. Women must wrestle with immune problems that do not seem to affect men's bodies. The reason for this vulnerability is unclear. Women's immune systems attack invaders more aggressively than do men's, but the response is dampened during pregnancy. Perhaps owing to this on-off intensity, women are more prone to develop autoimmune disorders such as lupus, rheumatoid arthritis, and multiple sclerosis, conditions in which the immune system attacks healthy tissue. Women also deal with health concerns related to potentially embarrassing topics such as menstruation and breast exams.

Gloria Steinem (1978, p. 110) once wrote that if men could menstruate, "Street guys would brag ('I'm a three-pad man') or answer praise from a buddy ('Man, you lookin' good!') by giving fives and saying, 'Yeah, man, I'm on the rag!'" Okay, so maybe that wouldn't happen. It is interesting that milestones of normal male development such as voice changes, increased muscle tone, body mass, and even ejaculation, are accepted as positive stages of development, but menstruation is mentioned only in private.

Lara Owen (1993) wrote a fascinating book about her experiences with menstruation. Like most women, she grew up thinking of her period as a "nuisance." It was just a messy intrusion that caused unpleasant symptoms, forced her to do her laundry more often, interfered with her sex life, and drained her energy. Still, even from adolescence, there was always a part of her that was relieved. She simultaneously felt a sense of achievement, excitement, curiosity, and embarrassment. Her first menses signaled something new—the beginning of womanhood—but everyone around her treated the event as commonplace.

As time progressed, her early pride and excitement were replaced with shame. She could not discuss the topic with her brothers or father, and the monthly event was never discussed in school, except in biology class. She kept trying to understand why she felt differently from the women in tampon advertisements, who were shown running gleefully toward the ocean and wearing tight white pants while jumping onto horses. She felt inadequate and weak.

As an adult, she began to study the way other cultures viewed menstruation. She studied goddess religious practices and found that ritual practices were connected to the monthly bleeding of women, and menstrual blood itself was highly valued as possessing magical power. She also found that many Native American tribes honored women during menstruation. Women would traditionally go to a menstrual hut or "moon lodge" to pass the time of their bleeding. During this time, they reached the zenith of their spiritual power. They concentrated all their energies towards meditation and the accumulation of spiritual energy.

Owen notes that many women might have trouble taking a positive view of menstruation, and she adds that she had the same difficulty accepting this perspective. When attending a workshop on Native American menstruation views, she encountered Harley Swiftdeer Reagan. At the time, Owen suffered from cervical dysplasia and severe cramps. She asked Swiftdeer what she could do to heal herself. His advice was to dig a hole in her garden and release her negative thoughts about her womanhood into the hole. Unsurprisingly, she felt silly talking into a hole, but she was amazed at how many thoughts sprang to mind. When she finished, she covered the hole and felt more connected to herself and the earth. Her youthful resentment about being female vanished and was replaced with a growing sense of wonder at the intricacies and depths and possibilities offered by the monthly cycle. Her depression lifted, she had more energy, and she seemed to understand her anger better. Owen's positive views of menstruation are not unique. Angier (Ehrenreich, 1999) claims that premenstrual symptoms are experienced by many as a state of heightened activity, intellectual clarity, and feelings of well-being.

Although views of menstruation can become more positive, they should not overshadow the potential difficulties caused by monthly hormonal fluctuations. Premenstrual syndrome (PMS) is a cluster of physical and emotional symptoms that appear on a regular basis before the onset of menstrual bleeding. Common symptoms include water retention, breast pain, ankle swelling, increased body weight, irritability, aggressiveness, depression, lethargy, and food cravings (Deuster, Tilahun, & South-Paul, 1999). Barnhart, Freeman, and Sondheimer (1995) argue that approximately 75 percent of women complain of some PMS symptoms, but only 3 to 8 percent suffer from a more severe condition known as premenstrual dysphoric disorder (PMDD).

To be diagnosed with PMDD, a woman must experience symptoms during most menstrual cycles over the course of a year. The symptoms must begin to remit within a few days after the end of menstrual discharge. Common symptoms include depression, anxiety, mood swings, anger or irritability, decreased interest in usual activities, difficulty concentrating, lethargy, change in appetite, hypersomnia or insomnia, sense of being overwhelmed, and physical symptoms such as breast tenderness or swelling, headaches, joint or muscle pain, and a sensation of "bloating."

Even if all these symptoms are present, the diagnosis cannot be made unless the disturbance markedly interferes with work, school, or relationships. These problems create a vicious cycle in the disorder because women reporting significant life stresses are universally more likely to rate premenstrual symptoms as severe. Deuster, Tilahun and South-Paul (1999) found that after controlling for a variety of biological, social, and behavioral factors, perceived stress was still the strongest predictor of PMDD. So, as women experience difficulties with work, school, or relationships, they are likely to experience anxiety, which is likely to increase their premenstrual symptoms.

For many years, the symptoms of PMDD appeared untreatable. The assumption was that providing estrogen and other female hormones would eliminate the hormonally related symptoms. However, there is now sufficient evidence to suggest that estrogen may actually increase premenstrual problems (Mortola, 1998), and diuretics, progesterone, mineral or herbal mixtures, and vitamins seem to have little effect as well. Rather than continue to treat the syndrome with traditional hormones, researchers are beginning to propose alternatives. Sertraline and Selective Serotonin Reuptake Inhibitors (SSRIs) have been shown to be effective in managing PMS/PMDD symptoms (Yonkers et al., 1997). SSRIs such as the FDA-approved drug Sarafem (which is chemically similar to Prozac and also produced by Lilly) may treat PMDD the way anticonvulsants treat epilepsy, by decreasing sensitivity to stress and raising the threshold for symptoms. The most promising treatments, however, involve drugs such as leuprolide that appear to regulate hormonal changes and attenuate many PMS-related symptoms (Schmidt et al., 1998).

Some feminists have argued that PMS, however severe, should not be considered an illness; they fear that women's normal biology will be stigmatized and be used against them to limit employment opportunities. Others have argued that forms of PMS must be defined as an illness in order for the condition to receive adequate insurance coverage and research funding. Should we allow medication response to define pathology? Mood conditions such as PMDD (premenstrual dysphoric disorder) respond well to Prozac, but does this response make the condition an illness? These issues may take a few more years to resolve.

Although medical and mental health professionals have only recently championed the legitimacy of PMS symptoms, other female health issues have long been taken seriously. Breast cancer takes a severe toll on the lives of many women. For many, it is a mysterious enemy that relentlessly stalks its prey. That was the view Susan Ballard took. While she was in her twenties, she nursed her mother through the agonizing process of breast cancer until she died an excruciating death. The process inspired her to completely change her lifestyle. She switched to a vegetarian diet, eating only whole grains, fruits, vegetables, and soy products. She took up yoga and exercise, and followed a variety of other health-promoting practices. Still, at age 56, she was diagnosed with breast cancer.

Susan's story is not uncommon. Judith Hirshfield-Bartek, a nurse manager for the breast care center at Beth Israel Deaconess Medical Center, said, "All I see is women with breast cancer, and so often they say, 'I ate a healthy diet, I don't smoke, I did all the right things, and I still got breast cancer'" (Saltus, 1997). Environmental factors, such as diet, do affect the likelihood of cancer, but genetic influences are equally important, if not more so. If a woman inherits a mutant form of the BRCA1 gene and her family history includes many cases of breast or ovarian cancer, she has nearly an 85 percent lifetime chance of developing breast cancer and a 50 percent chance of ovarian cancer. A second gene, BRCA2, also plays a role in elevating a woman's risk.

There also seem to be cultural factors involved in breast cancer development. Mexican Americans, Japanese and Filipino women living in Hawaii, American Indians, Seventh-Day Adventists, and Mormons are less likely to contract the disease, while Jewish women have a higher than average risk. The reasons for these differences are still unclear. However, studies conducted in China found that women who breastfed for at least 24 months were 54 percent less likely to develop breast cancer than women who breastfed for less than 6 months. Women who spent at least 74 months breastfeeding during their lifetimes had an even lower risk of developing breast cancer before or after menopause (Reuters Health Information, 2000). Few women in Western countries nurse their babies for more than four months. An American woman has a 1 in 9 risk of developing breast cancer over the course of her lifetime, and she is more likely to develop the disease later in life. Two-thirds of all breast cancer cases are diagnosed in women aged 50 or older, with the mean age of diagnosis being 64.

To combat breast cancer, breast self-examinations (BSE) should be practiced beginning in early adulthood. According to the American Cancer Society (Tittle & Torre, 1996), women self-diagnose nearly 95 percent of breast abnormalities. Breast changes such as lumps, thickening, swelling, dimpling, skin irritation, distortion, retraction, scaliness and tenderness or unusual discharge should be immediately reported to a physician.

Finding breast abnormalities, however, is only half of the battle. When Donna (Torre, 1997), found a lump in her breast at age 55, she attempted to ignore it. She did not call a doctor, telling herself, "It will go away." Sadly, it did not go away—it grew. Within six months the lump was three-fourths of an inch in diameter. Eventually, she underwent a lumpectomy (having the lump surgically removed) and chemotherapy to get rid of the cancer. Later, Donna commented, "You stick your head in the sand and think it won't happen to you—I felt like I was totally stupid for not believing I could get it."

Even after successful treatment for breast cancer, other concerns remain. Weijmar Schultz, van de Wiel, Hahn, and Wouda (1995) found that after undergoing treatment for cancer of the breast or reproductive organs, a woman's motivation to resume sexual contact was the most important component to returning to adequate sexual functioning. This psychological motivation was even more significant than the physical handicaps caused by the treatment. For this reason, women can benefit from joining a support group of cancer survivors in which they are free to express their feelings and regain their confidence. Losing a breast can have a powerful effect on a woman's sense of self. Discussing their loss with others who have successfully adapted can speed the healing process.

Breast cancer is not the only cancer plaguing women. Similar hormonal changes are also responsible for cancers of the uterus, ovaries, and cervix, although recent advances in diagnostic exams and hormone treatments have drastically cut the incidence of these disorders over the past five decades. Pap smears that detect abnormal cells in the cervix before they become malignant have contributed to a 75 percent drop in cervical cancer since the 1950s (Park, 1999). Even changes in birth control pills and hormone replacement therapy (with estrogen and progestin) have contributed to better treatment of ovarian and uterine cancers.

Hormonal changes are also partly responsible for heart attacks. Typically, heart trouble is considered a male problem, and this myth has caused many women to ignore the risks. On average, women tend to suffer their first heart attack ten years later than men do, but because they are often older when these occur, they are also more likely to die from it. Approximately 24 percent of men will die within a year after a heart attack (Park, 1999). Nearly twice as many women (42 percent) will die within the same time frame. The cause may stem from changes in a woman's hormonal levels. Women who elect not to undergo postmenopausal hormonal treatments are at greater risk for heart failure. Estrogen keeps blood vessels elastic and free of hardened-plaque formations and instructs the liver to churn out more good cholesterol (HDL), which pulls plaque away from artery walls. A lack of estrogen in postmenopausal women is also responsible for changes in the skeletal structure of women, leading to osteoporosis. Estrogen slows down bone loss and even helps create additional bone mass. The effect is so significant that women can cut their risk of a hip fracture in half simply by undergoing estrogen-replacement therapy (Park, 1999).

Some women fear that taking estrogen will increase their risk for breast cancer. While it is true that there is a correlation between breast cancer and estrogen replacement therapy, new forms of estrogen-like supplements may actually prevent the growth of breast tumors. Taking the drug tamoxifen concurrently with estrogen-type treatments can significantly reduce the risk of developing cancer (Park, 1999), but there are still risks. A huge study (16,608 women) by the Women's Health Initiative found that hormone replacement therapy increased a woman's risk for breast cancer, heart disease, and stroke (Smith, 2002). Teaching behavioral skills like healthy eating, regular exercise, and stress management skills are better interventions for offsetting cancer and cardiovascular threats.

When problems such as breast cancer arise, mortality issues are rarely the presenting problem. The more immediate concern is one of identity. After losing their breasts, some complain about losing their womanhood. Similar complaints are made by women undergoing hysterectomies or radiation therapy (which inevitably involves hair loss). Other women may question their womanhood because they are unable to have children. Mary Ellen Williams (1997) interviewed 15 infertile women and found 11 repeating patterns: negative identity; worthlessness/inadequacy; lack of personal control; anger/resentment; grief/depression; anxiety/stress; lower life satisfaction; envy of other mothers; loss of the dream of co-creating; "emotional roller coaster" of mood swings; and isolation. Similar findings have been reported for Chinese women (Lu, Yang, Lu, & Sun, 1996).

Many of these emotional factors can hinder a woman's identity development. If she focuses on the anger, she may find herself admonished to "get over it." If she begins to envy women who have children, she may retreat from social contact and become isolated and withdrawn. Of all the emotional reactions to infertility, the most painful is anxiety. Most women realize their anxiety may increase the difficulty of becoming pregnant (Domar, 1997), but their inability to release their fears and anxiety creates guilt and additional stress. One infertile woman summed up her feelings in this way:

> I knew things were getting bad when I couldn't attend Mother's Day ceremonies at church any more. It was just too painful. Person after person came up to me with flowers and, while smiling, asked, "Are you a mother?" Once I just said "Yes" so no one else would offer me one. The following year, the first happy volunteer who discovered that I wasn't a mother gave me a flower any-

way. She just smiled knowingly and said, "Well, you'll be a mother someday." That was the last Mother's Day service I attended—I couldn't take the stress.

How do we help ease the emotions enveloping infertile women? McQueeney, Stanton, and Sigmon (1997) compared the efficacy of emotion-focused and problem-focused group therapies for 29 infertile females (aged 24 to 38 years) who had been attempting to have children for an average of four years. The problem-solving group produced improvements in general distress and infertility-specific well-being. However, emotion-focused training resulted in greater improvement at a one-month follow-up. The women in this latter group were less depressed and felt better about their infertility. At 18 months, however, problem-focused group members were more likely to have a child. These differing outcomes create a dilemma for the counselor. Should we assume the couple cannot have children and focus on their emotional well-being, or should we help them understand all the possible alternatives and continue to provide hope? There is no clear answer, but many practitioners feel more comfortable pumping their clients with hope. It is important for therapists to realize, however, that sometimes their clients will simply need to learn acceptance and discover how to create new goals.

Cultural Uniqueness

Judy Mann (1994) tells the story of watching a mother learn how to braid her daughter's hair. The little girl remained relatively motionless, but was admonished when she made any movement. Mann noted that such a lesson in forced femininity included many different elements. The girl appeared exhausted and pained from the experience, but she was still coaxed into thanking the hairdresser for the treatment. Such experiences help to create "good little girls" who are grateful, polite, still, calm, and obedient.

These subordinating elements of feminine social conditioning are apparent in much of Western culture. Even the language used tends to view men as the representative humans, but, over the past few decades, this has changed. The pronoun "he" is no longer considered a universal referent. Instead, we often use "he or she" when referring to an unidentified or hypothetical individual. *Chairman* has changed to chairperson, chair, or moderator; *foreman* has become supervisor; *mankind* has become humanity, *manmade* is handcrafted, synthetic, handmade, or artificial; *newsmen* are reporters; *firemen* are firefighters; *mailmen* are mail carriers; *manpower* is labor, staffing, or work force; *forefathers* are ancestors or forebears. All of these changes encourage or reflect the growing equality of women.

Despite a greater sensitivity to women's issues and feminine culture, a rift between the sexes still exists. From early childhood, girls are treated differently from boys. Adults are more likely to play with girls gently and boys aggressively, even though girl babies are biologically tougher and hardier (Philpot,

Brooks, Lusterman, & Nutt, 1997). Fathers will throw their young boys into the air, while mothers will hug and coo at young girls. Even the way adults communicate with boys and girls differs. When examining the speech patterns of mothers and fathers, Leaper, Anderson, and Sanders (1998) found that mothers tended to talk more, use more supportive speech, and provide fewer directives than fathers. This tendency held true for both sons and daughters, but even though mothers were more likely than fathers to engage in such dialogue they still talked more and used more supportive speech when talking to their infant daughters than their sons.

The early treatment of girls creates some difficult paradoxes. A girl who adopts stereotypically feminine mannerisms is punished by society; e.g., girls who cry too often are mocked for their effusiveness. Girls who avoid crying are criticized for their lack of femininity. This double bind appears to stem from changing views of womanhood and a misunderstanding of feminine culture. Some strides are being made to appreciate and celebrate feminine culture, but these are still in their nascence.

The interpersonal dimension of womanhood has been wonderfully depicted in *Women's Ways of Knowing* by Field-Belenky et al. (1986). Here, the authors describe women's epistemological foundations (methods of learning) as differing from those of men. Rather than view knowledge as external facts, the women in their studies learned to interact with knowledge relationally. Furthermore, they argued, women appear to follow a different process of acquiring knowledge. The process described by Field-Belenky et al. is summarized below.

- First, women learn through silence. Their families, husbands, and others typically undervalue them, which leaves them feeling voiceless and unable to think.

- Second, in this quiet state, they learn to listen to the voices of others. Women at this stage had no respect for their own opinions and regarded other people and books as the source of all knowledge.

- Third, as their knowledge coalesced with their experiences, they begin to identify an inner voice, a form of subjective knowledge. At this point, some women may reject the masculine world as being alien and qualitatively different from their own experience of knowing.

- At this point, there are two options that some women take. We will call the first option stage 4a, and it is a type of doubting game. Only knowledge capable of standing up to the increased scrutiny is accepted.

- The alternative fourth stage, 4b, is a type of believing game. There is an attempt to get inside an idea—in a sense, to play with the possibilities and explore it experientially. Often this is accomplished through interaction with others who are also seeking truth through this means. The process resembles gossip more than debate. Fellow participants are viewed as colleagues seeking precious ways of knowing.

- Finally, the fifth stage is one of constructing knowledge by integrating the voices. Objectivity and subjectivity are blended together, but both must also be transcended to reach knowledge. In a sense, this is a trained subjectivity with its own heuristics and guidelines.

Women who reach the final stage can solve complex problems with this reasoned subjectivity. One example involves the process of buying cereal from a grocery story. Women were monitored and asked why they were buying a particular size, brand, or quantity of the products. Some women, with very little education, were able to deduce which product was the most economical by using simple heuristics and subjective measurements. Others were able to envision the space in their pantry and purchase the size of box that would fit into the available space. In other cases, women solved applied problems, which, from an objective point of view would require complex calculus or trigonometry and take several minutes to solve. These experienced women, however, could solve the problems accurately within seconds.

The foundations for feminine culture appear to stem from human evolution. Joseph (2000) argued that evolutionary neurology explains human sex differences in language, sexuality, and visual-spatial skills. Trends in the division of labor were established early in human development and became amplified with the emergence of the "big-brained" *Homo erectus*. Exaggerated sex differences in the division of labor derived from "innate" sex differences in visual-spatial versus language skills. "Women's work" such as child-rearing, food gathering, and domestic tool construction and manipulation contributed to the functional evolution of the angular gyrus. These activities gave rise, therefore, to a female superiority in grammatical vocabulary rich language. Hunting as a way of life does not require speech but relies on excellent visual-spatial skills and, thus, contributed to a male visual-spatial superiority and sex differences in the brain.

Whatever the reason for women's superior language skills, the sex difference plays a significant role in the culture of women. The tendency for women and girls to talk more and be more supportive with each other continues throughout their development. By the time they reach school age, girls are able to use communication to assist in their self-concept development. Lytle, Bakken, and Romig (1997) tested the communication patterns of 317 male students and 332 female students in grades 6, 8, 10, and 12 in small and a midsized Midwestern cities. The girls in their study were able to blend interpersonal and intrapersonal identity development. They based their identities on their cliques and social groups, but they also took pride in their individual abilities. The boys in this study, however, focused entirely on their personal thoughts and skills. They had friendships, but their friends had less of an influence on how they viewed themselves.

TABLE 9.1 *Womanist Identity Model (WIM)*

	Process
Stage 1: Pre-encounter	Accepts the limited roles prescribed for women and fails to recognize or accept institutional sexism.
Stage 2: Encounter	Sexual harassment, discrimination, or some other incident shocks the woman in accepting the fact that sexism exists.
Stage 3: Immersion-Emersion	There is an involvement in feminist or woman-oriented groups, and there is a clear effort to help women work towards their full potential.
Stage 4: Internalization	Femininity is accepted but there is also a willingness to participate in the positive elements of the dominant culture. Sexism is still viewed as an enemy, but masculine culture is not necessarily harmful.

With girls placing so much importance on social groups, their identity development is often complicated by conflicting social messages. The process of recognizing and dealing with sexist assumptions led Helms (1990) to create the Womanist Identity Model (WIM). Although it is sometimes associated with women of color (Crawford & Unger, 2000), it is also considered a general model of female identity development. Like the models for the development of ethnic and racial identity, this model consists of four stages, which are listed in Table 9.1.

As with the ethnicity models, the earliest stage involves a lack of awareness about the differences between male and female cultures. In the pre-encounter stage, a young woman fails to realize that she lives in a sexist world. She may simply believe that women must resign themselves to the roles assigned to them because things have always worked this way, or she will not acknowledge that her culture may limit her goals to feminine pursuits.

In the encounter stage, which is sometimes accompanied by anger, there is an awareness of sexism, often emerging from sexual harassment or discrimination. This awareness triggers the immersion-emersion stage, in which she may become involved in feminist groups and begin to identify with women who seek to realize their potential. Finally, for some, there is a period of internalization. Here, a woman realizes she is free to make her own choices and follow the path of her heart, but she moves beyond the anger present from the encounter stage. She understands the value of femininity and still seeks to defeat sexism, but also learns to appreciate the positive elements of the dominant culture.

African American and European American women have different patterns of responses to both feminist and mental health scales. For European American women, immersion-emersion and, to a lesser extent, encounter and pre-encounter attitudes have been found to be related to common psychological symptomatology. For African American women, no such relationship between womanist attitudes and mental health was found (Carter & Parks, 1996).

In this context, the term *womanist* is differentiated from feminist because the latter became associated with too many things, while the former was associated with African American women. Other movements include socialist feminism (emphasizing discrimination based on social structures), radical feminism (emphasizing the elimination of male domination of women), liberal feminism (striving for political equality), and cultural feminism (celebrating the differences between women and men). Although each of these is important and deserves attention, there are other cultural issues that must also be examined. For example, psychological variables such as fear of racism, anger, and stress often affect the health of ethnic-minority women more than that of ethnic-minority men and White women. More research is needed to develop effective prevention and intervention strategies for this population (Sanders-Phillips, 1996).

Feminist culture has also been responsible for a shift in the way some women view their spirituality. During the 1980s, a movement arose that attempted to explore feminine elements of the divine (Merchant, 1983). Feminist theology affirmed the necessity of feminine energy in spirituality. Nature (including the body) is seen as something that is born out of God. It is not alien to God, but flows out of God as if being formed through a process of gestation (McFague, 1988). This spirituality is nature-based, earth-grounded, and cosmically conscious. It does not look for an external God who transcends the world, but attempts to find a union with God in the creation process of the life cycle (Weber, 1987). This panentheistic theology embodies a rebellion against the transcendence of patriarchical religions. The entire cosmos is seen as a passageway in which the ineffable Mystery of Being (sometimes called God) flows in and through us.

This sense of relatedness seems to embody much of feminine culture. Frequently, man's sense of creativity involves making things work. Masculine professions emphasize tools; masculine philosophy emphasizes structure. Women, on the other hand, as real or potential mothers, possess a sense of relatedness by which they let something grow, nurture it, and allow it to follow the mysterious law of becoming.

Although the sisterhood advocated by feminism helps women to group together and fight for equality, this ideal is seldom met, and the culture of womanhood has historically been one of the obstacles in the fight for women's equality. Chesler's (2001) thought-provoking text, *Woman's Inhumanity to Woman*, challenges popular notions about women's lack of aggressiveness. She admits that women's violence is usually less direct than men's tactics, but the results can be extremely damaging. Women and girls judge each other harshly, in life and on juries, hold grudges, gossip, exclude, envy, and compete against each other. These harmful behaviors, Chesler argues, stem from a feminine culture advocating emotional and physical intimacy with other women. The desire to bond with other females leads to the formation of cliques and "in groups." Such elitism creates a power structure that enforces female conformity and discourages female independence.

Psychological Issues

When addressing the psychology of women, it is important to point out that research biases have long pathologized women for acting the way society wanted them to act (Collier, 1982). Even traditional psychotherapies have an obvious androcentric orientation. Freud (1932) argued that women secretly rebelled against their femininity and desired to possess a penis to experience manhood. According to Freud's theory, girls realized that boys had something that they lacked, which led them to develop penis envy. A girl would blame her mother for this physical inadequacy and turn to the father for love. In this process, she underwent a loss of the mother's support and attempted to identify with her to retain the mother's support. The girl's lack of castration anxiety meant that she had no reason to resolve the Oedipal complex. As a result, Freud argued, girls had weaker superegos, and were likely to wish to have a baby boy of their own to finally possess a penis.

These impulses, Freud argued, made women prone to hysterical reactions because they could not express their sexuality freely. From his point of view, women would not even allow themselves to contemplate the sexual side of their nature. Decades later, Betty Friedan (1963), while politely admitting that sexual repression might have caused hysterical reactions in the past, noted that such complications had become much less common for liberated women. She suggested that Freud's entire notion of developmental psychology as a sexual process no longer seemed accurate.

Adding to the difficulties of understanding women is confusion regarding how to define positive mental health traits. Bem (1974) conducted a study to discover the most used adjectives to describe the typical male or female. Feminine adjectives included *gentle, yielding, understanding, naive, childlike,* and *sensitive to the needs of others.* Masculine adjectives included *ambitious, athletic, self-reliant, independent, dominant,* and *competitive.* When comparing these qualities with what is considered "mentally healthy" for all people, the masculine adjectives, in general, are typically more positive. This poses a dilemma for women. They can either become more masculine and "healthy" or more feminine and needy (Collier, 1982). Sadly, it appears that Bem's stereotypical adjectives used to describe women are still applied today, although men are now expected to be more androgynous (Auster, 2000).

Kaplan (Collier, 1982) argued that women can learn to appreciate their femininity while adding traditionally masculine features. This process usually involves assertiveness training, where women continue to view themselves as relational beings while also appreciating the value of independence. The purpose of such training is to reach a form of sex-role transcendence in which women view gender as one component of their identity. Ideally, women learn to view themselves as people first and women second. This has led to the feminist belief that therapies should emphasize the social origins of differences between the sexes, when differences are noted at all. The differences created by nature or heredity, while recognized, have been viewed as less important to the identity of women (Collier, 1982).

With today's increased emphasis on biochemical roots of behavior, however, there is more and more evidence of hormonal and genetic differences that may explain some of the differences between the sexes. Psychological issues are also being described physiologically, and it would be a travesty to ignore the research in this developing field. At the same time, the socially created differences between the sexes are important and likely to explain more than we realize. Sociological causes can be difficult to discover because of the notorious complexities inherent in the study of people. For these reasons, our discussion of psychological issues will be dedicated more to biological causes than social ones, although we should always keep in mind that biology and environment do not operate independently.

Depression

Because women have been socialized to interact more with others, they are also more likely to become dependent upon others. This limited self-autonomy is associated with increased risk of depression. During the 1970s, most of the research on women and sadness addressed this social component (Collier, 1982). This research has continued into the new millennium, but the perspective has changed somewhat. Atwood (2001), for example, found that girls coming from abusive or otherwise sexist households were more likely to have problems with gender role socialization, depression in adulthood, involvement in demeaning intimate relationships, self-doubt, and a tendency to sacrifice their own personal and relational development for the sake of others. In addition to looking at familial and social influences, a new branch of research has explored the biological roots of depression. Evidence is mounting that the brains of females may respond differently to hormones and brain chemicals than those of males. Women produce less serotonin, a mood-regulating chemical, than men, and they are more sensitive to changes in serotonin levels, which are in turn regulated by estrogen (Park, 1999). It should be noted, however, that the existence of chemical differences between the brains of men and women does not imply that social causes are unimportant. In all likelihood, social causes interact with genetic or chemical predispositions to depression. One of the clearest examples of this interrelationship is found in the existence of seasonal affective disorder or SAD.

Women's reduced serotonin production also makes them more sensitive to changes in the weather. Women appear to seek treatment for depression more often in the winter, and they seek treatment for bipolar disorder in the summer, but no such pattern has been found for men (Park, 1999). Women are also more likely than men to experience SAD. Symptoms include depressed mood, fatigue, lack of energy, sleeping disturbances (either too much or too little sleep, or difficulty awakening in the morning), increased appetite (often including carbohydrate craving), weight gain, and reduced work productivity. For the diagnosis to be made, these symptoms must be absent in the late spring and summer months but return during the fall or winter.

SAD is somewhat more common for people who live farthest from the Equator, because of shortened days during the winter months. It has been estimated that SAD affects less than 1 percent of the population in Florida, while in Alaska as many as 10 percent of people may suffer. In America, as much as 25 percent of the population at the middle-to-northern latitudes of the United States experience many of the symptoms of SAD.

The most important factor in seasonal depression seems to be exposure to sunlight. Some research suggests that the brain may produce less serotonin in some people during short days. Schwartz et al. (1997) investigated whether the central nervous system appeared to generate less serotonin during the winter. They found moderate support for their theory, which suggests that sunlight absorbed from the skin and eyes helps to maintain a balanced flow of serotonin. However, others have argued that SAD is unrelated to serotonin production. Neumeister et al. (1997), for example, experimented with levels of tryptophan depletion to exacerbate the depressive symptoms of SAD. They found that serotonergic activity does not play a primary, direct role in the pathogenesis of winter depression.

The treatment for SAD often includes light therapy. Clients sit in front of bright light generated by a "light box" for approximately 30 minutes every day. The treatment is highly effective and relatively inexpensive. Originally, only special lights that mimicked sunlight were used, but it appears that any light exposure is adequate. The findings are so encouraging that Beauchemin and Hays (1997) suggest that light treatment may even benefit people suffering from other forms of depression. In some cases, the only treatment is to brighten a person's room. In one study, inpatient clients staying in sunny rooms had an average stay of 16.9 days compared to 19.5 days for those in rooms that received little or no sunlight (Beauchemin & Hays, 1996).

Eating Disorders

Although depressive symptoms are often devastating to women, another disorder tends to cripple nearly every component of their identity. According to the National Institute of Mental Health (American Psychological Association, 1998), adolescents and young women account for 90 percent of those with eating disorders, which leaves only 10 percent accounted for by older women, men, and boys. For many years, it was generally regarded to be a problem afflicting only White women, but it appears that other ethnic groups may be similarly affected. Specifically, Mukai and McCloskey (1996) found that Japanese schoolgirls were just as likely as White American girls to view their weight as a problem. Approximately half of the girls from each country expressed a desire to be thinner, and about a third of both groups reporting having tried to lose weight.

The causes associated with eating disorders are diverse, but contemporary views of attractiveness play a significant role. Adolescent girls are still introduced to their own sexuality in terms of how they should look. Regan (1996) examined the extent to which a person's body weight influences perceptions of his or her sexuality and sexual experiences. Ninety-six undergraduates (aged 17 to 23 years) received information about a male or female person who was obese or of normal weight, and then evaluated that person along several dimensions related to sexuality. The participants rated the obese man's sexual experiences as similar to those of the normal-weight man, but they viewed the obese woman differently. They described the obese woman as less sexually attractive, skilled, warm, and responsive than her thinner peer. They also viewed her as less likely to experience desire and various sexual behaviors than a normal-weight woman or an obese man.

The influence of beauty on feminine acceptance is significant. Efrat Tseelon (1992) argued that physical attractiveness, for women, functions as a stigma. She believes that beauty defines a woman's identity and often places her in a stigmatized position. Such findings are not surprising, but the extent to which the "beauty myth" affects women might not be fully understood. Henss (2000) examined how men viewed the attractiveness of women based on waist-to-hip ratio. In accordance with evolutionary psychological expectations, a lower ratio was more attractive than a higher one. In addition to body shape, there is evidence that facial attractiveness plays an important role in the treatment of women. Thornhill and Grammer (1999) argued against the notion that facial attractiveness in women is a deceptive signal of youth, unrelated to phenotypic and genetic quality. Their study of 30 Viennese and 30 American men's ratings of the attractiveness of photographs of 92 nude women revealed that men judged the entire presentation of women when ranking attractiveness. The correlation between the ratings of different photos implies that men view women's faces and external bodies as a collective whole, rather than focusing on any particular feature.

Evolutionary psychology assumes that men view women's bodies in terms of how fertile they appear. Signs of fertility are culturally determined, but they often involve such elements as waist-to-hip ratios, large breasts, youthful skin, and an engaging face (i.e., open to conversation and relationships). Women often accept these cultural mandates as well. The correlation between women's self-perceptions of their body image and evolutionary psychology has long been established (Wade & Abetz, 1997). Women are encouraged to become "objects of desire" instead of agents of their own pleasures and desires. Weight and body size is an important factor in these perceptions and roles.

There is a dangerous contradiction at work regarding weight and self-perception. Society encourages women to look youthful (i.e., fertile), which includes having a small or thin body. For some women, controlling their weight is one of the only daily routines that provides them with a sense of power. Dieting advertisements are everywhere, and women come to believe that being thin is equivalent to being successful. Naomi Wolf (1991) emphasizes the effects of TV and advertisements in this socialization process: "Girls learn to watch their sex along with the boys; that takes up the space that should be devoted to finding out about what they are wanting, and reading and writing about it, seeking it and getting it. Sex is held hostage by beauty and its ransom terms are engraved in girls' minds early and deeply" (p. 157). It is not surprising that women who are physically more attractive than their peers are also more likely to be preoccupied with their weight, putting them at increased risk for eating disorders (Davis, Claridge, & Fox, 2000).

The connection between physical beauty and eating disorders may explain the emergence of studies indicating a genetic predisposition towards eating disorders, especially bulimia nervosa. After studying nearly 2,000 identical and fraternal twins, Bulik, Sullivan, Wade, and Kendler (2000) concluded that genes account for 83 percent of female susceptibility to bulimia. However, they noted that these genetic influences interact with known environmental factors in unpredictable ways. Prior to discussing this topic, we need to provide a little background about the various types of eating disorders.

Individuals with bulimia nervosa tend to eat excessively and then purge the food from their bodies. The methods used for purging vary. Some will use laxatives, enemas, or diuretics. They may also attempt self-induced vomiting or excessive exercise. Whatever the mechanism, the behaviors are performed in secrecy, which aggravates the diagnostic process. Guilt and shame permeate their sense of self, but the act also provides a sense of relief when they purge their bodies of the food. It is as if they use the food as a means of stuffing their emotional hardships and then expunge the symbolic conflict in hopes of feeling better. The excitement/shame cycle can become so intense that some clients might eroticize their binging. Maguire (1995) noted that one client described how her excitement came to a climax when she vomited only to be followed by a post-prandial depression.

Despite the psychological stress of bulimic compulsions, few bulimic women admit to needing help until signs of physical damage appear. A number of physical concerns are present with bulimia. If vomiting is the primary mechanism of expulsion, the esophagus can degrade and eventually rupture, the stomach lining can tear, and tooth enamel can be eroded by stomach acids. Although these are real and potentially life-threatening risks, the most serious eating-related health risks stem from anorexia nervosa.

Anorexia nervosa is the refusal to maintain body weight at or above a minimally normal weight for age and height. The diagnosis is made when an intense fear of becoming fat causes a person to weigh less than 85 percent of expected weight. Self-starvation is an intentional act. "Anna" was 19 when she wrote the following:

> Sometimes, when I get really down, I just go for days without eating. Once, I went three weeks and no one seemed to notice. I would just chew gum or drink water. Sometimes people would ask if that was all I was planning to eat. I would just tell them I wasn't hungry.

Even after treatment, Anna confessed that she had to "force" herself to eat. As her disorder progressed, she felt disgusted with herself and the way she ate. She found it virtually impossible to eat in the presence of other people, especially strangers.

It is important to realize that the conditions leading to eating disorders go beyond dieting or genetics. Horesh et al. (1996) examined a huge number of variables and compared eating disordered populations with other psychiatric clients and a control group. The eating disordered clients and the psychiatric groups shared the following characteristics: lack of warmth in parent-child relations, parental discord, hostility, physical abuse, parent mental disorder, distorted communication, inadequate parental control, hazardous living conditions, negative change in family relations, loss of self-esteem, and frightening experience. The only characteristic in which the eating disorder group significantly differed from both the control and psychiatric groups involved parental pressures. Inappropriate parental pressure was specific to adolescent girls with eating disorders. The pressures included gender-related pressure (e.g., girls felt "forced into an exaggerated feminine style of behavior"), age-inappropriate pressure (e.g., parents discussed sex with the child before she was ready for such topics), and pressure inappropriate to the child's abilities (e.g., forcing children to engage in activities to fulfill the parents' ambitions rather than the child's).

The dysfunctional quality of the families led the American Psychological Association (1998) to provide a fact sheet on the subject. The APA argued that there were a number of factors that predisposed people to developing eating disorders. Dysfunctional families or relationships are one factor, but they admitted that there were personality traits that contributed as well. Both must be considered when treating such individuals.

Regardless of the etiology of the disorder, one of the most important interventions involves a direct attack on the client's sense of self-inadequacy and shame. Burney and Irwin (2000) explored the relationship between the guilt women feel regarding their eating behaviors and an underlying sense of shame. Guilt, which is defined as feelings of culpability especially for imagined offenses, was an effective predictor of developing an eating disorder when the feelings were associated with eating behavior. Shame, which is defined as a condition of humiliating disgrace or disrepute, was the strongest predictor of the severity of eating-disorder symptomatology when the feelings were specifically associated with the body or eating behaviors. Shame and guilt were only predictive of eating disturbances, however, when specifically associated with the body or eating. The women in this study were not prone to shame and guilt in a global sense. The same has been found for issues of perfectionism. Perfectionism itself is not a risk factor for eating disorders. It is only when high standards are combined with a tendency to be hypercritical or extremely anxious that the risk increases (Davis, Claridge, & Fox, 2000).

As the disorder progresses, distortions in self-perception lead to increased problems with disordered eating (Noll & Fredrickson, 1998). These misconceptions of self are not entirely related to distorted body images. There is a significant association between bodily shame and childhood abuse, which does not appear to be explained by bodily dissatisfaction (Andrews, 1997). Andrews suggests that bodily shame may act as a mediator between early abuse and bulimia. The shame becomes a mechanism for coping with earlier physical, emotional, or sexual trauma. This would explain why Sanftner et al. (1995) found a significant correlation between bodily shame and drive for thinness, bulimia, body dissatisfaction, ineffectiveness, interpersonal distrust, asceticism, difficulties with impulse regulation, and social insecurity. It is a paradox. Clients feel intense shame, which they believe is directly related to their physical appearance, but it probably stems from an inability to cope with the pressures of their past—a limitation that eventually interferes with their ability to function socially, occupationally, or academically. This progression is depicted in the case of 21-year-old Sissy:

> I don't know how to describe it. I just feel "bad" when I eat. I feel the fat inside of me, and it hurts. It like, attacks me, and makes me feel like I'm going to explode. Then I look at myself, and it's like I can see the fat I just ate building on my hips. I can't take it any more. I have to get rid of it.
>
> I'm starting to pull away from everyone in my life, because they are always telling me to just "get over it" and start eating. Even my dad tells me that. He can't understand why it's taken me this long to get over the stuff he did to me. Even now, when I walk by a closet I feel uncomfortable. He would take me in there and put sex toys into me. I know I should have stopped him; I was just too weak. And now, it seems that I'm too weak to get better, but I'm trying. I really am.

Sissy was unaware of the relationship between her body image and her sexual history. All she knew was that she hated herself. She hated herself for being sexually abused as a girl, and she hated herself for being hospitalized for anorexia (binge-eating/purging type). Together these forces combined to obstruct her recovery. If she started to eat, she felt shame from her past. If she worked on the past, she found her eating disorders worsened. The intervention that finally proved successful kept both components ever present. She needed to be able to focus on her pain without focusing on her diet.

Cognitive-behavioral interventions also appear useful. Hilde Bruch (1993) laid the foundations for cognitive therapy in her book, *Eating Disorders*. She stated that therapy with eating disordered clients must progress slowly and requires careful, concrete interventions for each event that arises. For example, in the early stages, just getting clients to eat is a major accomplishment. Using small increments, clinicians help clients increase their diets. Weight gain is especially difficult because anorexic patients often have a higher metabolism than normal individuals and more calories are required to put on weight. Eventually, the patient is given foods containing as many as 3,500 calories or more a day. Dietary supplements are not usually recommended because the patient needs to resume normal eating patterns as soon as possible.

It is also important to shift tension away from eating. Discussions of the disorder should never be held during meals, which are times for relaxed social interaction. Additionally, tube or intravenous feeding is rarely needed or recommended unless the patient's condition is life-threatening, because they remove the client's sense of control and fail to address the systemic, underlying issues.

When a client's weight begins to improve, other serious issues are likely to persist. Anorexia causes low levels of reproductive hormones, changes in thyroid hormones, and increased levels of the stress hormones. Long-term irregular or absent menstruation (amenorrhea) is common, which eventually may cause infertility and bone loss. When a client's weight improves, menstruation may not resume spontaneously. Hormonal therapy may be necessary, or, at the minimum, use of herbs such as Black or Blue Cohosh.

Within-Group Differences

As discussed in the section on African Americans, women of minority groups struggle to define themselves both as women and as members of a cultural minority. In a racist and misogynistic society, a European American woman may be considered inferior because of her sex but also superior because of her race. Sadly, early feminism did little to address this situation. As women attempted to fight for liberation, they failed to realize that minority women would require additional support. Feminists tended to evoke an image of women as a collective group, and they were compared with "Blacks" as two distinct groups. This constant comparison between "women" and "Blacks" deflected attention away from the fact that Black women were victimized by both racism and sexism—a fact which, had it been emphasized, might have diverted public attention away from the complaints of middle- and upper-class White feminists (hooks, 1991).

The plight of minority women has made it difficult for mental health professionals to effectively intervene with some groups. Sanders-Phillips (1996), a psychologist at the King/Drew Medical Center in South Central Los Angeles, studied African American, Mexican-immigrant and Mexican American women over a ten-year period. She found that ethnic-minority women have little trust in the health-care system and often believe they will encounter racism if they seek treatment. These perceptions also decrease the chances that the women will comply with a medical regimen, whether it's visiting with a psychologist, taking prescribed medications, or avoiding drugs and alcohol.

In some ways, differences between ethnic minority women are easier to understand than differences between lesbian and heterosexual women. The early feminist movement often promoted lesbianism (Brown, 1994), viewing oppression against lesbians as a sign of misogyny. The emphasis on sexuality created some distance between women who were comfortable with their roles as wives and mothers and those who sought political and economic changes (Williams & Wittig, 1997). In many ways, contemporary heterosexual women view lesbianism the way the ancient Greeks did. In ancient texts, *Lesbiazein* connoted female lasciviousness and especially fellatio. It basically included any kind of promiscuity. The Romans later added the homoerotic connotation (Rabinowitz, 2002). Although most Americans view lesbianism as a valid alternative lifestyle, a large minority still equates the practice with perversion (Newport, 2001). These social perceptions make it difficult for lesbian women to find acceptance from heterosexual women and men.

For all minority groups, the pressures of discrimination often produce feelings of rage and resentment. These emotions are especially important within women's groups, because of the social intolerance against women displaying anger. Sanders-Phillips (1996) found a direct, positive relationship between female anger and smoking. The angrier smokers became, the more they smoked. Women who were exposed to more life stressors were also more likely to drink. Sanders-Phillips noted that these issues appeared to be connected to the environmental conflicts; i.e., the more often women were mistreated, the more likely they were to use tobacco or alcohol.

There is some evidence that ethnic minority women may learn to cope with discrimination and prejudice earlier in life, which creates a helpful foundation for later life experiences. African American college women tend to receive the highest self-esteem and appearance evaluation scores when compared to their education-matched peers (Lennon, Rudd, Sloan, & Kim, 1999). When self-esteem rises, there is usually a corresponding elevation in positive body images and nontraditional attitudes toward gender roles. Statistics such as these may help to explain why White women are more likely to suffer from eating disorders. Their initial encounters with discrimination happen at puberty, a time that is fraught with emotional and physical changes.

Women with triple minority status also evidence unique strengths and coping skills. The most striking of these are Muslim women who attempt to maintain their traditional Islamic appearance while residing in Western countries. In order to better understand this population, I met with a group of European American women who had spent a month in Iran. They had all experienced intense frustration from the moment their plane had landed. It had been their intention to live among the native women and adopt their standards. Although they had thought they were well prepared, they found that they didn't understand the culture as well as they thought they did. They were expected to keep their hair, ankles, and wrists covered at all times, avoid any public eye contact with men, avoid addressing a man before being addressed, and never walk in front of, sit in front of, or walk across a man's path in public.

From the outside, it may appear that the treatment of Iranian women is harsh, but the women within that environment viewed it otherwise. They reported a type of sisterhood and stated that they felt extremely safe. Some of the women discussed how they were able to roam the streets at night without any fear of attack. They also reported fewer crimes against women in general because Islamic codes strongly condemn any such crimes. Are these benefits worth the costs? Some women clearly believe they are. When such women emigrate to the west, they often find that their clothing offers a weaker protection against masculine crimes, which was the original intention for the clothing. Western women may view their attire as "strange." One of the women from the tourism group mentioned above decided to continue wearing the *burka* after returning from her pilgrimage. She reported that she lost her job within a week. "It's okay," she said, "I found something more important."

Although ethnic culture clearly plays a role in the way gender culture is formed, there does appear to be something unique about the way women function. Singh-Manoux (2000) conducted a study to explore the effect of gender on the emotional processes of social sharing and mental rumination. She created a questionnaire and administered it to Indian, immigrant Indian, and English adolescents. As predicted, she found that females were more likely to initiate sharing, to share feelings, and to realize the relational benefits of sharing. The surveyed girls were also more likely to report being affected by their emotions, and they had more mental ruminations. Interestingly, the cultures that were examined viewed male and female roles differently. Singh-Manoux concluded that gender and cultural differences cannot be explained by the same psychological dimensions.

Counseling Issues

At the beginning of this chapter, it was argued that the differences, and sometimes the similarities, between men and women have been exaggerated. Sadly, both errors appear necessary to provide a realistic perspective on the cultural issues involved in therapy. It is important to realize that women and men are capable of the same emotions, thoughts, and behaviors. Nevertheless, there are cultural, social, and biological differences between the sexes that cannot be overlooked.

Although medical interventions are usually outside the scope of a therapist's practice, a brief comment about gender differences in medicine may shed some light on the uniqueness of women's bodies. Women have a slower metabolism than men do, which causes them to metabolize drugs differently. Even if a man and a woman eat the same thing, it may take the woman much longer to digest it. This difference leaves women three times as vulnerable to chronic constipation as men and twice as likely to develop intestinal disorders. They also feel the effects of alcohol more quickly, and aspirin stays in their systems longer.

Other biochemical differences allow women to respond better to drugs affecting serotonin production (such as Prozac), while men tend to respond better to drugs that also affect norepinephrine, a neurotransmitter secreted by the adrenal glands and by nerve endings during stress. Other drugs, including beta blockers and tricyclics, also affect women and men differently (Park, 1999). Drugs such as Inderal, prescribed to reduce blood pressure and migraine pain, take longer to metabolize in women than in men, and the dosage must be more carefully monitored to avoid side effects. With tricyclics, women taking oral contraceptives may need lower doses of these drugs to treat their depression, since the Pill keeps levels of the drugs in the body high (Park, 1999).

In light of the differences between women's and men's bodies, therapeutic interventions for women should also be unique. Awareness of differences between the sexes led to the development of feminist psychology, but the term still frightens away many women. Buschman and Lenart (1996) conducted a study to see if women felt differently about the terms "women's movement" and "feminist movement." Less positive statements were made about the feminist movement than about the women's movement, even though the two terms refer to the same series of events and philosophy. Something about the word *feminism* causes people to react negatively. Feminists were viewed as man-hating, masculine extremists, and a vocal minority may have fit this description. This negative image has left many women, even some who are at the heart of the women's movement and who endorse feminist goals, reluctant to label themselves feminists (Williams & Wittig, 1997).

The fear of feminism (sometimes referred to as "the f-word") has had a deleterious effect on therapeutic interventions. Fundamentally, feminism argues that women deserve and require equal rights with men without being forced to lose the culture of womanhood. Feminist therapy, since its establishment, has sought to help clients have equal opportunity for personal power, economic well-being, and political/institutional influence. A feminist approach requires that interactions between individuals be egalitarian (Collier, 1982).

Adrienne Smith and Ruth Siegel (1985) outlined three fundamental stages for feminist therapy. Two decades later, these basic stages still seem applicable to helping women understand the social politics that create pathology.

Stage One (the personal is political): The woman comes to recognize the social etiology of her so-called pathology; i.e., she understands that there are political and social influences in all personal problems. For example, a girl is told she is more fragile and less capable than a boy. By affirming a social context of the woman's feelings, we enable the woman to recognize her fears of leaving the familiar world of dependent females to risk the judgments of the establishment, both female and male, as she enters the world of achievement.

The central dilemma of women's lives, as Simone de Beauvoir viewed it, is that women do not shape their own experience, but allow their life choices to be made for them by others. Pleasing their fathers, lovers, husbands, defining themselves through them and through their children become ways of achieving justification at different stages of women's lives (Plaskow, 2001). Because marriage and motherhood have depended (and in great measure still depend) upon a profound male-female inequality of power, status, and economic reward, any critique is bound to be opposed by powerful elements within our society.

Stage Two: This stage focuses on those aspects of female development that become distorted, e.g., power, dependency, or responsibility. In this stage, the woman learns to recognize the conflict between autonomy and dependency as evidenced in her particular family dynamics, and in general, as she grew up. The idea of victim is shifted to one of survivor, and definitions of "mental illness" are reformulated. In this stage, there is no "disease model" of mental illness. Instead, psychological distress is viewed as a means of coping with harsh conditions. Depression may simply be an expression of an unjust system. Resistance may be a way for the woman to remain alive and powerful in the face of oppression (Brown, 1994). One way to think about this topic may be to consider the possibility that psychological pitfalls may be different for women and men. For men, the greatest sin may be pride, but for women, who are often belittled, raped, controlled, or abused, it may be a greater sin to succumb to oppression and fail to realize one's freedom.

Stage Three: This final stage involves liberating oneself from gender stereotypes. At this stage, a woman is increasingly able to recognize the legitimacy of her needs and to establish her personal power in a healthy manner. She is able to accept her feelings as valid, find ways of pleasing herself, identify personal strengths, and accept her personal imperfections. The following techniques may be helpful in reaching this stage.

- Countering negative self-statements.
- Identifying perfectionism in self.
- Defining social and cultural sources of the devaluation of women.
- Modeling exercises (women receive admiration from each member of the group).
- Self-appreciation and compliments exercise: Share positive thoughts about the strengths of others in the group.
- Celebrating women's experience: patriarchal, objective truth must give way to a feminist consciousness that encourages women to express their emotions and intuition.
- Boasting (three minutes of boasting before the group).

There are considerable obstacles that can prevent clients from reaching Stage Three. In *The Cinderella Complex,* Dowling (1994) suggested that living in a patriarchal society keeps women in a state of dependence, not unlike what is expected of a child. Dependent women do not feel free to make their own choices and come to believe that they need direction from men. The shining prince coming to save them is also a captor preventing them from actualizing their autonomy and learning how to support themselves. They invest in this hope and support the dream even when it interferes with achieving their occupational, vocational, and social goals.

Often, the best way to begin assisting a client who is mired in dependency is by helping her feel more aware of her environment and her desires. In a basic assertiveness training model, there is a progression from accepting feelings toward working on weaknesses. For example,

- *Week 1:* Acceptance of feelings as being valid. Anger, frustration, fear, and other "negative" emotions are part of interacting with the world. If we turn these off, we take away some of our power.
- *Week 2:* Finding ways of pleasing self. What would we like to see changed in the world? How would things be different if we had what we wanted?
- *Week 3:* Identifying personal strengths. These may include typically feminine tasks, such as raising children, cooking, or cleaning, but it could also include anything else. The point is to expand the possibilities for each individual, unlimited by sex-typed roles.
- *Week 4:* Recognize and accept personal imperfections. Once talents are identified, their application must be realistic. If someone is direct and assertive, using these skills to confront an abusive husband is unlikely to be productive. Similarly, attempting to fulfill all the demands placed on wife, mother, and employee can often require readjusting priorities and learning how to say "No."

When creating an intervention, the counselor must be careful to avoid fostering passivity and dependence by taking too dominant a role. The client may feel that she cannot find health on her own and requires the assistance of the counselor. In extreme cases, the woman may feel paralyzed and completely incapable of helping herself. This should be evident in the following scenario. Maria came to counseling because she "could not deal with the stress of college," and she was suffering from bulimia. During the early stages of counseling, she was introduced to biofeedback. During her first biofeedback experience, we reviewed the various controls and sensors. She watched the screen as it depicted her heart rate, skin temperature, pulse, etc. As the calming music started and she noticed her heart rate decrease, she burst into tears. "What's the matter?" I asked. Maria looked up, smiling proudly but still crying. "I didn't know I could do that!" It was the first time she realized she had control over her body, and it was her first step toward becoming a self-sufficient woman.

Maria's lack of self-efficacy is commonly observed in women with eating disorders. Self-doubt and shame can cripple the individual and lead to social isolation. They may withdraw from social contact, hide their behavior, and deny their eating patterns. For these reasons, changing thoughts and behaviors is not enough. Achieving lasting improvement requires an exploration into the issues underlying the eating disorder. Psychotherapy often focuses on improving the individual's personal relationships, medication, and learning new techniques for coping with anxiety and depression.

Sharf (2000) examined many of the disorders predominantly diagnosed in women. In addition to eating disorders, common DSM-IV diagnoses include depression, post-traumatic stress disorder, borderline personality disorder, and generalized anxiety disorder. Why are these more common among women? Perhaps because women have been taught to be dependent, submissive, and self-sacrificing. Herlihy and Corey (2001) suggest that the main goal of feminist therapy is empowerment, which often stems from promoting self-acceptance, self-confidence, joy, and self-actualization. In order to become empowered, clients must understand their anxiety and defenses. They must gain an understanding of power issues and examine the external forces that influence their behaviors.

In order to reach self-awareness and conceptualize how gender biases have helped create the "pathology" women experience, therapists can help their clients undergo *gender role analysis*. In this process, the therapist helps the client explore the gender messages that have been communicated. Without judgment, counselors simply explore some of the comments that have been offered during the session, and then seek to reinterpret them. In the case of Elizabeth, a 32-year-old woman who has been working as a waitress, gender role analysis might proceed as follows.

Matthew: Do you want to tell me more about that conversation with your father?

Elizabeth: Not really. (pause) It's not really important. (pause) Well, if you really want me to tell you.

Matthew: (smiles) It's okay not to talk about it if you are uncomfortable. This is your time. Feel free to discuss what you want. (pause)

Elizabeth: (sighs) Well, okay, but it really wasn't a big deal. It happened about two months after I started my period. I ran up to my father, who was sitting in his chair watching TV, and I flung myself onto his lap. I had done it countless times before, and he would usually embrace me with a bear hug. This time, he stiffened up, looked around me to the game, and tried not to notice me. I was a little stunned. I didn't say anything. I didn't move. Finally, he started talking about the cheerleaders on the screen and blurted out that I had better watch my weight if I wanted to be on a team like that.

Matthew: That's not the message a 12-year-old wants to hear.

Elizabeth: No! (pause) It's not.

Matthew: How did that conversation affect what happened next in your life?

Elizabeth: Oddly enough, I stayed with cheerleading. I liked dancing, and cheerleading was a good way to increase my dancing skills. But I think this was a mistake. When I started college, I started thinking of myself as fat, and I felt like I just didn't care about anything any more.

Matthew: I wonder how your life would be different if he had just loved you when you ran to him.

Elizabeth: I wouldn't have become a cheerleader—that's for sure.

Matthew: What about the dancing?

Elizabeth: It was too much work—emotional work. It left me feeling like I was just a *thing* who supported others. I did like the dancing, but I hated the ever-present requirement for happiness.

Matthew: Is that what society expects of cheerleaders—for them to become vapid, eternally happy things?

Elizabeth: Well, (pause) yeah. (laughs)

Matthew: It seems like the thing you enjoy most, dancing, became just another feminine entrapment. It's as if society said, "feel free to dance, but only in the prison we designed for you."

Elizabeth: Well, maybe it wasn't a prison.

Matthew: There were some positive elements?

Elizabeth: (tosses her head) I . . . I liked the attention, and being in front of the crowds.

Matthew: You seem to feel guilty saying that.

Elizabeth: I am—I don't want to be thought of as a cheerleader.

Matthew: Maybe what we have to do is redefine what the experience meant to you. You don't like being thought of as vapid because you are creative and dynamic. You enjoy feeling happy but want, as all humans do, moments to process pain. Society tried to stick you in a small box, but you know there is more to life than what fits in that box—there is more to you. Let's explore what society missed in you and what you hope to become.

As this session ends, Matthew has directed Elizabeth to reframe her gender-prescribed experiences. She learns to accept her past and focus on breaking away from the prescribed roles that followed her throughout adolescence. Although the session was positive, there were serious problems. Matthew's gender, for instance, may have contributed to Elizabeth's growth and simultaneously hindered it. Elizabeth deferred to his authority at the beginning of the session and discussed the topic he initiated. This should have been explored in more detail, and eventually, Elizabeth should have been encouraged to take control of the session. However, despite this weakness, Elizabeth was also able to define her gender role with a sympathetic and generally empowering man.

The power issues associated with mixed-gender relationships, of any type, cannot be overlooked. Lesbian relationships can also involve physical violence (which is usually predicted by a controlling partner), but female-to-female relationships are more likely to involve emotional aggression (which is predicted by fusion, poor self-esteem, and a lack of independence). Emotional aggression, which is most likely evidenced through verbal abuse, is important, but it is rarely life threatening. The male abuse of women has more life-threatening consequences and warrants in-depth attention (Miller et al., 2001). Careful attention to gender role awareness and empowerment are especially important and difficult when women find themselves involved in controlling and abusive intimate relationships. Probably the most severe form of control involves rape. Rape can include all of the following definitions:

- Having sex with a minor.
- Forcing someone to have sex, or continuing with a sex act after the individual has requested an end to the act.
- Having sex with someone who is unable to consent to the act (e.g., people who are drugged or mentally ill).
- Having sex with someone who has not verbal given consent. (*Note:* Lack of verbal or physical resistance by the victim, resulting from the use of force or threat by the accused, *does not* constitute consent.)

When rape occurs, women are likely to feel an overpowering sense of shame. They may try to "cleanse" themselves from the assault by showering, throwing away clothes, or washing bed sheets, but these actions will only hinder prosecution of the offender. The best action to follow is to call the police, write down anything that can be remembered about the assailant (e.g., height in reference to something at the scene, hair and eye color, scars, tattoos, physical defects, what the offender sounded like, or what he smelled like). However, most women will feel uncomfortable reporting the crime. Whether the rape was violent or not, a woman may enter a type of emotional shock. She may experience self-blame, vulnerability, a loss of power and control, and fear/anger toward all men (Resnick, 2001). The idea of reporting the crime and reliving the event is not appealing to any victim.

Counselors can help clients cope with the emotions caused by sexual assault, and they can also answer important questions. Survivors of rape are often concerned about the possibility of contracting HIV/AIDS or other diseases, or becoming pregnant. The hospital will probably not test for diseases during the first visit, which places the burden on the client to find a physician to help. One of the best places to start is to call the National AIDS Hotline (1-800-342-AIDS) or the National STD Hotline (1-800-227-8922). These agencies are usually able to offer a referral to confidential clinics in most states.

Therapists can assist the client in dealing with the range of emotions that will likely follow a sexual trauma. Although individuals respond to crises differently, the following reactions are common:

- Embarrassment
- Anger/Revenge
- Self-blame/Guilt/Shame/Humiliation
- Fear/Helplessness/Vulnerability
- Anxiety/Irritability
- Confusion/Poor concentration
- Dramatic and intense mood swings
- Nightmares
- Distrust of others
- Overreacting to everyday occurrences
- Loss of previous coping skills
- Flashbacks
- Persistent discomfort at the site of attack (e.g., swollen glands or sore throat if victim was orally assaulted)
- Denial or minimization of the problem
- Physical problems (e.g., nausea or upset stomach, soreness and bruising, infections, or tension headaches)
- Sleep disturbances
- Eating disturbances
- Pregnancy concerns
- Fears of venereal disease or HIV/AIDS
- Menstrual cycle disruption and genitourinary difficulties

Therapists can help their clients realize that all of these reactions are common and, to some degree, expected. Problems arise, not with the manifestation of symptoms *per se*, but with minimizing or denying the event. Sometimes, clients will compare their trauma to someone else's and conclude that their ordeal "wasn't as bad." When this happens, therapists must ensure that the client realizes that any rape or molestation is traumatic.

Society also plays a role in the way rape victims are perceived. Sometimes people will wonder why the female survivor was unable to stop the perpetrator. If this question is brought up by the counselor, the client will likely internalize the guilt she feels more intensely, and virtually any benefit from the sessions will be lost.

Women should understand that violence against them is common but not found in every relationship. They should also understand that genuine danger exists, and they should literally fear for their lives. It is important for survivors to realize that there is a strong correlation between the frequency of abuse and its severity (Straus, Gelles, & Steinmetz, 1980). Rape by a stranger is much less common than date rape, and violence within a relationship, whether sexual or physical, becomes more life-threatening with each attack.

When clients are known to be in abusive relationships, Walker (1985) suggests working with them to devise an escape plan. The plan should include all of the following:

- Developing cognitive recognition of signs of an impending battering incident (e.g., face turning red, eyes looking menacing, fingers twitching, etc.).
- Method of and timing for leaving the house safely.
- Items she would need to bring with her (car keys, spare cash, etc.).
- Provisions for children.
- Location of nearest public telephone or neighbor to whom she can run for help.

When all of these components are included, the client should rehearse the plan with the therapist in much the same manner as a fire drill. Ask the client to review every possible scenario. What might happen if the abuser returned when you were moving toward the door? How should you get the children out of the house? What would you do if your abuser found out where you were going? Many clients may view these provisions as unnecessary, but therapists should explain that even the possibility of violence is life-threatening.

After establishing an escape plan, therapy with women clients should address the role they play in the family. Survivors of spousal abuse often come to view themselves as peacemakers. They view themselves as being responsible for violence in the family, and they feel that they must exude forgiveness, patience, love, and support at all times.

Women have internalized the roles of caretaker and nurturer; abused men also take responsibility for the abuse from a caretaking perspective (Leeder, 1994). With male and female survivors caring for the needs of others before their own, a primary task in therapy is for the survivor to assert her or his rights and demand safety. These issues are best addressed in individual therapy, where the abused partner feels safe enough to share her fear. For some, this may include assertiveness training. For others, bibliotherapy (therapy through reading) and learning about the success of others may prove more beneficial. Some clients may benefit from interacting with others in a support group, which teaches them they are not alone. Whatever the tactic used, the powerless partner must find a way to reclaim a sense of self and re-ignite the spark of life, and the controlling partner must learn how to find inner peace without needing to steal it away from others.

Hope's Story

Hope and Mark provide a common story of abuse with wonderful insight and depth. As you read their story, notice how Hope describes how she knew of Mark's tendencies for abuse before she married him and how, when the abuse appeared, it took many forms. In many ways, Hope deteriorates through the story. She begins with anger towards her husband and ends with fear. Mark's story, which is provided at the end of the chapter on men, is remarkable for its de-emphasis of abuse. His story begins with his treatment and never elaborates on the abuse.

In some ways, most abusive families provide similar stories. The survivor is often trapped in the past and must use the past to understand her future. The abuser's life begins with the emergence of a new self; the old self is swept away or hidden from the world.

> People always ask me how I ended up with Mark. I suppose, to them, any rational woman would have seen the abuse coming, but I don't think it is ever that easy. I was a little concerned about how controlling he was, but there were contrasting elements. When we were on a date, he devoted all his attention to me, encouraged me, and protected me. I felt safe, even if I was a little disempowered.
>
> In many ways, Mark was the first man who sincerely cared about me. Maybe his care actually created some of the problems. He frequently attempted to "improve" me. He would drop subtle hints about the way I dressed, my deportment, vocabulary, and friends. In each of these suggestions, there was an element of truth. Maybe he was entirely correct with some of his ideas, but with each suggestion, I lost part of myself. I didn't realize until later that he added less than he took, and my identity dwindled away into dependence.
>
> Our relationship continued to "blossom," and in a couple of years, we were married. We had a daughter, and I stayed at home to play full-time mom. This change in status radically changed our relationship. With only one income, finances became tight, and neither of us expected how much our daughter would cost. That's when it happened.
>
> We started arguing about the rent and I suggested (demanded) that we start a budget. I wanted to tell him that he could no longer spend money on his automobile hobbies, but we didn't get to that. He started yelling, "You don't know how hard it is for me to earn all the money here—I'm doing the best I can . . ." The argument didn't last long. The more I demanded a change in our spending, the angrier he became, until the moment that he hit me. He struck me hard across the cheek, but I didn't feel the pain. I think I entered a state of shock—almost like a soldier shot in the jungle. I couldn't believe it happened to me. I fell to the ground and closed my eyes.
>
> I don't remember what happened next, but I know I was furious and he was apologetic. When I finally regained my senses, I verbally struck back and threatened to leave him. At that moment, he agreed to everything. He wanted to start the budget. He suggested we start therapy (which we never did). He wanted to create a fresh start.

For the next few months, everything, or at least most things, went well. He bought me cards, wrote me poems, and even brought me breakfast in bed. He apologized for hitting me, promised never to do it again, and tried "rebuilding" what we had.

It all happened so slowly. I never realized the subtle attempts to "fix" me as he continued to woo my heart. What I now regard as the "critical" conversation really didn't seem very important at the time. We started talking about the night of the fight. He said he felt "vulnerable" and "weak" when I yelled at him. He lashed out because he felt his masculinity was threatened. When I think about it now, it's almost laughable, but at the time, I understood his point. I challenged his ability to provide for the family, and he reacted by acting like a Neanderthal.

This courtship blended with wife repair continued for a few months. After awhile, the courtship melted away and the wife repair intensified. That's when it happened again.

Chelsea, our daughter, knocked her milk over. It damaged some of Mark's official documents and probably cost him a few days worth of work. I just picked up the documents, shook off the milk, and attempted to comfort Chelsea, who seemed to think the world had come to an end. Mark asked, "Aren't you going to punish her?" The question took me aback. "No," I replied, "It was an accident." Mark started fuming and he stood up from the table. "By that logic," he continued, "It would be an accident if I ripped the paper in half." He grabbed one of the forms and angrily tore it to shreds. This action sent Chelsea into hysterics, but I was still focused on the documents. I reached down to pick them up and when I came up, I felt a blow to the back of my head. He claims it was an "accident," which seemed ironic given the events of the evening. I just felt I couldn't do anything right and fell deeper into despair. The more "perfect" I attempted to become, the more I felt my spirit chipped away. I cowered at everything, and started to fear making any kind of mistake. Eventually, I even started to fear myself.

What finally brought me to my senses was taking a psychology course at the local junior college. The professor started talking about "battered women," and I felt my heart sink. I wrote a paper on the subject, and found myself completely stunned at what I had become. Even worse, I shuddered to think that Chelsea could become the weak-minded fool her mother was. This insight led me to seek out a counselor, which helped me reprioritize my life, and, eventually, find the strength to leave Mark. He still talks to me—still hopes to reconcile, but I can't help but remember how easily he blanketed my eyes. He stole the only part of me that really belonged to me—my soul. How could I give it back to him again?

Questions to Consider

1. Women were once described as a "a necessary evil." Do you believe that sentiment still exists today? Why or why not?

2. Hare-Mustin (1978) wrote that the family has been the principle arena for the exploitation of women. Do you think this opinion is accurate?

3. How common is child sexual abuse against girls, and what are the probable consequences of such acts?

4. Are women likely to earn as much as men? Traditionally, what were the reasons for women earning less?

5. Even though girls are more interested in careers than ever before, women still find themselves torn between their responsibilities to their families and occupations. What advice would you give to a young woman wrestling with such conflicts?

6. Girls often devalue their ability to succeed in math and science, and they tend to view professions related to these subjects as masculine. With this being the case, how would you explain their great success in college?

7. Why are girls uncomfortable talking about menstruation, and what might be done to help them become more comfortable with the topic?

8. Should premenstrual dysphoric disorder be considered a psychiatric disorder?

9. What are the chief health risks for women? What can be done to prevent these health problems?

10. How is evolutionary psychology used to explain the relationship between low body weight and women's self-perceptions of body image?

11. Do women still undergo the stages outlined by the Womanist Identity Model (WIM)?

12. Why are women more likely than men to experience clinical levels of depression?

13. What is wrong with the phrase "women and minorities"?

14. Iranian women reported belonging to a type of sisterhood and stated that they felt extremely safe. Are these benefits worth the costs of clearly defined gender roles?

15. Women tend to do better on certain psychiatric medications than others. Why is this the case?

16. What is feminism, and why is it viewed so negatively by many people?

17. What are the stages of feminist therapy? Are these more likely to be useful with women having certain diagnoses or social problems?

18. What should be done after determining the potential for violence in an abusive family?

19. When is conjoint therapy recommended for women in domestic violence situations?

10

Men and the Men's Movement

What does it mean to be male? Beats me—I'm still trying to figure out what it means to be human. Maybe it means being human with a penis. Wait, that didn't come across the way I had intended. Gender issues never really seemed very important to me, but now that I think about it, maybe they should be. I had always been expected to be the "responsible one" in our family. My wife stayed home with our children and I was expected to work harder to make this possible. When our marriage was in trouble, I was told to "get help" because I needed to learn how to communicate better. When our beloved cat died, *I* was expected to take the carcass to the vet for disposal. I guess these are all gender issues, but I never thought of them as such. I don't really mind being responsible for solving problems because, I think, with that responsibility comes the freedom to set priorities, goals, and direction—at least, in part.

What does it mean to be male? For now, I think it means being a savior and villain. I bear the responsibility for failures and the glory of success, even if, in either case, I had little to do with the process. Will this ever change? I guess that is somewhat up to you. Will men always live in this shadowy world between savior and villain? Are men the ones responsible for the world's problems and economic successes? There may not be a right answer to these questions, but they will be easier to solve if we work through them together.

One of the problems with referring to men and women as "opposite sexes" is the implied assumption that there are more differences than similarities. In reality, both genders are similar in intelligence, personality, abilities, and goals (Kimball, 1995). Many of the differences between the genders are rooted in cultural norms. Men involve themselves in different activities, have different traits, and possess different values from women.

In a society where sexist assumptions are accepted by many people, an overemphasis on differences could be construed as an argument for the superiority of men. Such a position would be ill-founded. Physical and mental differences between the genders have been researched for more than a hundred years. No one has ever discovered psychological traits or cognitive abilities on which men and women differ completely (Crawford & Unger, 2000). There may be slight, but statistically significant, differences in given abilities or traits, but these differences are usually less than 5 percent, which implies that men and women are more alike than they are different.

It is also important to note that feminine culture must continually battle the ongoing oppression contributed by a masculine culture. Although courses on gender issues are becoming increasingly popular, considerably more attention is paid to male minority issues than female issues. Hernandez (1997) points out that research and teaching interest in Mexican American male issues has not been accompanied by the allocation of similar resources to Latina studies.

Men's issues are difficult to address because of men's changing roles in society. Forty years ago, the roles men played (at least, European American men) were clearly defined, generally accepted, and, in some circles, considered divinely sanctioned. With the rise of civil rights and feminism, and the birth of the men's movement, men's roles are no longer as clear-cut as they once were. Today's men are more likely to act as primary caregivers for their children, to enter traditionally feminine occupations, and to express their feelings. Men's changing roles may, however, create a new set of prejudices that could evolve in unpredictable ways during the new millennium.

History of Oppression

"I was hoping we were going to study something boring today—like men. I have to study for a test." (Female graduate student in a multicultural class)

One of the primary difficulties involved in examining the oppression of men is the assumption that male privilege erases the possibility of hardship. Such a supposition is untrue. American males are subject to forms of oppression that often go unrecognized and unaddressed.

In the United States, oppression of males begins soon after birth, when more than half of infant boys (62 percent) are subjected to a painful, invasive, and medically unnecessary procedure called circumcision (Bollinger, 2001), in which the baby's arms and legs are strapped down while a doctor uses a hemostat or other probe to separate the protective prepuce of the penis from the underlying glans (head), often with little or no anesthesia. Tearing the normal protective adhesions between the glans and foreskin resembles ripping a fingernail from the quick. If a clamping method is used, the foreskin is crushed over a bell-shaped device to enable amputation (Boyle et al., 2000). The tissue is either discarded or sold to biotech firms.

Circumcision of male infants for nonreligious reasons is rare in most countries, including technologically advanced nations such as Japan and Sweden.

No medical organization in the world recommends circumcision, and several actively discourage it. American parents tend to have their sons circumcised mainly for cultural or "aesthetic" reasons rather than religious mandates. For example, the baby's father is circumcised, and he wants his son to look like him. Some parents believe circumcision is more hygienic or that an intact boy will be teased by his circumcised peers.

During the early years of the United States, most boys grew up with intact genitals. Around the middle of the nineteenth century, doctors began to circumcise young boys in an effort to prevent masturbation (Johnson, 1860), which was thought to be physically and mentally damaging. Later, a host of purported medical "benefits" were concocted to justify the procedure. Most of these have since been disproven, although Castellsagué et al. (2002) found that male circumcision is associated with a reduced risk of penile HPV infection and, in the case of men with a history of multiple sexual partners, a reduced risk of cervical cancer in their current female partners. However, the number of reasons to avoid the procedure is significantly greater than the potential benefits. The removal of normal erogenous tissue causes considerable pain during and after the procedure, and it leaves the raw glans open to infections, further compromising sexual sensitivity. Circumcision can lead to a host of medical problems immediately or in adulthood, including obstruction of the urinary opening (meatal stenosis), tissue adhesions, painful erections, chordee, permanent nerve damage, hemorrhage, necrotizing fasciitis, and even death.

In contrast to male circumcision, female genital cutting is rare in the United States, although it is common in parts of Africa and the Middle East. Many European countries and the U.S. have passed laws banning circumcision of females under the age of 18, but there are no comparable laws restricting male circumcision. There is even some debate whether the current laws will stop the practice of female circumcision among some cultural groups (Key, 1997).

Some types of female circumcision are more dangerous than male circumcision, but the added risk does not attenuate the risk to men. It seems that Western society feels a special duty to protect females, while men are expected to look after themselves. This statement may sound biased, but consider the way we treat domestic violence. Men are often assumed to be the perpetrators in all cases of domestic abuse, but violence directed at men is more prevalent than people realize. In 1988, 2 million men reported having been assaulted by a wife or girlfriend (Straus & Gelles, 1988). This figure is higher than the self-reported abuse experienced by women during the same year. Straus and Gelles also reported that women were more often the initiators of violence and were at least three times more likely than men to use a weapon against their spouse. There is little reason to believe that the conditions today are any different. The rate of female-to-male attacks remained constant between 1975 and 1985, while the rate of male-to-female abuse decreased by 50 percent during this same period (Leo, 1996). Magdol et al. (1997) found that 37.2 percent of women and only 21.8 percent of men reported having attacked their partners. Over the course of a lifetime, men and women report similar rates of emotional abuse. Although women are more likely to be the victims of physical abuse (25 percent of women report having been victimized by an intimate partner) the percentage of men who have experienced physical abuse from their female partners (13 percent) is not far behind (Coker, et al., 2000).

In November 1998, the Department of Justice (Tjaden & Thoennes, 1998) released the National Violence Against Women Survey, which stated that 36 percent of the victims of domestic violence were men. As evidenced by the title of the report, even this finding was obscured behind statistics on male-to-female violence. Very little is known about the actual number of men who are in a domestic relationship in which they are abused or treated violently by women. This lack of knowledge stems, in part, from the fact that virtually nothing has been done to encourage men to report abuse. Men may worry they will be regarded as "wimps" or "unmanly" if they report having been attacked by their partners. The police are likely to feel the same way when called to intervene. Police are more likely to arrest the abuser if the victim of spousal violence is a woman who is affluent, White, older, or suburban (Avakame & Fyfe, 2001). The police are not the only ones to treat males more harshly. Felson (2002) posited the radical theory that violent males are actually victims in our society. He believes our culture and legal system treat male abusers more harshly than female abusers, and we have continued to perpetrate the notion that violence against women is the result of sexism. His research, however, demonstrates that women in highly sexist societies are usually safer than in more liberal countries. This finding is not an endorsement of sexism, but it suggests that we may have misunderstood the source of domestic violence. Felson believes men abuse women for much the same reason that women abuse men: they become frustrated and seek control.

Despite the prevalence of female-to-male abuse, there is virtually no research on battered husband syndrome (Steinmetz & Lucca, 1988). The research is so scant, it is not even possible to say whether this condition exists (Lucal, 1995). Abused husbands are even the butt of many American jokes. Saenger (1963) reported that in newspaper comic strips, wives were the perpetrators in 73 percent of the domestic violence scenes depicted. Apparently, it is acceptable, and even humorous, for a woman to hit a man. The comic strips depict men who are never hurt or unable to defend themselves, and who are, in some ways, deserving of the abuse. These social messages add to the humiliation often felt by abused men. Even in films, such as Disney's *The Parent Trap*, abuse against men has been presented in a humorous light. In the 1961 version of the movie, the hot-tempered Irish wife punches her husband in the eye when their conversation becomes heated. After the assault, the husband simply puts his hand over his eye and says, "Why did you have to do something like that?"

Research conducted on personality correlates and life experiences of abusers has revealed a typology consisting of inexpressivity, rigidity in thinking, low self-esteem, alcohol/drug use, criminal acts, antisocial and sociopathic characteristics, a violent subculture, and a history of being abused (or witnessing abuse) during childhood (Dutton, 1988; Gondolf, 1988). Nonetheless, other researchers, such as Edleson, Eisikovitz, and Guttman (1985) contend that the personality differences between abusers and nonabusers are nonexistent. Given the difficulties in classification, many researchers (e.g., Ornduff, Kelsey, & O'Leary, 1995) argue for a variety of treatment methods depending on the individual.

It should be noted, however, that even if the number of violent incidents is similar between women and men, the consequences of violent acts are not. Men are more likely to hurt women when they attack. This fact led Campbell (1984) to admonish practitioners to refer to partner domestic violence as wife abuse. She admitted that men were exposed to physically dangerous acts of violence but felt that the incidence of such cases was "so low that its significance as a health problem can be considered negligible" (p. 76).

In addition to facing physical abuse, men face a unique and concomitant problem. In the past two decades, the status of being male has fallen. To be a man was once admired, perhaps even envied, but not any more. Bettina Arndt (1993) illustrates this point by describing the plot from a *Roseanne* episode. The 1990s American sitcom had Roseanne's husband, Dan, making an insensitive remark to one of their daughters, which caused the girl to flee in tears. Roseanne exclaims, "Oh Dan, you're such a . . . a *man*," as she leaves to comfort her daughter. D. J. (Dan Junior), who witnessed the incident, asks his father about what happened. "Dad," he inquires, "Why did Mom call you a man?" Dan sighs and replies, "Because she's mad at me." Still curious, the boy continues, "I thought it was good to be a man." The father quips, "Oh, no, son, not since the late sixties."

Most any magazine or newspaper is filled with evidence that masculinity is no longer respected. Men are portrayed as incompetent lovers, inept family members, emotionally bankrupt, and sometimes as violent and dangerous. Oddly enough, men seem reluctant to offer a contrary image. Some men are reluctant to comment on the changing gender roles because they wish to avoid the appearance of sexism. Any male promoting the role of fathers is seen as criticizing single mothers, while a husband who supports his wife's role as a full-time homemaker is suspected of thwarting her career ambitions.

Family

> "If a woman has to choose between catching a fly ball and saving an infant's life, she will choose to save the infant's life without even considering if there are men on base." (Dave Barry)

A man's position in family life is filled with paradoxes. On the one hand, men have long benefited from the family structure, and they are usually happier and healthier when they are married. On the other hand, fathers often spend less time with their family members than mothers do, and they are less likely to know the details of their children's lives. Men may state that their family is their top priority, but they may invest very little time at home.

The tendency for some fathers to provide financial support while remaining emotionally distant from their children has been addressed negatively in the literature. Near the beginning of the feminist movement, it was often argued that men instituted marriage for their own advantage. Consider the "traditional" family as an example of class structure. The woman typically feels more pressure to stay home with her children or at least earn less than her spouse. This imbalance of family power and class levels has led authors such as Bograd (1991) to strongly react to family therapy. Feminists such as Bograd argue that encouraging families to stay together perpetuates the subordinate role of women and fuels the potential for violence. It essentially legitimizes the current power structure and overlooks the danger women face.

In recent years, increased attention to domestic violence has led to negative views of traditional family structures. Theorists such as Harway and Evans (1996) argue that domestic violence is asystemic, meaning that a wife's behavior has little or no effect on the emergence of her partner's violence. There is a long history of research supporting this theory (Gottman et al., 1995; Jacobson, 1993). Despite the passive role of the survivor, violent men believe that their partner is the primary instigator of their own aggressive actions (Copenhaver, 2000). The role of therapy is to assist the abused client in learning how to act independently and apart from her controlling partner. Creating this independence requires therapists to understand the dynamics of abusive relationships, because starting independence at the wrong time in an abusive cycle could prove fatal.

Walker's (1979) classic text on battered women depicts three stages that commonly occur in male-to-female domestic violence. Early in the relationship, the couple enters **phase one**, the tension-building phase. During this time, minor verbal abuse or physical beatings occur. The survivor attempts to defuse the violence by trying to please her partner, by denying her own anger, and by attempting to pacify his anger. When she realizes the futility of her actions, and withdraws from the abuser, the abuser reacts and oppresses her more openly. The couple enters **phase two**, the acute battering incident. The abuser discharges tensions in an apparently uncontrollable manner. He realizes he is out of control, but both members continue to look for external causes such as work-related stress or alcohol use. Only the abuser can end this phase. The survivor simply has to find a safe place to hide. Survivors tend to downplay the extent of the violence and attempt to minimize the risks; e.g., "It's not like he used a knife—he didn't even break the skin." Such denial can be enormous, as in the case of Felicity.

> *Felicity:*   He really can't control it. He just gets so angry that he lets go.
> *Counselor:*   (sigh) So, he hit you on your head so hard that he left a soft spot on your skull and left you unconscious on the floor.
> *Felicity:*   Yeah.

Counselor:	Why do you think he hit you on the back of the head?
Felicity:	I don't know.
Counselor:	You were probably facing him when you argued with him, right?
Felicity:	Yeah.
Counselor:	So, it seems like he had to think about where he was going to hit you.
Felicity:	(long pause) Well, I suppose. (Tears form.)
Counselor:	(sigh) I'm really concerned that if you go back, he is going to kill you.
Felicity:	(weeping) I can't leave him!

Many couples presenting for therapy want the therapist to preserve the marriage (Leeder, 1994). This places the therapist in a difficult bind. Do you work on building the couple's relationship skills while placing the survivor at great risk, or do you assist the couple in accepting the permanence of abuse and help them to end the relationship? Such questions are especially difficult if the abuser has ended phase two and started to take some responsibility for his actions. In *phase three*, kindness and contrite loving behavior typify the relationship. During this "honeymoon" period, little energy is exerted toward solving significant problems in the relationship. The abuser acts like a little boy who is sorry for his actions and begs for forgiveness. The abuser may believe he will never attack his partner again, and may convince others by giving up drinking, visiting his mother, spending more time with his partner, buying expensive gifts, or any other temporary remedy. If his partner has left him, he may even volunteer for psychotherapy as a way of getting her back. Walker (1979) noted that this phase appears to last longer than phase two.

During the extended calm following the violence, the abuser may appear kinder and more willing to grow. These factors, combined with the desperation of the abuser, often compel the survivor to continue with the relationship. Without any distinct end to either the violence or the relationship, however, the couple finds itself back in phase one. When the aggressor begins to feel his control slip away, the likelihood of a violent episode increases. Violence becomes the primary method of maintaining control (Pence & Paymar, 1990).

The delicate balance between the abuser's sense of control and his insecurity is easily upset. Franchina, Eisler, and Moore (2001) investigated whether men who experienced gender-related stress would more likely abuse their partners. When the men in their study viewed their female partner's behavior as a threat to their masculinity, they were more likely to react with depression and verbal aggression. The greater the gender-related stress, the greater the potential for abuse. The most threatening topics to men, and ones most likely to result in violence, are those involving the management of children or finances (Martin, 1987). Women are likely to control the management of children and the family expenses. In a violent household, a woman may acquiesce to her husband's demands in an attempt to pacify him. When issues are important to both parties, however, it is unlikely that the woman will comply indefinitely. A confrontation is inevitable.

Arguments over the management of children are especially noteworthy because children are at greater risk of physical abuse when spouses use physical violence against each other (Martin, 1987). Violence frequently occurs when issues of control arise. Since boys may be more likely to challenge their fathers, they are more often victims of aggression than girls in families characterized by "more extreme" battering (Jouriles & Norwood, 1995).

Even when children are not physically abused, the effects of witnessing abuse may have severe consequences. Children who witness violence are more likely to externalize problems (Jouriles et al., 1996). This effect is greater for boys, which may be partly due to the increased abuse they face (Jouriles & Norwood, 1995). However, there is some evidence that girls are impacted more through witnessing violence and boys are impacted by concurrent problems such as alcohol use of the parent (Mihalic & Elliott, 1997).

Regardless of their gender, children who witness violence between their parents are more likely to have behavioral problems. Smith, Berthelsen, and O'Connor (1997) found that 42 percent of children aged three to six who have witnessed parental violence exhibited behavioral problems that warranted clinical intervention. The amount of violence that the child witnessed, the child's responses when the violence occurred, and whether or not the child copied the violent partner's behavior were associated with the child's behavioral adjustment scores. Once these processes have occurred, the family is often unable to correct the behavioral outbursts. Children are likely to act out in school, engage in inappropriate and violent behaviors with other children, or may appear withdrawn and depressed. Unfortunately, if one partner is abusive, the other parent cannot offset the effects through nurturing and compassion (Smith, Berthelsen, & O'Connor, 1997). The only clearly effective intervention is to prevent the abuse from occurring.

The problems with abuse may have led to a recent onslaught against fatherhood. In 1999, Louise Silverstein and Carl Auerbach wrote a powerful article called, "Deconstructing the Essential Father." The article appeared in psychology's premier journal, *The American Psychologist*, and argued that neither a mother nor a father is essential. While the authors admitted that there was a negative correlation between two-parent homes and child poverty, urban decay, societal violence, teenage pregnancy, and poor school performance, they also asserted that there is no clear evidence that fathers or mothers play a unique role in the parenting process. Their conclusions: "Taken as a whole, the empirical research does not support the idea that fathers make a unique and essential contribution to child development" (p. 402).

Silverstein and Auerbach's study started an intense debate about the role fathers play. Mackey (2001) seemed to put the topic to rest by looking at more than 55,000 adult-child dyads from 23 cultures and subcultures. Contrary to the earlier hypothesis, they found that fathers who participated actively in the lives of their families possessed a unique, predictable, and nontrivial affiliative bond with their children. This bond was, they argued, unique and separate from any man-woman bond or any woman-child bond. With regard to family development, there is emerging research indicating that fathers play an important role in the rearing of children. Lamb (1997) had previously found that with male infants from 7 to 13 months, fathers were recipients of more affiliative behaviors (e.g., smiling, looking at, vocalizing, laughing, and giving) than were mothers. Older infants (15 to 24 months) continued to exhibit more affiliative behaviors toward the father, but also demonstrated more attachment behaviors (e.g., seeking proximity, touching, approaching, wanting to be held) from the father than the mother.

The relationship fathers have with their children has been changing in recent years. Robertson and Verschelden (1993) investigated the experiences of voluntary male homemakers. These men spent most of their time working within the home, and their female partners were the primary wage earners. The couples reported their perceptions of social reactions to their nontraditional arrangement, and they completed several questionnaires that measured relevant personal attributes such as life and marital satisfaction, self-esteem, depression, self-reported symptoms of physical or emotional distress, and gender-related attitudes. This was one of the first studies that found that stay-at-home dads did not find the experience negative. In fact, they were assessed to be psychologically healthy and relatively happy with their lives and choices. They did not overwhelmingly experience tension relative to their gender role, although some men said others had evaluated them negatively. There is also some evidence that stay-at-home fathers find it difficult to maintain close social networks because most of the potential friends available during the day are women.

> "I come into these [online] chat rooms because I find that I don't really have anyone to talk to. It's kinda isolating, at times, being a stay-at-home dad. I hope it's okay for me to be here." (Anonymous male participant in a "women's" chat room)

Even when Dad is at home, working mothers tend to know what their child's daily schedule is (classes or doctor appointments), while traditional working fathers lack such basic information regarding their children's schedules (Frank & Kromelow, 1997). Additionally, fathers tend to lack the support they need to build a sense of community. Sixty-three percent of stay-at-home dads felt isolated, compared with only 37 percent of stay-at-home moms. The majority (65 percent) of stay-at-home dads chose this lifestyle because they did not want to put their children in day care. (Frank & Kromelow, 1997).

When husbands choose to work outside the home, those who learn to participate in domestic chores are most likely to report high levels of marital satisfaction. When one member of the partnership is left with an inequitable share of chores, the overburdened member is likely to report a diminished sense of self-worth and negative judgments about the relationship (Voydanoff & Donnelly, 1999). Not surprisingly, wives have fewer depressive symptoms when husbands help around the house. Wives' contentment is also directly associated with the quality of the relationship as a whole. Equality and respect appear to be the best measurable basis for marital satisfaction.

Johnson and Jacob (1997) investigated how couples regarded the state of their relationship when one member of the partnership was depressed. If the husband was depressed, the relationship was relatively unchanged. When the wife was depressed, the couple was more likely to report that the relationship was "negative." This finding implies that women are typically the emotional cornerstone of the relationship. It supports the old adage, "If Momma ain't happy, nobody is happy."

The importance of the wife's contentment does not imply that husbands play an insignificant role. Karney and Bradbury (1997) found that high levels of psychological distress (neuroticism) at the start of the marriage for both husbands and wives were linked to husbands having a low level of marital quality throughout their marriage. It did not matter whether the husband or wife improved during the marriage; the husband's satisfaction was determined by the couple's health early in the relationship. This finding might be related to the way a husband separates from his parents. Husbands who are able to begin married life without being overly dependent on their parents are much more likely to have a positive marriage. Both spouses reported higher levels of adjustment and satisfaction in their marriage when the husbands were free from excessive guilt, anxiety, mistrust, responsibility, inhibition, resentment, and anger in relation to their mothers (Amstutz-Haws & Mallinckrodt, 1998). Perhaps this study could be related to Karney and Bardbury's results, suggesting that healthy husbands are those who can care about their parents without feeling dependent upon them.

Increased attention to men's issues and the role they play in the family structure has led to renewed efforts to understand how to intervene with male victims of abuse. Abuse against men occurs with great frequency and requires targeted intervention. From my clinical experience with female spousal abusers, some common themes have arisen. The women speak about feeling "out of control" and distant from their spouse. Their hostility often stems from frustration rather than the rage reported by male abusers. These components are depicted well by "Maria's" remarks below:

> I don't really know why it happens. My mother used to hit me, and I guess it rubbed off. When I argue with my husband, I sometimes feel like he's mocking me. He doesn't say anything, but it seems like he isn't listening—or he doesn't care. Sometimes I just lose control. I get so angry I'll throw something at him. Maybe I just want to get his attention. I don't mean to hurt him, but I know it does.

These statements are different from those of men who tend to abuse their spouses. As indicated from Maria's comments, she accepts responsibility for her actions and views the cycle as her fault. The guilt improves the prognosis for successful intervention. For male abusers, however, a different cycle exists, and ultimately, the woman often blames herself for the crisis. Given that Maria is willing to take responsibility for the critical incident, the prognosis for therapy is improved. However, such cases are unlikely to reach a therapist's doors because neither party is likely to report the violence.

Economics

Men tend to view their occupation as a central part of their identity. In 1978, Levinson stated that men undergo three distinct stages in their occupational lives. In the first phase, the novice phase, the young adult explores various life choices. This phase often involves the formation of an adult dream (e.g., becoming a successful novelist, being promoted to vice president of a company, etc.), forming of mentor relationships, selecting an occupation, and finding a "special woman" who is lover, friend, and helper. The partner plays an important role, because she assists in the acquisition of the dream. As mentioned earlier, this developmental process is different from that of women, who are less likely to find a "special man" to assist with their dreams.

Even when men find that "special woman" to help with their career dreams, the men may find the stress of their employment overwhelming. Nordstrom et al. (2001) explored whether there was a connection between the existence of carotid lesions and intima-media thickness (both associated with artery hardening), with scores obtained from a state-anxiety test. Eighteen months after giving the questionnaires, they performed B-mode ultrasounds on their subjects. After adjusting for differences in age, they found that the prevalence of carotid lesions among men scoring in the highest stress quintile was 36 percent, as compared with 21 percent among men in the lowest quintile. These findings suggest that men with greater work-related stress are at increased risk for atherosclerotic disease. The interesting part of the study came when they also looked at women's scores. At the 18-month follow-up exam, they found no relationship between stress and lesions or intima-media thickness. For some reason, women were protected from the effects of work-related stress, whereas the environment was literally making men sick.

Men also face struggles in the workplace when they attempt to explore occupations that are traditionally considered feminine. Women have long suffered through the process of breaking into "men's" work and have met with considerable success. Men, however, are still struggling with obtaining the same vocational freedom. If a man's profession follows traditionally feminine paths, he may even question his identity. Consider Tom's vocational experiences, described below. Although he had successfully created an occupational identity, he continued to question his future and even his perception of himself.

> When I announced my decision, everyone gave me a strange look. "Why do you want to teach elementary school?" my mother asked. They didn't understand that I enjoyed being with children or that money wasn't very important to me. My mother thought I should become a doctor; my father thought I was nuts and should just go into the family business. I don't know if I can explain how I made the decision. Maybe it was partly to show them that I could do what I wanted to do.
>
> At the time, I thought telling my parents was the worst part of my decision. I was wrong. I will never forget applying to my first job. At my interview, my potential supervisor said, "It's so nice to have a man here." I didn't really know how to take that, but at least it sounded positive. After they offered me the job, I noticed that I was viewed as an outsider. Other than the principal, there were no men. Some of the children's parents even seemed uncomfortable with me, at least at first. Once a woman came in asking for the teacher. The receptionist pointed me out to her and she replied, "No, I need the teacher, not her husband."
>
> At my next school, I was literally the only male employed at the school. During my interview, I remarked that I thought I could contribute something to the office because I was involved with men's issues. The principal responded, "I would have hired you even if you weren't male."
>
> There is just something odd about being a man in a female-dominated profession that used to be male dominated. I don't think it would be so odd being a male psychologist or nurse. I could be wrong, but it seems like the women in those professions expect their male colleagues to be "different" from other men. In education, I think the women expected me to make some great contribution or to become power hungry. I became a symbol of the male dominated aspect of profession, and seemed to personify the positive and negative aspects of this.
>
> Maybe my parents were right. It seems hard, struggling to forge an identity though a profession that is less likely to accept men than women. But I guess that's what women have put up with for centuries. If nothing else, these experiences should help me understand what women in many professions still face daily.

Even in today's society where gender stereotypes are resisted more than ever before, men appear more comfortable than women have been with their stereotypical assignments and appear less likely to break free from them. Hensing, Alexanderson, Akerlind, and Bjurulf (1995) explored the factors associated with what they called minor psychiatric morbidity (MPM) and its relation to age, occupation, and gender. They found that individuals between the ages of 25 and 54 years working in industrial occupations were more likely to take sick leave. Women were also more likely than men to take sick leave. Interestingly, women working in extremely male-dominated occupations had the highest incidence of all groups, while men in extremely female-dominated occupations had the highest incidence of all men. Breaking societal mores is always difficult, but it appears that this struggle is especially traumatic when it involves work. Women and men who are employed in nontraditional occupations may be at higher risk of illness than those employed in more stereotypical occupations.

Sick leave is not the only financial issue affected by gender differences. As mentioned in the previous chapter, women typically earn less than men. Inderrieden and Keaveny (2000) studied the differences between men's and women's perceptions of their income. Women, they found, attached great importance to their occupation and future. They were also more likely to report greater satisfaction with their family financial situation. Men, on the other hand, reported higher pay expectations than women, which may help to explain why they are more likely to obtain higher incomes; i.e., they are more willing to fight for salary increases.

The perceived need for men to be the primary wage earners also creates problems for family dynamics. The greatest threat created by patriarchal family structures is an increased risk of domestic violence. In the past, it was commonly believed that families of lower socioeconomic status were more likely to engage in spousal abuse. McCloskey (1996), however, found that this perception failed to examine the effects of each partner's contribution to the family income. When a woman's income is higher than that of a potentially violent partner, she is significantly more likely to become a victim of abuse. Asymmetry favoring women, rather than total family income, predicts the frequency and severity of a husband's abuse toward his wife. It may be true that members of lower-class families are at greater risk of violence, but this appears to be related to the fact than both partners in these families must work to survive. The multi-income setting may increase a husband's insecurity and, consequently, his violence.

Women in abusive relationships may shy away from highly paid positions because they fear the wrath that may come from their increased power and independence. If this hypothesis is valid, it would explain why female victims of spousal abuse are usually ill-prepared to support themselves financially after their relationship ends (Wolf, 1991). Their economic dependence on their husband may force them to remain in an abusive relationship, even if they are aware of the harm it is causing. Abused women express stronger feelings of commitment when they have few economic alternatives. The more financially and emotionally invested they are in the relationship, the more likely that abused women will report satisfaction with their marriage (Rusbult & Martz, 1995).

When men are adequately employed, a number of other factors can affect their psychological well-being. Piotrkowski (1998) focused on gender harassment among 385 White and minority women in administrative and clerical jobs at a municipal agency. She found that more than 70 percent of the women, both minority and White, had experienced or heard offensive slurs or jokes or remarks about women. Although such findings are hardly surprising, a follow-up study revealed some interesting insights about men. The 113 minority men and 149 White men in her sample reported a level of workplace gender harassment that was similar to the level the women reported. Even the White men considered a gender-hostile workplace to be restrictive and to offer them fewer chances for advancement.

Hostility in the work force clearly harms minority men more than European Americans. Minority males are unlikely to be given the same opportunities that their European American peers receive. Researchers have found that homeless African American men tend to be more educated, less psychiatrically impaired, and have better job skills than their European American peers (Davis & Winkleby, 1993). Even when they are employed, income disparity contributes to the inability of many ethnic minority adults to maintain adequate housing. This finding suggests that discrimination might play a significant role in the onset of homelessness, which implies that teaching additional stress management skills may help keep some minority men off the streets. However, coping skills alone are unlikely to evoke lasting changes if the homeless remain underemployed for significant periods of time. Instead, clinicians should work with public and private organizations to help provide food, clothing, temporary shelter, and emergency financial support. Satisfying basic needs is an essential first step toward economic independence.

Education

Boys and girls are treated differently from infancy onward. Even prior to beginning school, parents have different expectations for their sons and daughters. Morrongiello and Dawber (1999) examined the treatment of preschool-aged boys and girls (between two and four years) in 48 families. They found that both mothers and fathers provided their sons with more directives, offered fewer explanations, and asked them more questions about their actions than they did their daughters. The boys were also expected to complete tasks without parental support, while the parents were more likely to intervene and help their daughters. These expectations were present despite the fact that the sons and daughters in the study possessed equivalent skills. The parents simply encouraged the boys to be independent risk takers.

During the preschool years, boys also spend more time in "rough-and-tumble play" and girls spend more time drawing or playing with stuffed animals (Lindsey & Mize, 2001; Maccoby, 1990). These differences perpetuate the stereotype that boys are less capable of fine motor skills and girls are physically weaker. In some ways, these early behaviors create societal stereotypes. The more the sexes engage in sex-matched behaviors, the more likely they are to continue these practices through adolescence. Even friendships are based on these factors. School-aged boys base friendships on similar physical abilities, while girls emphasize similarity of attractiveness of personality and social network size (Hartup & Stevens, 1997).

Boys are also more likely to base friendships on traditionally masculine traits, such as physical aggressiveness. Rodkin et al. (2000) studied the behavioral patterns of 452 fourth- through sixth-grade boys and found, as expected, that the popular but socially compliant boys were rated by teachers as cool, athletic, leaders, cooperative, studious, not shy, and nonaggressive. However, the boys their peers perceived as cool were tough, athletic, and antisocial. Teachers described the same boys as argumentative, disruptive, frequently in trouble, and often involved in fighting. Such findings suggest that highly aggressive boys can be among the most popular and socially connected children in elementary classrooms.

Rather than being viewed entirely as negative, it should be noted that aggressive behavior sometimes carries boys into successful careers. Power is often associated with status, prestige and social/professional connections. This association has been found to apply only to boys, however, and Rodkin noted that other studies have shown that the same findings do not apply to girls. Aggressive behavior usually makes girls unpopular.

In addition to aggressiveness, concentration difficulties and hyperactivity affect boys' educational experiences. There is some evidence to suggest that attention deficit hyperactivity disorder (ADHD) is frequently comorbid with oppositional defiant disorder, conduct disorder, and behavioral disturbances (Loeber et al., 2000). Emerging evidence indicates that these disturbances are associated with increased instability in sleep onset, sleep duration, and true sleep, especially among boys with ADHD (Gruber, Sadeh, & Raviv, 2000).

Conduct disorder is more prevalent in boys than girls and often wreaks havoc with their academic performance. Lahey et al. (1999) studied 347 seventh-grade boys over a period of six years. Their primary intent was to determine what factors were most closely associated with entering a gang. They concluded that an individual's first gang entry was predicted by both baseline conduct disorder (CD) behaviors and increasing levels of CD behaviors prior to gang entry. This suggests that the boys who enter aggressive gangs are furthering the development of their existing antisocial behavior. They found a critical window in this trend. Having friends prior to gang entry who engaged in aggressive delinquency increased the risk of gang entry further, but only during early adolescence. As the children aged, they were better able to fend off threats of gang involvement.

Gang involvement and antisocial behaviors may also be partly responsible for obstacles to academic success. Girls now make up 57 percent of straight-A students, while boys make up 57 percent of high school dropouts. Girls are also more likely to take upper-level courses in algebra, chemistry, and biology. Only physics is still dominated by males during high school (Young, 2001). These trends carry over to college, where women now make up 56 percent of college enrollment in America, and female college freshmen are more likely than men to earn a degree within four years. The gender gap in higher education also has differences among various cultural groups. African American men are earning significantly more bachelor's degrees than they did in 1977, but they are far outpaced by the increase among African American women (30 percent increase for Black men versus a 77 percent increase for Black women). This two-to-one margin between the rates of African American female and male college graduates has led the Urban League to express "concern" for Black males (Young, 2001).

Despite being more prone to behavioral and academic problems, by the time they reach college, boys outperform girls on all college aptitude tests. This is due in part because boys typically do better than girls on timed tests (Sadker & Sadker, 1994) and multiple-choice exams (Anderson, Benjamin, & Fuss, 1994). Girls excel on open-ended essay exams without time limits. For these reasons, boys tend to outperform girls on SAT measurements.

Little changes by the time students reach graduate school. Men outscore women on all three sections of the Graduate Record Examination (GRE) (Sadker & Sadker, 1994). Despite these trends, women tend to earn higher grades than their male counterparts during graduate school (House & Keely, 1995). Such disparities indicate that males have an unfair advantage getting into colleges. Their scores on the primary aptitude tests help them enter the better colleges, which in turn leads to higher-paying careers.

Although education may help expand men's views of the world, it appears to have limited efficacy on reducing violence or promoting acceptance of women's independence. Fagan, Stewart, and Hansen (1983) found that when men with higher educational attainment became violent, they tended to inflict *greater injury*. More recently, however, Magdol et al. (1997) found the opposite to be true: women and men were more likely to engage in severe acts of violence when they had less education. It is likely that the differences between the two studies involve the types of education discussed. Perhaps future studies will reveal that men with education related to topics such as women's issues, counseling, or psychology tend to gain greater insight and a higher capacity for empathy.

Health

> "The only time anybody mentions that men die eight years earlier than women is when they're telling us how women suffer from a shortage of eligible men." (Fred Hayward)

Benrud and Reddy (1998) conducted an interesting test regarding gender and physical health. They asked 433 people (301 women and 132 men) to read a description of a gender difference in acute and chronic conditions that placed either women or men at a health disadvantage. As the authors expected, when the woman was perceived to have the greater health disadvantage, the participants attributed it primarily to relatively uncontrollable, constitutional factors (e.g., biology). When the man was perceived as having the same physical illness, participants attributed it primarily to relatively controllable, nonconstitutional factors (e.g., behavior). Interestingly, both women and men demonstrated the same bias and held men more responsible for their physical health.

Men appear to have internalized the notion that sickness is something they should be able to control. This erroneous belief has made men reluctant to seek medical help. Women see a doctor almost three times as often as men, and live about seven years longer. It appears that women may become more involved with the health care system because they are typically the ones who care for their children's health. Men, on the other hand, are afraid of being considered weak and will ignore minor symptoms.

A collaborative survey by *Men's Health* magazine and CNN (Hendrick, 1997) found that 64 percent of the respondents said cost was a factor keeping them away from physicians, but other reasons were time, lack of faith in the healing ability of physicians, and men's discomfort with discussing their own health. Apparently, men often view physicians as adversaries. Going to a physician may indicate an inability to control internal processes. When men do seek help, it is more often for treatment of a specific problem than for a routine physical examination.

Infrequent contact with health care professionals also leaves men vulnerable to unexpected problems. For example, just as women often view heart attacks as a "male" problem, so men view cancer and especially breast cancer afflictions as only affecting women. In 1995, 1,400 American men discovered they had breast cancer. During the same year, 240 American men died of breast cancer, accounting for 0.5 percent of total breast cancer deaths and 0.08 percent of cancer deaths among men. Although the mortality risk for this disease in males is low, the incidence of breast cancer in men, like that in women, increases with age. Most men do not realize that they are even susceptible to the disease. Because of this, men often fail to seek medical assistance until they are in the advanced stages of breast cancer (Bunkley et al., 2000).

Even when men are aware of the risks, they may still lack the motivation to seek treatment. Prostate cancer is the single most common form of nonskin cancer in men in the United States. In the year 2000, approximately 180,400 men were diagnosed with prostate cancer, and at least 30,000 died of the disease (National Cancer Institute, 2001). This makes prostate cancer the number two killer of men. The National Cancer Institute (NCI) reports that most men (approximately 80 percent) who are diagnosed with prostate cancer have an early stage of the disease. However, even when the disease is discovered, the treatment is less clear than with breast cancer. Typical treatments include the following:

- radical prostatectomy, which is more frequent among men under age 70;
- radiation therapy for men between the ages of 70 and 79;
- conservative therapy (no treatment or hormonal therapy) in men over age 79.

Another treatment consideration, and one that has a direct bearing on mortality, involves the spread of cancerous tissue. If the disease is identified when the cancer is localized within the prostate, the ten-year survival rates are 75 percent. If the disease has spread to the surrounding tissue, survival rates fall to 55 percent. If the cancer has spread beyond the prostate area (distant metastases), survival rates fall to just 15 percent (Kramer, Brown, Prorok, Potosky, & Gohagan, 1993). The high mortality for distant metastases correlates with the male aversion for physicals. When the cancer spreads beyond the prostate, additional symptoms are rare. Because of this silent migration, between one-third and two-thirds of patients already have local extracapsular extension or distant metastases at the time of diagnosis (Mettlin, Jones, & Murphy, 1993).

In addition to mortality rates, prostate cancer creates a number of other medical complications requiring psychotherapeutic intervention. Treatment for distant metastases has not changed over time, with about 65 percent of patients receiving hormonal therapy. This treatment sometimes produces breast growth, which can seriously diminish the client's already threatened sense of masculinity. Radiation therapy and radical prostatectomy may have detrimental effects on urinary, bowel, and sexual functions, which can create feelings of helplessness, loss of control, and disturbances in self-concept. Stanford et al. (2000) found that even after 18 months or more had passed since their surgery, at least 8.4 percent of the patients were incontinent (lacked urinary control), and at least 59.9 percent were impotent (unable to achieve an erection sufficient for sexual intercourse). At 24 months after surgery, 8.7 percent of men were bothered by lack of urinary control, and 41.9 percent reported that sexual function was a moderate-to-major problem. Therapists should address these topics directly. No one likes to talk about impotence. Having an uncomfortable therapist just makes the subject all the more difficult to address.

Prostate cancer also appears to affect various cultural groups differently. The lowest incidence rates are found in Native Americans, and all other groups have lower rates than Whites and Blacks. African Americans, in contrast, are 60 percent more likely than European Americans to contract the disease. The reasons for these differences are not yet understood. Another confusing element is that Native Americans appear to have the poorest survival rates of all racial/ethnic groups when the cancer is localized within the prostate, while African Americans and Latinos have the lowest five-year relative survival rates among patients with distant metastatic prostate cancer (The Methodist Health Care System, 2001).

Skin cancer is also a significant threat to men's health. According to the American Cancer Society, more than 47,000 new cases of skin cancer were diagnosed in 2001 and nearly 8,000 will die from it (1.4 percent of cancer-related deaths, and 3.5 percent of cancer diagnoses). A recent study published in the *Journal of the National Cancer Institute* (Autier et al., 1999) found that skin cancer rates had increased by 191 percent in males and 84 percent in females from 1950 to 1994, with more Americans seeking to tan themselves. The reason for the higher rates among men is unclear but probably involves the increased likelihood of men working outside. Many men tend to dismiss skin problems (or ignore them), which significantly increases mortality rates. Survival rates can be as low as 20 percent for people with advanced melanoma.

The tendency for men to ignore early symptoms of cancer is a small component of a much larger problem. Some men believe there is no reason to seek medical assistance because their longevity is determined by their genes, but this is hardly the case. A study using the Danish twin registry (Bortz, 2001), one of the most comprehensive registries in the world, found that fewer than 10 percent of monozygotic twins died within a year of each other, and dizygotic twins were even less likely to die during the same year. The researchers concluded that heredity contributes somewhat to longevity, but it does not completely determine one's chances of survival. It appears that heredity explains 20 to 25 percent of the variance in mortality, which means that the environment and behavior play a greater role in determining longevity. Men should realize that reducing stress, choosing nutritious foods, and forming social connections could significantly extend their longevity regardless of their genetic history.

Cultural Uniqueness

One of the topics frequently mentioned with regard to gender differences is men's greater success in business pursuits. Although male privilege explains some of the discrepancy, there are cultural reasons for it as well. Barke, Jenkins-Smith, and Slovic (1997) studied how men and women view their susceptibility to risks. Gender significantly predicted whether people would agree with the phrase, "I often feel discriminated against." Women were more likely to sense discrimination, and, consequently, they had a higher perception of risk in nearly every area of life.

Men, on average, are more likely to regard their daily routine and the future of the world as safe (Slovic, 1999). Slovic's study revealed that men feel confident refraining from seat belt use, believe the world is safe from nuclear power accidents, and are more likely to view the world as fair. What is interesting about this finding is that the gender difference was generated by only a small subset of men. European American men lacked fear in almost every area, while most men of color expressed concerns that paralleled those of the women surveyed. The European American men were the ones, typically, who were more likely to take risks and tended to feel more in control of their lives. Minority men and most women viewed themselves as more vulnerable and to see the world as being more risky.

There are actually very few studies demonstrating gender differences that are independent of cultural differences. Lehr, Seiler, and Thomae (2000) believe ethnic and gender issues interconnect so thoroughly that no single predictor could be found for issues of contentment or longevity. They did find, however, that men and women advance divergent reasons for overall life satisfaction. Specifically, women tended to focus on social and familial networks, whereas men tended to stress material issues and economic security. The point is that men seek stability and feelings of accomplishment. They are less likely to find ways of forming intimate relationships with large numbers of people.

The tendency for women to emphasize interconnectedness and men to emphasize ideas or things is also evident in linguistic expression. Tannen (1996) argued that conversations among women are more likely to address feelings, make reference to the conversationalists, and to have an overall emphasis on relational concerns. Men's conversations, on the other hand, are more likely to focus on external matters, have a competitive tone, and to be task oriented. Even in the business world, men and women tend to use language in different ways. Mulac, Seibold, and Farris (2000) examined features of language used in managers' and professionals' criticism of coworkers. Their analysis revealed significant differences in language use, permitting 72 percent accuracy in gender reclassification. The language features associated with men were using more words, negations, questions, judgmental adjectives, references to emotion, and oppositions. Basically, men talked more than women and focused on confrontation over agreement. Women were more likely to use intensive adverbs (e.g., excellent, wonderful, exciting, etc.), longer sentences, hedges, directives, dependent clauses, and sentence initial adverbials (e.g., Wow, that's great!). Women tended to express their thoughts more colorfully and delicately. Although other studies found some of these indicators to be predictive of the opposite gender, the overall conclusions seem relatively constant. These cultural differences not only influence the way men and women view their occupational roles, but they also affect how the sexes view ethics and morality.

Kohlberg (Colby & Kohlberg, 1987) identified three levels and eight stages of moral development. Basically, people start life with a preconventional level of morality, which emphasizes avoiding punishments and acquiring rewards. When a child enters school age, there is a shift to a conventional level of functioning. Here, the emphasis is on following social rules and externally mediated moral guidelines. Some people will likely remain in this stage for the remainder of their lives, but others will progress to the postconventional level. At this stage, individually defined moral principles reshape the values provided by society. Ultimately, in the final stage of level three, the individual assumes a stance based on cosmic or eternal values. The individual internalizes principles that go beyond the teachings of an organized religion. Persons in stage 6 may be willing to die for their principles, but persons in stage 7 are more willing to change their daily routine to match their beliefs. A stage 6 person might be willing to become a martyr, while a stage 7 person will refrain from all harmful behaviors, seek growth, and set aside regular time for learning and meditation.

Carol Gilligan (1982) argued that Kohlberg's position was biased towards the male way of knowing. She argued that rather than operate from an ethic of justice, women operate from an ethic of caring. From Kohlberg's position, ethics are ultimately created around a personalized set of rules that can be universally applied to any given situation. In most cases, this ethical code will emphasize individual rights, equality before the law, and fair play. An ethic of justice is impersonal and objective. An ethics of caring, on the contrary, emphasizes sensitivity to others, loyalty, responsibility, self-sacrifice, and peacemaking. Care comes from connecting with others. Gilligan believes this ethical system develops because women, from early in their childhood, are more likely to be rewarded for comforting or soothing people in need (e.g., "you are such a good girl for helping that boy when he fell off his bike"). In short, males tend to be more concerned with getting the job done, while females tend to be concerned with holding the group together.

If Gilligan's position is accurate, the implications for male culture are profound. Moral problems, and possibly relationships themselves, become problems to be solved through calculations rather than situations to be lived. Women change the rules in order to preserve relationships; men abide by the rules and see relationships as replaceable. This difference, if true, could partially explain why men tend to emphasize ethical guidelines over relationships. For example, men who batter their wives are more likely to claim a religious affiliation than nonbatterers (Martin, 1987). On the other hand, women from any cultural group are safer when they live within a strong community. Levinson's (1989) worldwide study on spousal abuse indicates that the women least abused are active members within supportive communities, including religious groups. But men are less likely to benefit from the social contact.

Hintikka, Koskela, Kontula, and Viinamaeki (2000) investigated how men and women benefit from attendance in church. They surveyed 869 women and 773 men and gathered information about sociodemographic variables, frequency of religious attendance, social contacts, and perceived social and family support. They found that women not only attended religious events more often than men, but they were also more likely to attend regularly. Women who chose not to attend religious events were significantly more likely to suffer from "minor mental disorders" (such as adjustment disorders or mild depression) than those who attended regularly. However, among men, no such finding was present. The researchers' multivariate analysis revealed that women experienced increased social contacts through church attendance, and men gained a happier family life.

Cultural differences in the ways males and females form relationships can be seen from the earliest formation of social networks. During the early school years, boys are more likely to have one close friend, and their relationships are likely to be reciprocal. This means their communication is filled with statements such as, "I'll be your best friend if you'll be mine." Girls are better able to build relationships based on nonexclusive intimacy. They can have friendship groups and multiple close friends. They also form nonreciprocal triads (Rose & Asher, 2000). Such trends are consistent with Gilligan's ethical theory.

Psychological Issues

The tendency for men to focus on ideas and women to address relationships explains some of the differences in mental health. Women, as mentioned in the previous chapter, are more likely to have problems with social/physical issues such as eating disorders, as well as concerns with depression or affective lability (mood swings). Men tend to struggle with problems involving control, perception, or nonrelational excitement, such as drugs or harmful sexual practices (Tomori, Zalar, & Plesnicar, 2000). This is not to say that men deal with categorically different problems from women. Instead, the difference seems to stem from the way males cope with frustration, depression, and anxiety.

William Pollack (1999) wrote about the ongoing damage from the "Boy Code," which he defines as the outdated and constricting assumptions, models, and rules about boys that our society has used since the nineteenth century. Basically, the boy code tells young males that they should be "strong" and not show fear or sadness. When emotional pain arises, boys are expected to push it down so no one can see it. Although such behaviors may help men to appear functional, they also encourage boys to externalize their problems. This tendency means that males will often handle psychological issues differently from females, even when they are facing the same behavioral symptoms.

Back in 1694, Richard Morton, a London physician, announced the first case of anorexia nervosa in a 16-year-old male. After the initial treatment failed, Morgan admonished the patient to "abandon his studies, to go into the country air, and to use riding, and a milk diet . . . for a long time." Such advice would no longer be given, but the sentiment from Morton's comment still lingers. Eating disorders among women are taken seriously, while similar problems among men are given less significance.

Although the ratio of women to men being diagnosed with anorexia and bulimia is close to 10 to 1, there are certain groups of males with elevated risk. Male wrestlers, for example, often diet to make certain weight levels. Some boys will lose ten or more pounds in an attempt to reach their desired weight category. These repeated weight loss attempts can translate into a clinical eating disorder in which the client sees himself as "fat" (Andersen, 1995). By focusing on the parts of his body that tend to be overweight, his cognitive pattern shifts to believing that he *should* lose weight.

From early in life, boys are taught to value their physical prowess and to be strong (Silverman, 1990). If the desire to reach perfect masculinity continues unchecked, some men may start using anabolic steroids to improve muscle tone and build strength. Others may diet to improve sports performance, or they may have gender-identity conflicts. In the end, the co-morbid conditions common to females with eating disorders are present for males. Mood disorders (such as depression), personality disorders and some medical conditions (such as osteoporosis) are often present in males with eating disorders (Andersen, 1995).

Although male eating disorders are a serious threat, it is still uncertain why men are less likely than women to encounter such problems. One of the key influences appears to be mothers. Maureen Vincent and Marita McCabe (2000) studied 306 adolescent girls and 297 boys by having them complete a questionnaire exploring family and peer relationships. They found that the *quality* of relationships with family members and peers was less important than the discussion of diet. When fathers encouraged their daughters to diet and lose weight, the eating problems were more likely to be severe, but the paternal influence was weak for the development of problems with boys. Instead, maternal and peer encouragement predicted binge eating and weight loss behaviors in boys. Part of the difference stems from social expectations. Girls who struggle with bulimia tend to seek approval from their parents. Boys are more likely to be perfectionistic and fear that their parents are providing false information about food (Moulton, Moulton, & Roach, 1998).

Mental health differences between the sexes appear to stem from both social and biological origins. Zahn-Waxler, Robinson, and Emde (1992) compared the differences between monozygotic (identical) and dizygotic twins during the second year of life. At home and in a laboratory, the experimenters would simulate appearances of distress and gauge children's reactions. Girls scored higher than boys on most of these observational measures and the reactions of monozygotic twins were significantly more alike than those of dizygotic siblings. The researchers concluded that there was modest evidence for heritability of empathy, particularly for the affective component.

In addition to twin studies, evidence of affective differences in genders stems from emerging psychopharmacological research. Women tend to respond better to drugs affecting the serotonin system (such as Prozac), while men tend to respond better to drugs that affect norepinephrine, a neurotransmitter secreted by the adrenal glands and by nerve endings during stress (Park, 1999). These findings correspond directly to observable patterns of behavior. Norepinephrine is associated with alertness and wakefulness, and serotonin affects affective lability (mood swings).

Biological causes are relatively easy to study, but environmental forces are more difficult. Let's start with a basic physiological problem, such as heart disorders. As already mentioned, men are more likely than women to suffer from most cardiac problems. Gerdi Weidner (2000) believes these differences, while partially based on physical differences, are clearly linked to behavioral and psychosocial contributions. One reason for this conclusion is that coronary heart disease mortality rates between various countries are greater than those between men and women, suggesting that biological factors are not the sole influences on the gender gap in coronary heart disease. For example, eastern European men score higher on stress-related psychosocial coronary risk factors (e.g., social isolation, vital exhaustion) than men living in the West. Comparisons between the sexes also reveal gender differences in psychosocial and behavioral coronary risk factors, including excessive alcohol consumption and smoking, favoring women. Overall, it appears that men's coping with stressful events may be less adaptive physiologically, behaviorally, and emotionally, contributing to their increased risk for coronary heart disease.

What is most interesting about the factors predictive of heart problems is that men, overall, seem to have fewer affective or psychological symptoms. Coelho, Ramos, Prata, and Barros (2000) found that mean depression scores were significantly higher in women and in subjects with lower educational level. Interestingly, educational levels seemed to mitigate the effects of gender. The more education the study participants had, the lower their depression scores. Unfortunately, educational levels were not strong enough to erase the gender difference. Men with higher educational levels had the highest scores for general psychological well-being (PWB). This means that men, on average, and especially educated men scored higher on quality of life issues and psychopathology measures. Why is this the case? One theory involves the process of gender formation and identification.

Kohut (1978), an object relations theorist, stated that women develop more fluid ego boundaries because they are usually reared by women. They are allowed, possibly even compelled, to feel esteemed and loved through identification or "fusion" with others. Kohut argued that this process allows them to compensate for the problems with self-esteem by operating as continuations or extensions of others. Men, on the other hand, learn to view their mothers as "other." This means that they are more likely to form rigid ego boundaries and strive for independence. Kohut believes this leads men to develop feelings of grandiosity and extreme self-centeredness, as well as a need for admiration. For these reasons, from an object relations perspective, both men and women are re-enacting the experience of the maternal self-object—men as the other object of the mother, women as the subjective extension of the mother.

Although it would be difficult to find direct support for Kohut's position, there is indirect evidence. Julie Bingham Shiffler (1998) explored the way men and women handle self-conscious emotions (e.g., guilt, shame, depression, narcissism, anger, dysphoric affect, cooperation, need for affection, self-inspection, etc.), in a college population. After giving the Rorschach and the Test of Self-Conscious Affect—modified to 91 college students—she found some interesting gender differences. The women in her study reported higher levels of guilt and shame, but the men were more likely to demonstrate qualities of narcissism. When depression arose, men were more likely than women to also experience nonruminative guilt. Basically, when they did something they regretted, it brought on depression, but they were usually able to let the guilt go and continue with their lives. When ruminative guilt and shame arose in males, there was a corresponding link to narcissism. Such a finding was not present with women. Instead, women tended to handle their guilt by allowing themselves to feel negative emotions. It was only when there was an absence of dysphoric affect that women would feel nonruminative guilt. Although the relationship is complex, it basically implies that men deal with their shame by attempting to improve their perceptions of themselves, while women allow themselves to feel negative emotions such as depression.

Within-Group Differences

Masculinity is clearly defined differently in various cultures, but in many societies, masculinity appears to be associated with dismissing negative emotions and exercising one's independence. Fernandez et al. (2000) surveyed 4,784 people living in 21 countries. A variety of data were collected, including information on socio-demographics as well as information about verbal and nonverbal behavior. The primary focus of study was how people expressed three prototypical emotions (i.e., anger, sadness, and joy). They found that Asians have the strongest set of restrictions governing emotional displays, but their system also expects similar emotional expressions for men and woman. As they investigated this topic further, they found that societies that encouraged verbal and nonverbal emotional expression were most likely to also have a strong cultural concept of masculinity. When men are allowed to show anger or contentment but few negative emotions (e.g., crying, sadness, fear, etc.), the gender differences are more acute. The differences are so apparent that many have considered emotions to be the language of the genders, and these apparently biological features are reinforced and encouraged. Although babies and young children show no gender differences in crying frequency, girls start to cry more than boys beginning at about age 11 to 13 (prior to menarche), and the gap between the sexes widens through adulthood. Older boys cry less often than younger boys, while older girls cry more often than their younger cohorts (Van Tilburg, Unterberg, & Vingerhoets, 2002). Avoiding crying is so critical to manhood that Truijers and Vingerhoets (1999) found that adolescent boys scored higher than girls on only one item of their shame inventory: "I feel shame when I cry."

One difficulty with men being able to display fewer emotions has been evidenced in the way inner-city African American teenage boys deal with violence. Dawn Wilson (2001) studied 200 inner-city teens and observed that African American boys, who regularly witness neighborhood violence, are at higher risk of elevated blood pressure and possibly heart disease and stroke. These results may be expected, but the surprising element of the study involves

TABLE 10.1 *Ethnic Components of Manhood*

Group	Elements of Manhood
African Americans	*Macho:* African American males often view manhood in terms of strength, physical ability, or sexual prowess (Parker, Howard-Hamilton, & Parham, 1998). This viewpoint may be fostered by the media's portrayal of African American males.
Latinos	*Machismo:* This prevalent cultural ideal is intimately connected to family leadership. The closest European concept may be the idea of chivalry. Men are expected to care for and protect their families, especially women, while stoically defining selfhood through hard work, avoiding shame, and acting in a dignified manner.
Asian Americans	*Structure over Function:* There are expectations that an Asian male is expected to fulfill, but the actual performance of the job may fall to someone else. For example, a man is expected to care for his ailing parents, but the actual job of caregiving may fall to his wife or children.
European Americans	*Puritan:* Successful males are those who financially provide for their immediate families and succeed in their occupations.
Native Americans	*Interrelational:* Man's identity and sense of worth come from immersion with nature, providing for one's tribe/relatives, and gaining wisdom by communing with the spirits.

the observed gender differences. Girls with the same degree of exposure to violence did not evidence the same pattern of nondipping blood pressure. The implication is that girls may have better coping skills than boys. Girls may find it easier to walk away from violence, while boys are more likely to get involved, which appears, in part, to be based on hormonal influences (Sanchez-Martin et al., 2000).

One reason girls may cope with violence more effectively than boys may be the training they receive from their environment. Most girls know what is expected of them (which presents problems as well as benefits), but the definition of manhood is often less clear. Table 10.1 depicts some of the ethnic definitions of manhood. Although there are some similarities, the differences demonstrate the lack of uniformity in defining a universal form of masculinity.

Counseling Issues

If men primarily experience mental health issues in terms of receiving admiration from others and achieving intimacy in a single dyadic relationship, it is unlikely that they will present for counseling to deal with affective or emotional concerns. Instead, men often seek help for relationship issues such as infidelity, infertility, boundary issues, pornography, spousal abuse, and so on. It is important to realize that all of these issues involve relationships with others. As a result, therapists who counsel men frequently find themselves also working with the person responsible for his coming to therapy.

Marsha's Story

I have been through a lot this year. My husband, Mark, revealed to me that he was unhappy with our marriage, and I was four months pregnant with our second child. I was devastated. When I thought he was telling me this because he was leaving me, I told him that it would be easier to take if he could at least tell me that there was someone else. Well, he admitted to being "passionately in love" with a coworker with whom he had an affair four years ago. They supposedly stopped their affair, but of course his feelings for her never went away. I prayed to God for a miracle to keep our marriage together. My husband was willing to go to counseling. I figured that if he wasn't happy with our marriage it was something he had to figure out. He finally came around and began working with me on what he really wanted in our relationship.

Marsha was the reason for her husband coming to therapy. During the intake, Marsha repeatedly explained how Mark "agreed" to enter therapy. Mark demonstrated little desire to be there and almost appeared as though he was being dragged along. As Marsha continued to describe the condition of their marriage, Mark's face grew pale and he became very quiet. He had been "caught" and wanted to be anywhere other than where he was. For many men, this position of shame and embarrassment is equivalent to an alcoholic "hitting bottom." They will work to end this negative feeling, which is usually untenable and painful. It is the goal of ending this discomfort that often motivates them to work in therapy.

Shame is the key component in men's mental health. Some men are willing to address their feelings directly, but most men are only aware of anger and shame. Discussing shame becomes a way to help them understand other emotions that they have refused to examine. When shame begins to overwhelm men, they begin to feel a greater need for affection (Shiffler, 1998). This is sometimes sublimated into a compulsive need to work, but it may also take highly dysfunctional shapes such as voyeurism and child sexual abuse, which only increase the problem and create vicious circles. When a man feels inadequate, he may open himself up to negative behaviors he might not entertain otherwise. If a desire for having sex with children arises, shame is likely to compound his sense of inadequacy. He starts thinking, "Now I know why I'm a failure—I'm attracted to children." If he acts on his impulses, his shame and inadequacy increase, and he starts to feel "out of control." The cycle increases his shame, which leaves him vulnerable to more negative behaviors.

Paul's Story

I think my whole problem started when I was in college. I was dating this girl, Jennifer, and we had a thing. It was all going really well, and we were together for four years. Then, out of the blue, she just said that she was ready to move on. I couldn't believe it, but I told her that I understood. I'm not really sure that I've had a girlfriend since that time. Instead, I find myself addicted to pornography and I can't seem to break the habit. I know it's wrong and a sin, but I can't stop. I find myself driving by the liquor store and I know full well that if I go in, I will buy a magazine, but I convince myself that I just need some milk. I will only get milk. Once I'm inside, I convince myself that I could just walk down the magazine aisle, just to see if there is anything different and new. Inevitably, I will buy pornography and then I will go into my room and masturbate.

Paul was troubled by his lack of intimacy, and he felt unworthy of love. His method of dealing with loneliness was to create a fantasy. On the surface, the compulsion to view pornography appears to be about creating the illusion of being with beauty. For Paul, pornography was not a method of viewing himself with beautiful women, it was a means of creating a fantasy in which beautiful women were infatuated with him. He would view himself meeting the women in the pictures and rescuing them from their tawdry lives. The method of healing such pain is to address the shame.

Above all else, Paul wanted to stop his obsession, which he viewed as his sole downfall. He blamed his poor social skills, inability to date, problems at work, and inability to save money on his need to attend strip shows and buy dirty magazines and videos. He never once stopped to consider whether the pornography was actually a means of coping with his problems—whether, by submerging himself in these fantasies, he was able to accomplish two very important things.

The first coping skill Paul gained through pornography was an ability to protect himself from failure. Although he was failing in nearly every aspect of his life, he attributed these failures to a cause outside of himself. It was the pornography that led his boss to view him as passive, obedient, and uncreative. It was the vileness of pornography beneath his clean-cut persona that kept him from dating. No one could see the real Paul, and, as such, no one could blame him for failure. Others may believe they see him, but they see only the illusion—the tainted exterior.

The other benefit Paul gained through his addiction to pornography was an ability to view himself as more than he was. In his fantasies, he played the pure knight who rescued seductresses from themselves. In many ways, this fantasy was the only positive image he had of himself, even though he realized that it was illusory. Still, it allowed him to escape the drudgery of his daily life and enter into a world of excitement, strength, prowess, and honor. These are all noble dreams, but his method of achieving them would never reach fruition.

When working with someone like Paul, our primary task should not be to fight against the specific behavior—in this case, his use of pornography. Instead, we should focus on the goals behind the behaviors, i.e., find a way for the client to overcome his shame and begin to behave in ways that are proud, brave, strong, exciting, and honorable. For Paul, such a path began with the admission that women might find him attractive. We created lists of his positive qualities, delved into the strengths he lost when pornography took over his life, and discussed the things he would like to do with his life. Next, we attempted to find new ways in which he could protect himself from failure and open himself to taking risks. When he no longer felt "addicted" to pornography (whether or not he continued to use it), how would he defend himself against the pain of rejection, being passed over for a promotion, or feeling alone and isolated?

For some men, finding the answers to the existential questions around them rests in stereotypical masculine metaphors. For example, one client stated that he felt the world was constantly shooting arrows at him. He needed all the shields he could find to defend himself. We started to discuss what happens when an arrow enters the body. It's something every guy should be familiar with because it is an important scene in any action film depicting pre-twentieth-century events. The injured party does not rip the arrow out the moment it enters, because the arrow may have nicked a vital organ and removing it could spell death. Instead, the wounded hero must lay still and wait for his body to heal the damaged area. The same is true for all wounds, whether physical or psychological. Even when an assault causes our heart to break, if we can rest quietly for a moment, and not panic, the pain will usually subside and someone else will be along to help us recover.

Although shame and vulnerability appear to undergird many psychological problems, there are times when addressing such issues should be considered secondary. Two such areas are substance addition and domestic violence. In both cases, the threat from the behaviors overshadows the underlying causes. As such, the behaviors must stop before any long-term intervention can be made.

Dealing with substance abuse typically involves overcoming denial. Alcoholics, if they admit to struggling with alcohol, often deny any personal problems besides alcohol addiction (Blume, 1985). Denial, minimizing, blaming, excusing, generalizing, dodging, attacking, and repression of anger are common to alcoholics and their family members (Friends in Recovery, 1989). Alcoholics (and their families) learn to blame the "problem" on external and interpersonal difficulties (e.g., stress at work, marital incompatibility, or unruly children), and the alcohol itself is frequently looked upon as the cure to these "problems," rather than the cause (Wilson, 1989). Family members become obsessed with the process of solving these external pressures so that the alcoholic will not need to drink. By preventing alcoholics from experiencing the consequences of their excessive drinking, family members become enablers. They facilitate the drinking by shifting the responsibility away from the alcoholic (e.g., an enabling wife may excuse her alcoholic husband's absence from work as the result of the flu when he is actually hung over). Counselors who contribute to these systems of denial (either tacitly or directly) violate the principle of nonmaleficence (doing no harm) by reinforcing the dysfunctional structure.

Once denial has been overcome, however, shame can be addressed. I once witnessed a group counseling session at an inpatient treatment center for drug abusers who were military veterans. The therapist politely asked the relatively large group (more than 30 clients) how they were feeling. A few apathetically responded, "Fine." With this, the therapist's face changed, turning red with anger. His eyes open widely and pointed towards one of the group members who responded. Suddenly, he screamed out, "*FINE*? You're not *fine*, you're in an in-patient center for drug abusers!" After startling the members of the group, he continued. "Your lives are all full of shit and you are fucked up." The onslaught continued for two to three minutes, until the therapist quickly and unexpectedly changed gears. "I would imagine," he yelled, "Some of you are here because your childhoods were so screwed up that you never learned that you could amount to anything." Without pausing, he asked, "How many of you were sexually abused?" Remarkably, three people raised their hands. He pointed to one of them and said, "You! Tell us your story." The man spoke about being sexually molested by his uncle. During the story, the therapist's manner became more relaxed. His voice softened and he compassionately responded, "Yeah, that must have been hard."

What appears necessary, when confronting men with substance abuse, is to stay focused on the problem behavior while finding a way to approach negative feelings. The therapist from the Veterans Administration did this by taking clients off guard, using client-oriented language, and showing compassion. The mechanism that is used may be less important than reaching a balance between confrontation and compassion.

The same approach should be used with spousal abuse. There is a dearth of information demonstrating efficacy with any given program, which has led many texts to recommend methods of empowering the survivor and virtually ignore treatment methods for the abuser (Philpot et al., 1997). Sadly, this might be the best strategy. In the following paragraphs, we will note the advantages and disadvantages of individual, conjoint, and group therapy for abusers. Each can have an effect on deterring violence but, in most cases, abusive clients simply fail to complete the programs. Whatever the treatment modality, therapists must master an ability to build a strong rapport and simultaneously confront unacceptable behaviors to help reduce the tendency for abusers to drop out of treatment.

Individual therapy, while ineffective by itself, is recommended as an introduction to therapy. Meeting individually with clients may provide them with the necessary understanding and comfort level to stay with a treatment program. Such an intervention is not a sufficient treatment because it is unlikely to evoke lasting change. Instead, individual therapy can be used to provide the abuser with knowledge about the therapeutic process, goals for treatment, and possible outcomes associated with treatment. Once these components have been established, and a therapeutic alliance exists, clients should be moved toward either conjoint or group therapy.

When the ultimate goal is conjoint therapy, the individual intervention focuses on identifying the abuser's desires and goals for the relationship while helping him to become aware of the mechanisms that are likely to trigger a violent response. Many men come to therapy only because they want the health of their relationship restored. They are not interested in personal growth except insofar as it is necessary to preserve the relationship.

Often, effective interventions help the client to realize that the relationship may not be salvageable. Psychoeducation can be used to teach the client about battered-wife syndrome and other effects of abuse (e.g., depression, anxiety, powerlessness, and learned helplessness). Prior to conjoint sessions, the abuser must comprehend the consequences of his abusive behavior and realize that his wife is likely to change as she gains self-assurance, contentment, and a sense of peace.

In addition to educating the client about the effects of abuse, individual sessions can also address precipitating causes for violence. The etiology of violence differs from one couple to another. In systemic abusive relationships, the wife's actions may fuel the abuser's rage. For example, a failure to perform a task to the husband's standards, accidentally breaking something, spending time with other people, failing to show interest in the abuser, or some other action may result in abuse. In other cases, the violence may simply stem from the abuser's disposition. He may have been drinking, heard disappointing news, or experienced increased stress. Whatever the triggers may be, individual sessions can help the abuser become aware of the warning signs. Often, clients view their violent impulses as coming from outside themselves. When they can localize the impulses within themselves, they may be ready for a forum that will teach them how to cope with these feelings.

One of the benefits of conjoint sessions is the ability to work on communication issues. Even in asystemic cases, where the survivor's actions are irrelevant to the outbreak of violence, the presence of the victimized spouse can foster growth in the relationship, provide healthy communication boundaries, and educate both parties about each other's internal processes. Such growth is important to many couples because when they attend therapy voluntarily, they usually expect to stay together.

Many couples assume their counselor will encourage them to end their relationship, especially when the abuse spans several years. While this may be the case, couples strongly committed to the relationship are likely to terminate therapy if it fails to help them reach their goals. Rather than assuming that an abusive relationship should end, counselors can facilitate the therapeutic process by helping the counselees reassess the state of the relationship (Leeder, 1994). In any physically abusive relationship, the safety of the victim must be preserved.

Usually, this requires a temporary separation. Therapists must handle this stage well. There is some evidence that conjoint therapy does not increase violence within the household (Brannen & Rubin, 1996), but lethal violence is most common when the victim attempts to leave. Stressing the temporary nature of a separation should help to alleviate the abuser's feelings of rejection.

If the couple decides to stay together, and sufficient personal gains have been reached, conjoint sessions provide the opportunity for the couple to share what they have learned (Leeder, 1994). Certain guidelines will help in this process:

- *Establish guidelines for speaking.* For example, when one person is talking, the other cannot interrupt.
- *Create a sign to indicate when a violent action or phrase is used.* For example, the survivor could raise her hand whenever she felt threatened during the session. This is an important component. Most survivors are acutely aware of their partner's controlling behaviors, but the abusers lack such an awareness. Abusers will require special support during this phase, as it will be uncomfortable and threatening for them to see their partner's hand raise after every other sentence.

For many therapists and researchers, there are two implicit goals when working with the couple. First, the counselor should attempt to stop the violence, and second, the survivor needs to become less vulnerable and more powerful in the relationship (Wileman & Wileman, 1995). Both of these objectives are essential for the health of the relationship and well-being of both clients.

The necessary component of being violence-free cannot be overemphasized. Conjoint therapy is only recommended if the violence has ceased for at least 6 months, the abuser has accepted responsibility, and both parties have participated in individual treatment (Philpot et al., 1997). If conjoint therapy is attempted prematurely, the couple may lack the communication skills and emotional development to cope with the painful issues aroused in therapy. Considering the correlation between feelings of inadequacy and abuse, forcing a couple to address issues of abuse prematurely is harmful and unethical if the couple has yet to establish a violence-free environment. Consider the following transcript.

Husband:	I'm really concerned about my wife. She doesn't seem to trust me any more, and I don't know how to help.
Wife:	(looking at husband) I want to trust him again.
Husband:	(looking at wife) Just let me know what you want me to do.
Wife:	It's nothing. There's nothing—I . . . (pause) (silence)
Therapist:	John, when your wife was speaking just then, your expression started to change. It looked as though you were getting angry that she wouldn't tell you how you could help.
Husband:	(scowling) I . . . want . . . to . . . help.

Wife looks down and avoids all eye contact.

Fortunately, this session did not lead to violence, but this example should demonstrate the necessity for prior therapy. If the conditions for violence are still fertile, forcing couples to discuss their deepest concerns makes them vulnerable and unsure of themselves. When the abuser's sense of security comes from controlling another person, this form of therapy may actually contribute to abuse.

One exception may be when the violent partner also abuses alcohol. Recent research indicates that in such cases, conjoint sessions are more effective in the short term than individual sessions (Brannen & Rubin, 1996). The reasons for this phenomenon are not yet clear. If the abuse occurs only when the abuser is intoxicated, perhaps the survivor can confront the denial and help dissuade him from continued drinking. It is important to note, however, that Brannen and Rubin's study did not investigate the effects of group therapy, which often has the best results for any type of abuse.

Although conjoint sessions have unique strengths, the potential benefits of these sessions are vastly overshadowed by the benefits of group therapy. Group therapy is usually the most effective treatment mode for abusers (Geffner, Bartlett, & Rossman, 1995; Philpot et al., 1997). When dealing with men, the primary intervention is likely to be confronting their assumptions about gender. If they believe that men should control women, or that being vulnerable is a sign of weakness, their aggressive behavior likely flows out of these beliefs. Such men appear to use violence as means of controlling their environments. Rather than confront clients directly, which often leads to high dropout rates, the goal of these sessions is to foster an emotional vulnerability. Abusers are not used to expressing their feelings, admitting to wrongdoing, or giving up power (Harway & Evans, 1996). The group provides a context in which they are expected to share part of themselves. In healthy groups, experienced group members challenge men who refuse to share, and these members also serve as role models of abusers in recovery.

Philpot et al. (1997) provided a three-step model of group counseling for male abusers. First, attend to the client's crisis. Most men referred for therapy are nearing the end of a relationship or are sent to therapy by the courts. They are desperate, confused, and defensive. The therapist uses this phase to teach the men about violence control and to explore acceptable ways of channeling negative feelings.

The second phase, short-term counseling, begins to address the violence itself. Issues of abandonment, guilt, shame, anger, and fear are explored.

In the third and final phase, maintenance, the counselor works with the client to develop new relationship skills, and encourages the client to form relationships with other men. During this phase, the client should attempt to reconcile himself with his past. Amends with one's spouse, other friends, and other family members should be sought even if there is no hope of salvaging those relationships.

Even when programs offer effective long-term intervention, clients are unlikely to follow through to the point where they achieve these results.

Gondolf and Foster (1991) reported a 94 percent dropout rate after the first three months of a six-month treatment program. For those who finished the program, their physical outbursts decreased, but they continued to verbally abuse their spouses.

Madden (1987) notes that many violent persons use group therapy on an "as needed" basis. Regular attendance in any mental health program is preferred, but even irregular attendance often helps in the client's recovery. It seems reasonable to assume that an Alcoholics Anonymous approach would be successful in these cases as well. As mentioned above, effective groups provide a place for abusers to take responsibility for their violence. Peer groups could easily foster such accountability and provide an ongoing treatment setting. The AA 12-step approach also provides a forum for explaining how abusers are always in recovery and are always at risk.

Whatever the medium, effective programs will provide four essential components: (1) a productive therapeutic alliance, (2) effective confrontation of denial, (3) the elimination of alcohol consumption, and (4) a long-term, crisis intervention mechanism to handle violent impulses. Few programs offer all of these elements, which may explain why effective programs are virtually nonexistent.

Mark's Story

I often wonder what has affected my recovery as it has. I know attending group counseling has helped, and simply missing my family and wanting to get them back.

It's amazing how hard this process is. For the past two years, I attended a group for abusers. I went weekly for the first year, but I lost interest after awhile. A number of the guys who started with me simply dropped out. At first, some would just start attending every other week, then maybe once a month, and finally they would disappear.

I started looking in the paper to see if any of my fellow attendees were arrested. None of them have made the papers, so I hope they are doing well. It's hard to tell. For me, the groups, even though I only attend monthly now, are invaluable. They keep my thoughts in check. Well, I should say, it helps if I let it. In our meetings, if someone has "slipped" and verbally abused his spouse, we will work through it together and help him find ways to avoid such tactics in the future. It only works if you share, though, and sometimes the shame and guilt become overwhelming.

I keep wondering how many men are out there who have problems with abuse. I seem to run into them everywhere: online, in the grocery store, with e-mail. Everyone seems to have a unique opinion on how to stop the abuse. I wish someone could come up with something productive. For now, the key seems to be keeping yourself from believing you are "fixed."

I've been trying to build my peer group and get back into school. I want to surround myself with alternate views. I can't live in a world entirely dominated by abuse issues. Sometimes, I just want to escape.

Seeing my kids helps. I don't get to be with them as often as I'd like, but I savor any time I have with them. They make my world normal again. I must admit, sometimes spending time with them is a little depressing. They are growing so quickly, and I can't be there with them to experience each moment. Next week, they will be finished with elementary school, a week later high school, and within a month, married with children of their own. The pace is mind numbing; I need to slow it down.

I keep wondering what will happen in the future. Will Hope take me back? Will our marriage remain dissolved? Will my children forgive me? I really don't know what will happen, and the uncertainty is tearing me apart. How can I learn to grow when my foundation has been ripped away?

I also wonder what would have happened had none of this taken place. Would our family be stronger? Would there be other problems? I don't know the answers to these questions, but I suppose it really doesn't matter. I've run my course and now I have to find out where it leads. I'm trying to improve and change. I want my life back the way it was. I suppose only time will tell what happens next.

Questions to Consider

1. Do you believe male victims of domestic violence receive adequate psychological support? If not, what might need to change before this occurs?

2. Why do women stay with abusive husbands?

3. What is the value of fatherhood?

4. What needs to happen for men to feel more comfortable in traditionally feminine occupations?

5. What factors contribute to the disparity between the skills of European Americans and African Americans who are homeless?

6. How does sexual harassment affect men?

7. Girls now make up 57 percent of straight-A students, and boys make up 57 percent of high school dropouts. If this trend continues, how might it affect gender roles in the future?

8. Men tend to ignore health problems. What are the consequences of this tendency?

9. Men tend to believe their world is completely safe. What might be the possible advantages and consequences of such a belief?

10. Are there differences between masculine and feminine morality?

11. How would you counsel a man wrestling with "feminine" psychopathology such as anorexia?

12. Why are men more likely than women to display feelings of grandiosity?

13. How do various cultures dictate how men display emotions?

14. Shame is a key component in men's mental health. How would you use this concept in your therapeutic intervention?

15. Why are alcoholism and spousal abuse different from most other pathologies experienced by men?

PART IV

Exploring Cultural Complexity

Studying diversity presents a number of challenges for clinicians and students. One of the greatest potential pitfalls involves trying to pigeonhole a person into only one or two of the categories described in this text. Many people belong to several groups and are likely to resent being limited to one classification. Consider the ethnic origins of golfing legend Tiger Woods.

In 1997, pro golfer Fuzzy Zoeller uttered an offhand remark that was to change his life. Tiger Woods, an emerging golf champion, had recently won the Masters' Golf Tournament, one of the most prestigious competitions in the world of sports. Mr. Zoeller, commenting on the winners' privilege of selecting the ceremonial dinner, quipped that Mr. Woods would be likely to choose fried chicken and collard greens. The comment created a national debate about prejudice and discrimination, but there was another aspect to the incident that was virtually untouched by the media.

The comments offered by Mr. Zoeller were undoubtedly insensitive and demonstrated a lack of understanding concerning African Americans, but in this case, the victim of the slur was not predominantly African American. Tiger's father is half African American, a quarter Chinese, and a quarter Native American, and his mother is half Thai, a quarter Chinese, and a quarter White (Verdi, 1997). Ethnically, Tiger Woods is more Asian than Black. Given this information, does it seem surprising that no one made comments about Mr. Woods serving sushi? (By the way, referring to sushi would still have been inappropriate because it is a Japanese dish, not Chinese or Thai.) The reasons are likely two-fold: (1) Because of his skin tone, Mr. Woods looks more African American than Asian, and (2) Asians are less likely than African Americans to be chastised for their success in predominantly "White" activities.

As illustrated by the Tiger Woods example, multiple ethnicities may be present within a single individual. Many times, such a person may be pressured to identify with a single ethnic background rather than embracing more than one cultural heritage. Multiple minority status may also combine ethnic and sexual minorities, and it can encompass conditions that cross all ethnic and sexual boundaries, such as disability and age.

11

Mixed Cultural Identities

*C*ultural competency includes respecting the unique strengths and challenges of each individual. Instead of viewing people in stereotypical ways, we need to acknowledge the various factors that contribute to who they are.

People with Mixed Cultural Origins

Bicultural individuals have long had difficulty knowing where they belong. Should they identify with one part of their heritage and disregard the other? How do they determine their racial identity? These are difficult issues and ones the United States government has only recently addressed. For many years, the state of Virginia had a law on its books (the Virginia Racial Integrity Act) that made it a felony for a "White" person to marry a "Colored" person. The punishment for intermarriage was at least one and not more than five years in prison. A case was brought to the Supreme Court in 1967 regarding this statute, and Chief Justice Earl Warren delivered the opinion of the Court. For the first time, the prohibition against interracial marriage was lifted as the court determined that preventing marriages between persons solely on the basis of racial classifications violated the Equal Protection and Due Process Clauses of the Fourteenth Amendment.

Changes in immigration policies have also increased the number of bicultural Americans. For example, the Asian American population was quite small prior to amendments to U.S. immigration laws in 1965. Today, intermarriage rates among Asians and non-Asians are quite high, especially among native-born Asian Americans (Lee & Fernandez, 1998). In Maryland, for example, about 20 percent of Asian children were identified as multiracial in the 2000 census, compared with only 8 percent of Asians aged 18 and over.

Since the Supreme Court struck down the last state law forbidding interracial marriages in 1967, such unions have tripled, and the birth rate among interracial couples has more than doubled. The 1990 census found that nearly 2 million children under 18 were identified as "of a different race than one or both of their parents" (Beech, 1999). The numbers grew considerably in 2000, with about 4.0 percent of children identified as multiracial, compared with 1.9 percent of adults (Annie E. Casey Foundation, 2001). Most European Americans probably have yet to notice the changing demographics because society is still relatively segregated. About 30 percent of Whites live in cities, but they typically live in urban neighborhoods that are about 72 percent White. More than 60 percent of Blacks live in cities. The typical Black city dweller lives in a neighborhood that has about 75 percent minority residents and in which three out of five residents are Black (Schmitt, 2001).

These biological issues are blended with an increasing number of multicultural adoptions. This practice has been hotly debated, with vocal advocates on both sides. In October 1994, the Multiethnic Placement Act was passed in the United States Senate. The law prohibited public agencies from considering race in the placement of children with adoptive families, but it did not end the debate. The National Association of Black Social Workers (NABSW) strongly opposes the adoption of Black children by White families, and they have argued that placement agencies should use their discretion of acting in the "child's best interests" to oppose transracial adoption. The NABSW's position is so strong that it may be associated with some African American children growing up in foster care rather than going into adoptive placement. This outcome can be extremely harmful, because the longer a minority child remains in foster care, the less likely the child is to make a healthy adjustment into an adoptive family (George, 1996). Even without organizations like the NABSW arguing against transracial adoptions, African American children are less likely to be adopted early in life (Kim, Zrull, Davenport, & Weaver, 1992). Most of the time, when European American parents adopt African American children, the children fare well in educational attainment, peer relationships, self-esteem, and social competencies (Rushton & Minnis, 1997). In response to these findings, the Multiethnic Placement Act was amended in 1996 to become the Removal of Barriers to Interethnic Adoption Act. The 1996 law specifically prohibits delaying or denying the placement of a child for adoption or foster care on the basis of race, color, or national origin of the foster or adoptive parents or of the child involved.

Issues of transcultural adoption are becoming even more important as growing numbers of American couples strive to adopt children from other countries. According to U.S. Department of State data, the number of children adopted from other countries has grown substantially over the past three decades, from about 5,000 in 1975 to more than 19,000 in 2001 (U.S. Department of State, 2002). In recent years, nearly half of the children adopted from other countries have come from the People's Republic of China or Russia. The diversity of internationally adopted children has compounded the difficulty of compiling a list of competencies for parents who choose transcultural adoption. Currently, there is no consensus regarding the attitudes, skills, and knowledge needed to enhance adoptive parents' cultural competence. There are some important starting points, however, that all transcultural adoptive parents should address:

- Understand the history of oppression for members of your child's ethnic group (Greene, Watkins, McNutt, & Lopez, 1998), and be open to understanding racism. This includes learning about the benefits that European Americans experience daily. For example, most European Americans generally expect protection rather than harassment from police. Minority children, even if they live in a White household, are less likely to receive such benefits.

- Recognize your cultural biases/traditions and anticipate where these might conflict with the child's ethnic background (Vonk, 2001).

- Realize that gaining cultural competency is a long-term process and will require involvement in groups outside the dominant culture. Spend time in organizations associated with your child's ethnic background. Learn the culture by making friends.

- Celebrate the importance of an ethnic identity (McRoy, 1994), and integrate this with your family's developing cultural identities (e.g., religious, adopted ethnicity, etc.).

- Find ethnic role models for your child. This is often difficult for parents, because they want to be the primary teachers for their children. However, White parents cannot teach their children to be Black. Their children will need guidance from people who share their ethnicity (Huh, 1997).

This list of competencies should offset a common problem in transcultural adoptions: the tendency to raise adopted minority children as if they were not members of an ethnic minority. One of my European American clients was instructed by a therapist to treat her adopted Chinese daughter exactly the same way she treated her biological child. The therapist specifically told his client, "Your child is White now." This "culture-blind" approach robbed the child of her ethnic identity, which she later sought, much to the consternation of her adoptive mother. Parents who adopt cross-culturally must recognize and celebrate the fact that they are raising bicultural children. Helping children understand the advantages of a multicultural identity provides them with a stronger sense of self and a holistic sense of being.

In some cases, identifying with a single ethnicity may be difficult for people from diverse heritages. I tend to compare such a situation to a tree that has been grafted for several generations with other varieties. Earlier generations are relatively simple to identify, but the subsequent intermixing makes identification more complex. For humans, who thankfully have greater self-awareness than trees, the process of identification becomes an internal activity. We can choose to highlight the elements of our history that are most dear to us, but we should not reject any of the other elements. Each component is part of our history and our identity.

Multiracial ethnicity can pose unique challenges to an individual's identity, but other types of cultural blending can be even more difficult. Transgendered individuals, for example, spend their lives attempting to unify gender identifications within themselves. Imagine the struggles they must face to understand the cultural mores of both genders. Often, the culture of a gender is often assumed. If you ask a man or a woman to explain what seminal qualities define maleness or femaleness, they are unlikely to posit anything profound. They have been indoctrinated into those cultures from birth, and they have accepted many of the precepts without analyzing them. Transgendered individuals must learn these cultural facets as adults, without instruction from their parents.

There are also unique struggles for people who identify themselves with ethnic and sexual minority groups. Gays and lesbians who are members of ethnic minority groups often struggle with identity issues because they can never be sure if they are being discriminated against because of their ethnicity or their sexuality. This sense of vulnerability affects nearly every dimension of life. Even the way gays and lesbians come out to their parents is influenced by their ethnicity. Kennamer, Honnold, Bradford, and Hendricks (2000) interviewed gay and bisexual men (aged 15 to 77 years) concerning their disclosure to family members, heterosexual friends, gay friends, coworkers, health care workers, and members of their church. They found that European American men were much more likely than gay African Americans to disclose their sexuality, to join gay organizations, and to have gay/bisexual friends. What is even more interesting, and disconcerting, were the moderating effects. As education increased, European American men were *more* likely and African American men were *less* likely to disclose sexuality and associate with gay groups. In a sense, African Americans realized that their biculturalism would have a more negative effect on their lives. The findings from this study have serious implications regarding how biculturalism should be addressed. One of the most immediate concerns, however, is how these trends will affect research into African American gay issues. African American gay men may be less likely to participate in the fight against HIV/AIDS, and they may avoid involvement in gay issues as a means of protecting themselves from prejudice.

In addition to the groups discussed previously, there is another group of bicultural individuals who are more difficult to identify because they blend into the dominant culture. Nadya Fouad (2001), a psychologist and former president of the American Psychological Association's Division 17, recalls her confusion over how to view her ethnicity. Her mother was from Brazil and her father was Egyptian. Although she valued her Hispanic ancestry, most of her colleagues thought of her as "White." She had an Arab surname, she looked White, but there was more to her identity than she realized. When she was elected president of Division 17, she was introduced as the "second woman of color" elected to the position. The announcement surprised many of her friends and colleagues, who had never thought of her as a "person of color" or a member of a minority group. For Dr. Fouad, who had been raised in a small Iowa town with multicultural parents, discovering her own cultural identity seemed less important than learning how to blend into the dominant society. In a very real way, she became an invisible minority, struggling to create a cultural identity without distancing herself from the dominant culture that accepted her.

The influence of invisible minority status should not be overlooked. Bicultural individuals can include immigrants who take up residence in a country other than their birthplace. Sometimes we think of immigrants to the United States as people of non-English-speaking backgrounds, but this classification overlooks people who immigrate from Australia or England and encounter significant cultural differences when moving to the United States. For that matter, even people moving from California to the American South must contend with significant differences in culture. Southern culture in the U.S. is steeped in traditions and modes of communication that are often misunderstood by outsiders.

Wilson and Ferris (1989) helped edit an encyclopedia of Southern culture. The book helped familiarize readers with cultural elements such as fried chicken, mint juleps, the Dukes of Hazzard, Foxfire, the magazine *Southern Living*, the Lost Cause Myth, the Kentucky Derby, snake handlers, Texas Rangers, Indians, the Civil War, Industrialization, and country music. One of the interesting elements of the book, especially as we are discussing hidden minorities, is the authors' assertion that "Southern" culture can include people who live in northern states. The authors argue that there are "Southern" outposts in Midwestern and middle-Atlantic border states, and even in the southern pockets of Chicago. Ultimately, being Southern has more to do with a state of mind than a geographical boundary. The same can also be said for members of other invisible minorities.

People with Disabilities

Although they are certainly not invisible, there are other minority groups that society often refuses to identity or accept. One of the most overlooked groups includes people with physical or mental disabilities. Even the term "disabled" seems to imply an inability to function in the world, which, understandably, leaves many people with disabilities resentful of the impersonal terms used to describe them. Physical complications may limit some activities, but in reality we are all "differently abled." A rocket scientist is unlikely to be a professional athlete. An artist is unlikely to excel in politics. The important component, when dealing with any individual, is learning to emphasize the strengths of an individual rather than that person's limitations. For these reasons, the expression "people with disabilities" is preferred to terms such as "disabled," "handicapped," or "disabled people," because the former expression emphasizes the humanity of the individual and views the disability as a single characteristic of a person. Even better would be to use terms that refer to individuals wrestling with a specific disability; e.g., we could refer to "people with epilepsy" or "people who are hearing impaired" rather than "epileptics" or "the deaf."

If you find the use of the term "differently abled" confusing, keep in mind that it is just the tip of the iceberg. There are subtle differences between the terms *disadvantage*, *impairment*, and *disability*. If we are discussing someone with a spinal cord injury, all three of these terms can be used. If the spinal cord damage has created paraplegia, the paraplegia is an impairment. If that person had worked in a job requiring physical mobility (e.g., a firefighter), the effect of the impairment on the person's ability to walk is a disability. If the person lives in an area that lacks wheelchair accessibility or he/she is discriminated against because of the impairment, then he or she suffers a disadvantage.

Esses and Beaufoy (1994) argued that for individuals with physical disabilities, the negative attitudes of society often represent a more formidable barrier than the disability itself. Individuals who are dealing with mental illnesses face even greater stigma. In 1986, the National Institute of Mental Health (NIMH) reported that social stigma was the most debilitating handicap faced by former mental health patients. More recent reports confirm the ongoing negative effects of stigma on the quality of life for individuals with mental illnesses. Several researchers have claimed that the debilitating effects of stigma for current and former mental patients are as difficult to overcome as the illness itself (Granello & Wheaton, 2001). Consequently, for individuals with physical disabilities or mental illnesses, research has demonstrated that negative stereotypes have led to discrimination in housing, employment, schooling, and social interactions, even when their disability has had no bearing on the job or situation before them (Corrigan et al., 2000).

The discrimination leveled against differently abled individuals comes in many different forms, and it is not applied to all people equally. There is much evidence that rather than stigmatizing all persons with disabilities equally, the public makes distinctions between types of disabilities and reacts differently to people with different disabilities (Corrigan et al., 2000), but the way people stigmatize and discriminate against people with disabilities is often very subtle. The more "different" a person appears, the more likely they are to face prejudice. Imagine you are walking into a mall and you observe a person in a wheelchair. For many people, the first reaction would be to quickly avert their eyes in order to keep the person from feeling uncomfortable. Now switch places with that person, and imagine that you are walking through the store and everyone you pass quickly looks away as you approach. You would probably begin to wonder if there was something seriously wrong with your appearance. You might even rush into the restroom to examine yourself in the mirror.

Physical appearance is only one element people consider when viewing differently abled individuals. The other key component is the person's apparent ability to change. If the disability is viewed as something beyond the person's control, the public appears more willing to accept and interact with this individual. If the person could have avoided or controlled the disability, there is less sympathy. For example, participants in a study by Esses and Beaufoy (1994) were more accepting of persons who were amputees than those who were diagnosed with AIDS, reasoning that individuals with AIDS were more responsible for their disability. Similar studies have been done comparing mental with physical disabilities. Until recently, mental disabilities were viewed more negatively, apparently because they were considered to be more controllable (Granello & Wheaton, 2001), and there are still problems with the way our society addresses mental disabilities. Susan Stefan (2002) examined the failure of the Americans with Disabilities Act to help people with mental disabilities fight discrimination. People with mental disabilities still struggle to find employment, to get time off from work to attend therapy sessions, and to obtain fair treatment. Many times, discrimination is veiled behind the stipulation that employees must be "qualified individuals." The assumption behind this statement is that individuals who are experiencing intense anxiety are unable to perform their duties. This may be true in some instances, but often people with anxiety disorders can focus their energy on their work. Employers must learn to evaluate an individual's competencies based on the nature of the work rather than the person's diagnosis.

Working with differently abled individuals requires wide-ranging skills, ingenuity, and adaptability. Many of the issues confronted are multifaceted and will require diverse interventions. Consider the challenges faced by an individual recovering from a stroke. The brain trauma may have diminished the individual's mobility or cognitive functioning, which may require physical therapy or medical interventions. The individual may also be afraid of the physical, emotional, and financial consequences of trauma, which would require psychotherapeutic interventions. Clinicians expecting to work with such individuals would be wise to establish a clear multidisciplinary referral list.

Building a referral list of multidisciplinary professionals can be difficult when working with differently abled individuals. The most important difficulty to overcome is the problem of failing to recognize or value the culture of the differently abled. Cooke (2002) found that differently abled children who were screened for child abuse were less likely to be placed on a child protection register than a control group of nondisabled children. She noted that there was a tendency for professionals "not to see" the abuse of differently abled children. Despite this oversight, European American children with disabilities are more likely than nondisabled children to be physically abused by their parents (Randall, Sobsey, & Parrila, 2001).

Education can play an important role in increasing acceptance of people with disabilities. School counselors and therapists working with children can use techniques such as theatrical interventions to help shape the way children view differently abled persons. D'Amico et al. (2001) examined the attitudes of

84 children (aged 9 to 13 years) toward actors with disabilities. They exposed the children to a musical that incorporated a variety of differently abled individuals in positive situations. After viewing the musical, the researchers explored how the children viewed the actors. The play significantly influenced the way the children viewed differently abled individuals, and after the play, the children reported that differently abled people were capable of singing, acting, working cooperatively, and establishing friendships. Steward (2002) argues that confronting and eliminating prejudices against differently abled children is an important and necessary role for all school employees. At-risk children should never be overlooked, no matter how confident they may appear. Anything that makes adolescents appear different can interfere with the developmental process. Disabilities can increase the stress of this phase of life (Trevatt, 2001). Part of the challenge of functioning in an able-bodied culture involves maintaining a positive view of one's body. People with physical disabilities often struggle to maintain a positive view of their bodies, but there is evidence that having a disability does not preclude positive physical and global self-perceptions (Guthrie & Castelnuovo, 2001). There is often a grieving process if some of their physical beauty is lost, but therapists can help clients find parts of their bodies that had been underexplored. Some clients have never really considered the beauty of their eyes or the softness of their skin. They may not appreciate the texture of their hair, or the strength of their muscles. The trick is learning to value the positive aspects of one's body in order to build a new conception of the self.

Ageism and the Elderly

In 1968, Robert Butler (1993) coined the term *ageism*. He came up with the concept when he heard about a group of middle-aged citizens protesting the construction of a luxury apartment building for the elderly poor. The protesters were not fighting for the right to rent the proposed apartments. They simply wanted the structure to be built somewhere else. In many respects, ageism stems from society's struggle to find a balance between providing for the needs of vulnerable elders and maintaining "entitlement" programs, such as Medicare and Medicaid, at the expense of other groups, but it also reflects a limited understanding of the aging process and the special needs of the elderly. In addition to benefiting from perceived privileges, the elderly are more likely to face ambivalence or negativity because unlike gender, ethnicity, or sexual orientation, aging involves physical decline (Warren, 1998).

Geriatric clients are less likely to seek counseling than younger people (Weiss, 1995), and few studies have examined the efficacy of various interventions. Why do researchers often overlook this area of study? Perhaps it is because the issues confronting the elderly are often chronic and irresolvable.

Clinicians may feel at a loss to help their clients cope. For example, some of the serious issues related to geriatric mental health stem from inadequate financial resources, depression, loneliness, and decreased cognitive functioning. Financial issues are especially difficult for those facing double minority status. Most elderly minority members earn similar incomes, with Asian Americans earning slightly more than their peers. However, elderly European Americans have a long history of incomes that are 30 to 40 percent higher than those of any minority group (Baruth & Manning, 1991). These trends are not limited to finances. African American elderly, for example, are more likely to be physically ill or disabled, and they experience higher mortality rates. They are also more likely to be abused, which is yet another underexplored component of geriatric life. Whether elder abuse is defined in terms of physical maltreatment, financial exploitation, neglect, misuse of medication, violation of rights, or psychological abuse, elderly African Americans are more likely to experience abuse than are their European American peers (Baruth & Manning, 1999), although 4 to 10 percent of all elderly citizens will face abuse in America (Wolf, 1998). Latino elderly are more likely than other groups to be confined to bed because of an illness (AARP, 1995). Traditional screening tools are unlikely to detect depression in Asian Americans, especially Korean Americans (Pang, 1995). Native American elders have the highest mortality rate, in part because of their distrust of European healing interventions (Baruth & Manning, 1999). The estimated 3.5 million gays and lesbians over 60 often feel the need to create their own support groups in order to have their needs met (Slusher, Mayer, & Dunkle, 1996). All of these unique elements make geriatric issues difficult to address, but it is important to realize that geriatric issues are cultural issues, and cultural sensitivity is just as important in this arena as in any other.

Bicultural issues for geriatrics are complex, but there are a number of issues common to the geriatric minority that warrant attention. Table 11.1 depicts some of the common themes in geriatric psychotherapy. As with all developmental groups, there are physical, social, affective, and cognitive issues unique to this age group. The table provides introductory descriptions of common problems and some basic foundations or techniques to employ when dealing with each area.

Often, one of the most helpful interventions is to encourage or strengthen the client's religious ties. Religious values, beliefs, and rituals can help integrate members within a community and provide hope for the future. McCullough et al. (2000) conducted a meta-analysis of data from 42 independent samples examining the association of a measure of religious involvement and all-cause mortality. Religious involvement was significantly associated with lower mortality rates (odds ratio = 1.29; 95% confidence interval: 1.20-1.39). People who are religious are more likely to live longer than those who are not. An interesting aspect of the study was the fact that it explored both public and private religiosity. In the past, similar findings were attributed to the idea that people who

TABLE 11.1 *Geriatric Counseling Issues*

	Symptoms	Interventions
Physical Issues	Changes in appearance; feeling like you are not the same person	The most important element, when counseling someone who is feeling self-alienated, is finding the cause of the feeling. Sometimes subtle changes in voice or dexterity may be more significant than balding or wrinkles. Physical exercise and better nutrition can rejuvenate the skin and improve health, but ultimately, the client needs to shift to defining the self through *being* rather than *doing*. When clients base their identity on their level of activity, they will likely experience depression as their physical condition declines. Transpersonal/spiritual growth will assist clients in coping with physical changes. Effective therapy may incorporate personal myths and stories to explore the client's definition of self and the meaning of life.
	Diminished sensory functioning; loss of hearing or poor eyesight	Sensory perception changes can be significant for a number of reasons. They tend to isolate people from friends whose hearing and vision are not impaired, and the disability can lead to feelings of incompetence, shame, or inadequacy. Helping to find assistive technology (e.g., hearing aids) is often an important first step. Support groups may also help to provide an avenue in which people can share their concerns with others in similar situations. The key is finding a way to optimize existing physical abilities while compensating for deficits.
Social Issues	Loss of a spouse or close friend	The grieving process is different for every individual, but for an elderly spouse, losing one's partner creates a significant shift in identity. It is also important to realize that friendships provide helpful transitions into widowhood, and clients should be encouraged to spend more time with their friends and relatives. Therapists are strongly advised to incorporate the entire family when helping geriatric clients cope with bereavement, because the loss of a parent or grandparent may interfere with the family dynamic, which may leave the widow feeling more isolated or lonely. Individually, therapists can help clients continue to explore how they will address their sexual desires (which may remain strong well into the eighties).
	Limited mobility decreasing social outlets	Therapists must ascertain whether the client's limited social contact stems from shame or a lack of knowledge. Clients may simply be unaware of the things they can do without the use of their legs or arms. Occupational therapists may also be helpful in training elderly clients to explore new activities and daily routines.
Affective Issues	Possible changes in personality	Older adults show markedly consistent personality scores over time, and age appears to explain only about 4 percent of personality variance (Costa, Yang, & McCrae, 1998). When changes are observed, medical reasons should be explored before being ruled out. Clients should realize that personality changes are not a natural part of aging, and they are often able to continue developing positive traits.

attended church, synagogue, or mosque were conditioned to pursue more healthy lifestyles. This is why they are less likely to be obese, lonely, or immobile. They were more likely to have better social support networks, regular activities, and long-term friendships, which helped them remain physically healthy and mentally alert (Burgess, Schmeeckle, & Bengtson, 1998). But the benefit of private spirituality implies that there is some value in believing in a

TABLE 11.1 *Continued*

	Symptoms	Interventions
Affective Issues Continued	Depression	Depression in the elderly often remains undetected. Although older adults are less susceptible to depression and other mental health disorders (except dementia) than younger people, depression can have a powerful influence on their lives. Physicians may overlook depression in 90 percent of their African American male patients (Lichtenberg et al., 1996) and the Geriatric Depression Scale can miss depression at least 36 percent of the time, and perhaps even more often with minority elderly (Baruth & Manning, 1999). Diagnostic difficulties stem from the multiple causes of depression. Sometimes changes in estrogen levels or neurotransmitter functioning may create the need for pharmacological interventions. Functional depression may arise from changes in ability, performance, or relationships. The key intervention appears to be helping the client maintain ego integrity over despair. If they have a reason to hope, they can fight against depression, but they need something to hang onto. For example, depression often emerges as chronic illnesses develop. Providing hope may take the form of helping the client to connect with family members or to write out a positive narrative of his or her life.
Cognitive Issues	Memory loss	When memory loss occurs, it is usually a loss of recent memory rather than remote memory. In these cases, reminiscent therapy can be extremely beneficial. Clients can be encouraged to reflect on their past relationships, accomplishments, and acquisition of wisdom as a means of feeling integrated and whole.
	Difficulty learning	When learning new skills becomes increasingly difficult, maintaining the development of already acquired skills may be a helpful substitution. If a client has previously mastered quilting, piano playing, or cards, he or she can be encouraged to spend more time maintaining and perfecting this skill.
	Dementia	Families often treat dementia and cognitive malfunction as taboo topics. The family assumes nothing can be done and regards the problem as something best left alone. Avoidance of this topic tends to create divisions within the family, with the impaired client correctly assuming that his or her family is keeping secrets. The situation becomes even more complicated if the impaired individual is considered to be the head of the household. Although discussing the topic openly may produce considerable strife, it is the best way to help the family create a new homeostasis. The family can also help their loved one cope with changes in memory and affect (e.g., anger, frustration, and fear).

higher power (George et al., 2000). This is an area that requires considerably more attention, and the multicultural elements cannot be overlooked.

Practitioners can help their elderly clients by raising topics such as relationships with their children, estate planning, financial circumstances, career transitions and retirement, the effects of physical changes, and affective issues (especially depression). Even when working with depressed and anxious clients, psychotherapy is as effective as pharmacological interventions (Lebowitz et al., 1997). It is important to realize that therapy with geriatric clients must take an approach that differs from therapy with younger people. Instead of focusing on a linear goal, the intervention requires a cyclical perspective (Nordhus, Nielsen, & Kvale, 1998). Within this perspective, there is no immediate focus on reaching a certain level of insight or achieving a specific behavioral change. Instead, there is a mutual understanding that the cycle has no beginning or end. The client's condition may retrace the same path several times or start an entirely different cycle without warning. The client's ability to regulate the therapeutic process is encouraged, therapy is conducted through shorter and more frequent sessions, and the interactional style between client and counselor is often more relaxed and informal than with other clients.

Conclusions

In all multicultural contexts, flexibility, tolerance, and open-mindedness are essential components for working with clients. The cultural dimensions of counseling make the therapeutic process dynamic and ever-changing. In medical interventions, the physician's job involves examining the patient and narrowing down the possible diagnoses until only one remains. In multicultural therapy, the therapist must continue to expand the realm of possibility. Basically, we must realize that the assessment skills taught in general assessment classes may not always apply to multicultural clients. A depressed African American man may have a chemical imbalance, but he may also feel unable to cope with the pressures imposed by a racist society. A woman who is starving herself may be genetically predisposed to do so, but she may also have fallen prey to a cultural overemphasis on physical beauty.

In a sense, medical and general psychological training can provide helpful starting points when dealing with clients, but ongoing multicultural training allows therapists to transcend medical and general issues. Therapy becomes a sociological process in which the individual can only be understood within the culture and environments from which he or she has emerged. Ideally, you will continue to develop your multicultural skills throughout your career. To do so, you should spend as much time as possible with members of diverse cultures, become familiar with the myths and stories of different groups, and continue to examine the ways in which your cultural worldview has shaped your perspective on diverse individuals. By doing such things, you will foster your growth as a therapist and as a person.

Questions to Consider

1. Why was there a national outcry when Fuzzy Zoeller suggested that Tiger Woods might select fried chicken and collard greens at the Masters ceremonial dinner?

2. What are some examples of social trends that will influence the ways in which we view multiculturalism in the future?

3. Why are African American gay men less likely than their European American peers to disclose their sexual orientation and associate with gay groups?

4. Why is it often difficult for members of invisible minorities to create a clear cultural identity?

5. What are the advantages of using the term "differently abled" when referring to people with disabilities?

6. Esses and Beaufoy (1994) argued that for individuals with physical disabilities, the negative attitudes of society often represent a more formidable challenge than the disability itself. Do you agree with this statement? Why or why not?

7. Why are European American children with disabilities more likely to be physically abused than disabled children from other ethnic groups?

8. How can school counselors help to reduce stigma toward people with disabilities?

9. What is ageism, and why does it exist?

10. In what ways can religious involvement help elderly individuals?

11. How do older individuals tend to cope with depression and personality changes? Are these common facets of the aging process?

References

Abbott, M. W., Wong, S., Williams, M., Au, M., & Young, W. (1999). Chinese migrants' mental health and adjustment to life in New Zealand. *Australian & New Zealand Journal of Psychiatry, 33*(1), 13–21.

Aberle, D. (1966). *The peyote religion among the Navaho.* Chicago: Aldine.

Abraido-Lanza, A. F. (1997). Latinas with arthritis: Effects of illness, role identity, and competence on psychological well-being. *American Journal of Community Psychology, 25*(5), 601–627.

Adams, H. E., Wright, L. W., & Lohr, B. A. (1998). Is homophobia associated with homosexual arousal? *Journal of Abnormal Psychology, 105*(3), 440–445.

Agbayani-Siewert, P., & Revilla, L. (1995). Filipino Americans. In P. G. Min (Ed.), *Asian Americans: Contemporary trends and issues* (pp. 134–168). Thousand Oaks, CA: Sage.

Ailinger, R. L., & Dear, M. R. (1997). Latino immigrants' explanatory models of tuberculosis infection. *Qualitative Health Research, 7*(4), 521–531.

Ainsworth-Darnell, J., & Downey, D. B. (1998). Assessing the oppositional culture explanation for racial/ethnic differences in school performance. *American Sociological Review, 63*(4), 536–553.

Alexander, F. G., & Selesnick, S. T. (1966). *The history of psychiatry: An evaluation of psychiatric thought and practice from prehistoric times to the present.* New York: Harper & Row.

Allen, P. G. (1998). Angry women are building: Issues and struggles facing American Indian women today. In M. L. Anderson & P. H. Collins (Eds.), *Race, class, and gender: An anthology* (3rd ed., pp. 43–47). Belmont, CA: Wadsworth.

American Association of Retired Persons (AARP). (1995). *A portrait of older minorities.* Long Beach, CA: AARP.

American Psychological Association. (1992). *Ethical principles of psychologists and code of conduct.* Washington, DC: American Psychological Association. Retrieved February 12, 2002, from the World Wide Web: **http://www.apa.org/ethics/code.html**.

American Psychological Association. (1997). *Answers to your questions about sexual orientation and homosexuality.* Retrieved March 15, 2001, from the World Wide Web: **http://www.apa.org/pubinfo/orient.html**.

American Psychological Association. (1998a*). Eating disorders: Psychotherapy's role in effective treatment.* Retrieved August 2000 from the World Wide Web: **http://helping.apa.org/therapy/eating.html**.

American Psychological Association. (1998b). *Stereotypes may explain some Black boys' emotional withdrawal from academics. APA Monitor,* Retrieved April 7, 2000, from the World Wide Web: **http://www.apa.org/monitor/jan98/stereo.html**.

336

Amey, C. H., & Albrecht, S. L. (1998). Race and ethnic differences in adolescent drug use: The impact of family structure and the quantity and quality of parental interaction. *Journal of Drug Issues, 28*(2), 283–298.

Amstutz-Haws, W., & Mallinckrodt, B. (1998). Separation-individuation from family of origin and marital adjustment of recently married couples. *American Journal of Family Therapy, 26*(4), 293–306.

Andersen, A. (1995). Eating disorders in males. In K. Brownell & C. G. Fairburn, *Eating disorders and obesity: A comprehensive handbook* (pp. 177–182). Guilford: New York.

Anderson, G., Benjamin, H., & Fuss, M. A. (1994). The determinants of success in university introductory economics courses. *Journal of Economic Education, 25,* 99–119.

Anderson, M. J., & Ellis, R. (1995). On the reservation. In N. A. Vacc, S. B. DeVaney, & J. Wittmer (Eds.), *Experiencing and counseling multicultural and diverse populations* (3rd ed., pp. 179–198). Bristol, PA: Accelerated Development.

Andrews, B. (1997). Bodily shame in relation to abuse in childhood and bulimia: A preliminary investigation. *British Journal of Clinical Psychology, 36*(1), 41–49.

Annie E. Casey Foundation. (2001). *Using the new racial categories in the 2000 Census.* Retrieved June 15, 2001, from the World Wide Web: **http://www.aecf.org/ kidscount/categories/counts.htm**.

Anonymous. (1996). An ex-wife talks about losing her transitioning husband. *TGGuide.* Retrieved June 15, 2001, from the World Wide Web: **http://www.tgguide.com/ Library/fromthewife.txt**.

APA Task Force on Diversity Issues at the Pre-college and Undergraduate Levels of Education in Psychology. (1998, March). Enriching the focus on ethnicity and race. *APA Monitor, 29*(3), 43.

Aponte, J. F., & Crouch, R. T. (1995). The changing ethnic profile of the United States. In J. F. Aponte, R. Y. Rivers, & J. Wohl (Eds.), *Psychological interventions and cultural diversity* (pp. 1–18). Boston: Allyn & Bacon.

Aponte, J. F., & Morrow, C. A. (1995). Community approaches with ethnic groups. In J. F. Aponte, R. Y. Rivers, & J. Wohl (Eds.), *Psychological interventions and cultural diversity* (pp. 128–144). Boston: Allyn & Bacon.

Aries, E., Oliver, R. R., Blount, K., Christaldi, K., Friedman, S., & Lee, T. (1998). Race and gender as components of the working self-concept. *Journal of Social Psychology, 138*(3), 277–290.

Arndt, B. (1993). Men under siege. *The Weekend Australian.* Retrieved October 27, 2000, from the World Wide Web: **http://www.vix.com/men/articles/siege.html**.

Arroyo, J. A., Westerberg, V. S., & Tonigan, J. S. (1998). Comparison of treatment utilization and outcome for Hispanics and non-Hispanic Whites. *Journal of Studies on Alcohol, 59*(3), 286–291.

Asakawa, K., & Csikszentmihalyi, M. (1998). The quality of experience of Asian American adolescents in academic activities: An exploration of educational achievement. *Journal of Research on Adolescence, 8*(2), 241–262.

Asscheman, H., Gooren, L. J., & Eklund, P. L. (1989). Mortality and morbidity in transsexual patients with cross-gender hormone treatment. *Metabolism: Clinical and Experimental, 38*(9), 869–873.

Associated Press. (1997, February 23). Black-White gap over O.J.'s guilt narrows. *USA Today.* **http://167.8.29.8/form/results/oj2_results.html**.

Atienza, A. A., Stephens, M. A. P., & Townsend, A. L. (2002). Dispositional optimism, role-specific stress, and the well-being of adult daughter caregivers. *Research on Aging, 24*(2), 193–217.

Atkinson, D. R., Morton, G., & Sue, D. W. (1998). *Counseling American minorities: A cross-cultural perspective* (5th ed.). Boston: McGraw-Hill.

Atwood, N. C. (2001). Gender bias in families and its clinical implications for women. *Social Work, 46*(1), 23–36.

Auster, C. J. (2000). *Masculinity and femininity in contemporary American society: A reevaluation using the Bem Sex-Role Inventory.* Retrieved May 26, 2001, from the World Wide Web: **http://www.findarticles.com/cf_0/m2294/2000_Oct/71966971/print.jhtml**.

Autier, P., Doré, J-F., Négrier, S., Liénard, D., Panizzon, R., Lejeune, F. J., Guggisberg, D., & Eggermont, A. M. M. (1999). Sunscreen use and duration of sun exposure: A double-blind, randomized trial. *Journal of the National Cancer Institute, 91*(15), 1304–1309.

Avakame, E. F., & Fyfe, J. J. (2001). Differential police treatment of male-on-female spousal violence. *Violence Against Women, 7*(1), 22–45.

Axelson, J. A. (1999). *Counseling and development in a multicultural society* (3rd ed.). Pacific Grove, CA: Brooks/Cole.

Ayerst Laboratories, Inc. (1988). Hormones: Dream goal or time bomb? Retrieved June 2000 from the World Wide Web: **http://www.tgguide.com/Library/bbs/hormoneb.txt**.

Ayonrinde, O. (1999). Black, White, or shades of grey: The challenges of ethnic and cultural difference (or similarity) in the therapeutic process. *International Review of Psychiatry, 11*(2–3), 191–196.

Azar, B. (1998). Sex differences may not be set at birth. *APA Monitor, 29*(10).

Baharudin, R., & Luster, T. (1998). Factors related to the quality of the home environment and children's achievement. *Journal of Family Issues, 19*(4), 375–403.

Balagopal, S. S. (1999). The case of the brown memsahib: Issues that confront working South Asian wives and mothers. In S. R. Gupta (Ed.), *Emerging voices: South Asian American women redefine self, family, and community* (pp. 146–168). Walnut Creek, CA: Altamira Press.

Barke, R. P., Jenkins-Smith, H., & Slovic, P. (1997). Risk perceptions of men and women scientists. *Social Science Quarterly, 78*(1), 167–176.

Barnhart, K. T., Freeman E. W., & Sondheimer, S. J. (1995). A clinician's guide to the premenstrual syndrome. *Medical Clinics of North America, 79*, 1457–1472.

Barrett, J. (1998). Psychological and social function before and after phalloplasty. *The International Journal of Transgenderism, 2*. Retrieved January 10, 2001, from the World Wide Web: **http://www.symposion.com/ijt/ijtc0301.htm**.

Baruth, L. G., & Manning, M. L. (1991). *Multicultural counseling and psychotherapy: A lifespan perspective.* Englewood Cliffs, NJ: Prentice-Hall/Merrill.

Baruth, L. G., & Manning, M. L. (1999). *Multicultural counseling and psychotherapy: A lifespan perspective* (2nd ed.). Upper Saddle River, NJ: Prentice-Hall/Merrill.

Beauchemin, K. M., & Hays, P. (1996). Sunny hospital rooms expedite recovery from severe and refractory depressions. *Journal of Affective Disorders, 40*(1–2), 49–51.

Beauchemin, K. M., & Hays, P. (1997). Phototherapy is a useful adjunct in the treatment of depressed in-patients. *Acta Psychiatrica Scandinavica, 5*(5), 424–427.

Beaver, B., & Tuck, B. (1998). The adjustment of overseas students at a tertiary institution in New Zealand. *New Zealand Journal of Educational Studies, 33*(2), 167–179.

Beech, H. (1999). Don't you dare list them as "other": Multiracial Americans seek full recognition. *U.S. News & World Report.* Retrieved June 11, 2001, from the World Wide Web: **http://www.usnews.com/usnews/issue/birace.htm**.

Belfiglio, V. J. (1986). Cultural traits of Italian Americans which transcend generational differences. In R. Caporale (Ed.), *The Italian Americans through the generations*. New York: Italian American Historical Association.

Bell, D. A. (1994). Are Asian Americans a "model minority"? In R. C. Monk (Ed.), *Taking sides: Clashing views on controversial issues in race and ethnicity*. Guilford, CT: McGraw-Hill/Dushkin.

Bem, S. L. (1974). The measurement of psychological androgyny. *Journal of Consulting and Clinical Psychology, 42*, 155–162.

Benrud, L. M., & Reddy, D. M. (1998). Differential explanations of illness in women and men. *Sex Roles, 38*, 375–386.

Berg, I. K., & Jaya, A. (1993). Different and same: Family therapy with Asian-American families. *Journal of Marital and Family Therapy, 19*(1), 31–38.

Berger, R., & Kelly, J. (1996). Gay men and lesbians grown older. In R. Cabaj & T. Stein (Eds.), *Textbook of homosexuality and mental health* (pp. 305–316). Washington, DC: American Psychiatric Press.

Bergesen, A., & Herman, M. (1998). Immigration, race, and riot: The 1992 Los Angeles uprising. *American Sociological Review, 63*(1), 39–54.

Bergman, R. L. (1973). A school for medicine men. *American Journal of Psychiatry, 130*, 663–666.

Bernal, G., & Flores-Ortiz, Y. (1982). Latino families in therapy: Engagement and evaluation. *Journal of Marital and Family Therapy, 8*(3), 357–365.

Berry, E. H., Shillington, A. M., Peak, T., & Hohman, M. M. (2000). Multi-ethnic comparison of risk and protective factors for adolescent pregnancy. *Child and Adolescent Social Work Journal, 17*(2), 79–96.

Berry, M. (1995). The experience of being a woman student. *British Journal of Guidance and Counselling, 23*(2), 211–218.

Bhattacharjee, A. (1999). The habit of ex-nomination: Nation, woman, and the Indian immigrant bourgeoisie. In S. R. Gupta (Ed.), *Emerging voices: South Asian American women redefine self, family, and community* (pp. 229–252). Walnut Creek, CA: Altamira Press.

Blakes, J. S. (1994). Bridging the gender gap: Self-concept in the middle grades. *Schools in the Middle, 3*(3), 19–23

Blank, S. (1998). Hearth and home: The living arrangements of Mexican immigrants and U.S.-born Mexican Americans. *Sociological Forum, 13*(1), 35–57.

Blumberg, R. L. (1991). Afterword: Racial ethnic women's labor: Factoring in gender stratification. In R. L. Blumberg (Ed.), *Gender, family, and economy: The triple overlap* (pp. 201–208). Newbury Park, CA: Sage Publications.

Blume, S. B. (1985). Group psychotherapy in the treatment of alcoholism. In S. Zimberg, J. Wallace, & S. B. Blume (Eds.), *Practical approaches to alcoholism psychotherapy*. New York: Plenum Publishing Company.

Bograd, M. (Ed.). (1991). *Feminist approaches for men in family therapy*. New York: Harrington Park Press.

Bolin, A. (1988). *In search of Eve: Transsexual rites of passage*. South Hadley, MA: Bergin & Garvey Publishers.

Bolin, A. (1994). Transcending and transgendering: Male-to-female transsexuals, dichotomy and diversity. In G. Herdt (Ed.), *Third sex, third gender: Beyond sexual dimorphism in culture and history*. New York: Zone Books.

Bollinger, D. (2001). *Normal versus circumcised: U.S. neonatal male incidence ratio.* A white paper on circumcision incidence in the United States. An original publication by the Circumcision Information Resource Pages. Retrieved June 9, 2002, from the World Wide Web: **http://www.cirp.org/library/statistics/USA**.

Boodoo, G., Bouchard, T., Boykin, W., Brody, N., Ceci, S., Loehlin, J., Perloff, R., Sternberg, R., & Urbina, S. (1995). *Intelligence: Knowns and unknowns.* Washington, DC: American Psychological Association.

Bornstein, K. (1994). *Gender outlaw: On men, women, and the rest of us.* New York: Routledge.

Bortz II, W. M. (2001). *Living longer for dummies.* New York: Hungry Minds.

Boutte, G. (1999). *Multicultural education: Raising consciousness.* Belmont, CA: Wadsworth.

Boyle, G. J., Svoboda, J. S., Price, C. P., & Tuner, J. N. (2000). Circumcision of healthy boys: Criminal assault? *Journal of Law and Medicine, 7,* 301–310.

Bradford, J., & Ryan, C. (1994). National lesbian health survey: Implications for mental health. *Journal of Consulting and Clinical Psychology, 62,* 228–242.

Brammer, R. (1994). *Interviews with Californians.* Unpublished manuscript.

Brammer, R. (1997). Interview with Cathy Harris. Unpublished manuscript.

Brannen, S. J., & Rubin, A. (1996). Comparing the effectiveness of gender-specific and couples groups in a court-mandated spouse abuse treatment program. *Research on Social Work Practice, 6*(4) 405–424.

Britt, D. (1994, March 15). Lights, camera, sad reaction. *Washington Post,* B01.

Brooke, J. (1998, April 9). Indians strive to save their languages. *The New York Times,* A1.

Brookeman, C. (1990). *The Native American Peoples of The United States.* Liverpool: American Studies Resources Centre.

Brooks, G. R. (2000). The role of gender in marital dysfunction. In R. M. Eisler & M. Hersen (Eds.), *Handbook of gender, culture, and health* (pp. 449–470). Mahwah, NJ: Lawrence Erlbaum Associates.

Brown, D. (1979). *Bury my heart at Wounded Knee: An Indian history of the American West.* New York: Holt, Rinehart & Winston.

Brown, L. W. (1994). *Subversive dialogues: Theory in feminist theory.* New York: Basic Books.

Bruch, H. (1993). *Eating disorders.* New York, NY: Basic Books.

Bryan, C. A. (1997). *Working moms turn traditional when they're home.* American Psychological Association. Retrieved August 1, 2000, from the World Wide Web: **http://www.apa.org/releases/dad.html**.

Bryant, A. (1977). *The Anita Bryant story: The survival of our nation's families and the threat of militant homosexuality.* Old Tappan, NJ: Fleming H. Revell.

Buchanan, C. M., Eccles, J. S., & Becker, J. B. (1992) Are adolescents the victims of raging hormones? Evidence for activational effects of hormones on moods and behavior at adolescence. *Psychological Bulletin, 111,* 62–107.

Buhrich, N. (1978). Motivation for cross-dressing in heterosexual transvestism. *Acta Psychiatrica Scandinavica, 57*(2), 145–152.

Buhrich, N. (1996). A heterosexual transvestite club. In R. Ekins & D. King (Eds.), *Blending Genders* (pp. 63–69). London: Routledge.

Bulik, C. M., Sullivan, P. F., Wade, T. D., & Kendler, K. S. (2000). Twin studies of eating disorders: A review. *International Journal of Eating Disorders, 27*(1), 2–20.

Bullough, V. L., & Bullough, B. (1993). *Cross dressing, sex, and gender.* Philadelphia: University of Pennsylvania Press.

Bunch, C. (1972). Lesbians in revolt: Male supremacy quakes and quivers. *The Furies: Lesbian/Feminist Monthly, 1*, 8–9.

Bunkley, D. T., Robinson, J. D., Bennett, N. E., Jr., & Gordon, S. (2000). Breast cancer in men: Emasculation by association? *Journal of Clinical Psychology in Medical Settings, 7*(2), 91–97.

Burgess, E. O., Schmeeckle, M., & Bengtson, V. L. (1998). Aging individuals and societal contexts. In I. H. Nordhus, G. R. VandenBos, S. Berg, & P. Fromholt (Eds.), *Clinical Geropsychology* (pp. 15–32). Washington, DC: American Psychological Association.

Buriel, R., & De Ment, T. (1997). Immigration and sociocultural change in Mexican, Chinese, and Vietnamese American families. In A. Booth & A. C. Crouter (Eds.), *Immigration and the family: Research and policy on U.S. immigrants* (pp. 165–200). Mahwah, NJ: Lawrence Erlbaum Associates.

Burke, L. K., & Follingstad, D. R. (1999). Violence in lesbian and gay relationships: Theory, prevalence, and correlational factors. *Clinical Psychology Review, 19*(5), 487–512.

Burnette, E. (1997). A psychologist seeks to overcome the language barriers he faced in high school by advocating for Ebonics. *APA Monitor*. Retrieved November 2000 from the World Wide Web: **http://www.apa.org/monitor/apr97/profile.html**.

Burney, J., & Irwin, H. J. (2000). Shame and guilt in women with eating-disorder symptomatology. *Journal of Clinical Psychology, 56*(1), 51-61.

Buschman, J. K., & Lenart, S. (1996). I am not a feminist, but . . .: College women, feminism, and negative experiences. *Political Psychology, 17*, 59–75.

Butler, R. N. (1993). Dispelling ageism: The cross-cutting intervention. *Generations, 17*(2), 75–78.

Bylsma, W. H., & Major, B. (1992). Two routes to eliminating gender differences in personal entitlement: Social comparisons and performance evaluations. *Psychology of Women Quarterly, 16*(2), 193–200.

Cabaj, R. P. (1996). Native Two-Spirit People. In R. P. Cabaj & T. S. Stein (Eds.), *Textbook of homosexuality and mental health* (pp. 103–620). Washington, DC: American Psychiatric Press.

Caetano, R., & Clark, C. L. (1998). Trends in alcohol-related problems among Whites, Blacks, and Hispanics, 1984–1995. *Alcoholism, Clinical and Experimental Research, 22*(2), 534–538.

Cameron, A. (1996). *Daughters of copper women.* Vancouver, BC: Press Gang Publishers.

Campbell, J. (1984). Abuse of female partners. In J. Campbell & J. Humphreys (Eds.), *Nursing care of victims of family violence.* Reston, VA: Reston Publishing Company.

Caputo, R. (2000). Race and marital history as correlates of women's access to family-friendly employee benefits. *Journal of Family and Economic Issues, 21*(4), 365–385.

Carroll, L., & Gilroy, P. J. (2002). Transgender issues in counselor preparation. *Counselor Education and Supervision, 41*(3), 233–242.

Carter, R. T., & Parks, E. E. (1996). Womanist identity and mental health. *Journal of Counseling and Development, 74*(5), 484–489.

Castellsagué, X., Bosch, F. X., Muñoz, N., Meijer, C. J. L. M., Shah, K. V., de Sanjosé, S., Eluf-Neto, J., Ngelangel, C. A., Chichareon, S., Smith, J. S., Herrero, R., Moreno, V., & Franceschi, S. (2002). Male circumcision, penile human papillomavirus infection, and cervical cancer in female partners. *The New England Journal of Medicine, 346*, 1105–1112.

Cecchin, M. L. (2001). Reconsidering the role of being a daughter of a mother with dementia. *Journal of Family Studies, 7*(1), 101–107.

Center for Mental Health Services. (2000). *Alternative approaches to mental health care.* Retrieved September 10, 2000, from the World Wide Web: **http://www.mentalhealth. org/publications//allpubs/ken98-0044/ken980044.htm**.

Centers for Disease Control and Prevention. (2000). National Center for HIV, STD, and TB Prevention, Division of HIV/AIDS Prevention—Surveillance and Epidemiology. Retrieved March 29, 2002, from the World Wide Web: **http://www. cdc.gov/nchs/products/pubs/pubd/hus/tables/2001/01hus053.pdf**.

Chadiha, L. A., Veroff, J., & Leber, D. (1998). Newlyweds' narrative themes: Meaning in the first year of marriage for African American and White couples. *Journal of Comparative Family Studies, 29*(1), 115–130.

Chafe, W. H. (1977). *Women and equality: Changing patterns in American culture.* New York: Oxford University Press.

Chan, S. (1991). *Asian Americans: An interpretive history.* Boston: Twayne Publishers.

Chandler, B. (1996). *Can religion change your sexuality?* Retrieved December 1999 from the World Wide Web: **http://www.cmhc.com/perspectives/articles/art07966.htm**.

Chandler, M. J., & Lalonde, C. (1998). Cultural continuity as a hedge against suicide in Canada's First Nations. *Transcultural Psychiatry, 35*(2), 191–219.

Chen, C., Greenberger, E., Lester, J., Dong, Q., & Guo, M-S. (1998). A cross-cultural study of family and peer correlates of adolescent misconduct. *Developmental Psychology, 34*(4), 770–781.

Chesler, P. (2001). *Woman's inhumanity to woman.* New York: Avalon Publishing Group.

Chodorow, N. (1978). *The reproduction of mothering.* Berkeley, CA: University of California Press.

Choi, K., Yep, G. A., & Kumekawa, E. (1998). HIV prevention among Asian and Pacific Islander American men who have sex with men: A critical review of theoretical models and directions for future research. *AIDS Education and Prevention, 10* (Supplement 3), 19–30.

Churchill, W., & LaDuke, W. (1992). Native North America: The political economy of radioactive colonialism. In M. A. Jaimes (Ed.), *The state of Native America: Genocide, colonization, and resistance.* Boston: South End Press.

Cimmarusti, R. A. (1999). Exploring aspects of Filipino American families. In K. S. Ng (Ed.), *Counseling Asian families from a systems perspective* (pp. 63–81). Alexandria, VA: American Counseling Association.

Clark, K. B., & Clark, M. K. (1947). Racial identification and preference in Negro children. In T. M. Newcomb & E. L. Hartley (Eds.), *Readings in social psychology* (pp. 169-178). New York: Holt, Rinehart, & Winston.

Coats, P. B., & Overman, S. J. (1992). Childhood play experiences of women in traditional and nontraditional professions. *Sex Roles, 26*(7-8), 261–271.

Coelho, R., Ramos, E., Prata, J., & Barros, H. (2000) Psychosocial indexes and cardiovascular risk factors in a community sample. *Psychotherapy & Psychosomatics, 69*(5), 261–274.

Cohen-Kettenis, P. T., & Gooren, L. J. G. (1999). Transsexualism: A review of etiology, diagnosis, and treatment. *Journal of Psychosomatic Research, 46*, 315–333.

Cohen-Kettenis, P. T., & van Goozen, S. H. M. (1997). Sex reassignment of adolescent transsexuals: A follow-up study. *Journal of the American Academy of Child and Adolescent Psychiatry, 36*(2), 263–271.

Coker, A. L., Derrick, C., Lumpkin, J. L., Aldrich, T. E., & Oldendick, R. (2000). Help-seeking for intimate partner violence and forced sex in South Carolina. *American Journal of Preventive Medicine, 19*(4), 316–320.

Colapinto, J. (1997, December 11). The true story of John/Joan. *The Rolling Stone,* 54–97.

Colasanto, D. (1989, October 25). Gay rights support has grown since 1982, Gallup poll finds. *San Francisco Chronicle,* p. A21.

Colby, A., & Kohlberg, L. (1987). *The measurement of moral judgment.* Cambridge, UK: Cambridge University Press.

Cole, H. W. (1877). *Saint Augustine: A poem in eight books.* Edinburgh: T. & T. Clark.

Cole, S. S., Denny, D., Eyler, A. E., & Samons, S. L. (2000). Issues of transgender. In T. Szuchman & F. Muscarella (Eds.), *Psychological perspectives in human sexuality* (pp. 149–195). New York: Wiley.

Collier, H. V. (1982). *Counseling women: A guide for therapists.* New York: Free Press.

Comas-Díaz, L., & Jacobsen, F. M. (1991). Ethnocultural transference and countertransference in the therapeutic dyad. *American Journal of Orthopsychiatry, 61,* 392–402.

Conlon, M. (1997). Sex change theories shaken by boy raised as girl. Reuters. Retrieved August 2000 from the World Wide Web: **http://www.christgen.org/reuters.txt**.

Constantino, G., & Rivera, C. (1994). Culturally sensitive treatment modalities for Puerto Rican children. *Journal of Consulting and Clinical Psychology, 54*(5), 639–645.

Cook, A., & Jordan, M. (1997). Explaining variation in income between Hispanic and white female-headed households in Washington. *Hispanic Journal of Behavioral Sciences, 19,* 433–445.

Cook, E. A., Jelen, T. G., Wilcox, C. (1993). Catholicism and abortion attitudes in the American states: A contextual analysis. *Journal for the Scientific Study of Religion, 32*(3), 223–230.

Cooke, P. (2002). Abuse and disabled children: Hidden needs . . .? *Child Abuse Review, 11*(1), 1–18.

Cooper, M. (2000, January 13). *Whites now minority of gay men with aids in U.S.* Reuters. Retrieved January 21, 2001, from the World Wide Web: **http://www.foxnews.com/fn99/health/011300/aids.sml**.

Copenhaver, M. M. (2000). Testing a social-cognitive model of intimate abusiveness among substance-dependent males. *American Journal of Drug and Alcohol Abuse, 26*(4), 603–628.

Cornwell, J. (1998). Do GPs prescribe antidepressants differently for South Asian patients? *Family Practice, 15*(Supplement 1), S16-S18.

Corrigan, P. W., River, L. P., Lundin, R. K., Wasowski, K. U., Campion, J., Mathisen, J., Goldstein, H., Bergman, M., Gagnon, C., & Kubiak, M. A. (2000). Stigmatizing attributions about mental illness. *Journal of Community Psychology, 28,* 91–102.

Costa, P. T., Jr., Yang, J., & McCrae, R. R. (1998). Aging and personality traits: Generalizations and clinical implications. In I. H. Nordhus, G. R. VandenBos, S. Berg, & P. Fromholt (Eds.), *Clinical Geropsychology* (pp. 33-48). Washington, DC: American Psychological Association.

Cowan, G., Martinez, L., & Mendiola, S. (1997). Predictors of attitudes toward illegal Latino immigrants. *Hispanic Journal of Behavioral Sciences, 19*(4), 403–415.

Coyle, A. (1993). A study of psychological well-being among gay men using the GHQ-30. *British Journal of Clinical Psychology, 32*(2), 218–220.

Coyne, J. C. (2002). Marital quality, coping with conflict, marital complaints, and affection in couples with a depressed wife. *Journal of Family Psychology, 16*(1), 26–37.

Crawford, M., & Unger, R. (2000). *Women and gender* (3rd ed.). Boston: McGraw-Hill.

Creighton, S., & Minto, C. (2001). Managing intersex. *British Medical Journal, 323*(7324), 1264–1265.

Cross, W. E. (1971). The Negro-to-Black conversion experience: Towards a psychology of Black liberation. *Black World, 20,* 13–27.

Cross, W. E. (1991). *Shades of Black: Diversity in African American identity.* Philadelphia: Temple University Press.

Cross, W. E. (1995). The psychology of nigrescence: Revising the Cross model. In J. G. Ponterotto, J. M. Casas, L. A. Suzuki, & C. M. Alexander (Eds.), *Handbook of Multicultural Counseling* (pp. 93–122). Thousand Oaks, CA: Sage.

Cross, W. E. (2001). Encountering nigrescence. In J. G. Ponterotto, J. M. Casas, L. A. Suzuki, & C. M. Alexander (Eds.), *Handbook of multicultural counseling* (2nd ed., pp. 30–44). Thousand Oaks, CA: Sage.

Croughan, J. L., Saghir, M., Cohen, R., & Robins, E. (1980). *A comparison of treated and untreated male crossdressers.* Feminet. Retrieved May 24, 2001, from the World Wide Web: **http://www.tgguide.com/Library/bbs/mcross.txt**.

Crouter, A. C., Head, M. R., Bumpus, M. F., & McHale, S. M. (2001). Household chores: Under what conditions do mothers lean on daughters? In A. J. Fuligni (Ed.), *Family obligation and assistance during adolescence: Contextual variations and developmental implication* (pp. 23–41). New York: Wiley.

Daly, M., & Wilson, M. (1990). *Homicide: Foundations of human behavior.* New York: Aldine de Gruyter.

D'Amico, M., Barrafato, A., Peterson, L., Snow, S., & Tanguay, D. (2001). Using theatre to examine children's attitudes toward individuals with disabilities. *Developmental Disabilities Bulletin, 29*(1), pp. 231–238.

Daniluk, J. C. (1996). When treatment fails: The transition to biological childlessness for infertile women. *Women and Therapy, 19*(2), 81–98.

Das, S. A. (2001). *What is yoga?* Retrieved December 13, 2001, from the World Wide Web: **http://www.indiadivine.com/yoga1.htm**.

Davis, C., Claridge, G., & Fox, J. (2000). Not just a pretty face: Physical attractiveness and perfectionism in the risk for eating disorders. *International Journal of Eating Disorders, 27*(1), 67–73.

Davis, L. A., & Winkleby, M. A. (1993). Sociodemographic and health-related risk factors among African-American, Caucasian, and Hispanic homeless men: A comparative study. *Journal of Social Distress and Homelessness, 2,* 83–102.

Davis, M. P. (1990). *Mexican voices, American dreams: An oral history of Mexican immigration to the United States.* New York: Holt.

Davison-Aviles, R. M., & Spokane, A. R. (1999). The vocational interests of Hispanic, African American, and White middle school students. *Measurement and Evaluation in Counseling and Development, 32*(3), 138–148.

DeAngelis, T. (1996a, October). Better research being done on gay men and lesbians: Past research has not adequately defined lesbian, gay male and bisexual groups. *APA Monitor.* Retrieved July 11, 2000, from the World Wide Web: **http://www.apa.org/monitor/oct96/improve.html**.

DeAngelis, T. (1996b, October). Data are emerging on the psychology of bisexuals: Researchers are finding out more about bisexual men and how to craft interventions for them. *APA Monitor.* Retrieved April 29, 1999, from the World Wide Web: **http://www.apa.org/monitor/oct96/improve.html**.

DeAngelis, T. (1997). Women unwittingly uphold wage gap between the sexes. *APA Monitor.* Retrieved March 1, 2001, from the World Wide Web: **http://www.apa.org/monitor/aug97/worth.html**.

Deater-Deckard, K., Dodge, K. A., Bates, J. E., & Pettit, G. S. (1998). Physical discipline among African American and European American mothers: Links to children's externalizing behaviors. *Developmental Psychology, 32*(6), 1–8.

Decade of the woman. (1992, December 31). *Providence Journal Bulletin,* p. A8.

Denny, D. (1997). *Transgendered youth at risk for exploitation, HIV, hate crimes.* Unpublished manuscript.

Denny, D., & Green, J. (1996). Gender identity and bisexuality. In B. Firestein (Ed.), *Bisexuality: The psychology and politics of an invisible minority* (pp. 84–102). Thousand Oaks, CA: Sage.

Depp, M. (2001, May 9). Studies conflict on whether homosexuals can change. Reuters. Retrieved December 8, 2000, from the World Wide Web: **http://dailynews.yahoo.com/h/nm/20010509/ts/life_gays_dc_1.html**.

Deuster, P. A., Tilahun, A., & South-Paul, J. (1999). Biological, social, and behavioral factors associated with premenstrual syndrome. *Archives of Family Medicine, 8,* 122–128.

Devji, M. S. (1999). The paradoxes of the Kama Sutra and the veil: Asian-Indian women and marital sexuality. In S. R. Gupta (Ed.), *Emerging voices: South Asian American women redefine self, family, and community* (pp. 169–192). Walnut Creek, CA: Altamira Press.

Devor, H. (1989). *Gender bending: Confronting the limits of duality.* Bloomington: Indiana University Press.

Dexheimer-Pharris, M., Resnick, M. D., & Blum, R. W. (1997). Protecting against hopelessness and suicidality in sexually abused American Indian adolescents. *Journal of Adolescent Health, 21*(6), 400–406.

Diamond, M. (1996). Prenatal predisposition and the clinical management of some pediatric conditions. *Journal of Sex and Marital Therapy, 22,* 139–147.

DiPlacido, J. (1998). Minority stress among lesbians, gay men and bisexuals: A consequence of heterosexism, homophobia, and stigmatization. In G. Herek (Ed.), *Psychological perspectives on lesbian and gay issues: Vol. 4. Stigma and sexual orientation: Understanding prejudice against lesbians, gay men, and bisexuals* (pp. 138–159). Thousand Oaks, CA: Sage.

Domar, A. D. (1997). Stress and infertility in women. In S. R. Leiblum et al. (Eds.), *Infertility: Psychological issues and counseling strategies. Wiley series in couples and family dynamics and treatment* (pp. 67–82). New York: Wiley.

Dörner, G., Geier, T. H., Athrens, L., Krell, L., Münx., G., Sieler, H., Kittner, E., & Müller, H. (1980). Prenatal stress as possible aetiogenetic factor of homosexuality in human males. *Endokrinologie, 75,* 205–212.

Dörner, G., Götz, F., & Docke, W. D. (1982). Prevention of demasculinization and the feminization of the brain in prenatally stressed male rats by perinatal androgen treatment. *Experimental Clinical Endocrinology, 81,* 88–90.

Dowling, C. (1994). *The Cinderella complex: Women's hidden fear of independence.* London: HarperCollins.

Draguns, J. G. (1989). Dilemmas and choices in cross-cultural counseling. In P. B. Pedersen, J. G. Draguns, W. J. Lonner, & J. E. Trimble (Eds.), *Counseling across cultures* (2nd ed., pp. 3–22). Honolulu: University of Hawaii Press.

Draper, T. W., & Gordon, T. (1984). Ichabod Crane, in day care: Prospective child care professionals' concerns about male caregivers. *Academic Psychology Bulletin, 6*(3), 301–308.

Dutton, M. (1988). Profiling of wife assaulters: Preliminary evidence for a trimodal analysis. *Violence and Victims, 3,* 5–30.

Dutton, S. E., Singer, J. A., & Devlin, A. S. (1998). Racial identity of children in integrated, predominantly White, and Black schools. *Journal of Social Psychology, 138*(1), 41–53.

Eccles, J. S. (1989). Bringing young women to math and science. In M. Crawford & M. Gentry (Eds.), *Gender and thought: Psychological perspectives* (pp. 36–58). New York: Springer-Verlag.

EchoHawk, M. (1997). Suicide: The scourge of Native American people. *Suicide and Life-Threatening Behavior, 27*(1), 60–67.

Eckman, M., Kotsiopulos, A., & Bickle, M. C. (1997). Store patronage behavior of Hispanic versus non-Hispanic consumers: Comparative analyses of demographics, psychographics, store attributes, and information sources. *Hispanic Journal of Behavioral Sciences, 19*(1), 69–83.

Edelman, H. (1995). *Motherless daughters: The legacy of loss.* New York: Dell.

Edleson, J., Eisikovitz, Z., & Guttman, E. (1985). Men who batter women: A critical review of the evidence. *Journal of Family Issues, 6,* 229–247.

Edmo, E. (1989, December 26). Finding the best of two worlds: Teaching children about prejudices. *Lakota Times.*

Edwards, R. (1996, September). Can sexual orientation change with therapy? APA ponders its stance on a therapy designed to convert gay men and lesbians into heterosexuals. *APA Monitor.* Retrieved May 10, 2000, from the World Wide Web: **http://www.apa.org/monitor/sep96/converta.html**.

Ehrenreich, B. (1999, March 8). The real truth about the female body. *Time Magazine, 153*(9). Retrieved August 15, 2000, from the World Wide Web: **http://cgi.pathfinder.com/time/magazine/articles/0,3266,20616-7,00.html**.

Ekins, R., & King, D. (1997). Blending genders: Contributions to the emerging field of transgender studies. *The International Journal of Transgenderism.* Retrieved July 16, 2000, from the World Wide Web: **http://www.symposion.com/ijt/ijtc0101.htm**.

Ekins, R., & King, D. (2001) Transgendering, migrating and love of oneself as a woman: A contribution to a sociology of autogynephilia. *The International Journal of Transgenderism, 5*(3), **http://www.symposion.com/ijt/ijtvo05no03_01.htm**.

Ellickson, P. L., Collins, R., & Bell, R. (1999). Adolescent use of illicit drugs other than marijuana: How important is social bonding and for which ethnic groups? *Substance Use and Misuse, 34*(3), 317–346.

Epiro, S. (1995). *Foetal Decision: Another side to choice.* Retrieved May 11, 2001, from the World Wide Web: **http://www.curtin.edu.au/curtin/guild/grok/grok95/vol27/9/abort.htm**.

Erikson, E. (1950). *Childhood and Society.* New York: Norton.

Esses, V. M., & Beaufoy, S. L. (1994). Determinants of attitudes toward people with disabilities. *Journal of Social Behavior and Personality, 9*(5), 43–64.

Estiritu, Y. L. (1999). Gender and labor in Asian immigrant families. *American Behavioral Scientist, 42*(4), 628–647.

Ettner, R. (1996). Confessions of a gender defender: A psychologist's reflections on life among the transgendered. Evanston, IL: Chicago Spectrum Press.

Evanzz, K. (1999). *The messenger: The rise and fall of Elijah Muhammad.* New York: Pantheon Books.

Eyler, A. E., & Wright, K. (1997). Gender identification and sexual orientation among genetic females with gender-blended self-perception in childhood and adolescence. *The International Journal of Transgenderism.* Retrieved May 11, 2001, from the World Wide Web: **http://www.symposion.com/ijt/ijtc0102.htm**.

Fagan, J., Stewart, D., & Hansen, K. (1983). Violent men or violent husbands? Background factors and situational correlates. In D. Finkelhor, R. Gelles, G. Hotaling, & M. Staus (Eds.), *The dark side of families* (pp. 31–67). Beverly Hills: Sage.

Falicov, C. J. (1998). *Latino families in therapy: A guide to multicultural practice.* New York: Guildford Press.

Farrer, P. (1996). In female attire. In R. Ekins & D. King (Eds.), *Blending genders* (pp. 9–26). London: Routledge.

Faulkner, A. H., & Cranston, K. (1998, February). Correlates of same-sex sexual behavior in a random sample of Massachusetts high school students. *American Journal of Public Health, 88*(2), 262–266.

Fausto-Sterling, A. (2000). *Sexing the body: Gender politics and the construction of sexuality.* New York: Basic Books.

Feinberg, L. (1996). *Transgender warriors: Making history from Joan of Arc to Ru Paul.* Boston: Beacon Press.

Feinbloom, D. H. (1976). *Transvestites and transsexuals: Mixed views.* New York: Delacorte Press/Seymour Lawrence.

Felson, R. B. (2002). *Violence and gender reexamined.* Washington, DC: American Psychological Association.

Fernandez, I., Carrera, P., Sanchez, F., Paez, D., & Candia, L. (2000). Differences between cultures in emotional verbal and nonverbal reactions. *Psicothema, 12,* 83–92.

Field-Belenky, M., McVicker-Clinchy, B., Rule-Goldberger, N., & Mattuck-Tarule, J. (1986). *Women's ways of knowing.* New York: Basic Books.

Fischer, P., Schwartz, M., Richards, J., Goldstein, A., & Rojas, T. (1991). Brand logo recognition by children aged 3 to 6 years: Mickey Mouse and Old Joe the Camel. *Journal of the American Medical Association, 3145–3148.*

Fisher, M. A. (1999, April 14). The color chasm. *The Columbus Dispatch.* Retrieved June 14, 2001, from the World Wide Web: **http://www.dispatch.com/news/special/race/day4/day4.html**.

Fitzgibbon, M. L., Spring, B., Avellone, M. E., Blackman, L. R., Pingitore, R., & Stolley, M. R. (1998). Correlates of binge eating in Hispanic, Black, and White women. *International Journal of Eating Disorders, 24*(1), 43–52.

Flaskerud, J. H., & Liu, P. Y. (1991). Effects of an Asian client-therapist language, ethnicity and gender match on utilization and outcome of therapy. *Community Mental Health Journal, 27*(1), 31–42.

Flint, A. J., Yamada, E. G., & Novotny, T. E. (1998). Black-White differences in cigarette smoking uptake: Progression from adolescent experimentation to regular use. *Preventive Medicine: An International Devoted to Practice and Theory, 27*(3), 358–364.

Flynn, C. P. (1998). To spank or not to spank: The effect of situation and age of child on support for corporal punishment. *Journal of Family Violence, 13*(1), 21–37.

Folkman, S., Chesney, M. A., Pollack, L., & Phillips, C. (1992). Stress, coping, and high-risk sexual behavior. *Health Psychology, 11*(4), 218–222.

Fontaine, J. H. (1998). Evidencing a need: School counselors' experiences with gay and lesbian students. *Professional School Counseling, 11*(3), 8–14.

Ford, C. Y., & Harris, J. J. (1995). Underachievement among gifted African American students: Implications for school counselors. *School Counselor, 42,* 196–203.

Ford, K., & Norris, A. E. (1993). Knowledge of AIDS transmission, risk behavior, and perceptions of risk among urban, low-income, African-American and Hispanic youth. *American Journal of Preventive Medicine, 9*(5), 297–306.

Ford, K., Rubinstein, S., & Norris, A. (1994). Sexual behavior and condom use among urban, low-income, African American and Hispanic youth. *AIDS Education and Prevention, 6*(3), 219–229.

Foss, G. F. (1996). A conceptual model for studying parenting behaviors in immigrant populations. *Advances in Nursing Science, 19*(2), 74–87.

Fouad, N. A. (2001). Reflections of a nonvisible racial/ethnic minority. In J. G. Ponterotto, J. M. Casas, L. A. Suzuki, & C. M. Alexander (Eds.), *Handbook of multicultural counseling* (2nd ed., pp. 55–63). Thousand Oaks, CA: Sage.

Fox, R. (1996). Bisexuality in perspective: A review of theory and research. In B. Firestein (Ed.), *Bisexuality: The psychology and politics of an invisible minority* (pp. 3–50). Newbury Park, CA: Sage.

Fox News Online. (1998, October 21). *Surgeon General unveils national suicide prevention strategy.* News America Digital Publishing, Inc. Retrieved October 15, 2000, from the World Wide Web: **http://www.foxnews.com:80/js_index.sml?content=/health/102198/suicide.sml**.

Fracasso, M. P., Lamb, M. E., Schoelmerich, A., & Leyendecker, B. (1997). The ecology of mother-infant interaction in Euro-American and immigrant Central American families living in the United States. *International Journal of Behavioral Development, 20*(2), 207–217.

Franchina, J. J., Eisler, R. M., & Moore, T. M. (2001). Masculine gender role stress and intimate abuse: Effects of masculine gender relevance of dating situations and female threat on men's attributions and affective responses. *Psychology of Men and Masculinity, 2*(1), 34–41.

Frank, R. A., & Kromelow, S. (1997). *Primary caregiving father families: Do they differ in parental activities?* Paper presented at the 105th Annual Convention for the American Psychological Association in Chicago, Illinois.

Freiberg, P. (1995, June). Gays and lesbians bore the brunt of hate violence in 1994 compared to their relative numbers in society. *APA Monitor.* Retrieved June 17, 2000, from the World Wide Web: **http://www.apa.org/monitor/jun95/hatea.html**.

Freud, S. (1905). Three essays in the theory of sexuality. In J. Strachey (Ed.), *The standard edition of the complete works of Sigmund Freud,* Vol. 7. London: Hogarth Press.

Freud, S. (1932). *Lecture XXXV: A philosophy of life.* Retrieved May 11, 2001, from the World Wide Web: **http://werple.net.au/~gaffcam/phil/freud.htm**.

Friedan, B. (1963). The sexual solipsism of Sigmund Freud. *The Feminine Mystique.* Retrieved December 8, 2000, from the World Wide Web: **http://werple.net.au/~lynnbea/lib/friedan.htm**.

Friends in Recovery. (1989). *The 12 steps for adult children from addictive and other dysfunctional families.* San Diego: Recovery Publications.

Fuligni, A. J. (1997). The academic achievement of adolescents from immigrant families: The roles of family background, attitudes, and behavior. *Child Development, 68*(2), 351–363.

Fuller, J. (1995). Getting in touch with your heritage. In N. Vacc, S. DeVaney, & J. Wittmer (Eds.), *Experiencing and counseling multicultural and diverse populations* (3rd ed., pp. 9–27). Bristol, PA: Accelerated Development.

Gabriel, K. (1998). *Gambling and spirituality: A new anthropological perspective.* Retrieved September 11, 2000, from the World Wide Web: **http://www.nmia.com/~kgabriel/myths.html**.

Galaif, E. R., Chou, C., Sussman, S., & Dent, C. W. (1998). Depression, suicidal ideation, and substance use among continuation high school students. *Journal of Youth and Adolescence, 27*(3), 275–299.

Gardner, R. (1998). *The parental alienation syndrome* (2nd ed.). Cresskill, NJ: Creative Therapeutics.

Gavora, J. (2001). *Tilting the playing field: Schools, sports, sex and Title IX.* San Francisco: Encounter Books.

Geffner, R., Bartlett, M. J., & Rossman, B. B. R. (1995). Domestic violence and sexual abuse: Multiple systems perspective. In R. Mikesell, D. D. Lusterman, & S. McDaniel (Eds.), *Integrating family therapy: A handbook of family psychology and systems therapy* (pp. 501–518). Washington, DC: American Psychological Association.

George, C. (1996). A representational perspective of child abuse and prevention: Internal working models of attachment and caregiving. *Child Abuse & Neglect, 20,* 411–424.

George, L. K., Larson, D. B., Koenig, H. G., & McCullough, M. E. (2000). Spirituality and health: What we know, what we need to know. *Journal of Social & Clinical Psychology, 19*(1), 102–116.

Giachello, A. L., & Belgrave, F. (1997). Task Group VI: Health care systems and behavior. *Journal of Gender, Culture, and Health, 2,* 163–173.

Gibson, M. A., & Ogbu, J. U. (1991). *Minority status and schooling: A comparative study of immigrant and involuntary minorities.* New York: Garland.

Gibson, R. L., & Mitchell, M. H. (2003). *Introduction to counseling and guidance* (6th ed.). Upper Saddle River, NJ: Pearson Education

Gil, A. G., Vega, W. A., & Biafora, F. (1998). Temporal influences of family structure and family risk factors on drug use initiation in a multiethnic sample of adolescent boys. *Journal of Youth and Adolescence, 27*(3), 373–393.

Gilligan, C. (1982). *In a different voice: Psychological theory and women's development.* Cambridge, MA: Harvard University Press.

Gil-Rivas, V., Anglin, M. D., & Annon, J. J. (1997). Patterns of drug use and criminal activities among Latino arrestees in California: Treatment and policy implications. *Journal of Psychopathology and Behavioral Assessment, 19*(2), 161–174.

Glazer, N., & Moynihan, D. P. (1970). Beyond the melting pot: Negroes, Puerto Ricans, Jews, Italians, and Irish of New York City. Cambridge, MA: M.I.T. Press.

Goldenberg, C. H. (1998). Methods, early literacy, and home-school compatibilities: A response to Sledge et al. *Anthropology and Education Quarterly, 19*(4): 425–432.

Goldwyn, R. (1998, July 21). Straight and narrow the only path? Many are questioning whether gay and Christian lifestyles can coexist. *Philadelphia Daily News.* Retrieved May 11, 2001, from the World Wide Web: **http://www.phillynews.com:80/daily_news/98/Jul/21/features/FCOV21.htm**.

Golombok, S., & Tasker, F. (1996). Do parents influence the sexual orientation of their children? Findings from a longitudinal study of lesbian families. *Developmental Psychology, 32*(1), 3–11.

Gondolf, E. (1988). Who are those guys? Towards a behavioral typology of men who batter. *Violence and Victims, 3,* 187–203.

Gondolf, E., & Foster, R. (1991). Preprogram attrition in batterer programs. *Journal of Family Violence, 6,* 337–349.

González de Alba, L. (1994, January 17). Todos somos blancos. *La Jornade,* 28–29.

Gonzalez-Ramos, G., Zayas, L. H., & Cohen, E. V. (1998). Child-rearing values of low-income, urban Puerto Rican mothers of preschool children. *Professional Psychology—Research and Practice, 29*(4), 377–382.

Gottman, J., Jacobson, N., Rushe, R., Shortt, J., Babcock, J., La Taillade, J., & Waltz, J. (1995). The relationship between heart rate reactivity, emotionally aggressive behavior, and general violence in batterers. *Journal of Family Psychology, 9,* 227-248.

Granello, D. H., & Wheaton, J. E. (2001). Attitudes of undergraduate students towards persons with physical disabilities and mental illness. *Journal of Applied Rehabilitation Counseling, 32*(3), 9–21.

Green, R. (1987). *The "sissy boy syndrome" and the development of homosexuality.* New Haven: Yale University Press.

Green, R. (1998). Transsexuals' children. *International Journal of Transgenderism, 2*(4). Retrieved May 11, 2001, from the World Wide Web: **http://www.symposion.com/ijt/ijtc0601.htm**.

Green, R., & Fleming, D. (1990). Transsexual surgery follow-up: Status in the 1990s. *Annual Review of Sex Research, 7,* 351–369.

Greene, R. R., Watkins, M., McNutt, J., & Lopez, L. (1998). Diversity defined. In R. R. Greene & M. Watkins (Eds.), *Serving diverse constituencies* (pp. 29–57). New York: Aldine de Gruyter.

Greenslade, L., Pearson, M., & Madden, M. (1995). A good man's fault: Alcohol and Irish people at home and abroad. *Alcohol and Alcoholism, 30*(4), 407–417.

Griesler, P. C., & Kandel, D. B. (1998). Ethnic differences in correlates of adolescent cigarette smoking. *Journal of Adolescent Health, 23*(3), 167–180.

Griesler, P. C., Kandel, D. B., Davies, M. (2002). Ethnic differences in predictors of initiation and persistence of adolescent cigarette smoking in the National Longitudinal Survey of Youth. *Nicotine & Tobacco Research, 4*(1), 79–93.

Gritz, E. R., Prokhorov, A. V., Hudmon, K. S., Chamberlain, R. M., Taylor, W. C., DiClemente, C. C., Johnston, D. A., Hu, S., Jones, L. A., Jones, M. M., Rosenblum, C. K., Ayars, C. L., & Amos, C. I. (1998). Cigarette smoking in a multiethnic population of youth: Methods and baseline findings. *Preventive Medicine: An International Devoted to Practice and Theory, 27*(3), 365–384.

Groth, A. N., & Birnbaum, H. J. (1978). Adult sexual orientation and attraction to underage persons. *Archives of Sexual Behavior, 7*(3), 175-181.

Gruber, R., Sadeh, A., & Raviv, A. (2000). Instability of sleep patterns in children with attention-deficit/hyperactivity disorder. *Journal of the American Academy of Child and Adolescent Psychiatry, 39*(4), 495–501.

Guild, P. (1994). The culture/learning style connection. *Educational Leardership, 51*(8): 16–21.

Gupta, S. R. (1999). Walking on the edge: Indian-American women speak out on dating and marriage. In S. R. Gupta (Ed.), *Emerging voices: South Asian American women redefine self, family, and community* (pp. 120–145). Walnut Creek, CA: Altamira Press.

Guthrie, S. R., & Castelnuovo, S. (2001). Disability management among women with physical impairments: The contribution of physical activity. *Sociology of Sport Journal, 18*(1), 5–20.

Gutierres, S. F., & Todd, M. (1997). The impact of childhood abuse on treatment outcomes. *Professional Psychology: Research and Practice, 28,* 348-654.

Gutmann, M. C. (1996). *The meanings of macho: Being a man in Mexico City.* Berkeley: University of California Press.

Haaken, J. (1990). A critical analysis of the co-dependency construct. *Psychiatry, 53*(4), 396–406.

Haaken, J. (1995). A critical analysis of the codependency construct. M. Babcock & M. C. McKay (Eds.), *Challenging codependency: Feminist critiques* (pp. 53–69). Toronto, ON, Canada: University of Toronto Press.

Haberman, M. A., & Michael, R. P. (1979). Autocastration in transsexualism. *American Journal of Psychiatry, 136*(3), 347–348.

Haley, A. (1976). *Roots.* Garden City, NY: Doubleday.

Hallinan, M. T., & Williams, R. A. (1989). Interracial friendship choices in secondary schools. *American Sociological Review, 54*(1), 67–78.

Hammelman, T. (1993). Gay and lesbian youth contributing factors to serious attempts or considerations of suicide. *Journal of Gay and Lesbian Psychotherapy, 2*(l), 77–89.

Hanna, F. J., Bemak, F., & Chung, R. C-Y. (1999). Toward a new paradigm for multicultural counseling. *Journal of Counseling and Development, 77,* 125–134.

Hao, L., & Bonstead-Bruns, M. (1998). Parent-child differences in educational expectations and the academic achievement of immigrant and native students. *Sociology of Education, 71*(3), 175–198.

Hare-Mustin, R. T. (1978). A feminist approach to family therapy. *Family Process, 17,* 181–194.

Harju, B. L., Long, T. E., & Allred, L. J. (1998). Cross-cultural reactions of international students to US health care. *College Student Journal, 32*(1), 112–120.

Harrison, J. (1987). Counseling gay men. In M. Scher, M. Stevens, G. Good, & G. A. Eichenfield (Eds.), *Handbook of counseling and psychotherapy with men.* Newbury Park: Sage.

Hart, J. (1978). *A Companion to California.* New York: Oxford University Press.

Hartmann, U., Becker, H., & Rueffer-Hesse, C. (1997). Self and gender: Narcissistic pathology and personality factors in gender-dysphoric patients. *The International Journal of Transgenderism, 1*(1). Retrieved December 8, 2000, from the World Wide Web: **http://www.symposion.com/ijt/ijtc0103.htm.**

Hartup, W. W., & Stevens, N. (1997). Friendships and adaptation in the life course. *Psychological Bulletin, 121*(3), 355–370.

Harway, M., & Evans, K. (1996). Working in groups with men who batter. In M. Andronico (Ed.), *Men in groups: Insights, interventions, and psychoeducational work* (pp. 357-375). Washington, DC: American Psychological Association.

Harwood, R. L., Schoelmerich, A., Schulze, P. A., & Gonzalez, Z. (1999). Cultural differences in maternal beliefs and behaviors: A study of middle-class Anglo and Puerto Rican mother-infant pairs in four everyday situations. *Child Development, 70*(4), 1005–1016.

Hawthorne, K. (1994). Accessibility and use of health care services in the British Asian community. *Family Practice, 11*(4), 453–459.

Headden, S. (1997). The Hispanic dropout mystery. *U.S. News & World Report, 123,* 64–65.

Hebl, M. R., & Heatherton, T. F. (1998). The stigma of obesity in women: The difference is Black and White. *Personality and Social Psychology Bulletin, 24*(4), 417–426.

Heller, K. A., & Ziegler, A. (1996). Gender differences in mathematics and the sciences: Can attributional retraining improve the performance of gifted females? *Gifted Child Quarterly, 40*(4), 200–210.

Helms, J. E. (1990). *Black and White racial identity: Theory, research, and practice.* New York: Greenwood Press.

Henderson-King, D., & Stewart, A. J. (1999). Educational experiences and shifts in group consciousness: Studying women. *Personality and Social Psychology Bulletin, 25*(3), 390–399.

Hendrick, B. (1997, May 20). Men need to face up to doctor visits. *The New York Times.* Retrieved May 11, 2001, from the World Wide Web: **http://www.coxnews.com**.

Hensing, G., Alexanderson, K., Akerlind, I., & Bjurulf, P. (1995). Sick-leave due to minor psychiatric morbidity: Role of sex integration. *Social Psychiatry and Psychiatric Epidemiology, 30*(1), 39–43.

Henss, R. (2000). Waist-to-hip ratio and female attractiveness. Evidence from photographic stimuli and methodological considerations. *Personality and Individual Differences, 28*(3), 501–513.

Herdt, G. H. (Ed.). (1982). *Rituals of manhood: Male initiation in Papua, New Guinea.* Berkeley: University of California Press.

Herek, G. (1991). Stigma, prejudice and violence against lesbians and gay men. In J. Gonsiorek & J. Weinrich (Eds.), *Homosexuality: Research implications for public policy* (pp. 60–80). Newbury Park, CA: Sage.

Herek, G. M. (1998). *Facts about homosexuality and child molestation.* Retrieved May 11, 2001, from the World Wide Web: **http://psychology.ucdavis.edu/rainbow/html/ facts_molestation.html**.

Herek, G. M., Gillis, J. R., Cogan, J. C., & Glunt, E. K. (1997). Hate crime victimization among lesbian, gay, and bisexual adults. *Journal of Interpersonal Violence, 12*(2), 195–215.

Herlihy, B., & Corey, G. (2001). Feminist therapy. In G. Corey (Ed.), *Theory and practice of counseling and psychotherapy* (6th ed., pp. 340–381). Belmont, CA: Wadsworth-Brooks/Cole.

Hernandez, F. (1997). Mexican gender studies and the American university. *American Behavioral Scientist, 40*(7), 968–974.

Hernandez, H. (1989). *Multicultural education: A teachers' guide to content and practice.* Upper Saddle River, NJ: Merrill/Prentice Hall.

Hernandez-Tristan, R., Arevalo, C., & Canals, S. (1999). Effect of prenatal uterine position on male and female rats' sexual behavior. *Physiology and Behavior, 67*(3), 401–408.

Herr, K. (1997). Learning lessons from school: Homophobia, heterosexism, and the construction of failure. In M. B. Harris, et al. (Eds.), *School experiences of gay and lesbian youth: The invisible minority* (pp. 51–64). New York: Harrington Park Press/The Haworth Press, Inc.

Herrnstein, R. J., & Murray, C. A. (1996). *The bell curve: Intelligence and class structure in American life* (2nd ed.). New York: First Free Press.

Herskovits, M. J. (1948). *Man and his works: The science of cultural anthropology.* New York: Knopf.

Hewlett, S. A. (2002). *Creating a life: Professional women and the quest for children.* New York: Talk Miramax Books.

Highleyman, L. A. (1993). *A brief history of the bisexual movement.* Retrieved May 11, 2001, from the World Wide Web: **http://www.ncf.carleton.ca/freenet/rootdir/ menus/sigs/life/gay/bi/bi**.

Hildebrand, V., Phenice, L. A., Gray, M. M., & Hines, R. P. (1996). *Knowing and serving diverse families.* Englewood Cliffs, NJ: Prentice-Hall.

Hintikka, J., Koskela, K., Kontula, O., & Viinamaeki, H. (2000). Gender differences in associations between religious attendance and mental health in Finland. *Journal of Nervous and Mental Disease, 188,* 772–776.

Hirschauer, S. (1997). The medicalization of gender migration. *The International Journal of Transgenderism, 2.* Retrieved December 8, 2000, from the World Wide Web: **http://www.symposion.com/ijtc0502.htm**.

Hirschfelder, A. (2000). *Native Americans.* London: Dorling Kindersley.

Ho, C. (1990). An analysis of domestic violence in Asian American communities: A multicultural approach to counseling. In L. Brown & M. Root (Eds.), *Diversity and complexity in feminist therapy* (pp. 129–149). New York: Harrington Park.

Hoellinger, F. (1991). Frauenerwerbstaetigkeit und Wandel der Geschlechtsrollen im internationalen Vergleich (Female employment and changing sex roles: An international comparison). *Koelner Zeitschrift Fuer Soziologie und Sozialpsychologie, 43*(4), 753–771.

Holcomb-McCoy, C. C. (2000). Multicultural counseling competencies: An exploratory factor analysis. *Journal of Multicultural Counseling and Development, 28*(2), 83–97.

Holden, C. (12 October 2001). General contentment masks gender gap in first AAAS Salary and Job Survey. *Science Magazine, 294*(554), 396–411. Retrieved October 17, 2002, from the World Wide Web: **http://recruit.sciencemag.org/feature/salsurvey/v294i5541p396.htm**.

Hooker, E. (1957). The adjustment of the male overt homosexual. *Journal of Projective Techniques, 21*(1), 18–31.

hooks, b., (1991). *Ain't I a woman: Black women and feminism* (2nd ed.). Boston: South End Press.

Horesh, N., Apter, A., Ishai, J., Danziger, Y., Michulincer, M., Stein, D., Lepkifker, E., & Minouni, M. (1996). Abnormal psychosocial situations and eating disorders in adolescence. *Journal of the American Academy of Child and Adolescent Psychiatry, 35*(7), 921–927.

Hornung, C. A., Eleazer, G. P., Strothers, H. S., III, Wieland, G. D., Eng, C., McCann, R., & Sapir, M. (1998). Ethnicity and decision-makers in a group of frail older people. *Journal of the American Geriatrics Society, 46*(3), 280–286.

House, J. D., & Keeley, E. J. (1995). Gender bias in prediction of graduate grade performance from Miller Analogies Test scores. *Journal of Psychology, 129*(3), 353–355.

Howard, C. (1991). Americans with Disabilities Act. *Journal of Gender Studies, 13,* 25–30.

Huang, A., & Oei, T. (1996). Behind the myth. *Teaching Tolerance, 5*(2), 56–57.

Huffcutt, A. I., & Roth, P. L. (1998). Racial group differences in employment interview evaluations. *Journal of Applied Psychology, 83*(2), 179–189.

Huh, N. S. (1997). Korean children's ethnic identity formation and understanding of adoption. *Dissertation Abstracts International, 58*(2), 586.

Hunt, D. D., & Hampson, J. L. (1980). Follow-up of 17 biologic male transsexuals after sex reassignment surgery. *American Journal of Psychiatry, 137,* 432–438.

Hunter, A. G., & Sellers, S. L. (1998). Feminist attitudes among African American women and men. *Gender and Society, 12*(1), 81–99.

Hurtado, M. T., & Gauvain, M. (1997). Acculturation and planning for college among youth of Mexican descent. *Hispanic Journal of Behavioral Sciences, 19*(4), 506–516.

Hussain, S., & Roberts, N. (1998). Psychiatric presentation of adolescent homosexuality. *Canadian Journal of Psychiatry, 43*(4), 420–421.

Ibrahim, F. A. (1985). Effective cross-cultural counseling and psychotherapy: A framework. *The Counseling Psychologist, 13,* 625–638.

Inderrieden, E. J., & Keaveny, T. J. (2000). Gender differences in pay satisfaction and pay expectations. *Journal of Managerial Issues, 12*(3), 363–379.

Interfaith Working Group. (1998, June). Religious marriage update. Retrieved February 2, 2001, from the World Wide Web: **http://www.libertynet.org/iwg/ktf.html**.

International Bill of Gender Rights. (1995, June). Proceedings from the Fourth International Conference on Transgender Law and Employment Policy (TRANS-GEN '95). Houston: International Conference on Transgender Law and Employment Policy.

Iritani, F., & Iritani, J. (1995). *Ten visits.* San Mateo, CA: Asian American Curriculum Project.

Ishii-Kuntz, M. (1997). Intergenerational relationships among Chinese, Japanese, and Korean Americans. *Family Relations: Interdisciplinary Journal of Applied Family Studies, 46*(1), 23–32.

Jackson, M. L. (2001). Multicultural counseling: Historical perspectives. In J. G. Ponterotto, J. M. Casas, L. A. Suzuki, & C. M. Alexander (Eds.), *Handbook of multicultural counseling* (2nd ed., pp. 3–16). Thousand Oaks, CA: Sage.

Jacobson, J. L. (1991). Gender bias causes poverty, population growth. Washington, DC: Worldwatch Institute. Retrieved February 15, 2001, from the World Wide Web: **http://english-www.hss.cmu.edu/feminism/gender-bias-causes-poverty.txt**.

Jacobson, N. S. (1993, October). Domestic violence: What the couples look like. Paper presented at the Annual Convention of the American Association for Marriage and Family Therapy, Anaheim, CA.

Jain, A. K., & Joy, A. (1997). Money matters: An exploratory study of the socio-cultural context of consumption, saving, and investment patterns. *Journal of Economic Psychology, 18*(6), 649–675.

Jang, M., Lee, E., & Woo, K. (1998). Income, language, and citizenship status: Factors affecting the health care access and utilization of Chinese Americans. *Health and Social Work, 23*(2), 136–145.

Jeffe, D. B. (1995). About girls' "difficulties" in science: A social, not a personal, matter. *Teachers College Record, 97*(2), 206–226.

Jenkins, C. N. H., McPhee, S. J., Bird, J. A., Pham, G. Q., Nguyen, B. H., Nguyen, T., Lai, K. Q., Wong, C., & Davis, T. B. (1999). Effect of a media-led education campaign on breast and cervical cancer screening among Vietnamese-American women. *Preventive Medicine: An International Devoted to Practice and Theory, 28*(4), 395–406.

Jenny, C., Roesler, T. A., & Poyer, K. L. (1994). Are children at risk for sexual abuse by homosexuals? *Pediatrics, 94*(1), 41–44.

Jensen, A. R. (1968). Social class, race and genetics: Implications for education. *American Educational Research Journal, 5*(1), 1–42.

Johnson, A. A. W. (1860, April 7). On an injurious habit occasionally met with in infancy and early childhood. *The Lancet, 1,* 344–345.

Johnson, D. (1994). Stress, depression, substance abuse, and racism. *American Indian and Alaska Native Mental Health Research, 6*(1), 29–33.

Johnson, S., & Jacob, T. (1997). Marital interactions of depressed men and women. *Journal of Consulting and Clinical Psychology, 65,* 15–23.

Jones, A., & Jacka, S. (1995). Discourse of disadvantage: Girls' school achievement. *New Zealand Journal of Educational Studies, 30*(2), 165–175.

Joseph, R. (2000). The evolution of sex differences in language, sexuality, and visual-spatial skills. *Archives of Sexual Behavior, 29*(1), 35–66.

Josephy, A. (1973). *Indian heritage of America.* New York: Knopf.

Jou, Y. H., & Fukada, H. (1997). Stress and social support in mental and physical health of Chinese students in Japan. *Psychological Reports, 81*(3, Part 2), 1303-1312.

Jouriles, E. N., & Norwood, W. D. (1995). Physical aggression toward boys and girls in families characterized by the battering of women. *Journal of Family Psychology, 9*(1), 69–78.

Jouriles, E. N., Norwood, W. D., McDonald, R., Vincent, J. P., & Mahoney, A. (1996). Physical violence and other forms of marital aggression: Links with children's behavior problems. *Journal of Family Psychology, 10*(2), 223–234.

Jung, M. (1998). Chinese American Family Therapy. *Treatment Today, 10*(1), 12–13.

Kakar, S. (1978). *The inner world: A psychoanalytic study of childhood and society in India.* Delhi: Oxford University Press.

Kalichman, S. C. (1998). *Understanding AIDS: Advances in research and treatment* (2nd ed.). Washington, DC: American Psychological Association.

Kamo, Y., & Cohen, E. L. (1998). Division of household work between partners: A comparison of Black and White couples. *Journal of Comparative Family Studies, 29*(1), 131–145.

Kanellos, N. (1994). *The Hispanic almanac: From Columbus to corporate America.* Mt. Kisco, NY: Visible Ink Press.

Kao, G., & Tienda, M. (1998). Educational aspirations of minority youth. *American Journal of Education, 106*(3), 349–384.

Kaplan-Sanoff, M., & Leib, S. A. (1995). Model intervention programs for mothers and children impacted by substance abuse. *School Psychology Review, 24*(2), 186–199.

Karney, B. R., & Bradbury, T. N. (1997). Neuroticism, marital interaction, and the trajectory of marital satisfaction. *Journal of Personality and Social Psychology, 72,* 1075–1092.

Kasten, W. C. (1992). Bridging the horizon: American Indian beliefs and whole language learning. *Anthropology and Education Quarterly, 23*(2), 108–119.

Katz, M. S. (1998). *American Psychiatric Association rebukes reparative therapy.* Retrieved June 2000 from the World Wide Web: **http://www.psych.org/**.

Kaufman, A. S. (1990). Assessing adolescent and adult intelligence. Boston: Allyn and Bacon.

Kaufman, A. S., & McLean, J. E. (1996). Profiles of Hispanic adolescents and adults on the Holland Themes and Basic Interest Scales of the Strong Interest Inventory. *Psychological Reports, 79,* 1279–1288.

Kauh, T. (1997). Intergenerational relations: Older Korean-Americans' experiences. *Journal of Cross-Cultural Gerontology, 12*(3), 245–271.

Kavanaugh, P. C., & Retish, P. M. (1991). The Mexican American ready for college. *Journal of Multicultural Counseling and Development, 19,* 136–144.

Kawanishi, Y. (1992). Somatization of Asians: An artifact of Western medicalization? *Transcultural Psychiatric Research Review, 29*(1), 5–36.

Keane, E. M., Dick, R. W., Bechtold, D. W., & Manson, S. M. (1996). Predictive and concurrent validity of the Suicide Ideation Questionnaire among American Indian adolescents. *Journal of Abnormal Child Psychology, 24,* 735–747.

Kelly, J. A., Hoffmann, R. G., Rompa, D., & Gray, M. (1998). Protease inhibitor combination therapies and perceptions of gay men regarding AIDS severity and the need to maintain safer sex. *AIDS, 12*(10), F91–F95.

Kennamer, J. D., Honnold, J., Bradford, J., & Hendricks, M. (2000). Differences in disclosure of sexuality among African American and White gay/bisexual men: Implications for HIV/AIDS prevention. *AIDS Education and Prevention, 12*(6), 519–531.

Key, F. L. (1997). Female circumcision/female genital mutilation in the United States: Legislation and its implications for health providers. *Journal of the American Medical Women's Association, 52,* 179–180.

Kim, H., Rendon, L., & Valadez, J. (1998). Student characteristics, school characteristics, and educational aspirations of six Asian American ethnic groups. *Journal of Multicultural Counseling and Development, 26*(3), 166–176.

Kim, S. C. (1985). Family therapy for Asian Americans: A strategic-structural framework. *Psychotherapy, 22*(2), 342–348.

Kim, W. J., Shin, Y., & Carey, M. P. (1999). Comparison of Korean-American adoptees and biological children of their adoptive parents: A pilot study. *Child Psychiatry and Human Development, 29*(3), 221–228.

Kim, W. J., Zrull, J. P., Davenport, C. W., & Weaver, M. (1992). Characteristics of adopted juvenile delinquents. *Journal of the American Academy of Child Adolescent Psychiatry, 31,* 525-532.

Kimball, M. M. (1995). *Feminist visions of gender similarities and differences.* New York: Harrington Park.

Kirschenbaum, R. J., & Reis, S. M. (1997). Conflicts in creativity: Talented female artists. *Creativity Research Journal, 10*(2–3), 251–263.

Kirschner-Cook, A., & Welsh-Jordan, M. (1997). Explaining variation in income between Hispanic and White female-headed households in Washington. *Hispanic Journal of Behavioral Sciences, 19*(4), 433–445.

Kitchener, K. S. (1984). Intuition, critical evaluation and ethical principles: The foundation for ethical decision in counseling psychology. *The Counseling Psychologist, 12*(3), 43–55.

Kitzinger, C. (2001). *Sexualities: Handbook of the psychology of women and gender* (pp. 272–285). New York: Wiley.

Kniffen, F. B., Gregory, H. F., & Stokes, G. A. (1987). *The historic tribes of Louisiana.* Baton Rouge: Louisiana State University Press.

Kogon, E. (1950). *The theory and practice of hell.* New York: Farrar, Straus.

Kohut, H. (1978). In P. Ornstein (Ed.), *The search for the self: Selected writings of Heinz Kohut, 1950–1978.* New York: International University Press.

Koss-Chioino, J. (1995). Traditional and folk approaches among ethnic minorities. In J. F. Aponte, R. Y. Rivers, & J. Wohl (Eds.), *Psychological interventions and cultural diversity* (pp. 145–163). Boston: Allyn & Bacon.

Kramer, B. S., Brown, M. L., Prorok, P. C., Potosky, A. L., & Gohagan, J. K. (1993). Prostate cancer screening: What we know and what we need to know. *Annals of Internal Medicine, 119,* 914–923.

Krause, I., Rosser, R. M., Khiani, M. L., & Lotay, N. S. (1990). Psychiatric morbidity among Punjabi medical patients in England, as measured by General Health Questionnaire. *Psychological Medicine, 20*(3), 711–719.

Krishnan, A., & Sweeney, C. J. (1997). Asian vs. non-Asian differences in achievement-related background variables of medical students. *Psychology and Developing Societies, 9*(2), 189–224.

Kuiper, A. J., & Cohen-Kettenis, P. T. (1998). Gender role reversal among postoperative transsexuals. *The International Journal of Transgenderism, 2.* Retrieved May 12, 2000, from the World Wide Web: **http://www.symposion.com/ijt/ijtc0502.htm**.

Kulik, L. (1998). Effect of gender and social environment on gender role perceptions and identity: Comparative study of kibbutz and urban adolescents in Israel. *Journal of Community Psychology, 26,* 533–548.

Kung, H. C., Liu, X., & Juon, H. S. (1998). Risk factors for suicide in Caucasians and in African-Americans: A matched case-control study. *Social Psychiatry, 33*(4), 155–161.

Kurdek, L. A. (1999). The nature and predictors of the trajectory of change in marital quality for husbands and wives over the first 10 years of marriage. *Developmental Psychology, 35*(5), 1283–1296.

LaFromboise, T. D., Trimble, J. E., & Mohatt, G. V. (1990). Counseling intervention and American Indian tradition: An integrative approach. *The Counseling Psychologist, 18*, 628–654.

Lahey, B. B., Gordon, R. A., Loeber, R., Stouthamer-Loeber, M., & Farrington, D. P. (1999). Boys who join gangs: A prospective study of predictors of first gang entry. *Journal of Abnormal Child Psychology, 27*(4), 261–276.

Lai, T. (1998). Asian American women: Not for sale. In M. L. Anderson & P. H. Collins (Eds.), *Race, class, and gender: An anthology* (3rd ed., pp. 209–216). Belmont, CA: Wadsworth.

Lamb, M. E. (1997). *The role of the father in child development* (3rd ed.). New York: Wiley.

Lang, P., & Torres, M. I. (1997–1998). Vietnamese perceptions of community and health: Implications for the practice of community health education. *International Quarterly of Community Health Education, 17*(4), 389–404.

Langman, P. F. (1997). White culture, Jewish culture, and the origins of psychotherapy. *Psychotherapy, 34*(2), 207–218.

Larzelere, R. E. (2000). Child outcomes of nonabusive and customary physical punishment by parents: An updated literature review. *Clinical Child and Family Psychology Review, 3*(4), 199–221.

Latz, S., Wolf, A. W., & Lozoff, B. (1999). Sleep practices and problems in young children in Japan and the United States. *Archives of Pediatric Adolescent Medicine, 153*, 339–346.

Law, C. K., & Schneiderman, L. (1992). Policy implications of factors associated with economic self-sufficiency of Southeast Asian refugees. In S. M. Maeda & R. B. Renuka (Eds.), *Social work practice with Asian Americans, Sage sourcebooks for the human services series, Vol. 20* (pp. 167–183). Newbury Park, CA: Sage.

Leaper, C., Anderson, K. J., & Sanders, P. (1998). Moderators of gender effects on parents' talk to their children: A meta-analysis. *Developmental Psychology, 34*(1), 3–27.

Lebowitz, B. D., Pearson, J. L., Schneider, L. S., Reynolds, C. F., III, Alexopoulos, G. S., Bruce, M. L., Conwell, Y., Katz, I. R., Meyers, B. S., Morrison, M. F., Mossey, J., Niederehe, G., & Parmelee, P. (1997). Diagnosis and treatment of depression in late life: Consensus statement update. *Journal of the American Medical Association, 278*(14), 1186–1190.

Lee, E. (1997a). Overview: Assessment and treatment. In E. Lee (Ed.), *Working with Asian Americans* (pp. 3–35). New York: Guildford Press.

Lee, E. (1997b). Chinese American Families. In E. Lee (Ed.), *Working with Asian Americans* (pp. 47–77). New York: Guildford Press.

Lee, G. R., Peek, C. W., & Coward, R. T. (1998). Race differences in filial responsibility expectations among older parents. *Journal of Marriage and the Family, 60*(2), 404–412.

Lee, S. M., & Fernandez, M. (1998). Trends in Asian American racial/ethnic intermarriage: A comparison of 1980 and 1990 census data. *Sociological Perspectives, 41*(2), 323–342.

Leeder, E. (1994). Treating abuse in families: A feminist and community approach. New York: Springer.

Lehr, U., Seiler, E., & Thomae, H. (2000). Aging in a cross-cultural perspective. In A. Comunian & U. P. Gielen (Eds.), *International perspectives on human development* (pp. 571–589). Lengerich, Germany: Pabst Science Publishers.

Leland, J., & Miller, M. (1998, August). Can gays convert? *Newsweek, 47–52*.

Leland, S. (1992). *Coming of age.* Retrieved September 23, 2000 from the World Wide Web: **http://www.earthcircle.org/sadiemoon.html**.

Lennon, S. J., Rudd, N. A., Sloan, B., & Kim, J. S. (1999). Attitudes toward gender roles, self-esteem, and body image: Application of a model. *Clothing and Textiles Research Journal, 17*(4), 191–202.

Lester, D. (1994). Suicide rates in Native Americans by state and size of population. *Perceptual and Motor Skills, 78,* 954.

Lester, D. (1996). American Indian suicide and homicide rates and unemployment. *Perceptual and Motor Skills, 83,* 1170.

Lester, D. (1997). Note on a Mohave theory of suicide. *Cross-Cultural Research: The Journal of Comparative Social Science, 31*(3), 268–272.

Lester, D. (1999). Native American suicide rates, acculturation stress and traditional integration. *Psychological Reports, 84*(2), 398.

Levant, R. F., & Philpot, C. L. (2002). Conceptualizing gender in marital and family therapy research: The gender role strain paradigm. In H. A. Liddle, R. F. Levant, D. A. Santisteban, & J. H. Bray (Eds.), *Family psychology: Science-based interventions* (301–329). Washington, DC: American Psychological Association.

Leveille, S. G., Guralnik, J. M., Ferrucci, L., Corti, M. C., Kasper, J., & Fried, L. P. (1998). Black/White differences in the relationship between MMSE scores and disability: The Women's Health and Aging Study. *Journals of Gerontology Series B— Psychological Sciences and Social Sciences, 53B*(3), 201-208.

Levinson, D. J. (1978). *The seasons of a man's life.* New York: Knopf.

Levinson, D. J. (1989). *Family violence in cross-cultural perspective.* Newbury Park: Sage.

Levinson, D. J. (1996). *The seasons of a woman's life.* New York: Knopf.

Lewis, E. W., Duran, E., & Woodis, W. (1999). Psychotherapy in the American Indian population. *Psychiatric Annals, 29*(8), 477–479.

Lichtenberg, P. A., Kimbarow, M. I., Morris, P., & Vangel, S. J. (1996). Behavioral treatment of depression in predominantly African American medical patients. *Clinical Gerontologists, 17,* 15–32.

Liem, R. (1997). Shame and guilt among first- and second-generation Asian Americans and European Americans. *Journal of Cross-Cultural Psychology, 28*(4), 365–392.

Light, R. J., & Smith, P. V. (1969). Social allocation models of intelligence: A methodological inquiry. *Harvard Educational Review, 39*(3), 484–510.

Lim, I. (1999). Korean immigrant women's challenge to gender inequality at home: The interplay of economic resources, gender and family. In L. A. Peplau & S. C. DeBro (Eds.), *Gender, culture, and ethnicity: Current research about women and men* (pp. 208–227). Mountain View, CA: Mayfield.

Lindsey, E. W., & Mize, J. (2001). Contextual differences in parent-child play: Implications for children's gender role development. *Sex Roles, 44,* 155–176.

Little, J. (2001). Embracing gay, lesbian, bisexual, and transgendered youth in school-based settings. *Child and Youth Care Forum, 30*(2), 99–110.

Litton, E. (2001) Voices of courage and hope: Gay and lesbian Catholic elementary school teachers. *International Journal of Sexuality and Gender Studies, 6*(3), 193–205.

Liu, L. L., Slap, G. B., Kinsman, S. B., & Khalid, N. (1994). Pregnancy among American

Indian adolescents: Reactions and prenatal care. *Journal of Adolescent Health, 15*(4), 336–341.

Locke, D. C. (1998). *Increasing multicultural understanding* (2nd ed). Newbury Park, CA: Sage.

Leo, J. (1996, May 13). Things that go bump in the home. *U.S. News and World Report,* 25.

Loeber, R., Green, S. M., Lahey, B. B., Frick, P. J., & McBurnett, K. (2000). Findings on disruptive behavior disorders from the first decade of the Developmental Trends Study. *Clinical Child and Family Psychology Review, 3*(1), 37–60.

Lomawaima, K. T. (1995). Educating Native Americans. In J. A. Banks & C. A. M. Banks (Eds.), *Handbook of research on multicultural education.* New York: Macmillian.

Lombardi, E. L. (1999). Integration within a transgender social network and its effect upon members' social and political activity. *Journal of Homosexuality, 37,* 109–126.

Lonegren, S. (1996). *Spiritual dowsing.* Glastonbury: Gothic Image.

Lorch, B. R., & Hughes, R. H. (1988). Church, youth, alcohol and drug education programs, and youth substance use. *Journal of Alcohol and Drug Education, 33*(2), 14–26.

Lovinger, R. J. (1996). *Religion and the clinical practice of psychology.* Washington, DC: American Psychological Association Books.

Lowy, F. H., & Kolivakis, T. L. (1971). Autocastration by a male transsexual. *Canadian Psychiatric Association Journal, 16*(5), 399–405.

Lu, Y., Yang, L., Lu, G., & Sun, Q. (1996). Mental status and coping style of infertile women. *Chinese Mental Health Journal, 10*(4), 169–170.

Lucal, B. (1995). The problem with "battered husbands." *Deviant Behavior, 16*(2), 95–112.

Lukianowicz, N. (1959). Transvestism and psychosis. *Psychiatria et Neurologia, 138,* 64–78.

Lutwak, N., Razzino, B. E., & Ferrari, J. R. (1998). Self-perceptions and moral affect: An exploratory analysis of subcultural diversity in guilt and shame emotions. *Journal of Social Behavior and Personality, 13*(2), 333–348.

Lynch, M. A., & Ferri, R. S. (1997). Health needs of lesbian women and gay men: Providing quality care. *Mental Health Net.* Retrieved February 2001 from the World Wide Web: **http://www.medscape.com/CPG/ClinReviews/1997/v07.n01/c0701. 2.lynch/c0701.2.lynch.html**.

Lytle, L. J., Bakken, L., & Romig, C. (1997). Adolescent female identity development. *Sex Roles, 37*(3-4), 175–185.

Maccoby, E. E. (1990). Gender and relationships. *American Psychologist, 45,* 513–520.

MacKenzie, G. O. (1994). *Transgender nation.* Bowling Green, OH: Bowling Green University Popular Press.

Mackey, W. C. (2001). Support for the existence of an independent man-to-child affiliative bond: Fatherhood as a biocultural invention. *Psychology of Men and Masculinity, 2*(1), 51–66.

MacPhee, D., Fritz, J., & Miller-Heyl, J. (1996, December). Ethnic variations in personal social networks and parenting. *Child Development, 67*(6), 3278–3295.

MADD. (1999, February 22). *New federal statistics show Native and Mexican Americans have highest rates for alcohol-related traffic deaths.* Retrieved May 22, 2001, from the World Wide Web: **http://www.tbhonline.com/cns/9902/990222native_mexican_ americans.htm**.

Madden, D. J. (1987). Psychotherapeutic approaches in the treatment of violent persons. In L. J. Roth (Ed.), *Clinical treatment of the violent person* (pp. 54–78). New York: Guilford Press.

Magdol, L., Moffitt, T. E., Caspi, A., Newman, D. L., Fagan, J., & Silva, P.A. (1997). Gender differences in partner violence in a birth cohort of 21-year-olds: Bridging the gap between clinical and epidemiological approaches. *Journal of Consulting and Clinical Psychology, 65*(1), 68–78.

Maguire, M. (1995). *Men, women, passion, and power: Gender issues in psychotherapy.* London: Routledge.

Manaster, G. J., Rhodes, C., Marcus, M. B., & Chan, J. C. (1998). The role of birth order in the acculturation of Japanese Americans. *Psychologia: An International Journal of Psychology in the Orient, 41*(3), 155–170.

Manly, J. J., Jacobs, D. M., Sano, M., Bell, K., Merchant, C. A., Small, S. A., & Stern, Y. (1998). Cognitive test performance among nondemented elderly African Americans and Whites. *Neurology, 50*(5), 1238–1245.

Mann, D. (1996, July 17). Gender wars at the office can be unhealthy. *Medical Tribune News Service.*

Mann, J. (1994). *The difference: Growing up female in America.* New York: Warner Books.

Marmor, J. (1965). *Sexual inversion: The multiple roots of homosexuality.* New York: Basic Books.

Martin, G. L. (1987). *Counseling for family violence and abuse.* Waco, TX: Word Books.

Martin, S. (1995). Practitioners may misunderstand Black families. *APA Monitor.* Retrieved January 7, 2001, from the World Wide Web: **http://www.apa.org/monitor/oct95/strength.html**.

Martini, M. (1996). "What's new?" at the dinner table: Family dynamics during mealtimes in two cultural groups in Hawaii. *Early Development and Parenting, 5*(1), 23–34.

Massey, D. S., & Denton, N. A. (1993). *American apartheid: Segregation and the making of the underclass.* Cambridge, MA: Harvard University Press.

Maton, K. I., Hrabowski, F. A., & Greif, G. L. (1998). Preparing the way: A qualitative study of high-achieving African American males and the role of the family. *American Journal of Community Psychology, 26*(4), 639–668.

Matsuoka, J. K., Breaux, C., & Ryujin, D. H. (1997). National utilization of mental health services by Asian Americans/Pacific Islanders. *Journal of Community Psychology, 25*(2), 141–145.

Mays, V. M., Chatters, L. M., Cochran, S. D., & Mackness, J. (1998). African American families in diversity: Gay men and lesbians as participants in family networks. *Journal of Comparative Family Studies, 29*(1), 73–87.

McCarn, S. R., & Fassinger, R. E. (1996). Revisioning sexual minority identity formation: A new model of lesbian identity and its implications for counseling and research. *Counseling Psychologist, 24*(3), 508–534.

McClain, E. (2001, May 31). New study sees AIDS rates jump. *Associated Press.* Retrieved June 4, 2001, from the World Wide Web: **http://dailynews.yahoo.com/h/ap/20010531/hl/cdc_aids.html**.

McCloskey, L. A. (1996). Socioeconomic and coercive power within the family. *Gender and Society, 10*(4), 449–463.

McCullough, M. E., Hoyt, W. T., Larson, D. B., Koenig, H. G., & Thoresen, C. (2000). Religious involvement and mortality: A meta-analytic review. *Health Psychology, 19*(3), 211–222.

McCunn, R. L. (1981). *Thousand pieces of gold: A biographical novel.* San Francisco: Design Enterprises of San Francisco.

McDonald, H. B., & Steinhorn, A. I. (1990). *Homosexuality: A practical guide to counseling lesbians, gay men, and their families.* New York: Continuum.

McFadden, J. (1999). *Transcultural counseling.* Alexandria, VA: American Counseling Association.

McFague, S. (1988). Models of God for an ecological, evolutionary era: God as mother of the universe. In R. J. Russell, W. R. Stoeger, & G. V. Coyne (Eds.), *Physics, philosophy, and theology: A common quest for understanding.* Vatican City State: Vatican Observatory.

McFalls, J. A., Jr., Halluska, M., & Gallagher, B. J. (1996). Preliminary results from a national survey of psychiatrists concerning the etiology of transsexualism. *Psychology, 33,* 12–15.

McFarlane, J., & Wiist, W. (1997). Preventing abuse to pregnant women: Implementation of a "mentor mother" advocacy model. *Journal of Community Health Nursing, 14*(4), 237–249.

McGinnis, J. R., & Pearsall, M. (1998). Teaching elementary science methods to women: A male professor's experience from two perspectives. *Journal of Research in Science Teaching, 35*(8), 919–949.

McQueeney, D. A., Stanton, A. L., & Sigmon, S. (1997). Efficacy of emotion-focused and problem-focused group therapies for women with fertility problems. *Journal of Behavioral Medicine, 20*(4), 313–331.

McRoy, R. G. (1994). Attachment and racial identity issues: Implications for child placement decision making. *Journal of Multicultural Social Work, 3*(3), 59–74.

Mental Health Net. (1996). *AIDS infections in young U.S. women fall in northeast.* Retrieved April 10, 2001, from the World Wide Web: **http://www.cmhc.com/articles/aids3.htm**.

Merchant, C. (1983). Mining the earth's womb. In J. Rothschild (Ed.), *Machina ex dea: Feminist perspectives on technology.* New York: Pergamon.

Methodist Health Care System. (2001). Prostate cancer statistics. Retrieved February 7, 2001, from the World Wide Web: **http://www.methodisthealth.com/Urology/MthTopics/prostat.htm**.

Mettlin, C., Jones, G. W., & Murphy, G. P. (1993). Trends in prostate cancer care in the United States, 1974-1990: Observations from the patient care evaluation studies of the American College of Surgeons Commission on Cancer. *A Cancer Journal for Clinicians, 43,* 83–91.

Meyer, I. (1995). Minority stress and mental health in gay men. *Journal of Health and Social Behavior, 7,* 9–25.

Meyer, W., Bockting, W., Cohen-Kettenis, P., Coleman, E., DiCeglie, D., Devor, H., et al. (2001, January-March). Harry Benjamin International Gender Dysphoria Association's Standards of Care for Gender Identity Disorders, Sixth Version. *International Journal of Transgenderism, 5,* 1. Retrieved May 2, 2002, from the World Wide Web: **http://www.symposion.com/ijt/soc_2001/index.htm**.

Mihalic, S. W., & Elliott, D. (1997). A social learning theory model of marital violence. *Journal of Family Violence, 12*(1), 21–47.

Mikulas, W. L. (2002). *The integrative helper: Convergence of Eastern and Western traditions.* Pacific Grove, CA: Brooks/Cole.

Miller, A. J., Bobner, R. F., & Zarski, J. J. (2000). Sexual identity development: A base for work with same-sex couple partner abuse. *Contemporary Family Therapy, 22*(2), 189–200.

Miller, B. (1979). Unpromised paternity: Lifestyles of gay fathers. In N. M. Levine (Ed.), *Gay men: The sociology of male homosexuality* (pp. 239–252). New York: Harper & Row.

Miller, D. G., & Kastberg, S. M. (1995). Of blue collars and ivory towers: Women from blue-collar backgrounds in higher education. *Roeper Review, 18*(1), 27–33.

Miller, D. H., Greene, K., Causby, V., White, B. W., & Lockhart, L. L. (2001). Domestic violence in lesbian relationships. *Women & Therapy, 23*(3), 107–127.

Miller, G. M., & Larrabee, M. J. (1995). Sexual intimacy in counselor education and supervision: A national survey. *Counselor Education and Supervision, 34*(4), 332–343.

Miller, L., Sung, S. H., & Seligman, M. E. P. (1999). Beliefs about responsibility and improvement associated with success among Korean American immigrants. *Journal of Social Psychology, 139*(2), 221–228.

Moisan, P. A., Sanders-Phillips, K., & Moisan, P. M. (1997). Ethnic differences in circumstances of abuse and symptoms of depression and anger among sexually abused Black and Latino boys. *Child Abuse and Neglect, 21*(5), 473–488.

Money, J. (1974). Two names, two wardrobes, two personalities. *Journal of Homosexuality, 1*, 65–70.

Money, J., & Ehrhardt, A. (1972). *Man and woman / boy and girl: Differentiation and dimorphism of gender identity from conception to maturity*. Baltimore: Johns Hopkins Press.

Moon, A. (1999). Elder abuse and neglect among the Korean elderly in the United States. In Toshio Tatara (Ed.), *Understanding elder abuse in minority populations* (pp. 109–118). Philadelphia: Brunner/Mazel.

Moore, K. A., Manlove, J., Glei, D. A., & Morrison, D. R. (1998). Nonmarital school-age motherhood: Family, individual, and school characteristics. *Journal of Adolescent Research, 13*(4), 433–457.

Morain, D. (2000, September 10). State baffled by casinos' check for $34 million gaming: Tribes send in the payment without a breakdown of what it's for. Critics say problem shows ambiguities in the law regulating gambling. *Los Angeles Times.* Retrieved September 11, 2000, from the World Wide Web: **http://www.latimes.com:80/news/state/20000910/t000085287.html**.

Morrongiello, B. A., & Dawber, T. (1999). Parental influences on toddlers' injury-risk behaviors: Are sons and daughters socialized differently? *Journal of Applied Developmental Psychology, 20*(2), 227–251.

Mortola, J. F. (1998). Premenstrual syndrome: Pathophysiologic considerations. *The New England Journal of Medicine, 338*(4), 256. Retrieved August 31, 2000, from the World Wide Web: **http://www.nejm.org/content/1998/0338/0004/0256.asp**.

Morton, S. B. (1998). Lesbian divorce. *American Journal of Orthopsychiatry, 68*(3), 410–419.

Moulton, P., Moulton, M., & Roach, S. (1998). Eating disorders: A means for seeking approval? *Eating Disorders: The Journal of Treatment and Prevention, 6*, 319–327.

Mueller, K. A., & Yoder, J. D. (1997). Gendered norms for family size, employment, and occupation: Are there personal costs for violating them? *Sex Roles, 36*(3-4), 207–220.

Muhammad, E. (1997). *The supreme wisdom* (Vol. 1). Atlanta, GA: MEMPS Publications.

Mukai, T., & McCloskey, L. A. (1996). Eating attributes among Japanese and American elementary school girls. *Journal of Cross-Cultural Psychology, 27*, 424–435.

Mulac, A., Seibold, D. R., & Farris, J. L. (2000). Female and male managers' and professionals' criticism giving: Differences in language use and effects. *Journal of Language and Social Psychology, 19*(4), 389–415.

Munoz, R. F., VanOss-Marin, B., Posner, S. F., & Perez-Stable, E. J. (1997). Mood management mail intervention increases abstinence rates for Spanish-speaking Latino smokers. *American Journal of Community Psychology, 25*(3), 325–343.

Munro, R. (1996, March 14). State of Washington Initiative 669. Retrieved June 27, 1999, from the World Wide Web: **http://www.leg.wa.gov/pub/billinfo/initiatives/ 650-674/initiative_669_031496**.

Murphy, B. C. (1992). Counseling lesbian couples: Sexism, heterosexism, and homophobia. *Counseling gay men and lesbians: Journey to the end of the rainbow* (pp. 63–80). Alexandria, VA: American Counseling Association.

Murray, B. (1996). Self-esteem varies among ethnic-minority girls. *APA Monitor.* Retrieved April 22, 2000, from the World Wide Web: **http://www.apa.org/ monitor/nov96/esteem.html**.

Murray, B. (1998). Survey reveals concerns of today's girls. *APA Monitor, 29*(10).

Myaskovsky, L., & Wittig, M. A. (1997). Predictors of feminist social identity among college women. *Sex Roles, 37*(11–12), 861-883.

Myerson, J., Rank, M. R., Raines, F. Q., & Schnitzler, M. A. (1998). Race and general cognitive ability: The myth of diminishing returns to education. *Psychological Science, 9*(2), 139–142.

Nagoshi, C. T. (1997). g–loadings and the nature and salience of intelligence in the Hawaii family study of cognition. *Cahiers de Psychologie Cognitive, 16*(6), 758-761.

Nahulu, L. B., Andrade, N. N., Makini, G. K., Jr., Yuen, N. Y. C., McDermott, J. F., Jr., Danko, G. P., Johnson, R. C., & Waldron, J. A. (1996). Psychosocial risk and protective influences in Hawaiian adolescent psychopathology. *Cultural Diversity and Mental Health, 2*(2), 107–114.

Nation of Islam. (1991). *The secret relationship between Blacks and Jews* (Vol. 1). Chicago: The Historical Research Department.

National Cancer Institute. (2001). *The prostate cancer outcomes study*. Retrieved February 7, 2001, from the World Wide Web: **http://rex.nci.nih.gov/massmedia/ pressreleases/prost_outcome.html**.

National Institutes of Health. (2001). *Changing adolescent smoking prevalence*. Retrieved April 10, 2002, from the World Wide Web: **http://cancercontrol.cancer.gov/tcrb/ monographs/14/index.html**.

Naylor, G. (1993). The myth of matriarch. In J. Madden & S. M. Blake, *Emerging voices: Readings in the American experience* (2nd ed., pp. 13–15). Fort Worth: Harcourt Brace.

Neff, J. A., & Dassori, A. L. (1998). Age and maturing out of heavy drinking among Anglo and minority male drinkers: A comparison of cross-sectional data and retrospective drinking history techniques. *Hispanic Journal of Behavioral Sciences, 20*(2), 225–240.

Neisser, U. (Ed.). (1998). *The rising curve: Long-term gains in IQ and related measures.* Washington, DC: American Psychological Association.

Neumeister, A., Praschak-Rieder, N., Hesselmann, B., Vitouch, O., Rauh, M., Barocka, A., & Kasper, S. (1997). Rapid Tryptophan depletion in drug-free depressed patients with seasonal affective disorder. *American Journal of Psychiatry 154*(8), 1153–1155.

Newport, F. (2001, June 4). *American attitudes toward homosexuality continue to become more tolerant.* Princeton, NJ: Gallup News Service.

Nguyen, H. H., Messe, L. A., & Stollak, G. E. (1999). Toward a more complex under-standing of acculturation and adjustment: Cultural involvements and psychoso-cial functioning in Vietnamese youth. *Journal of Cross-Cultural Psychology, 30*(1), 5–31.

Nicholson, B. L. (1997). The influence of pre-emigration and postemigration stressors on mental health: A study of Southeast Asian refugees. *Social Work Research, 21*(1), 19–31.

Nicolosi, J. (1991). *Reparative therapy of male homosexuality: A new clinical approach.* North Vale, NJ: Jason Aronson Publishers.

Nicolosi, J. (1997). *Healing homosexuality: Case studies of reparative therapy.* North Vale, NJ: Jason Aronson Publishers.

1927 Grand Council of American Indians. (2002). *Sacred Lands.* Retrieved March 23, 2002, from the World Wide Web: **http://www.sacredlands.org/problem.htm**.

Noel, R. C., & Smith, S. S. (1996). Self-disclosure of college students to faculty: The influence of ethnicity. *Journal of College Student Development, 37*(1), 88–94.

Noll, S. M., & Fredrickson, B. L. (1998). A mediational model linking self-objectifica-tion, body shame, and disordered eating. *Psychology of Women Quarterly, 22*(4), 623–636.

Nordhus, I. H., Nielsen, G. J., & Kvale, G. (1998). Psychotherapy with older adults. In I. H. Nordhus, G. R. VandenBos, S. Berg, & P. Fromholt (Eds.), *Clinical geropsychol-ogy* (pp. 289-311). Washington, DC: American Psychological Association.

Nordstrom, C. K., Dwyer, K. M., Merz, C. N., Shircore, A., & Dwyer, J. H. (2001). Work-related stress and early atherosclerosis. *Epidemiology, 12*(2), 180–185.

Novas, H. (1994). *Everything you need to know about Latino history* (2nd ed.). New York: Penguin.

Oetting, E. R. (1992). Planning programs for prevention of deviant behavior: A psy-chosocial model. In J. Trimble, C. Bolek, & S. Niemcryk (Eds.), *Ethnic and multicul-tural drug abuse: Perspectives on current research* (pp. 313–344). Binghamton, NY: Harrington Park.

O'Faolin, J., & Matines, L. (1973). *Not in God's image.* New York: Harper & Row.

Ogbu, J. U. (1990). Literacy and schooling in subordinate cultures: The case of Black Americans. In K. Lomotey (Ed.), *Going to school: The African-American experience* (pp. 113–131). Albany: State University of New York Press.

Ogden, J., & Elder, C. (1998). The role of family status and ethnic group on body image and eating behavior. *Source International Journal of Eating Disorders, 23*(3), 309–315.

Ohtake, N., Itoh, M., & Shioya, N. (1992). Postoperative disorders of augmentation mammaplasty by the injection method in Japan. In U. T. Hinderer (Ed.), *Plastic surgery 1992* (Vol. 2, pp. 677–678). New York: Elsevier.

Okakok, L. (1989). Serving the purpose of education. *Harvard Educational Review, 59*(4), 401–422.

Old Dog Cross, P. (1982). Sexual abuse, a new threat to the Native American woman: An overview. *Listening Post: A periodical of the mental health programs of Indian health services, 6*(2), 18.

Olson, J. E., Frieze, I. H., & Detlefsen, E. G. (1990). Having it all? Combining work and family in a male and a female profession. *Sex Roles, 23*(9–10), 515–533.

Ontario Consultants on Religious Tolerance. (1998a). *Southern Baptist Convention and Homosexuality.* Retrieved August 2000 from the World Wide Web: **http://www. religioustolerance.org/hom_sbc.htm**.

Ontario Consultants on Religious Tolerance. (1998b). *Genocide of gay and lesbian youth.*

Retrieved January 15, 2000, from the World Wide Web: **http://www.religioustolerance.org/hom_suic.htm**.

Ordonez, R. Z. (1997). Mail-order brides: An emerging community. In M. P. P. Root (Ed.), *Filipino Americans: Transformation and identity* (pp. 121–142). Thousand Oaks, CA: Sage.

Orenstein, P. (2000). Unbalanced equations: Girls, math, and the confidence gap. In R. Satow & G. Vastola (Eds.), *Gender and social life: A workbook* (pp. 149–152). Boston: Allyn & Bacon.

Ornduff, S., Kelsey, R., & O'Leary, D. (1995). What do we know about typologies of batterers? Comment on Gottman et al. *Journal of Family Psychology, 9,* 249–252.

Osborne, J. W. (1998). Race and academic disidentification. *Journal of Educational Psychology, 89*(4).

Ottavi, T. M., Pope-Davis, D. B., & Dings, J. G. (1994). Relationship between White racial identity attitudes and self-reported multicultural counseling competencies. *Journal of Counseling Psychology, 41*(2), 149–154.

Owen, L. (1993). *Her blood is gold: Celebrating the power of menstruation.* San Francisco: Harper & Row.

Padilla, Y. C. (1997). Determinants of Hispanic poverty in the course of the transition to adulthood. *Hispanic Journal of Behavioral Sciences, 19,* 416–432.

Pang, K. U. (1995). A cross-cultural understanding of depression among elderly Korean immigrants: Prevalence, symptoms, and diagnosis. *Clinical Gerontologists, 15,* 3–20.

Park, A. (1999, March). Diagnosis: Female. *Time Magazine, 153*(9). Retrieved May 11, 2001, from the World Wide Web: **http://cgi.pathfinder.com/time/magazine/articles/0,3266,20620-2,00.html**.

Parker, W. M., Howard-Hamilton, M., & Parham, G. (1998). Counseling interventions with African American males. In W. M. Parker (Ed.), *Consciousness-raising: A primer for multicultural counseling* (2nd ed., pp. 147–175). Springfield, IL: Charles C. Thomas.

Paschall, M. J., & Hubbard, M. L. (1998). Effects of neighborhood and family stressors on African American male adolescents' self-worth and propensity for violent behavior. *Journal of Consulting and Clinical Psychology, 66*(5), 825–831.

Passano, P. (1995). Taking care of one's own: A conversation with Shamita Das Dasgupta. *Manushi Magazine, 89,* 17–26.

Pedersen, P. (2000). *A handbook for developing multicultural awareness* (3rd ed.). Alexandria, VA: American Counseling Association.

Peirce, K. (1993). Socialization of teenage girls through teen-magazine fiction: The making of a new woman or an old lady? *Sex Roles, 29*(1–2), 59–68.

Pence, E., & Paymar, M. (1990). *Power and control, tactics of men who batter: An educational curriculum.* Duluth, MN: Minnesota Program Development.

Peterson, J. V., & Nisenholz, B. (1987). *Orientation to counseling.* Boston: Allyn & Bacon.

Philpot, C. L., Brooks, G. R., Lusterman, D. D., & Nutt, R. L. (1997). *Bridging separate gender worlds: Why men and women clash and how therapists can bring them together.* Washington, DC: American Psychological Association.

Phinney, J. S., Ferguson, D. L., & Tate, J. D. (1997) Intergroup attitudes among ethnic minority adolescents: A causal model. *Child Development, 68*(5), 955–969.

Phipps, E., Cohen, M. H., Sorn, R., & Braitman, L. E. (1999). A pilot study of cancer knowledge and screening behaviors of Vietnamese and Cambodian women. *Health Care for Women International, 20*(2), 195–207.

Pilling, A. R. (1997). Cross-dressing and shamanism among selected western and North American tribes. In S. E. Jacobs, W. Thomas, & S. Lang (Eds.), *Two-spirit people: Native American gender identity, sexuality, and spirituality* (pp. 67–99). Chicago: University of Illinois Press.

Pinderhughes, E., Dodge, K., Bates, J., Pettit, G., & Zelli, A. (2000). Discipline responses: Influences of parents' socioeconomic status, ethnicity, beliefs about parenting, stress, and cognitive-emotional processes. *Journal of Family Psychology, 14*(3), 380–400.

Piotrkowski, C. S. (1998). Gender harassment, job satisfaction, and distress among employed White and minority women. *Journal of Occupational Health Psychology, 3*(1), 33–43.

Plaskow, J. (2001). Setting the problem, laying the ground. R. Satow (Ed.), *Gender and social life* (pp. 239–244). Boston: Allyn & Bacon.

Polednak, A. P. (1997). Gender and acculturation in relation to alcohol use among Hispanic (Latino) adults in two areas of the northeastern United States. *Substance Use and Misuse, 32*(11), 1513–1524.

Pollack, W. S. (1999). *Real boys: Rescuing our sons from the myths of boyhood.* New York: Holt.

Pope, M. (1995). The "salad bowl" is big enough for us all: An argument for the inclusion of lesbians and gay men in any definition of multiculturalism. *Journal of Counseling and Development, 73*(3), 301–304.

Powell-Hopson, D., & Derek, S. (1988). Implications of doll color preferences among Black preschool children and White preschool children. *Journal of Black Psychology, 14*(2) 57–63.

Prathikanti, S. (1997). East Indian American families. In E. Lee (Ed.), *Working with Asian Americans* (pp. 79–99). New York: Guildford Press.

Prince, V. (1976). *Understanding cross dressing.* Los Angeles: Chevalier.

Rabinowitz, N. S. (2002). Introduction. In N. S. Rabinowitz & L. Auanger (Eds.), *Among women: From the homosocial to the homoerotic in the ancient world* (pp. 1–24). Austin: University of Texas Press.

Rabkin, J., & Struening, E. L. (1976). *Ethnicity, social class and mental illness.* (Paper Series no. 17). New York: Institute of Pluralism and Group Identity.

Randall, W., Sobsey, D., & Parrila, R. (2001). Ethnicity, disability, and risk for abuse. *Developmental Disabilities Bulletin, 29*(1), 60–80.

Rector, F. (1981). *The Nazi extermination of homosexuals.* New York: Stein and Day.

Reed, M. K., McLeod, S., Randall, Y., & Walker, B. (1996). Depressive symptoms in African American women. *Journal of Multicultural Counseling and Development, 24*, 6–14.

Regan, P. C. (1996). Sexual outcasts: The perceived impact of body weight and gender on sexuality. *Journal of Applied Social Psychology, 26*(20), 1803–1815.

Religious institutions play a central role in African-American life. (1996). *APA Monitor.* Retrieved May 11, 2001, from the World Wide Web: **http://www.apa.org/monitor/aug96/faithb.html**.

Remafedi, G. (1999). Sexual orientation and youth suicide. *Journal of the American Medical Association, 282*(13), 1291–1292.

Rennison, C. M. (2000). *Crime Victimization 1999.* U.S. Department of Justice. NCJ 182734. Retrieved September 11, 2000, from the World Wide Web: **http://www.ojp.usdoj.gov/bjs/pub/pdf/cv99.pdf**.

Resnick, J. L. (2001). From hate to healing: Sexual assault recovery. *Journal of College Student Psychotherapy, 16*(1-2), 43–63.

Resnicow, K., Futterman, R., Weston, R. E., Royce, J., et al. (1996). Smoking prevalence in Harlem, New York. *American Journal of Health Promotion, 10*(5), 343–346.

Retish, P. M., & Kavanaugh, P. C. (1992). Myth: America's public schools are educating Mexican American students. *Journal of Multicultural Counseling and Development, 20,* 89–96.

Reuters Health Information. (2000). Long-term breastfeeding lowers breast cancer risk. Based on a study reported in the *American Journal of Epidemiology, 152,* 1129–1135. Retrieved June 5, 2002, from the World Wide Web: **http://www.cancerpage.com/cancernews/cancernews2291.htm**.

Rey, A. M., & Gibson, P. R. (1997). Beyond high school: Heterosexuals' self-reported anti-gay/lesbian behaviors and attitudes. In Mary Bierman Harris et al. (Eds.), *School experiences of gay and lesbian youth: The invisible minority* (pp. 65–84). New York: Harrington Park/Haworth.

Rice, F. P. (2001). *Human development: A life-span approach* (4th ed). Upper Saddle River, NJ: Prentice Hall.

Richman, C. L., Bovelsky, S., Kroovand, N., Vacca, J., & West, T. (1997). Racism 102: The classroom. *Journal of Black Psychology, 23*(4), 378–387.

Ridley, C. R. (1989). Racism in counseling as an adversive behavior process. In P. B. Pedersen, J. G. Draguns, W. J. Lonner, & J. E. Trimble (Eds.), *Counseling across cultures* (2nd ed., pp. 55–78). Honolulu: University of Hawaii Press.

Riley, L. (2002). You can't always get what you want—Infant care preferences and use among employed mothers. *Journal of Marriage & Family, 64*(1), 2–15.

Rivers, R. Y. (1995). Clinical issues and intervention with ethnic minority women. In J. F. Aponte, R. Y. Rivers, & J. Wohl (Eds.), *Psychological interventions and cultural diversity* (pp. 181–198). Boston: Allyn & Bacon.

Robertson, D. (1997). I ask you to listen to who I am. In S. E. Jacobs, W. Thomas, & S. Lang (Eds.), *Two-spirit people: Native American gender identity, sexuality, and spirituality* (pp. 228–235). Chicago: University of Illinois Press.

Robertson, J. M., & Verschelden, C. (1993). Voluntary male homemakers and female providers: Reported experiences and perceived social reactions. *Journal of Men's Studies, 1*(4), 383–402.

Rodkin, P. C., Farmer, T. W., Pearl, R., & Van Acker, R. (2000). Heterogeneity of popular boys: Antisocial and prosocial configurations. *Developmental Psychology, 36*(1), 14–24.

Rogers, R. G., Hummer, R. A., Nam, C. B., & Peters, K. (1996). Demographic, socioeconomic, and behavioral factors affecting ethnic mortality by cause. *Social Forces, 74*(4), 1419–1438.

Roscoe, W. (1987). Bibliography of berdache and alternative gender roles among American Indians. *Journal of Homosexuality, 14,* 81–171.

Roscoe, W. (1994). *Priests of the goddess: Gender transgression in the Ancient World.* Presented at the 109th Annual Meeting of the American Historical Association, San Francisco, CA.

Rose, A. J., & Asher, S. R. (2000). Children's friendships. In C. Hendrick & S. S. Hendrick, et al. (Eds.), *Close relationships: A sourcebook* (pp. 47–57). Thousand Oaks, CA: Sage.

Ross, M. W. (1990). The relationship between life events and mental health in homosexual men. *Journal of Clinical Psychology, 46*(4), 402–411.

Ross, S. M. (1996). Risk of physical abuse to children of spouse abusing parents. *Child Abuse and Neglect, 20*(7), 589–598.

Rotheram-Borus, M. J., Meyer-Bahlburg, H. F., Rosario, M., Koopman, C., et al. (1992). Lifetime sexual behaviors among predominantly minority male runaways and gay/bisexual adolescents in New York City. *AIDS Education and Prevention,* 34–42.

Ruiz, A. S. (1990). Ethnic identity: Crisis and resolution. *Journal of Multicultural Counseling and Development, 18,* 29-40.

Rusbult, C. E., & Martz, J. M. (1995). Remaining in an abusive relationship: An investment model analysis of nonvoluntary dependence. *Personality and Social Psychology Bulletin, 21*(6), 558–571.

Rushton, A., & Minnis, H. (1997). Annotation: Transracial family placements. *Journal of Child Psychology and Psychiatry, 38,* 147–159.

Russell, G. L., Fujino, D. C., Sue, S., Cheung, M-K., & Snowden, L. R. (1996). The effects of therapist-client ethnic match in the assessment of mental health functioning. *Journal of Cross-Cultural Psychology, 27*(5), 598–615.

Russo, N., & Dabul, A. (1997). The relationship of abortion to well-being: Do race and religion make a difference? *Professional Psychology: Research and Practice, 28*(1), 23–31.

Rybicki, L. (1997). Strong women alone. *VOW Journal.* Retrieved June 28, 2000, from the World Wide Web: **http://www.voiceofwomen.com/strongwomen.html**.

Saad, L. (2001). *Women see room for improvement in job equity but are generally satisfied with their lives. Poll Analysis.* The Gallup Organization. Retrieved August 2001 from the World Wide Web: **http://www.gallup.com/poll/releases/pr010629.asp**.

Saccuzzo, D. P., Johnson, N. E., & Russell, G. (1992). Verbal versus performance IQs for gifted African-American, Caucasian, Filipino, and Hispanic children. *Psychological Assessment, 4*(2), 239–244.

Sadker, M., & Sadker, D. (1994). *Failing at fairness: How America's schools cheat girls* (2nd ed.). New York: Scribner.

Saenger, G. (1963). Male and female relations in the American comic strips. In M. White & R. H. Abel (Eds.), *The funnies: An American idiom* (pp. 219–223). Glencoe, IL: Free Press.

Sales, J. (1995). Children of a transsexual father: A successful intervention. *European Child and Adolescent Psychiatry, 4,* 136–139.

Saltus, R. A. (1997, January 13). Breast cancer: The risk factors. *The Boston Globe.* Retrieved September 9, 2000, from the World Wide Web: **http://www.globe.com**.

Sanchez-Martin, J. R., Fano, E., Ahedo, L., Cardas, J., Brain, P. F., & Azpiroz, A. (2000). Relating testosterone levels and free play social behavior in male and female preschool children. *Psychoneuroendocrinology, 25*(8), 773–783.

Sanders-Phillips, K. (1996). The ecology of urban violence: Its relationship to health promotion behaviors in low-income Black and Latino communities. *American Journal of Health Promotion, 10*(4), 308–317.

Sanftner, J. L., Barlow, D., Hill, D., Marschall, D. E., & Tangney, J. (1995). The relation of shame and guilt to eating disorder symptomatology. *Journal of Social and Clinical Psychology, 14*(4), 315–324.

Sauerman, T. (1995). *A note for children thinking about telling their parents they are gay.* Titusville, NJ: PFLAG Philadelphia. Retrieved June 2000 from the World Wide Web: **http://www.libertynet.org/~pflag/brochure.html**.

Savina dot com. (1998). FAQ: Hormone therapy for F2M transsexuals. Retrieved April 2, 2001, from the World Wide Web: **http://www.savina.com/confluence/hormone/f2m/Hypertext**.

Schell, N. J., & Weisfeld, C. C. (1999). Marital power dynamics: A Darwinian perspective. In D. R. Wilson, D. Smillie, J. M. G. Dennen, & J. Van Dennen, *The Darwinian heritage and sociobiology* (pp. 253–259). Westport, CT: Greenwood Publishing Group.

Schmidt, P. J., Nieman, L. K., Danaceau, M. A., Adams, L. F., & Rubinow, D. R. (1998). Differential behavioral effects of gonadal steroids in women with and in those without premenstrual syndrome. *New England Journal of Medicine, 338*(4), 209–216.

Schmitt, E. (2001, April 4). Analysis of census finds segregation along with diversity. *New York Times.* Retrieved June 2, 2001, from the World Wide Web: **http://www.nytimes.com/2001/04/04/national/04CENS.html**.

Schneider, K. T., Fitzgerald, L. F., & Swan, S. (1997). Job-related and psychological effects of sexual harassment in the workplace: Empirical evidence from two organizations. *Journal of Applied Psychology, 82*(3), 401–415.

Schwartz, P. J., Murphy, D. L., Wehr, T. A., Garcia-Borreguero, D., Oren, D. A., Moul, D. E., Ozaki, N., Snelbaker, A. J., & Rosenthal, N. E. (1997). Effects of meta-chlorophenylpiperazine infusions in patients with seasonal affective disorder and healthy control subjects: Diurnal responses and nocturnal regulatory mechanisms. *Archives of General Psychiatry, 54*(4), 375–385.

Schweizer, T., Schnegg, M., & Berzborn, S. (1998). Personal networks and social support in a multiethnic community of southern California. *Social Networks, 20*(1), 1–21.

Sciarra, D. T. (1999). *Multiculturalism in counseling.* Itasca, IL: F. E. Peacock.

Scripps Howard News Service. (1998). Anglican conference splits on homosexuality: One bishop said to compare gays to child abusers. Retrieved March 10, 2001, from the World Wide Web: **http://www.desnews.com:80/tdy/wr178cok.htm**.

Scrivner, R., & Eldridge, N. (1995). Lesbian and gay family psychology. In R. Mikesell, D. D. Lusterman, & S. McDaniel (Eds.), *Integrating family therapy: Handbook of family psychology and systems theory.* Washington, DC: American Psychological Association.

Sellers, N., Satcher, J., & Comas, R. (1999). Children's occupational aspirations: Comparisons by gender, gender role identity, and socioeconomic status. *Professional School Counseling, 2*, 314–317.

Seppa, N. (1996). A multicultural guide to less spanking and yelling. *APA Monitor.* Retrieved February 14, 2001, from the World Wide Web: **http://www.apa.org/monitor/may96/kerby.html**.

Sharf, R. S. (2000). *Theories of psychotherapy and counseling: Concepts and cases* (2nd ed.). Pacific Grove, CA: Brooks-Cole Wadsworth.

Shea, C. (1994). "Gender gap" on examinations shrank again this year. *Chronicle of Higher Education, 41*, A54.

Shiang, J. (1998). Does culture make a difference? Racial/ethnic patterns of completed suicide in San Francisco, CA, 1987–1996, and clinical applications. *Suicide and Life-Threatening Behavior, 28*(4), 338–354.

Shiffler, J. B. (1998). The relationship between guilt- and shame-proneness and Rorschach indices of psychological functioning. *Dissertation Abstracts International: Section B: The Sciences and Engineering, 58*(11-B), 6247.

Shime, P. (1992). *Homophobia in the law: The experiences of lesbians and gay men in the legal profession.* Unpublished manuscript, p. 18.

Shorris, E. (1992). *Latinos: A biography of the people.* New York: Norton.

Siegel, R. J. (1985). Beyond homophobia: Learning to work with lesbian clients. In L. B. Rosewater & L. E. A. Walker (Eds.), *Handbook of feminist therapy: Women's issues in psychotherapy* (pp. 183–190). New York: Springer.

Silverman, J. A. (1990) Anorexia nervosa in males. In A. Anderson & A. E. Brunner (Eds.), *Males with eating disorders* (pp. 3–8). Mazel: New York.

Silverstein, L. B., & Auerbach, C. F. (1999). Deconstructing the essential father. *American Psychologist, 54*(6), 397–407.

Simms, W. F. (1999). The Native American Indian client: A tale of two cultures. In Y. M. Jenkins (Ed.), *Diversity in college settings: New directions for college mental health* (pp. 21–35). New York: Routledge.

Sinacore-Guinn, A. L., Akcali, F. O., & Fledderus, S. W. (1999). Employed women: Family and work—reciprocity and satisfaction. *Journal of Career Development, 25*(3), 187–201.

Singh-Manoux, A. (2000). Culture and gender issues in adolescence: Evidence from studies on emotion. *Psicothema, 12*(Supplement), 93–100.

Slabbekoorn, D., Van Goozen, S., Gooren, L., & Cohen-Kettenis, P. (2001). Effects of cross-sex hormone treatment on emotionality in transsexuals. *The International Journal of Transgenderism, 5*(3), Retrieved May 21, 2002, from the World Wide Web: **http://www.symposion.com/ijt/ijtvo05no03_02.htm**.

Slater, S. (1995). *The lesbian family life cycle.* New York: Free Press.

Sleek, S. (1996). Research identifies causes of internal homophobia: Gay men, lesbians and bisexuals not only face bigotry from society, but sometimes from their own psyches. *APA Monitor.* Retrieved March 2, 1999, from the World Wide Web: **http://www.apa.org/monitor/oct96/homophba.html**.

Slovic, P. (1999). Trust, emotion, sex, politics, and science: Surveying the risk-assessment battlefield. *Risk Analysis, 19*(4), 689–701.

Slusher, M. P., Mayer, C. J., & Dunkle, R. E. (1996). Gays and lesbians older and wiser (GLOW): A support group for older gay people. *Gerontologist, 36,* 118–123.

Smith, A. J., & Siegel, R. F. (1985). Feminist therapy: Redefining power for the powerless. In L. B. Rosewater & L. E. A. Walker (Eds.), *Handbook of feminist therapy: Women's issues in psychotherapy* (pp. 13–22). New York: Springer.

Smith, D. (2002). Canceled trial is yielding useful data: Behavioral scientists are busy mining data from the Women's Health Initiative's halted hormone-replacement therapy trial. *APA Monitor, 33,* 52.

Smith, E. J. (1991). Ethnic identity development: Toward the development of a theory within the context of majority/minority status. *Journal of Counseling and Development, 770,* 181–188.

Smith, J., Berthelsen, D., & O'Connor, I. (1997). Child adjustment in high-conflict families. *Child Care, Health and Development, 23*(2) 113–133.

Snider, K. (1998). Race and sexual orientation: The (im)possibility of these intersections in educational policy: Reply. *Harvard Educational Review, 68*(1), 103–105.

Snyder, G. (1998, January 10). Japanese culture. Available via e-mail: **rbrammer@wtamu.edu**.

Society for the Psychological Study of Ethical Minority Issues. (1982). *Guidelines for multicultural counseling proficiency for psychologists: Implications for education and training, research and clinical practice.* American Psychological Association.

Retrieved June 10, 2001, from the World Wide Web: **http://www.apa.org/ divisions/div45/resources.html**.

Sodowsky, G. R., & Parr, G. (1991). Cultural consistency and counselor credibility. *TACD Journal, 19*(1) 33–38.

South, S. J. & Crowder, K. D. (1998). Leaving the 'hood: Residential mobility between black, white, and integrated neighborhoods. *American Sociological Review, 63,* 17–26.

Sprecher, S. (1999). "I love you more today than yesterday": Romantic partners' perceptions of changes in love and related affect over time. *Journal of Personality and Social Psychology, 76* (1), 46–53.

Stanford, J. L., Feng, Z., Hamilton, A. S., Gilliland, F. D., Stephenson, R. A., Eley, J. W., Albertsen, P. C., Harlan, L. C., & Potosky, A. L. (2000). Urinary and sexual function after radical prostatectomy for clinically localized prostate cancer. *Journal of the American Medical Association, 283,* 354–360.

Staples, B. (1992). Black men and public space. In J. Madden & S. M. Blake. (1992). *Emerging voices: Readings in the American experience* (2nd ed., pp. 440–442). Fort Worth: Harcourt Brace.

Steele, C. M., & Aronson, J. (2000). Stereotype threat and the intellectual test performance of African Americans. In C. Stangor (Ed.), *Stereotypes and prejudice: Essential readings. Key readings in social psychology* (pp. 369–389). Philadelphia: Psychology Press/Taylor & Francis.

Steelman, L. C., & Doby, J. T. (1983). Family size and birth order as factors on the IQ performance of Black and White children. *Sociology of Education, 56*(2), 101–109.

Stefan, S. (2002). *Hollow promises: Employment discrimination against people with mental disabilities.* Washington, DC: American Psychological Association.

Steinem, G. (1978, October). If men could menstruate. *Ms., 8,* 100.

Steinmetz, S., & Lucca, J. (1988). Husband battering. In V. B. Van Hasselt (Ed.), *Handbook of family violence* (pp. 233–245). New York: Plenum Press.

Stevenson, W., Maton, K. I., & Teti, D. M. (1998). School importance and dropout among pregnant adolescents. *Journal of Adolescent Health, 22*(5), 376–382.

Steward, M. S. (2002). Illness: A crisis for children. In J. Sandoval (Ed.), *Handbook of crisis counseling, intervention, and prevention in the schools* (2nd ed., pp. 183–211). Mahwah, NJ: Lawrence Erlbaum Associates.

Stoller, R. (1968). *Sex and gender (Vol. I): The development of masculinity and femininity.* New York: Jason Aronson.

Stoller, R. (1985). *Presentations of gender.* New Haven: Yale University Press.

Stoller, R. (1997). *Splitting: A case of female masculinity.* New Haven: Yale University Press.

Straus, M. A., Gelles, R. J., & Steinmetz, S. K. (1980). *Behind closed doors: Violence in the American family.* Garden City, NY: Anchor.

Straus, M. A., & Gelles, R. J. (1988). Violence in American families: How much is there and why does it occur? In E. W. Nunnally & C. S. Chilman (Eds.), *Troubled relationships. Families in trouble series* (Vol. 3, pp. 141–162). Newbury Park, CA: Sage.

Strong, S. R. (1969). Counseling: An interpersonal influence process. *Journal of Counseling Psychology, 15,* 31–35.

Strong STARTS program combats unhappiness among Black youth. (1998). *APA Monitor.* Retrieved August 2000 from the World Wide Web: **http://www.apa.org/ monitor/feb98/Black.html**.

Subrahmanyan, L. (1999). A generation in transition: Gender ideology of graduate students from India at an American university. In S. R. Gupta (Ed.), *Emerging voices: South Asian American women redefine self, family, and community* (pp. 58–78). Walnut Creek, CA: Altamira Press.

Sue, D. W. (2001). Surviving monoculturalism and racism. In J. G. Ponterotto, J. M. Casas, L. A. Suzuki, & C. M. Alexander (Eds.), *Handbook of multicultural counseling* (2nd ed., pp. 45–54). Thousand Oaks, CA: Sage.

Sue, D. W., & Sue, D. (1990). *Counseling the culturally different: Theory and practice* (2nd ed.). New York: Wiley.

Sue, D. W., & Sue, D. (1999). *Counseling the culturally different: Theory and practice* (3rd ed.). New York: Wiley.

Sue, D., & Sundberg, N. D. (1996). Research and research hypotheses about effectiveness in intercultural counseling. In P. B. Pedersen, J. G. Draguns, W. J. Lonner, & J. E. Trimble (Eds.), *Counseling across cultures* (4th ed., pp. 323–352). Thousand Oaks, CA: Sage.

Sue, S. (1998). In search of cultural competence in psychotherapy and counseling. *American Psychologist, 53*(4), 440–448.

Sue, S., Chun, C., & Gee, K. (1995). Ethnic minority intervention and treatment research. In J. F. Aponte, R. Y. Rivers, & J. Wohl (Eds.), *Psychological interventions and cultural diversity* (pp. 266–282). Boston: Allyn & Bacon.

Suhail, K., & Cochrane, R. (1998). Seasonal variations in hospital admissions for affective disorders by gender and ethnicity. *Social Psychiatry and Psychiatric Epidemiology, 33,* 211–217.

Suinn, R. M. (1999). Scaling the summit: Valuing ethnicity. *APA Monitor.* Retrieved August 22, 2000, from the World Wide Web: **http://www.apa.org/monitor/mar99/pc.html**.

Sun, Y. (1998). The academic success of East-Asian-American students: An investment model. *Social Science Research, 27*(4), 432–456.

Svare, B., Betteridge, C., Katz, D., & Samuels, O. (1981). Some situational and experiential determinants of maternal aggression in mice. *Physiology and Behavior, 26,* 253–258.

Swaab, D. F., & Hofman, M. A. (1995). Sexual differentiation of the human hypothalamus in relation to gender and sexual orientation. *Trends in Neurosciences, 18,* 264–270.

Swaim, R. C., Oetting, E. R., Thurman, P. J., Beauvais, F., & Edwards, R. W. (1993). American Indian adolescent drug use and socialization characteristics: A cross-cultural comparison. *Journal of Cross Cultural Psychology, 24,* 53–70.

Sweezy, C. (1967). *The Arapaho way: A memoir of an Indian boyhood* (edited by A. Bass). New York: C. N. Potter.

Takaki, R. T. (1998). *Strangers from a different shore: A history of Asian Americans* (2nd ed.). Boston: Little, Brown.

Talvi, S. J. A. (1997). The silent epidemic: The challenge of HIV prevention within communities of color. *The Humanist, 57,* 6–10.

Tamaki, J. (2000, August 17). Indians find that money buys access. *Los Angeles Times.* Special Section, 1.

Tang, M., Fouad, N. A., & Smith, P. L. (1999). Asian Americans' career choices: A path model to examine factors influencing their career choices. *Journal of Vocational Behavior, 54*(1), 142–157.

Tannen, D. (1996). *Gender and discourse.* New York: Oxford University Press.

Telljohann, S. K., & Price, J. H. (1993). A qualitative examination of adolescent homosexuals' life experiences: Ramifications for secondary school personnel. *Journal of Homosexuality, 26*(1), 41–56.

Thandeka (1999). White racial induction and Christian shame theology: A primer. *Gender and Psychoanalysis, 4*(4), 455–495.

Thier, J. (1999). Vision quest: A journey of empowerment. *Montana Free Press.* Retrieved September 23, 2000, from the World Wide Web: **http://www.dreamweaverlodge.com/visionquestarticle.html**.

Thomas, A., & Sillen, S. (1972). *Racism and psychiatry.* Secaucus, NJ: Citadel Press.

Thomas, B. (1991). *A wives' bill of rights.* HCDA.

Thomas, S., & Larrabee, T. (2002). Gay, lesbian, bisexual, and questioning youth. *Handbook of crisis counseling, intervention, and prevention in the schools* (2nd ed., pp. 301–322). Mahwah, NJ: Lawrence Erlbaum Associates, Inc.

Thornhill, R., & Grammer, K. (1999). The body and face of woman: One ornament that signals quality? *Evolution and Human Behavior, 20*(2), 105–120.

Thurman, P. J., Swaim, R., & Plested, B. (1995). Intervention and treatment of ethnic minority substance abusers. In J. F. Aponte, R. Y. Rivers, & J. Wohl (Eds.), *Psychological interventions and cultural diversity* (pp. 215–233). Boston: Allyn & Bacon.

Ting-Toomey, S., Yee-Jung, K. K., Shapiro, R. B., Garcia, W., Wright, T. J., & Oetzel, J. G. (2000). Ethnic/cultural identity salience and conflict styles in four US ethnic groups. *International Journal of Intercultural Relations, 24*(1), 47–81.

Tittle, C., & Torre, V. (1996). Statistic and research on breast cancer. *The Lumberjack.* Retrieved June 10, 2001, from the World Wide Web: **http://www.thejack.nau.edu/0927/Life2.html**.

Tjaden, P., & Thoennes, N. (1998), Prevalence, incidence, and consequences of violence against women: Findings from the National Violence Against Women Survey. National Institute of Justice Centers for Disease Control and Prevention. Washington, DC: U.S. Department of Justice.

Tomes, H. (1998). Diversity: Psychology's life depends upon it. *APA Monitor, 29,* 12. Retrieved August 22, 2000, from the World Wide Web: **http://www.apa.org/monitor/dec98/pubint.html**.

Tomita, S. K. (1999). Exploration of elder mistreatment among the Japanese. In Toshio Tatara (Ed.), *Understanding elder abuse in minority populations* (pp. 119–139). Philadelphia: Brunner/Mazel.

Tomori, M., Zalar, B., & Plesnicar, B. K. (2000). Gender differences in psychosocial risk factors among Slovenian adolescents. *Adolescence, 35,* 431–443.

Torre, V. (1997). Real-life nightmares. *The Lumberjack.* Retrieved May 11, 2001, from the World Wide Web: **http://www.thejack.nau.edu/0927/Life1.html**.

Torres, S., Campbell, J., Campbell, D. W., Ryan, J., King, C., Price, P., Stallings, R. Y., Fuchs, S. C., & Laude, M. (2000). Abuse during and before pregnancy: Prevalence and cultural correlates. *Violence & Victims, 15*(3), 303–321.

Trevatt, D. (2001). Working in a school for severely physically disabled children. In G. Baruch (Ed.), *Community-based psychotherapy with young people: Evidence and innovation in practice* (pp. 89–102). Philadelphia: Brunner-Routledge.

Trimble, J. E., & LaFromboise, T. D. (1987). American Indians and the counseling process: Culture, adaptation, and style. In Paul Pedersen (Ed.), *Handbook of cross-cultural counseling and therapy* (pp. 127–133). New York: Greenwood.

True, R. H. (1990). Psychotherapeutic issues with Asian American women. *Sex Roles, 22*(7-8), 477–486.

Truijers, A., & Vingerhoets, J. J. M. (1999). Shame, embarrassment, personality and well-being. Second International Conference on the (Non) Expressions of Emotions in Health and Disease. Tilburg, The Netherlands.

Tseelon, E. (1992). What is beautiful is bad: Physical attractiveness as stigma. *Journal for the Theory of Social Behaviour, 22*(3), 295–309.

Turner, W. J. (1995). Homosexuality, Type 1: An Xq28 phenomenon. *Archives of Sexual Behavior, 24*(2), 109–134.

Unger, R. K. (1990). Imperfect reflections of reality: Psychology and the construction of gender. In R. Hare-Mustin & J. Marecek (Eds.), *Making a difference: Representations of gender in psychology* (pp. 102-149). New Haven: Yale University Press.

Updegraff, K. A., McHale, S. M., Crouter, A. C., & Kupanoff, K. (2001). Parents' involvement in adolescents' peer relationships: A comparison of mothers' and fathers' roles. *Journal of Marriage and Family, 63*(3), 655–668.

U.S. Bureau of the Census. (1991). *Statistical abstract.* Washington, DC: U.S. Government Printing Office.

U.S. Bureau of the Census. (1992). *Statistical abstract of the United States: The national data book* (112th ed.). Washington, DC: US Government Printing Office.

U.S. Bureau of the Census. (1995). *Population profile of the United States.* Washington, DC: U.S. Government Printing Office.

U.S. Department of Health and Human Services, Indian Health Service (1997). *Trends in Indian Health.* Washington, DC: United States Government Office of Planning, Evaluation, and Legislation, Division of Program Statistics.

U.S. Department of Labor, Bureau of Statistics. (2001). *Highlights of women's earnings in 2000.* Report 952. Retrieved May 24, 2002, from the World Wide Web: **http://www.bls.gov/cps/cpswom2000.pdf**.

U.S. Department of Labor, Women's Bureau. (2001). *Women's jobs, 1964-1999: More than 30 years of progress.* Retrieved May 25, 2002, from the World Wide Web: **http://www.dol.gov/wb/jobs6497.htm**.

U.S. Department of State. (2002). Immigrant visas issued to orphans coming to the U.S. Retrieved June 11, 2002, from the World Wide Web: **www.travel.state.gov/orphan_numbers.html**.

U.S. Environmental Protection Agency. (1984, November 8). *EPA policy for the administration of environmental programs on Indian reservations.* Washington, DC: EPA.

U.S. Environmental Protection Agency. (1999). *Understanding Native Americans.* Retrieved September 11, 2000, from the World Wide Web: **http://www.epa.gov/indian/resource/**.

Van Tilburg, M. A. L., Unterberg, M. L., & Vingerhoets, J. J. M. (2002). Crying during adolescence: The role of gender, menarche, and empathy. *The British Journal of Developmental Psychology, 20*, 1–77.

Varelas, N., & Foley, L. A. (1998). Blacks' and Whites' perceptions of interracial and intraracial date rape. *Journal of Social Psychology, 138*(3), 392–400.

Verdi, B. (1997, May 6). In Tiger Woods' case, perhaps we should remember the human race. *Chicago Tribune.* Retrieved June 11, 2001 from the World Wide Web: **http://www.texnews.com/tiger/verdi050697.html**.

Villarruel, A. M. (1998). Cultural influences on the sexual attitudes, beliefs, and norms of young Latina adolescents. *Journal of the Society of Pediatric Nurses, 3*(2), 69–79.

Vincent, K. R. (1991). Black/White IQ differences: Does age make the difference? *Journal of Clinical Psychology, 47*(2), 266–270.

Vincent, M. A., & McCabe, M. P. (2000). Gender differences among adolescents in family, and peer influences on body dissatisfaction, weight loss, and binge eating behaviors. *Journal of Youth and Adolescence, 29*, 205–221.

Vonk, M. E. (2001). Cultural competence for transracial adoptive parents. *Social Work, 46*(3), 246–255.

Voorhees, C. C., Yanek, L. R., Stillman, F. A., & Becker, D. M. (1998). Reducing cigarette sales to minors in an urban setting: Issues and opportunities for merchant intervention. *American Journal of Preventive Medicine, 14*(2), 138–142.

Voydanoff, P., & Donnelly, B. W. (1999). The intersection of time in activities and perceived unfairness in relation to psychological distress and marital quality. *Journal of Marriage and the Family, 61*(3), 739–751.

Wade, T. J., & Abetz, H. (1997). Social cognition and evolutionary psychology: Physical attractiveness and contrast effects on women's self-perceived body image. *International Journal of Psychology, 32*(1), 35–42.

Walker, L. E. (1979). *The battered woman.* New York: Harper & Row.

Walker, L. E. (1985). Feminist therapy with victims/survivors of interpersonal violence. In L. B. Rosewater & L. E. A. Walker (Eds.), *Handbook of feminist therapy: Women's issues in psychotherapy* (pp. 203–214). New York: Springer.

Walker, P. A., Berger, J. C., Green, R., Laub, D., Reynolds, C., & Wollman, L. (1984). Standards of care: The hormonal and surgical sex reassignment of gender dysphoric persons. *Annals of Plastic Surgery, 13*(6), 476–481.

Wallerstein, J. S. (1995). Nine "psychological tasks" needed for a good marriage. In *Family and relationships.* Washington, DC: American Psychological Association.

Ward, N. G. (1975). Single case study: Successful lithium treatment of transvestism associated with manic-depression. *Journal of Nervous and Mental Disease, 161*, 204–206.

Warren, C. A. B. (1998). Aging and identity in premodern times. *Research on Aging, 20*(1), 11–35.

Wasserstein, S. B., & La Greca, A. M. (1998). Hurricane Andrew: Parent conflict as a moderator of children's adjustment. *Hispanic Journal of Behavioral Sciences, 20*(2), 212–224.

Waters, M. (1998). Optional ethnicities: For Whites only? In M. L. Anderson & P. H. Collins (Eds.), *Race, class, and gender: An anthology* (3rd ed., pp. 403–412). Belmont, CA: Wadsworth.

Weatherburn, P., Hickson, F., Reid, D. S., Davies, P. M., & Crosier, A. (1998). Sexual HIV risk behaviour among men who have sex with both men and women. *AIDS Care, 10*(4), 463–471.

Weber, C. L. (1987). *WomanChrist: A new vision of feminist spirituality.* San Francisco: Harper & Row.

Weidner, G. (2000). Why do men get more heart disease than women? An international perspective. *Journal of American College Health, 48*(6), 291–294.

Weijmar Schultz, W. C. M., van de Wiel, H. B. M., Hahn, D. E. E., & Wouda, J. (1995). Sexual adjustment of women after gynecological and breast cancer. *Sexual and Marital Therapy, 10*(3), 293–306.

Weinberg, T. S., & Bullough, V. L. (1988). Alienation, self-image, and the importance of support groups for the wives of transvestites. *Journal of Sex Research, 24*, 262-268.

Weiss, J. (1995). Cognitive therapy and life review therapy: Theoretical and therapeutic implications for mental health counselors. *Journal of Mental Health Counseling, 17,* 157.

Wells, K. B., Hough, R. L., Golding, J. M., Burnam, M. A., & Karno, M. (1987). Which Mexican-Americans underutilize health services? *American Journal of Psychiatry, 144*(7), 918–922.

Whaley, A. (2000). Sociocultural differences in the developmental consequences of the use of physical discipline during childhood for African Americans. *Cultural Diversity and Ethnic Minority Psychology, 6,* 5–12.

Whaley, A. L., & Link, B. G. (1998). Racial categorization and stereotype-based judgments about homeless people. *Journal of Applied Social Psychology, 28*(3), 189–205.

Wileman, R., & Wileman, B. (1995). Towards balancing power in domestic violence relationships. *Australian and New Zealand Journal of Family Therapy, 16*(4), 165–176.

Williams, D., & Jackson, J. (1997). Racial tension undermines the health of Blacks. *APA Monitor.* Retrieved May 11, 2001, from the World Wide Web: **http://www.apa. org/monitor/dec97/race.html**.

Williams, D. R., Takeuchi, D. T., & Adair, R. K. (1992). Socioeconomic status and psychiatric disorder among Blacks and Whites. *Social Forces, 71*(1), 179–194.

Williams, M. E. (1997). Toward greater understanding of the psychological effects of infertility on women. *Psychotherapy in Private Practice, 16*(3), 7–26.

Williams, R., & Wittig, M. A. (1997). "I'm not a feminist but . . .": Factors contributing to the discrepancy between pro-feminist orientation and feminist social identity. *Sex Roles, 37,* 885–904.

Wilson, C. R., & Ferris, W. (Eds.). (1989). *The encyclopedia of Southern culture.* Raleigh, NC: University of North Carolina Press.

Wilson, D. K. (2001). *Violence may affect blood pressure in Black boys.* Presented at the sixteenth scientific meeting and exposition of the American Society of Hypertension, San Francisco, California.

Wilson, S. D. (1989). *Counseling adult children of alcoholics.* Dallas: Word Publishing.

Wolf, N. (1991). *The beauty myth.* New York: Morrow.

Wolf, R. S. (1998). Domestic elder abuse and neglect. In I. H. Nordhus, G. R. VandenBos, S. Berg, & P. Fromholt (Eds.), *Clinical Geropsychology* (pp. 161–165). Washington, DC: American Psychological Association.

Wong, P., Lai, C. F., Nagasawa, R., & Lin, T. (1998). Asian Americans as a model minority: Self-perceptions and perceptions by other racial groups. *Sociological Perspectives, 41*(1), 95–118.

Wood, P. B., & Clay, W. C. (1996). Perceived structural barriers and academic performance among American Indian high school students. *Youth and Society, 28,* 40–61.

Woodhouse, A. (1985). Forgotten women: Transvestism and marriage. *Women's Studies International Forum, 8,* 583–592.

Woodman, R. (2001, June 1). *British HIV infections hit record high in 2000.* ABCNEWS.com. Retrieved June 4, 2001, from the World Wide Web: **http://dailynews.yahoo.com/h/ nm/20010601/hl/britain_aids_1.html**.

Worell, J., & Remer, P. (1992). *Feminist perspectives in therapy: An empowerment model for women.* New York: Wiley.

Wyatt, G. E., Forge, N. G., & Guthrie, D. (1998). Family constellation and ethnicity: Current and lifetime HIV-related risk taking. *Journal of Family Psychology, 12*(1), 93–101.

Xu, Y., & Burleson, B. R. (2001). Effects of sex, culture, and support type on perceptions of spousal social support: An assessment of the "support gap" hypothesis in early marriage. *Human Communication Research, 27*(4), 535–566.

Yeh, M., Eastman, K., & Cheung, M. (1994). Children and adolescents in community health centers: Does the ethnicity or the language of the therapist matter? *Journal of Community Psychology, 22*(2) 153–163.

Yi, J. K. (1998). Vietnamese American college students' knowledge and attitudes toward HIV/AIDS. *Journal of American College Health, 47*(1), 37–42.

Ying, Y., & Akutsu, P. D. (1997). Psychological adjustment of Southeast Asian refugees: The contribution of a sense of coherence. *Journal of Community Psychology, 25*(2), 125–139.

Yoder, J. D., & Schleicher, T. L. (1996). Undergraduates regard deviation from occupational gender stereotypes as costly for women. *Sex Roles, 34*(3-4), 171–188.

Yonkers, K. A., Halbreich, U., Freeman, E., Brown, C., Endicott, J., Frank, E., Parry, B., Pearlstein, T., Severino, S., Stout, A., Stone, A., & Harrison, W. (1997). Sertraline Premenstrual Dysphoric Collaborative Study: Symptomatic improvement of premenstrual dysphoric disorder with sertraline treatment: A randomized controlled trial. *Journal of the American Medical Association, 278*(12), 983–988.

Young, C. (2001). Where the boys are: Is America shortchanging male children? *Reason.* Retrieved January 22, 2000, from the World Wide Web: **http://www.reason.com: 80/0102/fe.cy.where.html.**

Young, T. J. (1990). Poverty, suicide, and homicide among Native Americans. *Psychological Reports, 67,* 1153–1154.

Young, T. J., & French, L. A. (1996). Suicide and homicide rates among U.S. Indian Health Service areas: The income inequality hypothesis. *Social Behavior and Personality, 24*(4), 365–366.

Yuen, F. K. O., & Nakano-Matsumoto, N. (1998). Effective substance abuse treatment for Asian American adolescents. *Early Child Development and Care, 147,* 43–54.

Zahn-Waxler, C., Robinson, J. L., & Emde, R. N. (1992). The development of empathy in twins. *Developmental Psychology, 28,* 1038–1047.

Zane, N., Enomoto, K., & Chun, C. A. (1994). Treatment outcomes of Asian- and White-American clients in outpatient therapy. *Journal of Community Psychology, 22*(2) 177–191.

Zhou, J. N., Hofman, M. A., Gooren, L. J., & Swaab, D. F. (1997). A sex difference in the human brain and its relation to transsexuality. *The International Journal of Transgenderism, 1.* Retrieved May 22, 2001, from the World Wide Web: **http://www.symposion.com/ijt/ijtc0106.htm.**

Name Index

Subject Index

Abortion, 243–244
Abuse. *See also* Domestic violence; Spousal abuse; Violence
  case study of, 282–283
  elder, 331
  against gays and lesbians, 179
  of men, 287–289, 294
  sexual, 63–64
  of women, 279–281, 287
Academic performance. *See also* Education
  by African Americans, 40
  by Asian Americans, 94–95
  by boys, 299
  by Latinos, 66–68
  self-esteem and grades in, 41
Acceptance, in counseling Asians, 109
Acculturation
  Asian Americans and, 89–92, 108–109
  Cross's Black identity model and, 47–48
  intensity of cultural differences and, 47
  of Latinos, 67, 70, 72, 77
  of Native Americans, 118, 123, 126
  Ruiz's model of, 72–73
Acculturation theory, 3–5
Achievement. *See also* Academic performance
  among African American girls, 41
  among Asian Americans, 94–95
  in European American culture, 143
Action-oriented techniques, with Asians, 108
Actions
  judging, 6
  value orientation of, 17
Adaptability, in counseling Asians, 110
ADHD. *See* Attention deficit hyperactivity disorder (ADHD)
Adolescents
  African American, 41–42, 51
  eating disorders in, 266–267
  economic conditions, violence, and, 38–39
  misconduct by Chinese, 142
  Native American pregnancies and, 118
  smoking by, 97, 145
  transgendered, 229–230
"Adopted Whites," Asians as, 97, 99

Adoption
  of culturally diverse children, 90–91
  multicultural and transcultural, 324–325
Adrenal hyperplasia, 205
Advertising, European American susceptibility to, 145
Affective/spiritual domain, Native American acculturation and, 126
Affect-oriented approach, in African American therapy, 53
Affluence. *See also* Wealth
  race and, 37
African Americans, 31–57. *See also* specific issues
  adoption of, 324
  alcohol and, 146
  assimilation of, 3
  context for therapy, 54
  control of feelings by, 5–6
  counseling issues for, 52–55
  Cross's identity model of, 47–48
  cultural separateness of, 5
  cultural uniqueness of, 44–48
  developmental cycle of, 51–52
  Ebonics and, 44–45
  economic status of, 36–39
  ethnicities of, 50
  family and, 34–36
  feminist and mental health scale patterns, 262–263
  gender issues among, 51
  health and, 42–44
  homosexual behavior and, 186
  intelligence measures and, 14, 48–50
  language skills of, 15–16
  manhood and, 310
  men and women in higher education and, 299–300
  myth of matriarch and, 36
  oppositional culture of, 14–15
  physical punishment among, 35, 141
  problem attribution by, 53
  prostate cancer among, 302
  psychological issues for, 48–50
  purpose for entering therapy, 53–54